LITERATURE AND WORK

Thomas M. Kitts
St. John's University, NY

Longman

Boston   Columbus   Indianapolis   New York   San Francisco
Upper Saddle River   Amsterdam   Cape Town   Dubai   London   Madrid
Milan   Munich   Paris   Montreal   Toronto   Delhi   Mexico City   Sao Paulo
Sydney Hong Kong Seoul Singapore Taipei Tokyo

for Lisa Rosenberg

Senior Acquisitions Editor: Vivian Garcia
Editorial Assistant: Heather Vomero
Executive Marketing Manager: Joyce Nilsen
Production Manager: Meghan DeMaio
Creative Director: Jayne Conte
Cover Designer: Bruce Kenselaar
Cover Illustration/Photo: Fotolia
Project Coordination, Text Design, and Electronic Page Makeup: Niraj Bhatt/Aptara®, Inc.

For permission to use copyrighted material, we are grateful to all the copyright holders.

Library of Congress Cataloging-in-Publication Data
Literature and work / [edited by] Thomas M. Kitts.
   p. cm.
  An anthology.
  Summary: This book introduces students to work by having them read, discuss, and write about work-related topics. It features contemporary as well as classic literature with a global perspective. Each section is introduced by broad overviews of the subject, authors' biographies, short introductions to each work, the works themselves, and selections of study questions.
  ISBN-13: 978-0-205-68109-9
  ISBN-10: 0-205-68109-3
  1. College readers. 2. Readers—Work. 3. Work—Literary collections. 4. Work—Problems, exercises, etc. 5. Report writing—Problems, exercises, etc. 6. English language—Rhetoric— Problems, exercises, etc. 7. English language—Composition and exercises. I. Kitts, Thomas M.
  PE1127.W65L58 2011
  808'.0427—dc22

        2010040969

Longman
is an imprint of

www.pearsonhighered.com

ISBN-10:   0-205-68109-3
ISBN-13: 978-0-205-68109-9

CONTENTS

GENRE CONTENTS

Drama

Songs

NONFICTION

Autobiography/Biography

Essay

Speech

ALPHABETICAL ORDER BY AUTHOR WITHIN GENRE

Fiction

Poetry

Drama

Songs

NONFICTION

Autobiography/ Biography

Essay

Speech

ACKNOWLEDGMENTS

I would like to thank a number of people who helped this book come together. My colleagues in the Division of English and Speech at St. John's University were very generous with their suggestions. Many of the works that they recommended found their way into the text. Janice Shaman, also at St. John's, deserves my thanks and appreciation for her always very capable support and assistance with this and so many other projects, many happening concurrent with this book. I am also grateful to my student Keith Arias who suggested Cam'ron's "I Hate My Job," and to my good friends and colleagues Professor Stephen Paul Miller at St. John's for several suggestions and Professor Nick Baxter-Moore from Brock University for his excellent insight into the tentative reading list and for his recommendation of Bruce Springsteen's "Highway Patrolman."

At Pearson Education, I had the great pleasure of working on this text with Vivian Garcia, Senior Editor of Literature and Creative Writing. Vivian was always insightful, encouraging, and inspiring. She also assembled an outstanding team of reviewers, whose suggestions and recommendations led to a more dynamic text. To each of the reviewers, I am grateful: Rynetta Davis, University of Kentucky; William DeGenaro, The University of Michigan, Dearborn; Larnell Dunkley Jr., Harold Washington College; Norma J. Honaker, University of South Carolina; Sherry Lee Linkon, Youngstown State University; Price McMurray, Texas Wesleyan University; Neil Plakcy, Broward College; Donna Potts, Kansas State University; Aimee Pozorski, Central Connecticut State University; Nancy Sorkin, Philadelphia University, Philadelphia; and James Wallace, King's College. I must also thank Heather N. Vomero, editorial assistant at Pearson, for seeing this text through to completion.

On a personal note, I thank my extremely supportive partner Lisa Rosenberg, to whom this book is dedicated. Lisa gave me all of the space and time that I needed to bring the book to completion. I also thank my children, Dylan and Holly, and Lisa's children, Hayley and Julia Gordin, for understanding that my availability and, sometimes, my concentration were limited. All of their support is very much appreciated and inspiring.

ABOUT THE AUTHOR

Thomas M. Kitts, PhD, is a professor of English and chair of the Division of English and Speech at St. John's University, New York City. He is the author of *Ray Davies: Not Like Everybody Else, The Theatrical Life of George Henry Boker,* articles on American literature and popular culture; reviews of books, CDs, and performances; and *Gypsies* (a play). The co-editor of *Living on a Thin Line: Crossing Aesthetic Borders with The Kinks,* he currently edits *The Mid-Atlantic Almanack* and co-edits *Popular Music and Society.*

INTRODUCTION

Even in the meanest sorts of Labor, the whole soul of man is composed into a kind of real harmony the instant he sets himself to work.

—Thomas Carlyle

In this quotation, Thomas Carlyle, a nineteenth-century Scottish Romantic, advances an idealistic concept of work, one in which individuals find self-fulfillment and harmony with the world. Carlyle may seem far reaching, but we generally agree that such intense satisfaction is possible from work, otherwise why would we strive for our ideal job? Most of us realize soon enough that financial benefits are not enough from a job. As Henry David Thoreau, an American contemporary of Carlyle, wrote, "If the laborer gets no more than the wages which his employer pays him, he is cheated, he cheats himself."

But while work, this inescapable and almost all-consuming human activity, can be a source of tremendous self- and communal-fulfillment, satisfying in perhaps every way—emotionally, spiritually, physically, and financially—it can also be tedious, routine, and painful in the same ways it is satisfying and, for some, overwhelmingly stressful and a source of continual conflict, internal and external. It is no wonder why the topic has attracted all great writers and thinkers.

We so completely invest ourselves in our work that it is often how we define ourselves not just to others but also to ourselves—and, unfairly or not, our occupation will provoke strong initial impressions in others. On many levels, therefore, work can be a great source of not only satisfaction but also tension and anxiety. How do we respond, for instance, to conflicts with supervisors and coworkers? What happens when our work is no longer fulfilling but we need its financial compensation? Do we invest too much of our self-worth in our work? How do we respond if our work compromises our integrity? This anthology raises these and many other issues as it explores the dynamics of work from diverse perspectives.

Many of the writers in this text struggle for a definition of work. Poet Seamus Heaney ("Digging") considers writing poetry in light of the manual and more practical labors of his father and grandfather. Is writing work? In "What Work Is," Philip Levine's protagonist has to reconcile his definition of work with his brother's studying German and singing Wagner, and in "Marks," Linda Pastan presents an unappreciated housewife on the verge of revolt.

However, many writers celebrate work, echoing Carlyle. Walt Whitman celebrates the harmony of a nation at work in "I Hear America Singing"; Frost, the harmony of the individual and nature in "The Tuft of Flowers"; and Salvatore La Puma, a profound moment at work between a father and son in "Cakes." In Ernest Hemingway's "A Clean Well-Lighted Place," the old waiter finds meaning in the management of a café in much the same way as Dolores

Dante in Studs Terkel's "Waitress"—although Kraft Rompf's waiter finds no such satisfaction in "Waiting Table."

While we may find self-definition in work, we can, if not careful, define ourselves too rigidly and confine our impulse for development. The job and the culture around it can seduce us into becoming merely an extension of the task, whereby we gradually and often unknowingly surrender the deepest parts of ourselves. The results can be disastrous as indicated by Shu Ting ("Assembly Line") and James Wright ("Autumn in Martins Ferry"). In "Bartleby the Scrivener," Herman Melville presents characters (yes, the narrator and Bartleby) who have used work to withdraw from vital human relationships. More tragically, perhaps, children and spouses can fall victim to a strict class culture and strong gender prescriptions. Consider, for instance, both William Blake's chimney sweepers and Chitra Banerjee Divakaruni's "Song of the Fisher Wife."

In an increasingly shrinking world, workers often experience cultural collisions as they adapt to not only different workplaces but also different cultures. The resulting tensions are explored in Jimmy Santiago Baca's "So Mexicans Are Taking Jobs from Americans" and Jamaica Kincaid's "Mariah," among others. Of course, discrimination has long been an unfortunate part of human existence, a theme of Woody Guthrie's "Plane Wreck at Los Gatos (Deportee)" and Martín Espada's "Jorge the Church Janitor Finally Quits." In literature, as in actuality, too often those empowered use their work and cultural positionings to abuse the unempowered, usually minorities, as we see in the excerpt from Richard Wright's *Black Boy* ("Five Dollar Fight"). Occasionally, however, after continued discrimination and harassment, individuals stage frightening rebellions, as in John Cheever's "The Five-Forty-Eight." As these selections indicate, those in power have failed to consider what Ralph Waldo Emerson wrote some 150 years ago: ". . . just as the hand was divided into fingers, the better to answer its end . . . the individual to possess himself, must sometimes return from his own labor to embrace all the other laborers."

Some authors in the text deal with seemingly mundane work matters, like commuting and first days. However, even the mundane holds large implications, as we see in Ezra Pound's "In a Station of the Metro" and Daniel Orozco's "Orientation." Sometimes, as Antonya Nelson and John Updike suggest respectively in "Goodfellows" and "A & P," first jobs can be shaping experiences as they lead to greater self- and cultural awareness. In *The Hairy Ape*, Eugene O'Neill reveals how coworkers become intimates and the workplace a forum for debating significant cultural issues—which is inevitable since many adults spend more waking hours with coworkers than with family and friends.

I hope that after reading selections from this anthology that the reader will come to a greater understanding and appreciation of all work and workers. Perhaps, too, readers will be aided in their own quests for satisfying careers. As Robert Louis Stevenson said, "If a man loves the labor of his trade apart from any question of success or fame, the Gods have called him."

Thomas M. Kitts
St. John's University, NY

PART I

WORK: DEFINITIONS AND IDEALS

Introduction

The essays, short story, and poems in this section offer different perspectives on the meaning of work, perspectives that may serve us in reaching our own definition and realizing our own purpose of work. Most of us, like the speaker in Philip Levine's "What Work Is," think we know what work is, and think that, again like Levine's speaker, we have known for many years—since as long as we have been able to read. However, as we read these selections our definitions, attitudes, and goals may be thrown into flux. Certainly, they will be challenged and perhaps emerge more complex yet more focused and complete.

Benjamin Franklin, a leading figure during the Age of Enlightenment, begins the section with a very methodical approach to not only work but also moral development. His charts and ledgers make the complex seem simple and achievable. Yet, as he notes, his approach does not quite pan out. What interferes with his plans in his moral development? What unforeseen circumstances and complexities emerge? What Franklin is certain of, however, is that with focus and energy an individual can achieve wealth and that labor has a positive effect on human behavior.

In many ways, Henry David Thoreau rebukes Franklin's "Way to Wealth" with its emphasis on frugality and industry. Thoreau implies that he is living in an America that has been following Franklin's advice too literally. Thoreau is distressed by the emphasis on the material and rails against a culture driven by commerce. He argues that there are other wealths, more personal ones, in need of cultivation. He challenges us individually and collectively to redefine the very purpose of work.

In "The Tuft of Flowers," Robert Frost presents a speaker who gains a new, perhaps Thoreauvian perspective on labor as he works in a hayfield. At first, a reluctant and lonely worker, the speaker comes to a fuller understanding about how work connects us to other individuals and a larger human and nonhuman community. In

"A Clean Well-Lighted Place," Ernest Hemingway presents two characters with very different perspectives on their jobs. With this story, Hemingway seems to examine Socrates's maxim that "the unexamined life is not worth living." As you read this selection, consider which character leads the fuller and more contented life.

Levine's "What Work Is" concludes this section. However, the speaker of the poem does not reach much of a conclusion. Just when the earlier selections might have moved us toward some certainty about our work and careers, Levine reopens the discussion. In this poem, the speaker asserts that work needs no definition. We all know what it is. However, through the course of the poem, he becomes less certain. Consider what complicates his perspective. By the end of the poem, he concludes that he does not know what work is at all.

Is work really such a simple activity to define?

Benjamin Franklin
(1706–1790)

An individual with great versatility, boundless curiosity, and tremendous energy, Benjamin Franklin exemplifies the Age of Enlightenment or what he calls the Age of Experiments. His accomplishments as a statesman, scientist, inventor, self-made man, and revolutionary hero are awe-inspiring.

Born in Boston on January 17, 1706, Franklin loved to read as a young man. At sixteen, he ran away from his apprenticeship in his brother's print shop, moving first to New York and then to Philadelphia, walking the city streets, he reports, with only pennies. But by the time of his marriage in 1730, Franklin owned his own printing press, edited the colonies' most successful newspaper (*The Pennsylvania Gazette*), and served as the official printer of Pennsylvania. By the age of forty-two, Franklin was able to retire from active business and dedicate himself to various pursuits.

The range of Franklin's achievements is the stuff of legend. He invented such diverse items as bifocals, a stove, and a glass harmonica. He developed the first circulating library, the first colonial hospital, the most efficient delivery system for mail until that time, and the first modern fire department, and he conducted experiments with electricity. Serving the revolutionary cause in various roles, Franklin, with John Jay and John Adams, in 1783, arranged the terms and signed the Treaty of Paris that formally ended the Revolution. Upon his return to Philadelphia, he continued public service in various capacities, sounding, for instance, a prominent anti-slavery voice. His death on April 17, 1790, was an occasion for international mourning.

Included here are excerpts from *The Autobiography*, his most successful literary accomplishment, and "The Way to Wealth," first published in 1758.

FROM *THE AUTOBIOGRAPHY*, CHAPTER 8
[ON MORAL PERFECTION]

It was about this time that I conceiv'd the bold and arduous Project of arriving at moral Perfection. I wish'd to live without committing any Fault at any time; I would conquer all that either Natural Inclination, Custom, or Company might lead me into. As I knew, or thought I knew, what was right and wrong, I did not see why I might not *always* do the one and avoid the other. But I soon found I had undertaken a Task of more Difficulty than I had imagined. While my *Attention was taken up* in guarding against one Fault, I was often surpriz'd by another. Habit took the Advantage of Inattention. Inclination was sometimes too strong for Reason. I concluded at length, that the mere speculative Conviction that it was our Interest to be compleatly virtuous, was not sufficient to prevent our Slipping, and that the contrary Habits must be broken and good ones acquired and established, before we can have any Dependance on a steady uniform Rectitude of Conduct. For this purpose I therefore contriv'd the following Method.

In the various Enumerations of the moral Virtues I had met with in my Reading, I found the Catalogue more or less numerous, as different Writers included more or fewer Ideas under the same Name. Temperance, for Example, was by some confin'd to Eating and Drinking, while by others it was extended to mean the moderating every other Pleasure, Appetite, Inclination or Passion, bodily or mental, even to our Avarice and Ambition. I propos'd to myself, for the sake of Clearness, to use rather more Names with fewer Ideas annex'd to each, than a few Names with more Ideas; and I included under Thirteen Names of Virtues all that at that time occurr'd to me as necessary or desirable, and annex'd to each a short Precept, which fully express'd the Extent I gave to its Meaning.

These Names of Virtues with their Precepts were

1. Temperance.
   Eat not to Dulness.
   Drink not to Elevation.
2. Silence.
   Speak not but what may benefit others or yourself. Avoid trifling Conversation.
3. Order.
   Let all your Things have their Places. Let each Part of your Business have
   its Time.
4. Resolution.
   Resolve to perform what you ought. Perform without fail what you resolve.
5. Frugality.
   Make no Expence but to do good to others or yourself: i.e., Waste nothing.
6. Industry.
   Lose no Time. Be always employ'd in something useful. Cut off all unnecessary Actions.
7. Sincerity.
   Use no hurtful Deceit.
   Think innocently and justly; and, if you speak, speak accordingly.
8. Justice.
   Wrong none, by doing Injuries or omitting the Benefits that are your Duty.
9. Moderation.
   Avoid Extreams. Forbear resenting Injuries so much as you think they
   deserve.

10. Cleanliness.
   Tolerate no Uncleanness in Body, Cloaths, or Habitation.
11. Tranquility.
   Be not disturbed at Trifles, or at Accidents common or unavoidable.
12. Chastity.
   Rarely use Venery but for Health or Offspring; Never to Dulness, Weakness, or the Injury of your own or another's Peace or Reputation.
13. Humility.
   Imitate Jesus and Socrates.

My Intention being to acquire the *Habitude* of all these Virtues, I judg'd it would be well not to distract my Attention by attempting the whole at once, but to fix it on one of them at a time, and when I should be Master of that, then to proceed to another, and so on till I should have gone thro' the thirteen. And as the previous Acquisition of some might facilitate the Acquisition of certain others, I arrang'd them with that View as they stand above. *Temperance* first, as it tends to produce that Coolness and Clearness of Head, which is so necessary where constant Vigilance was to be kept up, and Guard maintained, against the unremitting Attraction of ancient Habits, and the Force of perpetual Temptations. This being acquir'd and establish'd, *Silence* would be more easy, and my Desire being to gain Knowledge at the same time that I improv'd in Virtue, and considering that in Conversation it was obtain'd rather by use of the Ears than of the Tongue, and therefore wishing to break a Habit I was getting into of Prattling, Punning and Joking, which only made me acceptable to trifling Company, I gave *Silence* the second Place. This, and the next, *Order*, I expected would allow me more Time for attending to my Project and my Studies; RESOLUTION, once become habitual, would keep me firm in my Endeavours to obtain all the subsequent Virtues; *Frugality* and *Industry*, by freeing me from my remaining Debt, and producing Affluence and Independence, would make more easy the Practice of *Sincerity* and *Justice*, &c. Conceiving then that agreable to the Advice of Pythagoras in his Golden Verses[1] daily Examination would be necessary, I contriv'd the following Method for conducting that Examination.

I made a little Book in which I allotted a Page for each of the Virtues. I rul'd each Page with red Ink, so as to have seven Columns, one for each Day of the Week, marking each Column with a Letter for the Day. I cross'd these Columns with thirteen red Lines, marking the Beginning of each Line with the first Letter of one of the Virtues, on which Line and in its proper Column I might mark by a little black Spot every Fault I found upon Examination to have been committed respecting that Virtue upon that Day.

I determined to give a Week's strict Attention to each of the Virtues successively. Thus in the first Week my great Guard was to avoid every the least Offence against Temperance, leaving the other Virtues to their ordinary Chance, only marking every Evening the Faults of the Day. Thus if in the first Week I could keep my

---

[1]Pythagoras was an ancient Greek philosopher–mathematician, known especially for his principle of "passionate intellectual contemplation."

first Line marked T clear of Spots, I suppos'd the Habit of that Virtue so much strengthen'd and its opposite weaken'd, that I might venture extending my Attention to include the next, and for the following Week keep both Lines clear of Spots. Proceeding thus to the last, I could go thro' a Course compleat in Thirteen Weeks, and four Courses in a year. And like him who having a Garden to weed, does not attempt to eradicate all the bad Herbs at once, which would exceed his Reach and his Strength, but works on one of the Beds at a time, and having accomplish'd the first proceeds to a Second; so I should have, (I hoped) the encouraging Pleasure of seeing on my Pages the Progress I made in Virtue, by clearing successively my Lines of their Spots, till in the End by a Number of Courses, I should be happy in viewing a clean Book after a thirteen Weeks daily Examination.

Form of the Pages

Temperance							
Eat not to Dulness. *Drink not to Elevation*							
	S	M	T	W	T	F	S
T							
S	••	•		•		•	
O	•	•	•		•	•	•
R			•		•		
F		•		•			
I		•	•				
S							
I							
M							
Cl.							
T							
Ch.							
H							

This my little Book had for its Motto these Lines from Addison's Cato:

Here will I hold: If there is a Pow'r above us,
(And that there is, all Nature cries aloud
Thro' all her Works) he must delight in Virtue,
And that which he delights in must be happy.[2]

Another from Cicero.

O Vitæ Philosophia Dux! O Virtutum indagatrix, expultrixque vitiorum! Unus dies bene, et ex preceptis tuis actus, peccanti immortalitati est anteponendus.[3]

---

[2]Joseph Addison, *Cato. A Tragedy* (1713), Act V. Scene i, lines 15–18.
[3]Marcus Tullius Cicero (106–43 B.C.). Roman philosopher and orator. The quotation is from *Tusculan Disputations*, Act V. Scene ii, line 5. Several lines are omitted after *viturum.* "Oh philosophy, guide of life! Oh searcher out of virtues and expeller of vices! . . . One day lived well and according to thy precepts is to be preferred to an eternity of sin."

Another from the Proverbs of Solomon speaking of Wisdom or Virtue;

Length of Days is in her right hand, and in her Left Hand Riches and Honours; Her Ways are Ways of Pleasantness, and all her Paths are Peace.   III, 16, 17.

And conceiving God to be the Fountain of Wisdom, I thought it right and necessary to solicit his Assistance for obtaining it; to this End I form'd the following little Prayer, which was prefix'd to my Tables of Examination; for daily Use.

O Powerful Goodness! bountiful Father! merciful Guide! Increase in me that Wisdom which discovers my truest Interests; Strengthen my Resolutions to perform what that Wisdom dictates. Accept my kind Offices to thy other Children, as the only Return in my Power for thy continual Favours to me.

I us'd also sometimes a little Prayer which I took from Thomson's Poems, viz

Father of Light and Life, thou Good supreme,
  O teach me what is good, teach me thy self!
Save me from Folly, Vanity and Vice,
  From every low Pursuit, and fill my Soul

The Morning Question, What Good shall I do this Day?	5	Rise, wash, and address *Powerful Goodness;* Contrive Day's Business and take the Resolution of the Day; prosecute the present Study; and breakfast?
	6	
	7	
	8	
	9	Work.
	10	
	11	
	12	Read, or overlook my Accounts, and dine.
	1	
	2	
	3	Work.
	4	
	5	
	6	Put Things in their Places, Supper, Musick, or Diversion, or Conversation, Examination of the Day.
	7	
	8	
Evening Question, What Good have I done to day?	9	
	10	
	11	
	12	
	1	Sleep.
	2	
	3	
	4	

> *With Knowledge, conscious Peace, and Virtue pure,*
>   *Sacred, substantial, neverfading Bliss.*[4]

The Precept of *Order* requiring that *every Part of my Business should have its allotted Time*, one Page in my little Book contain'd the following Scheme of Employment for the Twenty-four Hours of a natural Day.

I enter'd upon the Execution of this Plan for Self-Examination, and continu'd it with occasional Intermissions for some time. I was surpriz'd to find myself so much fuller of Faults than I had imagined, but I had the Satisfaction of seeing them diminish. To avoid the Trouble of renewing now and then my little Book, which by scraping out the Marks on the Paper of old Faults to make room for new Ones in a new Course, became full of Holes: I transferr'd my Tables and Precepts to the Ivory Leaves of a Memorandum Book, on which the Lines were drawn with red Ink that made a durable Stain, and on those Lines I mark'd my Faults with a black Lead Pencil, which Marks I could easily wipe out with a wet Sponge. After a while I went thro' one Course only in a Year, and afterwards only one in several Years; till at length I omitted them entirely, being employ'd in Voyages and Business abroad with a Multiplicity of Affairs, that interfered. But I always carried my little Book with me.

My scheme of ORDER, gave me the most Trouble, and I found, that tho' it might be practicable where a Man's Business was such as to leave him the Disposition of his Time, that of a Journey-man Printer for instance, it was not possible to be exactly observ'd by a Master, who must mix with the World, and often receive People of Business at their own Hours. *Order* too, with regard to Places for Things, Papers, &c. I found extreamly difficult to acquire. I had not been early accustomed to *Method*, and having an exceeding good Memory, I was not so sensible of the Inconvenience attending Want of Method. This Article therefore cost me so much painful Attention and my Faults in it vex'd me so much, and I made so little Progress in Amendment, and had such frequent Relapses, that I was almost ready to give up the Attempt, and content my self with a faulty Character in that respect. Like the Man who in buying an Ax of a Smith my neighbour, desired to have the whole of its Surface as bright as the Edge; The Smith consented to grind it bright for him if he would turn the Wheel. He turn'd while the Smith press'd the broad Face of the Ax hard and heavily on the Stone, which made the Turning of it very fatiguing. The Man came every now and then from the Wheel to see how the Work went on; and at length would take his Ax as it was without farther Grinding. No, says the Smith, Turn on, turn on; we shall have it bright by and by; as yet 'tis only speckled. Yes, says the Man; but—*I think I like a speckled Ax best.* —And I believe this may have been the Case with many who having for want of some such Means as I employ'd found the Difficulty of obtaining good, and breaking bad Habits, in other Points of Vice and Virtue, have given up the Struggle, and concluded that *a speckled Ax was best.* For something that pretended to be Reason was every now and then suggesting

---

[4]From James Thomson (1700–1748), *The Seasons*, "Winter" (1726), lines 218–23.

to me, that such extream nicety as I exacted of my self might be a kind of Foppery in Morals, which if it were known, would make me ridiculous; that a perfect Character might be attended with the Inconvenience of being envied and hated; and that a benevolent Man should allow a few Faults in himself, to keep his Friends in Countenance.

In Truth I found myself incorrigible with respect to *Order;* and now I am grown old, and my Memory bad, I feel very sensibly the want of it. But on the whole, tho' I never arrived at the Perfection I had been so ambitious of obtaining, but fell far short of it, yet I was by the Endeavour a better and a happier Man than I otherwise should have been if I had not attempted it; As those who aim at perfect Writing by imitating the engraved Copies, tho' they never reach the wish'd for Excellence of those Copies, their Hand is mended by the Endeavour, and is tolerable while it continues fair and legible.

1771

Questions

1. How is "moral perfection" like a job that Franklin undertakes? How would you characterize his approach to himself and this undertaking?
2. Characterize Franklin's definitions of the virtues. How are they all similar?
3. What are the strengths and weaknesses of Franklin's plan to obtain "moral perfection?"
4. Review Franklin's chart. Create a chart of a somewhat typical day in your life. Then create a chart of *how* a typical day in your life should be. Are there many inconsistencies between your two charts?
5. Franklin admits he does not reach "moral perfection," but was his plan at least somewhat successful? What were the benefits of the attempt?
6. How does Franklin regard himself in this excerpt?
7. Consider novelist and essayist D. H. Lawrence's response to Franklin in *Studies in Classic American Literature*: "The Perfectibility of Man! Ah what a dreary theme! . . . The perfectibility of which man? I am many men. Which of them are you going to perfect? I am not a mechanical contrivance."

THE WAY TO WEALTH: PREFACE TO POOR RICHARD, 1758

Benjamin Franklin published Poor Richard's Almanack annually from 1733 to 1758 before he sold it. It continued publication until 1796. The Almanack included the usual astronomical and agricultural information of a typical almanac, but Franklin added literary selections and editorials for which Franklin created the persona of Richard Saunders. Through Poor Richard, Franklin presented proverbs, old and new, but always with a homespun American sensibility and pragmatism. "The Way to Wealth" collects many of Richard's best remembered maxims.

Courteous Reader

I have heard that nothing gives an Author so great Pleasure, as to find his Works respectfully quoted by other learned Authors. This Pleasure I have seldom enjoyed; for tho' I have been, if I may say it without Vanity, an *eminent Author* of Almanacks annually now a full Quarter of a Century, my Brother Authors in the same Way, for what Reason I know not, have ever been very sparing in their Applauses; and no other Author has taken the least Notice of me, so that did not my Writings produce me some *solid Pudding,* the great Deficiency of *Praise* would have quite discouraged me.

I concluded at length, that the People were the best Judges of my Merit; for they buy my Works; and besides, in my Rambles, where I am not personally known, I have frequently heard one or other of my Adages repeated, with, *as Poor Richard says,* at the End on't; this gave me some Satisfaction, as it showed not only that my Instructions were regarded, but discovered likewise some Respect for my Authority; and I own, that to encourage the Practice of remembering and repeating those wise Sentences, I have sometimes *quoted* myself with great Gravity.

Judge then how much I must have been gratified by an Incident I am going to relate to you. I stopt my Horse lately where a great Number of People were collected at a Vendue of Merchant Goods. The Hour of Sale not being come, they were conversing on the Badness of the Times, and one of the Company call'd to a plain clean old Man, with white Locks, *Pray, Father* Abraham, *what think you of the Times? Won't these heavy Taxes quite ruin the Country? How shall we ever be able to pay them? What would you advise us to?*— Father *Abraham* stood up, and reply'd, If you'd have my Advice, I'll give it you in short, for a *Word to the Wise is enough,* and *many Words won't fill a Bushel,* as *Poor Richard says.* They join'd in desiring him to speak his Mind, and gathering round him, he proceeded as follows;

"Friends," says he, and Neighbours, the Taxes are indeed very heavy, and if those laid on by the Government were the only Ones we had to pay, we might more easily discharge them; but we have many others, and much more grievous to some of us. We are taxed twice as much by our *Idleness,* three times as much by our *Pride,* and four times as much by our *Folly,* and from these Taxes the Commissioners cannot ease or deliver us by allowing an Abatement. However, let us hearken to good Advice, and something may be done for us; *God helps them that help themselves,* as *Poor Richard* says, in his Almanack of 1733.

It would be thought a hard Government that should tax its People one tenth Part of their *Time,* to be employed in its Service. But *Idleness* taxes many of us much more if we reckon all that is spent in absolute *Sloth,* or doing of nothing, with that which is spent in idle Employments or Amusements, that amount to nothing. *Sloth,* by bringing on Diseases, absolutely shortens Life. *Sloth, like Rust, consumes faster than Labour wears, while the used Key is always bright,* as *Poor Richard* says. But *dost thou love Life, then do not squander Time, for that's the Stuff Life is made of,* as *Poor Richard* says.—How much more than is necessary do we spend in Sleep! forgetting that *The sleeping Fox catches no Poultry,* and that *there will be sleeping enough in the Grave,* as *Poor Richard* says. If Time be of all

Things the most precious, *wasting Time* must be, as *Poor Richard* says, *the greatest Prodigality*, since, as he elsewhere tells us, *Lost Time is never found again;* and what we call *Time-enough, always proves little enough*. Let us then up and be doing, and doing to the Purpose; so by Diligence shall we do more with less Perplexity. *Sloth makes all Things difficult, but Industry all easy*, as *Poor Richard* says; and *He that riseth late, must trot all Day, and shall scarce overtake his Business at Night*. While *Laziness travels so slowly, that Poverty soon overtakes him*, as we read in *Poor Richard*, who adds, *Drive thy Business, let not that drive thee;* and *Early to Bed, and early to rise, makes a Man healthy, wealthy, and wise*.

So what signifies *wishing* and *hoping* for better Times. We may make these Times better if we bestir ourselves. *Industry need not wish*, as *Poor Richard* says, and *He that lives upon Hope will die fasting. There are no Gains, without Pains;* then *Help Hands, for I have no Lands*, or if I have, they are smartly taxed. And, as *Poor Richard* likewise observes, *He that hath a Trade hath an Estate*, and *He that hath a Calling, hath an Office of Profit and Honour;* but then the *Trade* must be worked at, and the *Calling* well followed, or neither the *Estate*, nor the *Office*, will enable us to pay our Taxes.—If we are industrious we shall never starve; for, as *Poor Richard* says, *At the working Man's House* Hunger *looks in, but dares not enter*. Nor will the Bailiff or the Constable enter, for *Industry pays Debts, while Despair encreaseth them*, says *Poor Richard*.—What though you have found no Treasure, nor has any rich Relation left you a Legacy, *Diligence is the Mother of Good luck*, as *Poor Richard* says, *and God gives all Things to Industry. Then plough deep, while Sluggards sleep, and you shall have Corn to sell and to keep*, says *Poor Dick*. Work while it is called To-day, for you know not how much you may be hindered To morrow, which makes *Poor Richard* say, *One To-day is worth two To-morrows;* and farther, *Have you somewhat to do To-morrow, do it To-day*. If you were a Servant, would you not be ashamed that a good Master should catch you idle? Are you then your own Master, *be ashamed to catch yourself idle*, as *Poor Dick* says. When there is so much to be done for yourself, your Family, your Country, and your gracious King, be up by Peep of Day; *Let not the Sun look down and say, Inglorious here he lies*. Handle your Tools without Mittens; remember that *the Cat in Gloves catches no Mice*, as *Poor Richard* says. 'Tis true there is much to be done, and perhaps you are weak handed, but stick to it steadily, and you will see great Effects, for constant *Dropping wears away Stones*, and by *Diligence and Patience the Mouse ate in two the Cable;* and *little Strokes fell great Oaks*, as *Poor Richard* says in his Almanack, the Year I cannot just now remember.

Methinks I hear some of you say, *Must a Man afford himself no Leisure?*—I will tell thee, my Friend, what *Poor Richard* says, *Employ thy Time well if thou meanest to gain Leisure;* and, *since thou art not sure of a Minute, throw not away an Hour*. Leisure, is Time for doing something useful; this Leisure the diligent Man will obtain, but the lazy Man never; so that, as *Poor Richard* says, a *Life of Leisure and a Life of Laziness are two Things*. Do you imagine that Sloth will afford you more Comfort than Labour? No, for as *Poor Richard* says, *Trouble springs from Idleness, and grievous Toil from needless Ease. Many without Labour, would live by their* WITS *only, but they break for want of Stock*. Whereas

Industry gives Comfort, and Plenty, and Respect: *Fly Pleasures, and they'll follow you. The diligent Spinner has a large Shift*, and *now I have a Sheep and a Cow, every Body bids me Good morrow*; all which is well said by *Poor Richard*.

But with our Industry, we must likewise be *steady, settled* and *careful*, and oversee our own Affairs *with our own Eyes*, and not trust too much to others; for, as *Poor Richard* says,

> *I never saw an oft removed Tree,*
> *Nor yet an oft removed Family,*
> *That throve so well as those that settled be.*

And again, *Three Removes is as bad as a Fire*; and again, *Keep thy Shop, and thy Shop will keep thee*; and again, *If you would have your Business done, go; If not, send.* And again,

> *He that by the Plough would thrive,*
> *Himself must either hold or drive.*

And again, *The Eye of a Master will do more Work than both his Hands*; and again, *Want of Care does us more Damage than Want of Knowledge*; and again, *Not to oversee Workmen, is to leave them your Purse open.* Trusting too much to others Care is the Ruin of many; for, as the *Almanack* says, *In the Affairs of this World, Men are saved, not by Faith, but by the Want of it*; but a Man's own Care is profitable; for, saith *Poor Dick, Learning is to the Studious*, and *Riches to the Careful*, as well as *Power to the Bold*, and *Heaven to the Virtuous.* And farther, *If you would have a faithful Servant, and one that you like, serve yourself.* And again, he adviseth to Circumspection and Care, even in the smallest Matters, because sometimes a *little Neglect may breed great Mischief*; adding, *For want of a Nail the Shoe was lost; for want of a Shoe the Horse was lost; and for want of a Horse the Rider was lost*, being overtaken and slain by the Enemy, all for want of Care about a Horse shoe Nail.

So much for Industry, my Friends, and Attention to one's own Business; but to these we must add *Frugality*, if we would make our *Industry* more certainly successful. A Man may, if he knows not how to save as he gets, *keep his Nose all his Life to the Grindstone*, and die not worth a *Groat* at last. *A fat Kitchen makes a lean Will*, as *Poor Richard* says; and,

> *Many Estates are spent in the Getting,*
> *Since Women for Tea forsook Spinning and Knitting,*
> *And Men for Punch forsook Hewing and Splitting.*

If you would be wealthy, says he, in another Almanack, *think of Saving as well as of Getting: The* Indies *have not made* Spain *rich, because her* Outgoes *are greater than her* Incomes. Away then with your expensive Follies, and you will not have so much Cause to complain of hard Times, heavy Taxes, and chargeable Families; for, as *Poor Dick* says,

> *Women and Wine, Game and Deceit,*
> *Make the Wealth small, and the Wants great.*

And farther, *What maintains one Vice, would bring up two Children.* You may think perhaps, That a *little* Tea, or a *little* Punch now and then, Diet a *little* more costly, Clothes a *little* finer, and a *little* Entertainment now and then, can be no great Matter; but remember what *Poor Richard* says, *Many a* Little *makes a Mickle,* and farther, *Beware of* little *Expences; a small Leak will sink a great Ship;* and again, *Who Dainties love, shall Beggars prove;* and moreover, *Fools make Feasts, and wise Men eat them.*

Here you are all got together at this Vendue of *Fineries* and *Knicknacks.* You call them *Goods,* but if you do not take Care, they will prove *Evils* to some of you. You expect they will be sold *cheap,* and perhaps they may for less than they cost; but if you have no Occasion for them, they must be *dear* to you. Remember what *Poor Richard* says, *Buy what thou hast no Need of, and ere long thou shalt sell thy Necessaries.* And again, *At a great Pennyworth pause a while·* He means, that perhaps the Cheapness is *apparent* only, and not *real;* or the Bargain, by straitning thee in thy Business, may do thee more Harm than Good. For in another place he says, *Many have been ruined by buying good Pennyworths.* Again, *Poor Richard* says, *'Tis foolish to lay out Money in a Purchase of Repentance;* and yet this Folly is practised every Day at Vendues, for want of minding the Almanack. *Wise Men,* as *Poor Dick* says, *learn by others Harms, Fools scarcely by their own;* but, *Felix quem faciunt aliena Pericula cautum.* Many a one, for the Sake of Finery on the Back, have gone with a hungry Belly, and half starved their Families; *Silks and Sattins, Scarlet and Velvets,* as *Poor Richard* says, *put out the Kitchen Fire.* These are not the *Necessaries* of Life; they can scarcely be called the *Conveniences,* and yet only because they look pretty, how many *want* to *have* them. The *artificial* Wants of Mankind thus become more numerous than the *natural;* and, as *Poor Dick* says, *For one* poor *Person, there are an hundred* indigent. By these, and other Extravagancies, the Genteel are reduced to Poverty, and forced to borrow of those whom they formerly despised, but who through *Industry* and *Frugality* have maintained their Standing; in which Case it appears plainly, that a *Ploughman on his Legs is higher than a Gentleman on his Knees,* as *Poor Richard* says. Perhaps they have had a small Estate left them, which they knew not the Getting of; they think *'tis Day, and will never be Night;* that a little to be spent out of *so much,* is not worth minding; (*a Child and a Fool,* as *Poor Richard* says, *imagine* Twenty Shillings *and Twenty Years can never be spent*) but, *always taking out of the Meal tub, and never putting in, soon comes to the Bottom;* then, as *Poor Dick* says, *When the Well's dry, they know the Worth of Water.* But this they might have known before, if they had taken his Advice; *If you would know the Value of Money, go and try to borrow some;* for, *he that goes a borrowing goes a sorrowing;* and indeed so does he that lends to such People, when he goes *to get it in again.*—*Poor Dick* farther advises, and says,

> *Fond* Pride of Dress, *is sure a very Curse;*
> *E'er* Fancy *you consult, consult your Purse.*

And again, *Pride is as loud a Beggar as Want, and a great deal more saucy.* When you have bought one fine Thing you must buy ten more, that your

Appearance may be all of a Piece; but *Poor Dick* says, *'Tis easier to suppress the first Desire, than to* satisfy *all that follow it*. And 'tis as truly Folly for the Poor to ape the Rich, as for the Frog to swell, in order to equal the Ox.

> *Great Estates may venture more,*
> *But little Boats should keep near Shore.*

'Tis, however, a Folly soon punished; for *Pride that dines on Vanity sups on Contempt*, as *Poor Richard* says. And in another Place, *Pride breakfasted with Plenty, dined with Poverty, and supped with Infamy*. And after all, of what Use is this *Pride of Appearance*, for which so much is risked, so much is suffered? It cannot promote Health, or ease Pain; it makes no Increase of Merit in the Person, it creates Envy, it hastens Misfortune.

> *What is a Butterfly? At best*
> *He's but a Caterpillar drest.*
> *The gaudy Fop's his Picture just,*

as *Poor Richard* says.

But what Madness must it be to *run in Debt* for these Superfluities! We are offered, by the Terms of this Vendue, *Six Months Credit*; and that perhaps has induced some of us to attend it, because we cannot spare the ready Money, and hope now to be fine without it. But, ah, think what you do when you run in Debt; *You give to another, Power over your Liberty*. If you cannot pay at the Time, you will be ashamed to see your Creditor; you will be in Fear when you speak to him; you will make poor pitiful sneaking Excuses, and by Degrees come to lose your Veracity, and sink into base downright lying; for, as *Poor Richard* says, *The second Vice is Lying, the first is running in Debt*. And again, to the same Purpose, *Lying rides upon Debt's Back*. Whereas a freeborn *Englishman* ought not to be ashamed or afraid to see or speak to any Man living. But Poverty often deprives a Man of all Spirit and Virtue: *'Tis hard for an empty Bag to stand upright*, as *Poor Richard* truly says. What would you think of that Prince, or that Government, who should issue an Edict forbid ding you to dress like a Gentleman or a Gentlewoman, on Pain of Imprisonment or Servitude? Would you not say, that you are free, have a Right to dress as you please, and that such an Edict would be a Breach of your Privileges, and such a Government tyrannical? And yet you are about to put yourself under that Tyranny when you run in Debt for such Dress! Your Creditor has Authority at his Pleasure to deprive you of your Liberty, by confining you in Gaol [*sic*] for Life, or to sell you for a Servant, if you should not be able to pay him! When you have got your Bargain, you may, perhaps; think little of Payment; but *Creditors, Poor Richard* tells us, *have better Memories than Debtors*; and in another Place says, *Creditors are a superstitious Sect, great Observers of set Days and Times*. The Day comes round before you are aware, and the Demand is made before you are prepared to satisfy it. Or if you bear your Debt in Mind, the Term, which at first seemed so long, will, as it lessens, appear extremely short. *Time* will seem to have added Wings to his Heels as well as Shoulders. *Those have a short Lent*, saith *Poor Richard, who owe Money to be paid at Easter*.

Then since, as he says, *The Borrower is a Slave to the Lender, and the Debtor to the Creditor*, disdain the Chain, preserve your Freedom; and maintain your Independence: Be *industrious* and *free*; be *frugal* and *free*. At present, perhaps, you may think yourself in thriving Circumstances, and that you can bear a little Extravagance without Injury;

> *For Age and Want, save while you may;*
> *No Morning Sun lasts a whole Day,*

as *Poor Richard* says—Gain may be temporary and uncertain, but ever while you live, Expence is constant and certain; and *'tis easier to build two Chimnies than to keep one in Fuel*, as *Poor Richard* says. *So rather go to Bed supperless than rise in Debt.*

> *Get what you can, and what you get hold;*
> *'Tis the Stone that will turn all your lead into Gold,*

as *Poor Richard* says. And when you have got the Philosopher's Stone, sure you will no longer complain of bad Times, or the Difficulty of paying Taxes.

This Doctrine, my Friends, is *Reason* and *Wisdom*; but after all, do not depend too much upon your own *Industry*, and *Frugality*, and *Prudence*, though excellent Things, for they may all be blasted without the Blessing of Heaven; and therefore ask that Blessing humbly, and be not uncharitable to those that at present seem to want it, but comfort and help them. Remember *Job* suffered, and was afterwards prosperous.

And now to conclude, *Experience keeps a dear School, but Fools will learn in no other, and scarce in that*; for it is true, *we may give Advice, but we cannot give Conduct*, as *Poor Richard* says: However, remember this, *They that won't be counselled, can't be helped*, as *Poor Richard* says: And farther, That *if you will not hear Reason, she'll surely rap your Knuckles.*"

Thus the old Gentleman ended his Harangue. The People heard it, and approved the Doctrine, and immediately practised the contrary, just as if it had been a common Sermon; for the Vendue opened, and they began to buy extravagantly, notwithstanding all his Cautions, and their own Fear of Taxes.—I found the good Man had thoroughly studied my Almanacks, and digested all I had dropt on those Topicks during the Course of Five-and-twenty Years. The frequent Mention he made of me must have tired any one else, but my Vanity was wonderfully delighted with it, though I was conscious that not a tenth Part of this Wisdom was my own which he ascribed to me, but rather the *Gleanings* I had made of the Sense of all Ages and Nations. However, I resolved to be the better for the Echo of it; and though I had at first determined to buy Stuff for a new Coat, I went away resolved to wear my old One a little longer, *Reader*, if thou wilt do the same, thy Profit will be as great as mine.

> *I am, as ever,*
> *Thine to serve thee,*

July 7, 1757.   *Richard Saunders.*

Questions

1. According to Franklin, what is the way to wealth? Is his advice still relevant today?
2. Select five proverbs from the selection and explain what each one recommends. Find at least two with which you disagree. Explain your answer.
3. Do you agree with Franklin that being in debt is worse than lying?
4. How does Franklin's advice in "The Way to Wealth" reflect the American work ethic and the American dream?
5. How does Franklin keep his advice from being pompous and overbearing? Consider his use of Father Abraham and the reaction of the crowd outside the store. How is Franklin ironic and self-deprecating?
6. Nathaniel Hawthorne said that Franklin's proverbs "teach men but a very small portion of their duties. . . . They are all about getting money or saving it." Explain Hawthorne's criticism. Do you agree?
7. Mark Twain said that Franklin was "full of animosity towards boys" because he was forever telling them how not to waste time. Is Twain's criticism fair? Do you agree with Twain or Franklin?

Henry David Thoreau (1817–1862)

Henry David Thoreau was one of America's leading proponents of transcendentalism, an eclectic and idealistic literary, philosophical, and political movement at the heart of American Romanticism. Born in Concord, Massachusetts, Thoreau was a naturalist who was especially familiar with the New England landscape. He is best known for *Walden*, a reflection on his two years of simple living in a self-built house near Walden's Pond in Massachusetts. But he was also a surveyor, social critic, abolitionist, tax resister, and defender of individual rights whose doctrine of passive resistance influenced Mahatma Gandhi and Martin Luther King, Jr.

Thoreau, regarded by many as an extremist, could be cantankerous and often had fierce arguments with his mentor, Ralph Waldo Emerson. The leading American intellectual of his day, Emerson was so disappointed by Thoreau, who he thought lacked ambition, that after Thoreau's death, Emerson said that "instead of engineering for all America, he was the captain of a huckleberry-party." Little did Emerson realize that Thoreau's work would endure along with his own. (In a journal entry, Thoreau wrote, "I doubt if Emerson could trundle a wheelbarrow through the streets.")

Thoreau, who had suffered with tuberculosis for years, succumbed to the disease in 1862. His decline was hastened when he caught a bad cold in December 1860 while spending a night in a storm counting tree rings. As his end approached, his aunt Louisa asked him whether he had made his peace with God, to which Thoreau gave his often quoted response, "I did not know we had ever quarreled."

In this excerpt from "Life without Principle," Thoreau questions the American work ethic and the way individuals go about choosing their life's work.

FROM LIFE WITHOUT PRINCIPLE

"Life without Principle" was originally delivered as a lecture under the title "Getting a Living" on December 26, 1854.

Let us consider the way in which we spend our lives.

This world is a place of business. What an infinite bustle! I am awaked almost every night by the panting of the locomotive. It interrupts my dreams. There is no sabbath. It would be glorious to see mankind at leisure for once. It is nothing but work, work, work. I cannot easily buy a blank-book to write thoughts in; they are commonly ruled for dollars and cents. An Irishman, seeing me making a minute[1] in the fields, took it for granted that I was calculating my wages. If a man was tossed out of a window when an infant, and so made a cripple for life, or scared out of his wits by the Indians, it is regretted chiefly because he was thus incapacitated for—business! I think that there is nothing, not even crime, more opposed to poetry, to philosophy, ay, to life itself, than this incessant business.

There is a coarse and boisterous money-making fellow in the outskirts of our town, who is going to build a bank-wall under the hill along the edge of his meadow. The powers have put this into his head to keep him out of mischief, and he wishes me to spend three weeks digging there with him. The result will be that he will perhaps get some more money to hoard, and leave for his heirs to spend foolishly. If I do this, most will commend me as an industrious and hard-working man; but if I choose to devote myself to certain labors, which yield more real profit, though but little money, they may be inclined to look on me as an idler. Nevertheless, as I do not need the police of meaningless labor to regulate me, and do not see anything absolutely praiseworthy in this fellow's undertaking any more than in many an enterprise of our own or foreign governments, however amusing it may be to him or them, I prefer to finish my education at a different school.

If a man walk in the woods for love of them half of each day, he is in danger of being regarded as a loafer; but if he spends his whole day as a speculator, shearing off those woods and making earth bald before her time, he is esteemed an industrious and enterprising citizen. As if a town had no interest in its forests but to cut them down!

The ways by which you may get money almost without exception lead downward. To have done anything by which you earned money *merely* is to have been truly idle or worse. If the laborer gets no more than the wages, which his employer pays him, he is cheated, he cheats himself. If you would get money as a writer or lecturer, you must be popular, which is to go down perpendicularly. Those services which the community will most readily pay for, it is most disagreeable to render. You are paid for being something less than a man. The state does not commonly reward a genius any more wisely. Even the poet laureate would rather not have to celebrate the accidents of royalty. He must be bribed with a pipe of wine;[2] and perhaps another poet is called away from his muse to gauge that very pipe. As for my own business, even that kind of surveying, which I could do with most satisfaction my employers do not want. They would prefer that I should do my work coarsely and not too well, ay, not well enough. When I observe that there are different ways of surveying, my employer commonly asks, which will give him the most land, not which is most correct. I once invented a rule for measuring cord-wood,

[1]notation
[2]The traditional annual stipend for the poet laureate in England was a pipe of wine, or a large cask containing 126 gallons.

and tried to introduce it in Boston; but the measurer there told me that the sellers did not wish to have their wood measured correctly—that he was already too accurate for them, and therefore they commonly got their wood measured in Charlestown before crossing the bridge.

The aim of the laborer should be, not to get his living, to get "a good job," but to perform well a certain work; and, even in a pecuniary sense, it would be economy for a town to pay its laborers so well that they would not feel that they were working for low ends, as for a livelihood merely, but for scientific, or even moral ends. Do not hire a man who does your work for money, but him who does it for love of it. . .

America is said to be the arena on which the battle of freedom is to be fought; but surely it cannot be freedom in a merely political sense that is meant. Even if we grant that the American has freed himself from a political tyrant, he is still the slave of an economical and moral tyrant. Now that the republic—the *res-publica*—has been settled, it is time to look after the *res-privata*,—the private state,—to see, as the Roman senate charged its consuls, "*ne quid res*-PRIVATA *detrimenti caperet*," that the *private* state receive no detriment.

Do we call this the land of the free? What is it to be free from King George and continue the slaves of King. Prejudice? What is it to be born free and not to live free? What is the value of any political freedom, but as a means to moral freedom? Is it a freedom to be slaves, or a freedom to be free, of which we boast? We are a nation of politicians, concerned about the outmost defenses only of freedom. It is our children's children who may perchance be really free. We tax ourselves unjustly. There is a part of us which is not represented. It is taxation without representation. We quarter troops, we quarter fools and cattle of all sorts upon ourselves. We quarter our gross bodies on our poor souls, till the former eat up all the latter's substance.

1863

Questions

1. What is Thoreau's principal complaint with the America of his time? Is Thoreau's complaint relevant today?
2. How does America's obsession with business and making money affect the individual?
3. What is the purpose of Thoreau's anecdote about the "coarse and boisterous money-making fellow?"
4. In the third paragraph, Thoreau says he "would prefer to finish my education at a different school." Explain what he means.
5. Thoreau writes that "to have done anything by which you earned money merely is to have been truly idle or worse." Explain his statement. Is Thoreau being ironic? What does he mean by *worse*?
6. What does Thoreau imply with his reference to accurate surveying and his method for weighing wood?
7. How does Thoreau distinguish between the private state and the public state? How are both "the slave of an economical and moral tyrant?"

8. Explain the analogy that Thoreau makes between his contemporary America and America at the time of the Revolution? What kind of revolution is he calling for?

9. How would you summarize what might be called Thoreau's "philosophy of labor?"

10. Contrast Franklin and Thoreau. Franklin is generally considered more pragmatic than Thoreau, and Thoreau more idealistic. Argue, however, that Thoreau is the pragmatist and Franklin the idealist. Based on the excerpts in the text, who would you choose to consult for career advice?

11. How do you think Thoreau would have responded to the following remarks of President Calvin Coolidge (1872–1933; U.S. president, 1923–1929)?

> After all, the chief business of the American people is business. . . . Of course the accumulation of wealth cannot be justified as the chief end of existence. We make no concealment of the fact that we want wealth, but there are many other things that we want very much more. We want peace and honor, and that charity, which is so strong an element of all civilization. The chief ideal of the American people is idealism. I cannot repeat too often that America is a nation of idealists. That is the only motive to which they ever give any strong and lasting reaction. . . . The man who builds a factory builds a temple. The man who works there worships there.

Robert Frost (1874–1963)

Although he is considered the quintessential New England farmer–poet, Robert Frost was actually born in San Francisco and lived there until the age of eleven. After his father died, Frost's mother moved the family east where she and her husband had their roots. Frost graduated high school in Lawrence, Massachusetts, as co-valedictorian with Elinor White, his future wife. He briefly attended Dartmouth College before taking a job at a newspaper and then teaching school. In 1900, his grandfather gave him a farm in Derry, New Hampshire. For the next dozen years, Frost raised chickens and grew apples, wrote poetry, and taught at Pinkerton Academy from 1906–1910.

In 1912, anxious to develop a career as a poet, Frost sold the farm and moved his wife and four children to England, where he met several emerging poets, including William Butler Yeats, T. S. Eliot, and Ezra Pound. Pound helped him secure a publisher for his first two volumes, *A Boy's Will* (1913) and *North of Boston* (1914). With two critically acclaimed volumes, Frost returned to America in 1915 and settled on a New Hampshire farm. His fame grew with the publication of *Mountain Interval* in 1916.

Like Whitman before him, Frost cultivated his image, presenting himself as a folksy, affable, and modest sage who recited his poems in an avuncular voice. His life, however, was filled with tragedy, and he could be a bitter and spiteful competitor. In his poetry, Frost used an everyday vocabulary and a conversational tone, yet his poems insisted on established meter and sometimes rhyme. He once said that writing in free verse is like playing tennis without a net. For Frost, a poem "begins in delight and ends in wisdom" and represents a "momentary stay against confusion."

"The Tuft of Flowers" first appeared in *A Boy's Will*.

THE TUFT OF FLOWERS
The Tuft of Flowers (1913)

I went to turn the grass once after one
Who mowed it in the dew before the sun.

The dew was gone that made his blade so keen
Before I came to view the leveled scene.

5   I looked for him behind an isle of trees;
I listened for his whetstone in the breeze.

But he had gone his way, the grass all mown,
And I must be, as he had been,—alone,

"As all must be," I said within my heart,
10   "Whether they work together or apart."

But as I said it, swift there passed me by
On noiseless wing a bewildered butterfly,

Seeking with memories grown dim o'er night
Some resting flower of yesterday's delight.

15   And once I marked his flight go round and round,
As where some flower lay withering on the ground.

And then he flew as far as eye could see,
And then on tremulous wing came back to me.

I thought of questions that have no reply,
20   And would have turned to toss the grass to dry;

But he turned first, and led my eye to look
At a tall tuft of flowers beside a brook,

A leaping tongue of bloom the scythe had spared
Beside a reedy brook the scythe had bared.

25   The mower in the dew had loved them thus,
By leaving them to flourish, not for us,

Nor yet to draw one thought of ours to him,
But from sheer morning gladness at the brim.

The butterfly and I had lit upon,
30   Nevertheless, a message from the dawn,

That made me hear the wakening birds around,
And hear his long scythe whispering to the ground,

And feel a spirit kindred to my own;
So that henceforth I worked no more alone;

35   But glad with him, I worked as with his aid,
And weary, sought at noon with him the shade;

And dreaming, as it were, held brotherly speech
With one whose thought I had not hoped to reach.

"Men work together," I told him from the heart,
40   "Whether they work together or apart."

1913

Questions

1. The speaker of the poem seems profoundly lonely. What realization does the speaker achieve about work, which makes him less lonely?
2. Explain the shift in the author's attitude toward work and the human condition by focusing on lines 9–10 and the closing couplet.
3. What role does the butterfly play in the poem? Is the butterfly a kind of emissary? How does the speaker project his own feelings onto those of the butterfly? How does the butterfly help the speaker shift his attention off himself and onto the tuft of flowers? What does the butterfly connect the speaker with?
4. How is the poem a tribute to work? Do you agree with the speaker's vision of work?
5. Compare Frost's speaker in light of Franklin's closing paragraph from Chapter 13 [on "building forts"] in *The Autobiography*.
6. Consider the effect that form has on the revelation of character and theme. "The Tuft of Flowers" is written in heroic couplets—paired lines of iambic pentameter, rhymed and end-stopped.

Ernest Hemingway
(1899-1961)

Upon his graduation from high school, Ernest Hemingway opted for a job as a cub reporter for the *Kansas City Star*. But after only six months with the newspaper and at only eighteen years of age, the Illinois native volunteered as an ambulance driver in Italy during World War I. Shortly after his arrival, he was seriously wounded while delivering supplies to soldiers. He returned to America before accepting a job as a reporter for the *Toronto Star*. In 1921, he settled in Paris and began his literary career. In a short time, he became a celebrity, one whose rugged individualism, outdoor adventurousness, and colorful personality threatened to eclipse his work. In 1937, he was featured on the cover of *Time* magazine.

Hemingway won early critical acclaim for his short stories, collected in the book *In Our Time* (1925), and for several novels, including *The Sun Also Rises*, perhaps his finest (1926), *A Farewell to Arms* (1929), and *For Whom the Bell Tolls* (1940). A fan of bullfighting, he wrote two nonfiction books on the subject. After World War II, he moved with his fourth wife to Cuba, where he wrote *The Old Man and the Sea* (1952), which earned him a Pulitzer Prize. He was awarded the Nobel Prize for Literature in 1954. Depressed and physically ailing, he committed suicide in 1961. Hemingway created one of literature's most influential styles, noted for its crisp terseness and understatement, with much of the meaning of the text beneath the surface. He is one of America's most influential stylists.

First published in 1926, "A Clean Well-Lighted Place" later appeared in Hemingway's collection *Winner Take Nothing*.

A CLEAN WELL-LIGHTED PLACE*

It was late and every one had left the café except an old man who sat in the shadow the leaves of the tree made against the electric light: In the day time the street was dusty, but at night the dew settled the dust and the old man liked to sit late because he was deaf and now at night it was quiet and he felt the difference. The two waiters inside the café knew that the old man was a little drunk, and while he was a good client they knew that if he became too drunk he would leave without paying, so they kept watch on him.

"Last week he tried to commit suicide," one waiter said.

"Why?"

"He was in despair."

"What about?"   5

"Nothing."

"How do you know it was nothing?"

"He has plenty of money."

They sat together at a table that was close against the wall near the door of the café and looked at the terrace where the tables were all empty except where the old man sat in the shadow of the leaves of the tree that moved slightly in the wind. A girl and a soldier went by in the street. The street light shone on the brass number on his collar. The girl wore no head covering and hurried beside him.

"The guard will pick him up," one waiter said.   10

"What does it matter if he gets what he's after?"

"He had better get off the street now. The guard will get him. They went by five minutes ago."

The old man sitting in the shadow rapped on his saucer with his glass. The younger waiter went over to him.

"What do you want?"

The old man looked at him. "Another brandy," he said.   15

"You'll be drunk," the waiter said. The old man looked at him. The waiter went away.

"He'll stay all night," he said to his colleague. "I'm sleepy now. I never get into bed before three o'clock. He should have killed himself last week."

The waiter took the brandy bottle and another saucer from the counter inside the café and marched out to the old man's table. He put down the saucer and poured the glass full of brandy.

"You should have killed yourself last week," he said to the deaf man. The old man motioned with his finger. "A little more," he said. The waiter poured on into the glass so that the brandy slopped over and ran down the stem into the top saucer of the pile. "Thank you," the old man said. The waiter took the bottle back inside the café. He sat down at the table with his colleague again.

"He's drunk now," he said.   20

"He's drunk every night."[1]

"What did he want to kill himself for?"

"How should I know?"

"How did he do it?"

"He hung himself with a rope."   25

"Who cut him down?"

---

[1]The young waiter says both these lines. To represent a pause, Hemingway will sometimes begin a new paragraph and have the speaker resume talking.

"His niece."

"Why did they do it?"

"Fear for his soul."

30   "How much money has he got?"

"He's got plenty."

"He must be eighty years old."

"Anyway I should say he was eighty."*

"I wish he would go home. I never get to bed before three o'clock. What kind of hour is that to go to bed?"

35   "He stays up because he likes it."

"He's lonely. I'm not lonely. I have a wife waiting in bed for me."

"He had a wife once too."

"A wife would be no good to him now."

"You can't tell. He might be better with a wife."

40   "His niece looks after him."

"I know. You said she cut him down."

"I wouldn't want to be that old. An old man is a nasty thing."

"Not always. This old man is clean. He drinks without spilling. Even now, drunk. Look at him."

"I don't want to look at him. I wish he would go home. He has no regard for those who must work."

The old man looked from his glass across the square, then over at the 45 waiters.

"Another brandy," he said, pointing to his glass. The waiter who was in a hurry came over.

"Finished," he said, speaking with that omission of syntax stupid people employ when talking to drunken people or foreigners. "No more tonight. Close now."

"Another," said the old man.

"No. Finished." The waiter wiped the edge of the table with a towel and 50 shook his head.

The old man stood up, slowly counted the saucers, took a leather coin purse from his pocket and paid for the drinks, leaving half a peseta tip.

The waiter watched him go down the street, a very old man walking unsteadily but with dignity.

"Why didn't you let him stay and drink?" the unhurried waiter asked. They were putting up the shutters. "It is not half-past two."

"I want to go home to bed."

"What is an hour?"

55   "More to me than to him."

"An hour is the same."

"You talk like an old man yourself. He can buy a bottle and drink at home."

---

*"*He must be eighty years old.*" "*Anyway I should say he was eighty*"*: Is this another instance of the same character's speaking twice? Clearly, it is the younger waiter who says the next line, "I wish he would go home."

"It's not the same."

"No, it is not," agreed the waiter with a wife. He did not wish to be unjust. He was only in a hurry.

"And you? You have no fear of going home before the usual hour?"   60

"Are you trying to insult me?"

"No, hombre, only to make a joke."

"No," the waiter who was in a hurry said, rising from pulling down the metal shutters. "I have confidence. I am all confidence."

"You have youth, confidence, and a job," the older waiter said. "You have everything."   65

"And what do you lack?"

"Everything but work."

"You have everything I have."

"No. I have never had confidence and I am not young."

"Come on. Stop talking nonsense and lock up."

"I am of those who like to stay late at the café," the older waiter said.   70 "With all those who do not want to go to bed. With all those who need a light for the night."

"I want to go home and into bed."

"We are of two different kinds," the older waiter said. He was not dressed to go home. "It is not only a question of youth and confidence although those things are very beautiful. Each night I am reluctant to close up because there may be some one who needs the café."

"Hombre, there are bodegas² open all night long."

"You do not understand. This is a clean and pleasant café. It is well lighted. The light is very good and also, now, there are shadows of the leaves." 75

"Good night," said the younger waiter.

"Good night," the other said. Turning off the electric light he continued the conversation with himself. It is the light of course but it is necessary that the place be clean and pleasant. You do not want music. Certainly you do not want music. Nor can you stand before a bar with dignity although that is all that is provided for these hours. What did he fear? It was not fear or dread. It was a nothing that he knew too well. It was all a nothing and a man was nothing too. It was only that and light was all it needed and a certain cleanness and order. Some lived in it and never felt it but he knew it all was nada y pues nada y nada y pues nada. Our nada who are in nada, nada be thy name thy kingdom nada thy will be nada in nada as it is in nada. Give us this nada our daily nada and nada us our nada as we nada our nadas and nada us not into nada but deliver us from nada; pues nada. Hail nothing full of nothing, nothing is with thee. He smiled and stood before a bar with a shining steam pressure coffee machine.

"What's yours?" asked the barman.

"Nada."

"Otro loco más³," said the barman and turned away.

"A little cup," said the waiter.   80

---

²In this context, a bar.
³Another lunatic.

The barman poured it for him.

"The light is very bright and pleasant but the bar is unpolished," the waiter said.

"The barman looked at him but did not answer. It was too late at night for conversation.

"You want another copita?[4]" the barman asked.

85   "No, thank you," said the waiter and went out. He disliked bars and bodegas. A clean, well-lighted café was a very different thing. Now, without thinking further, he would go home to his room. He would lie in the bed and finally, with daylight, he would go to sleep. After all, he said to himself, it is probably only insomnia. Many must have it.

1926

Questions

1. Compare and contrast the younger waiter and the older waiter. List the differences.
2. Focus on the waiters' contrasting attitudes toward their jobs. How would each define work? How are their attitudes toward work consistent with their other attitudes, especially spirituality? Who leads a more satisfying life?
3. Does the older waiter have an almost religious attitude toward the café? How does his attitude demonstrate itself?
4. How do they respond differently to the elderly customer?
5. How does the scene in the coffee bar at the end of the story parallel the scene in the café involving the young waiter and the old man?
6. Why do you think the older waiter suffers from insomnia?
7. Which of the two waiters lives a fuller and more contented life?
8. Ford Madox Ford said that "Hemingway's words strike you, each one, as if they were pebbles fetched fresh from a brook." What are the implications behind some of his more prominent "pebbles," like *light, dark, clean, late, shadow, leaves,* and *nada*?
9. Hemingway once compared good writing to an iceberg, with the power coming from the unseen or unsaid. He congratulated himself on this skill of omission: "Another time I was leaving out good was in 'A Clean Well-Lighted Place.' There I really had luck. I left out everything." What does he omit from the story?

[4]Little cup.

Philip Levine (b. 1928)

P hilip Levine is one of America's most highly regarded poets. He has won major awards for his many volumes, including the Pulitzer Prize for Poetry (*The Simple Truth*, 1995), the National Book Critics Circle Award and the American Book Award for *Ashes: Poems New and Old* (1991), the National Book Award (for *What Work Is*, 1991), the Ruth Lilly Poetry Prize, the Harriet Monroe Memorial Prize for *Poetry*, the Frank O'Hara Prize, and two Guggenheim Foundation fellowships. For two years he served as chair of the Literature Panel of the National Endowment for the Arts, and he was elected a Chancellor of the Academy of American Poets in 2000.

The son of Russian–Jewish immigrants who settled in Detroit, Levine attended local schools right through to Wayne State University, which he attended at night while working in an automobile manufacturing plant. Later, he attended the University of Iowa. He began writing poetry while at Wayne State, focusing on Detroit, the Jewish immigrant experience, and working-class life. He continued to work various industrial jobs until he became a professor at Fresno State in California. He currently lives in Fresno and New York City, where he teaches at New York University as Distinguished Poet in Residence for the Creative Writing Program. Through his directness, simple syntax, and theme, Levine sounds a voice for ordinary, working-class people.

"What Work Is" is the title poem in his 1991 collection.

WHAT WORK IS

We stand in the rain in a long line
waiting at Ford Highland Park. For work.
You know what work is—if you're
old enough to read this you know what
work is, although you may not do it.   5
Forget you. This is about waiting,
shifting from one foot to another.
Feeling the light rain falling like mist
into your hair, blurring your vision
until you think you see your own brother   10

ahead of you, maybe ten places.
You rub your glasses with your fingers,
and of course it's someone else's brother,
narrower across the shoulders than
15 yours but with the same sad slouch, the grin
that does not hide the stubbornness,
the sad refusal to give in to
rain, to the hours wasted waiting,
to the knowledge that somewhere ahead
20 a man is waiting who will say, "No,
we're not hiring today," for any
reason he wants. You love your brother,
now suddenly you can hardly stand
the love flooding you for your brother,
25 who's not beside you or behind or
ahead because he's home trying to
sleep off a miserable night shift
it Cadillac so he can get up
before noon to study his German.
30 Works eight hours a night so he can sing
Wagner, the opera you hate most,
the worst music ever invented.
How long has it been since you told him
you loved him, held his wide shoulders,
35 opened your eyes wide and said those words,
and maybe kissed his cheek? You've never
done something so simple, so obvious,
not because you're too young or too dumb,
not because you're jealous or even mean
40 or incapable of crying in
the presence of another man, no,
just because you don't know what work is.

1991

Questions

1. The speaker says that we all know what work is. How would you define *work*?
2. Describe the speaker. What is his situation? What does the tone of the poem reveal about the speaker?
3. How does work, at least in part, define his relationship with his brother as well as his attitude? Does he admire his brother?
4. Explain the poem's surprising last line. Why is the speaker no longer so sure of what work is?

PART II

ENTERING THE WORKFORCE

Introduction

The three stories in this section focus on work firsts: a first job, a first day on a new job, and a first profound work experience.

For young workers, jobs open new worlds that are generally far more educative than they anticipate. Besides learning the tasks of a specific job, young workers learn about the expectations of employers and fellow workers; they learn to navigate the politics of the workplace (are workplace politics really much different anywhere?); they learn to deal with different personalities who may be coworkers, customers, or clients; and they learn about themselves, deepening their self-awareness and self-knowledge and perhaps sharpening their future self-expectations in the process.

In many ways, Sammy in John Updike's "A & P" is a typical nineteen-year-old. He is bright, observant, witty if not sarcastic, and a bit superior. He takes a job in a local supermarket, apparently for some extra spending money and perhaps to take some of the financial burden off his working-class family. His day proceeds typically: he sneers at the customers and his fellow employees and he eyes the young women. Then, a seemingly internal force swells within him and he abruptly quits his job in protest of his boss's unjust treatment of the young women. In that confused moment, Sammy surprises himself. He experiences an epiphany, a defining moment in which he realizes something about the world and his place in it. The recognition is so profound for him that he needs to make sense of it, so he reflects on it through the story.

Everyone remembers his or her first job. Not only because it is the first, but also because we learn so much from it. In Antonya Nelson's "Goodfellows," the narrator takes her first job at a franchised pizzeria. Roberta, who has decided to go by her middle name Jane, is similar to Sammy in that she, too, is in the process of self-discovery and self-definition. Through the course of the story, she may learn, whether she realizes it or not, what a successful business plan requires, but she is also learning about her strengths and weaknesses and about human decorum. She realizes, for instance, that she erred when she told her grieving boss that his newborn probably died as a result of his wife's smoking. As the story comes to a close, Roberta (or Jane) heads off to college a little more worldly and compassionate.

In Daniel Orozco's "Orientation," readers tend to put themselves in the place of the new employee, almost certainly not the worker's first job, who listens to an orientation delivered by a more experienced employee, perhaps an office manager, who zealously informs the new worker of the office's ground rules (those written and those understood) while passing on intimate information about the other employees. Orozco's inspiration for the story comes from his eleven years of office work. "The drama is large in an office, huge and momentous," says Orozco. "You hear a little bit about everybody in an office—more than you ever want to know." Learning to handle the drama and the often unwanted information can be problematic.

Each workplace will develop its own culture. The challenge for new employees is to define the culture and determine whether or not they can be comfortable and thrive within it. Sammy makes his decision in the story; Roberta (or Jane) has her decision made for her, and the speaker in "Orientation" seems to thrive on the atmosphere while the listener silently contemplates the presentation and the office atmosphere.

John Updike (1932–2009)

A native of Shillington, Pennsylvania, John Updike became one of America's most prolific and important literary figures of the second half of the twentieth century. He published more than twenty novels, more than a dozen short story collections, volumes of poetry, art criticism, literary criticism, children's books, and edited collections. He was a regular contributor to *The New Yorker* and *The New York Review of Books*. He is best known for his series of novels featuring Rabbit Angstrom as the protagonist. Two of the novels, *Rabbit Rich* and *Rabbit at Rest*, won Pulitzer Prizes.

Updike described his subject as "the American small town, Protestant middle class" and his typical characters as those who "frequently experience personal turmoil and must respond to crises relating to religion, family obligations, and marital infidelity." When writing in the third person, Updike generally employs a dense vocabulary, highly polished sentences, and an often poetic but lucid style, which results in more of an intellectual than emotional engagement for his readers.

"A & P," perhaps his most famous story, first appeared in *The New Yorker* in 1961 before being collected in *Pigeon Feathers and Other Stories* in 1962.

A & P

In walks these three girls in nothing but bathing suits. I'm in the second checkout slot, with my back to the door, so I don't see them until they're over by the bread. The one that caught my eye first was the one in the plaid green two-piece. She was a chunky kid, with a good tan and a sweet broad soft-looking can with those two crescents of white just under it, where the sun never seems to hit, at the top of the backs of her legs. I stood there with my hand on a box of Hi Ho crackers trying to remember if I rang it up or not. I ring it up again and the customer starts giving me hell. She's one of these cash-register-watchers, a witch about fifty with rouge on her cheekbones and no eyebrows, and I know it made her day to trip me up. She'd been watching cash registers for fifty years and probably never seen a mistake before.

By the time I got her feathers smoothed and her goodies into a bag—she gives me a little snort in passing if she'd been born at the right time they would have hung her over in Salem—by the time I get her on her way the girls had circled around the bread and were coming back, without a pushcart, back my way along the counters, in the aisle between the checkouts and the Special bins. They didn't even have shoes on. There was this chunky one, with the two-piece—it was bright green and the seams on the bra were still sharp and her belly was still pretty pale so I guessed she just got it (the suit)—there was this one, with one of those chubby berry-faces, the lips all bunched together under her nose, this one, and a tall one, with black hair that hadn't quite frizzed right, and one of these sunburns right across under the eyes, and a chin that was too long—you know, the kind of girl that other girls think is very "striking" and "attractive" but never quite makes it, as they very well know, which is why they like her so much—and then the third one, who wasn't quite so tall. She was the queen. She kind of led them, the other two peeking around and hunching over a little. She didn't look around, not this queen, she just walked straight on slowly, on these long white prima-donna legs. She came down a little hard on her heels, as if she didn't walk in her bare feet that much, putting down her heels and then letting the weight move along to her toes as if she was testing the floor with every step, putting a little deliberate extra action into it. You never know for sure how girls' minds work (do you really think it's a mind in there or just a little buzz like a bee in a glass jar?) but you got the idea she had talked the other two into coming in here with her, and now she was showing them how to do it, walk slow and hold yourself straight.

She had on a kind of dirty-pink—beige maybe, I don't know—bathing suit with a little nubble all over it and, what got me, the straps were down. They were off her shoulders looped loose around the cool tops of her arms, and I guess as a result the suit had slipped a little on her, so all around the top of the cloth there was this shining rim. If it hadn't been there, you wouldn't have known there could have been anything whiter than those shoulders. With the straps pushed off, there was nothing between the top of the suit and the top of her head except just *her,* this clean bare plane of the top of her chest down from the shoulder bones like a dented sheet of metal tilted in the light. I mean, it was more than pretty.

She had sort of oaky hair that the sun and salt had bleached, done up in a bun that was unravelling, and a kind of prim face. Walking into the A & P with your straps down, I suppose it's the only kind of face you *can* have. She held her head so high her neck, coming up out of those white shoulders, looked kind of stretched, but I didn't mind. The longer her neck was, the more of her there was.

She must have felt in the corner of her eye me and over my shoulder Stokesie in the first slot watching, but she didn't tip. Not this queen. She kept her eyes moving across the racks, and stopped, and turned so slow it made my stomach rub the inside of my apron, and buzzed to the other two, who kind of huddled against her for relief, and then they all three of them went up the cat-and-dog-food-breakfast-cereal-macaroni-rice-raisins-seasonings-spreads-spaghetti-soft-drinks-crackers-and-cookies aisle. From my slot I look straight up this aisle to the meat counter, and I watched them all the way. The fat one with the tan sort of fumbled with the cookies, but on second thought she put the package back. The sheep pushing their carts down the aisle—the girls were walking against the usual traffic (not that we have one-way signs or anything)—were pretty hilarious. You could see them, when Queenie's white shoulders dawned on them, kind of jerk, or hop, or hiccup, but their eyes snapped back to their own baskets and on they pushed. I bet you could set off dynamite in an A & P and the people would by and large keep reaching and checking oatmeal off their lists and muttering "Let me see, there was a third thing, began with *A*, asparagus, no, ah yes, applesauce!" or whatever it is they do mutter. But there was no doubt, this jiggled them. A few houseslaves in pin curlers even looked around after pushing their carts past to make sure what they had seen was correct.

You know, it's one thing to have a girl in a bathing suit down on the beach, where what with the glare nobody can look at each other much anyway, and another thing in the cool of the A & P, under the fluorescent lights, against all those stacked packages, with her feet paddling along naked over our checkerboard green-and-cream rubber-tile floor.

"Oh Daddy," Stokesie said beside me. "I feel so faint."

"Darling," I said. "Hold me tight." Stokesie's married, with two babies chalked up on his fuselage already, but as far as I can tell that's the only difference. He's twenty-two, and I was nineteen this April.

"Is it done?" he asks, the responsible married man finding his voice. I forgot to say he thinks he's going to be manager some sunny day, maybe in 1990 when it's called the Great Alexandrov and Petrooshki Tea Company or something.

What he meant was, our town is five miles from a beach, with a big summer colony out on the Point, but we're right in the middle of town, and the women generally put on a shirt or shorts or something before they get out of the car into the street. And anyway these are usually women with six children and varicose veins mapping their legs and nobody, including them, could care less. As I say, we're right in the middle of town, and if you stand at our front doors, you can see two banks and the Congregational church and the newspaper store and three real-estate offices and about twenty-seven old freeloaders tearing up Central Street because the sewer broke again. It's not as if we're on the Cape; we're north of Boston and there's people in this town haven't seen the ocean for twenty years.

The girls had reached the meat counter and were asking McMahon something. He pointed, they pointed, and they shuffled out of sight behind a pyramid of Diet Delight peaches. All that was left for us to see was old McMahon patting his mouth and looking after them sizing up their joints. Poor kids, I began to feel sorry for them, they couldn't help it.

Now here comes the sad part of the story, at least my family says it's sad, but I don't think it's sad myself. The store's pretty empty, it being Thursday afternoon, so there was nothing much to do except lean on the register and wait for the girls to show up again. The whole store was like a pinball machine and I didn't know which tunnel they'd come out of. After a while they come around out of the far aisle, around the lightbulbs, records at discount of the Caribbean Six or Tony Martin Sings or some such gunk you wonder they waste the wax on, six-packs of candy bars, and plastic toys done up in cellophane that fall apart when a kid looks at them anyway. Around they come, Queenie still leading the way, and holding a little gray jar in her hand. Slots Three through Seven are unmanned and I could see her wondering between Stokes and me, but Stokesie with his usual luck draws an old party in baggy gray pants who stumbles up with four giant cans of pineapple juice (what do these bums *do* with all that pineapple juice? I've often asked myself) so the girls come to me. Queenie puts down the jar and I take it into my fingers icy cold. Kingfish Fancy Herring Snacks in Pure Sour Cream: 49¢. Now her hands are empty, not a ring or a bracelet, bare as God made them, and I wonder where the money's coming from. Still with that prim look she lifts a folded dollar bill out of the hollow at the center of her nubbled pink top. The jar went heavy in my hand. Really, I thought that was so cute.

Then everybody's luck begins to run out. Lengel comes in from haggling with a truck full of cabbages on the lot and is about to scuttle into that door marked MANAGER behind which he hides all day when the girls touch his eye. Lengel's pretty dreary, teaches Sunday school and the rest, but he doesn't miss that much. He comes over and says, "Girls, this isn't the beach."

Queenie blushes, though maybe it's just a brush of sunburn I was noticing for the first time, now that she was so close. "My mother asked me to pick up a jar of herring snacks." Her voice kind of startled me, the way voices do when you see the people first, coming out so flat and dumb yet kind of tony, too, the way it ticked over "pick up" and "snacks." All of a sudden I slid right down her voice into her living room. Her father and the other men were standing around in ice-cream coats and bow ties and the women were in sandals picking up herring snacks on toothpicks off a big plate and they were all holding drinks the color of water with olives and sprigs of mint in them. When my parents have somebody over they get lemonade and if it's a real racy affair Schlitz in tall glasses with "They'll Do It Every Time" cartoons stenciled on.

"That's all right," Lengel said. "But this isn't the beach." His repeating this struck me as funny, as if it had just occurred to him, and he had been thinking all these years the A & P was a great big dune and he was the head lifeguard. He didn't like my smiling—as I say, he doesn't miss much—but he concentrates on giving the girls that sad Sunday-school-superintendent stare.

Queenie's blush is no sunburn now, and the plump one in plaid, that I liked better from the back—a really sweet can—pipes up. "We weren't doing any shopping. We just came in for the one thing."

"That makes no difference," Lengel tells her, and I could see from the way his eyes went that he hadn't noticed she was wearing a two-piece before. "We want you decently dressed when you come in here."

"We *are* decent," Queenie says suddenly, her lower lip pushing, getting sore now that she remembers her place, a place from which the crowd that runs the A & P must look pretty crummy. Fancy Herring Snacks flashed in her very blue eyes.

"Girls, I don't want to argue with you. After this come in here with your shoulders covered. It's our policy." He turns his back. That's policy for you. Policy is what the kingpins want. What the others want is juvenile delinquency.

All this while, the customers had been showing up with their carts but, you know, sheep, seeing a scene, they had all bunched up on Stokesie, who shook open a paper bag as gently as peeling a peach, not wanting to miss a word. I could feel in the silence everybody getting nervous, most of all Lengel, who asks me, "Sammy, have you rung up this purchase?"

I thought and said, "No" but it wasn't about that I was thinking. I go through the punches, 4, 9, GROC, TOT—it's more complicated than you think, and after you do it often enough, it begins to make a little song, that you hear words to, in my case "Hello (*bing*) there, you (*gung*) hap-py *pee-pul* (*splat*)!"— the *splat* being the drawer flying out. I uncrease the bill, tenderly as you may imagine, it just having come from between the two smoothest scoops of vanilla I had ever known were there, and pass a half and a penny into her narrow pink palm, and nestle the herrings in a bag and twist its neck and hand it over, all the time thinking.

The girls, and who'd blame them, are in a hurry to get out, so I say "I quit" to Lengel quick enough for them to hear, hoping they'll stop and watch me, their unsuspected hero. They keep right on going, into the electric eye; the door flies open and they flicker across the lot to their car, Queenie and Plaid and Big Tall Goony-Goony (not that as raw material she was so bad), leaving me with Lengel and a kink in his eyebrow.

"Did you say something, Sammy?"

"I said I quit."

"I thought you did."

"You didn't have to embarrass them."

"It was they who were embarrassing us."

I started to say something that came out "Fiddle-de-doo." It's a saying of my grandmother's, and I know she would have been pleased.

"I don't think you know what you're saying," Lengel said.

"I know you don't," I said. "But I do." I pull the bow at the back of my apron and start shrugging it off my shoulders. A couple customers that had been heading for my slot begin to knock against each other, like scared pigs in a chute.

Lengel sighs and begins to look very patient and old and gray. He's been a friend of my parents for years. "Sammy, you don't want to do this to your mom and dad," he tells me. It's true, I don't. But it seems to me that once you begin a gesture it's fatal not to go through with it. I fold the apron, "Sammy" stitched in red on the pocket, and put it on the counter, and drop the bow tie on top of it. The bow tie is theirs if you've ever wondered. "You'll feel this for the rest of your life," Lengel says, and I know that's true, too, but remembering how he made that pretty girl blush makes me so scrunchy inside I punch the No Sale tab and the machine whirs "*pee-*pul" and the drawer splats out. One advantage to this scene taking place in summer, I can follow it up with a clean exit, there's no fumbling around getting your coat and galoshes, I just saunter into the electric eye in my white shirt that my mother ironed the night before, and the door heaves itself open, and outside the sunshine is skating around on the asphalt.

I look around for my girls, but they're gone, of course. There wasn't anybody but some young married screaming with her children about some candy they didn't get by the door of a powder-blue Falcon station wagon. Looking back in the big windows, over the bags of peat moss and aluminum lawn furniture stacked on the pavement, I could see Lengel in my place in the second slot, checking the sheep through. His face was dark gray and his back stiff, as if he'd just had an injection of iron, and my stomach kind of fell as I felt how hard the world was going to be to me from here on in.

1962

Questions

1. Describe Sammy. What do you learn about him from the language he uses and the details that he provides?
2. What is Sammy's attitude toward his job? Did it change from the time that he entered his workplace that day to the time that he left?
3. Consider Sammy's closing statement. Why is life, "hereafter," going to be harder for him?
4. Does Sammy's attitude toward work in general change as a result of the incident with the young women? Will work be an extension of himself from here on and not just a way in which to make money?
5. Does Updike seem to endorse Sammy's response to the situation or does he remain neutral?
6. What does Sammy learn about himself from this experience?
7. What do you think is Stokesie's and Lengel's perspectives on their jobs? Whose work attitude, Sammy's, Stokesie's, or Lengel's is more common in America?
8. How do you characterize Sammy's decision to quit? Is it heroic? Silly? Impractical? Idealistic? Something else? Explain your answer.
9. The story takes place in approximately 1960. From your perspective, is the supermarket experience for the shopper and the worker much different today? Explain your answer.
10. Readers have complained about Updike's portrayal of women throughout his fiction. How are the women portrayed here? Is his portrayal of women in "A & P" offensive? Why or why not?

Antonya Nelson (b. 1961)

Born in Wichita, Kansas, in 1961, Antonya Nelson earned a BA from the University of Kansas and an MFA from the University of Arizona. Nelson's short stories have appeared in *The New Yorker*, *Esquire*, *Harper's Magazine*, and other prestigious publications. Her stories have been represented in *Prize Stories: The O. Henry Awards* and *The Best American Short Stories*. In 1999, *The New Yorker* selected Nelson as one of the "twenty best young fiction writers in America today."

Nelson has published three novels and six collections of short stories, including her latest, *Nothing Right* (2009). She lives in Telluride, Colorado, and in Las Cruces, New Mexico, and teaches in the Warren Wilson College MFA program and at New Mexico State University. "Goodfellows" is included in her 2002 collection, *Female Trouble*.

GOODFELLOWS

Anybody who ever worked for long making minimum wage at a little business knows how the family thing gets going: you all play a part. Somebody acts like Mom, keeping track of your tardiness, commenting on the black circles under your eyes, tsk-tsk-tsking. And then there's always Dad, the guy who can have you fired, whose nasty masculine office you have to visit to get a reprimand or a paycheck. Around you swarm your coworkers—younger, older, dumber, prettier—with whom you compete and spat and ally yourself, like siblings, like a gaggle of goslings. On the fringes, in the back, at the odd hours, are the eccentric in-laws, uncles, and other random black sheep.

The summer I was eighteen I worked at Goodfellows pizzeria. We were the prairie outpost of a Chicago-based chain, pioneering westward with our cornmeal crust and blend of four cheeses. Our product cost twice what the competition charged, yet the Kansas customer never quite bought the logic that it also weighed twice as much and fed twice as many. A pizza, the plains state consumer reasoned, was a pizza. Goodfellows was destined to go belly up after only one summer.

But for that summer I was employed at my first real job. Goodfellows had advertised for "those interested in ground-floor entry to an exciting new business!" They were moving into what had most recently been the Szechwan Palace: out went the fragile screens with dragons and Asian women coyly waving their fans, in came the Chianti bottles and red-and-white cafe curtains. I was interviewed by Marvin as he stood on chairs cutting tassels from light fixtures, collecting the Chinese characters in his left hand. He hired me because he didn't care whether the business made it or not. He was a sort of reluctant, distant Dad figure, one I recognized from my real-life family. You felt like you needed to snap your fingers in his face sometimes to bring his gaze into focus. He'd been sent to Kansas against his wishes and he missed Chicago. Mostly, Marvin was not a career pizza man. He planned to return to school for a master's in math as soon as he made enough money, and his true vocation, the one he kept looking toward, lay elsewhere.

"You like Bob Dylan?" he asked me as he leaned over the jukebox. "I got six Dylan records in here, so you better like Dylan."

"I can learn to like Bob Dylan," I said. At home we were never allowed to hate our food; we could only claim to be learning to like it.

"Raise your right hand," Marvin said. When I did, he grinned. "Nah, I'm just kidding around. You don't have to pledge allegiance." His assistant manager, however, had dedicated himself to pizza the minute he got the job. This was Steve Two. Steve Two was a fat guy just a year or two older than me who'd leapt into service for Goodfellows the way some boys join the army: with a righteous passion to go kick ass. The only thing that could distract him from pizza was racing hotrods. He built models and brought them in to decorate the restaurant kitchen. They were elaborate replicas, painstakingly glued and adorned, ridiculous but impressive, the way all miniatures are. It was hard to imagine Steve Two's broad stubby fingers capable of such intricacy, but there they were, complete with tiny steering wheels and hubcaps, occasionally a minuscule driver in a yellow helmet. On Friday nights, Steve Two's one night a week off, he would return to Goodfellows after the races in Augusta or Chanute[1] to tell us what had happened, his enthusiasm sending the spit flying while the rest of us maneuvered around him, closing the store. He wore his racing outfits on these nights, dirty white jumpsuits with too many pockets, and black protective eyeglasses held to his large round head with a rubber strap—dressed like a great big two year old.

Nobody really took Steve Two seriously except Annette, who put on a perplexed frown as she listened to him through the order window dividing front from back. Instead of leading him along his ludicrous yet entertaining narrative concerning the night the way the rest of us did—oh, those Kansas City boys and their hot shit engines, their hooker babes and their leather bikinis, the crack-ups and the anguish—Annette tried to compete. She was a kind of trashy twenty-five-year-old beauty school graduate with a sour outlook. She cut hair for five dollars and did not like me, even after I tried to get on her good side by

---

[1]race tracks in Kansas

letting her trim my bangs. Her own hair was a dramatic gleaming black, waved in one large stiff S-curve with a bright white stripe painted up the middle like the tail of a skunk. "Scary," Marvin had commented of her. Her jeans were faded white and stringy, and she'd taken her hair scissors to her green Goodfellows polo shirt, snipping fringe up to her navel. "Guess what these clippers cost," she challenged me.

I appraised them carefully, wondering aloud why they were ivory colored, and learned they were made of the same indestructible material used by NASA on the space shuttles.

"A hundred bucks," I guessed, aiming high so she could reveal her shrewd bargaining powers.

"For *these?* You couldn't touch 'em for less than three hundred fifty, and *I* got 'em for three even." Annette was always very busy catching people trying to rip her off. Most everyone fell into this category, grocery checkout clerks, insurance companies, the guy who owned the beauty parlor where she rented a station and from whom she'd bought the space clippers. While Steve Two told us about car crack-ups, Annette listed the offenses perpetrated against her that week by Hector, her other boss.

Our other boss was Steve One, the district manager, a large pear-shaped fellow who arrived apologetically every few days to check our percentages. Mumbling, he worried around the kitchen, his clipboard wedged against his big STEVE belt buckle, counting and weighing and adding, taking notes, then spending an anxious hour in Marvin's office on the second floor. Finally he would trundle heavily down the stairs, his computations showing us to still be, mercifully, operating in the black. Even though it didn't matter to Marvin how we fared each week, he had the good manners to fret a little while Steve One lowered his head over his calculator upstairs. Marvin seemed to respect Steve's limited expertise, his infinite stability. My mother's dull but reliable younger brother was just like this: instead of aspiring to become a medical doctor, he'd settled for driving around with a trunk full of drugs representing a pharmaceutical company.

On opening day, while Annette and I had filled pitchers of Diet Coke and Fanta, she told me she was sure Marvin would hit on her, it always happened, wherever she worked, that the boss came after her for sexual favors. She would have to watch her step. Favors, I kept thinking. "Also," she added as she cracked rolls of change into the cash register, "did you know there are more diseases on those forks out there than on this money? It's a common mistake to think money is dirty." She carelessly licked a quarter for emphasis, then pocketed it. When I pointed out that she'd misplaced the coin she began hating me.

So maybe I was the tattletale sister. Or maybe the family baby, as I was the youngest employee. At home, my other one, I was both. I'd been born late, after my parents' excitement for toddlers had worn thin, after the toys had broken and the dog had died. Everyone was gone—college, marriage, the West Coast. There, like here at Goodfellows, I most often felt like the ugly duckling, somehow never properly at home, honking when I should have been quacking.

I honestly *wanted* to fit. They fascinated me, I liked them, all of them, and wished to imprint.

Closing time made my heart pound: the dark vacant parking lot where trash blew under the vapor lights; inside, the loud jukebox, turned up using a crooked dime to a volume unsanctioned by Midwestern Sound Emporium; and the steady expressions on the faces of my new friends as they labored to restore order. There was something hellish and unreal about the empty business. It was my job to clean the salad bar, to wipe up coagulated dressing with a damp cloth diaper, to take buckets of dirty, half-melted ice to the sink in back.

One night a girl my age appeared at the locked front door and began pounding to be let in. She was banging with her wrists.

"We're closed!" I shouted at her over the din of the music, Annette's furious vacuuming. The girl wailed alarmingly on the other side of the glass, her skirt blowing around her thighs, their shape clear and beautiful beneath transparent material. I stared at her legs, mesmerized by their perfection, and somehow missed the blood, sticky and opaque, now on the glass.

"Hey!" I yelled, "Help!" I backed away as she held both wrists against the glass, flattening them white, the blood momentarily stanched—I thought of a stingray sliding eerily up an aquarium wall. Then she resumed pounding with the hands, smearing her blood between us. I had the greasy diaper at my mouth, the sweet-tart smell of Thousand Island in my face.

It was Marvin who let her in, Steve One who dialed the police, Luke who took her by the elbows and guided her to a seat, while I stood quaking, unbelieving. Her boyfriend had left her; she'd used a broken beer bottle. "A serious suicide follows the vein," Annette told me after the girl had been taken away, tracing a line from her own wrist to the soft inside of her elbow. "That chick just needed attention."

"She sure as heck got it," Steve One said, his hanky mopping his forehead. "You okay, Jane?"

I nodded, though I wasn't okay, and finding it hard though somehow necessary to hide my bewilderment. Steve Two muttered at being assigned to clean the glass; in the process he managed to drop and break the bottle of Windex, its clear shards on the concrete seeming an invitation of some kind. I never again reached for the Goodfellow's door without thinking just for an instant of her standing there in her skirt, beautiful, stricken, a catastrophe.

An interesting fact about the microcosmic job site is that you inevitably choose someone to love, even if you wouldn't give that person a second thought on the outside world. This, in my case, was Luke. He and Marvin had met at a used compact disc store buying jazz. Marvin was ecstatic to find a kindred spirit here in the milquetoast Midwest and hired him on the spot. Luke was wasting time between semesters, beginning graduate school in the fall, and decided he could save a lot of money by both collecting a paycheck from Goodfellows and eating three meals a day there. I was eight years younger than him, hopelessly tongue-tied in his presence, unable to speak a word that illustrated my maturity. He wasn't good looking (stooped, skinny like a crane, and embarrassed by it), and his sense of humor you had to coax like crazy. Unlike Steve Two, Luke was not actively seeking a girlfriend. He was more interested in pianos, in science fiction, in bantering with Marvin on a constantly evolving range of topics including *Star Trek*, Spinoza,[2] chaos, microbreweries, garlic therapy, hockey, William Casey, Thomas Merton, Bob Dylan, and many many others. I listened entranced, unable to enter. Annette, oblivious, never thought twice about tossing in an anecdote, as if all conversation were equal, every word its own gem, but I could not fathom the real rules of the game and would not try to play without knowing them. Only occasionally would Luke acknowledge me, leaning through the window separating front from back to ask me about an order I'd taken.

"Black olive?" he'd say, "or peppercorn?" I would look past his finger at the letters I'd scribbled.

"B.O."

"Sit or split?"

"Split," I'd say, pointing at the arrow I'd drawn at the bottom of the paper. I could never have explained to my friends how thrilling these exchanges were, the weight placed in a single acronym, Luke nodding sagely when everything had been deciphered. Only his barely quivering finger ever hinted at the possibility of his nervousness in my presence, and that gave me hope.

Though Annette claimed to have to fend off Marvin's interest in her, it was actually the reverse. She worked at getting his attention in a strategy directly opposed to my own in getting Luke's. She took every opportunity she could to touch him, to brush past and swat him, to lean through the window (her feet off the floor) while he sliced pie with a cleaver the length of his arm just under her face. These blatant overtures offended me. I felt my winning, subtle approach much the superior one. Of the two types of restaurant employee, she fell into the careerist category: she would stay in the service industry. And, as I mentioned before, Marvin was merely a tourist, like Luke, like me. I did not believe romance would transcend the line.

The four of us, plus Steve Two, constituted the late afternoon and nighttime Goodfellows staff. A large morose girl named Cherie (Cheri Amour, everyone called her) was the daytime waitress. It was she I relieved at four every afternoon, she whose African boyfriend leaned sucking a soda straw at the front counter each day, waiting. He was a striking molasses-colored man whose friendly expression seemed unshakably serene and self-satisfied. Cherie was not at all pretty, and I attributed her boyfriend's undiscriminating taste to the fact that he was foreign, never once thinking Cherie could have had anything to do with it. She hardly smiled until he was around; they walked out hip to hip, ambling in a frankly sexual manner. Steve Two would grab the mike in the back and make kissing noises over the sound system. The daytime cook told us her boyfriend had been waiting for her since Goodfellows opened at eleven.

"Nothing to do in the whole wide world but wait for that ugly girl," Steve Two marveled, rocking on his heels.

---

[2]These include Benedict de Spinoza (1632–1677), a Dutch-born philosopher; William Casey (1913–1987), the director of the Central Intelligence Agency under Ronald Reagan; and Thomas Merton (1915–1968), a monk and Roman Catholic author of the twentieth century.

Steve One, in the back checking our percentages, shook his head disapprovingly. "Watch your mouth," he told Steve Two.

Steve One had been in the Goodfellows business since he was sixteen. It had been his idea originally to open a Wichita branch; his wife was from here. His reprimand of Steve Two reminded me how unattractive Mrs. Steve One was, a woman so altogether fat you couldn't tell she was eight months pregnant on top of it. She never spoke when she visited the store, sitting at a table with her huge legs crossed, smoking cigarettes and drinking aspertame-filled, caffeinated Diet Coke in spite of her pregnancy. Fat couples always made me imagine comic sex.

"Jane," Steve One said. "Jane? Jane?" Finally I realized he was talking to me. My real name, Roberta, had lately begun to seem frumpy, so I'd asked everyone at work to call me by my middle one instead. Although I'd originally had the reputation of someone bright, the fact that I often forgot to respond to my own name made my coworkers suspicious. Luke thought I was being sly, which endeared me to him.

"Could you get me a water, Jane?" Steve One asked. He was sweating earnestly, weighing our bags of meat pellets and mushrooms. No one except the two Steves worried how Goodfellows fared. Annette could get temporarily excited by a profitable week, but she mostly was on the lookout for fake phone orders, ones designed by malcontents and misfits who wanted to humiliate us. We were located in a strip mall in a semiseedy neighborhood and much of our clientele made her suspicious. Wichita did not know what to do with our concept: gourmet pizza served on plastic tables, video games twirping and bleeping in the corner, waitresses who made you fetch your own meal and condiments, and prices higher than K-Bob's. Was one expected to leave a tip? Not without good reason did Goodfellows go under.

The thing was, we served great pizza. I ate pizza no fewer than five times a week that whole summer and never grew weary of it. Luke stopped by in the mornings to make little pizza dough rolls for his breakfast; at noon he had salad and a My Pie (pizza for one). He and I took our break together around eight, after the dinner rush, and split a small pizza in the back room while the Hobart[3] rumbled in the corner. Eating with him made me happy. Occasionally I will still try to imitate that Goodfellows flavor, but it can't be done. Something secret—a nonsequitous spice or lost baking tip—keeps me just this side of reviving it.

I looked forward to my job, bathing every afternoon before I went, washing and blow-drying my hair, making up my face. Despite the fact that I would stink of oregano and canned tomatoes five minutes after entering Goodfellows, I laundered my polo shirt every day, hoping to pass near enough to Luke early on so he could smell my cleanliness like a wafting breath of innocence. I liked our carryout rushes best, the times when I was asked to help in the back, working the assembly process with Marvin and Luke, Steve Two scurrying around doing the gopher jobs, fussing and muttering, Annette pacing the front in her surly predatory manner, squelching jokes by taking everything literally, telling long tedious anecdotes about her day, which revealed her as the person other

---

[3] a brand of kitchen equipment, probably a dishwasher here

people *thought* they might pull something over on. She was our mother, a necessary wet blanket, a source of constant conversational white noise.

"Wild Man," she yelled through the kitchen to the back one busy Friday night in late June. "You have three messages." Our day cook was Waldman. I never knew his first name, and hardly knew his last. Everyone called him Wild Man, though he seemed to me quite dull. He rarely spoke but always wore a quirky delighted grin like someone unabashedly stupid. He had long blond hair that Marvin, ever the inefficient Goodfellows manager, did not require be kept in a net, so Wild Man—or, *the* Wild Man, as the male employees called him—had to forever shake it from his eyes. He moved like a hoptoad pull toy I'd had when I was small, a kind of burping lurch that probably had to do with music, with the tiny headphones in his ears, two black buttons with a slack wire across the back of his pimply neck. He had stayed to wash pans that night, leaning over the big sinks, his long simian arms silver from the aluminum, marked with red slashes where he'd burned them pulling out pies. A mysterious woman kept phoning him and leaving urgent messages that he call. He wasn't responding.

"She's a nurse," Steve Two told me now, standing beside me feeding dough into the Hobart that flattened it. "I can't see why he won't even call her back. Man, if a babe wanted me that bad . . ." He popped his lips, leaving the thought unfinished, baffled by it.

Luke looked at the ceiling. "'Babe,'" he said. The previous Saturday night while Steve Two was at the Augusta track, Luke cooked a model car. It had had a Playboy bunny on the fender, tiny naked breasts just over the front wheels, flames and smoke on its long phallic hood. The car melted into a puddle of shining primary colors, the exhaust fan switched on high to suck up the fumes. Luke had put the mess in a to-go box with Steve Two's name on it, and Steve had had to accept it as a joke since Luke and Marvin were friends.

That evening, when the ringing phone wasn't a takeout order, Annette, who'd picked up, announced for all to hear: "Wild Man, I'm not gonna talk to that woman again! You think I'm your goddamned mother?"

Marvin clanged on the stainless steel shelf in our window with his huge class ring, and I jumped. "Hey," he said to Annette, "let's watch the language here." Marvin's temper was of the volcanic variety; he would preside sedately and then surprise us by exploding over nearly nothing. From my father I'd learned how to manage this kind of anger, staying out of the way, placating.

But Annette sparked right back at him. "Shit," she hissed, rising through the window. "He can get the damn phone back there!"

Marvin narrowed and then closed his eyes, twisting his head side to side to pop the joints in his stiff neck. He rolled his shoulders. When he opened his eyes, he was no longer mad. "Get the phone," he called out to Waldman. "Wild Man, pick up."

I went around back to find Waldman gone, the pans still dripping beside the sink. I picked up the rear extension. "He's gone," I told the nurse. She sighed over the line, as if she were heartbroken. It amazed me Waldman could elicit such feeling. I mean, he never washed his hair. Then she asked if she could leave him a message.

"Sure," I said, eager to keep her hopes up. She sounded nice.

"Just tell him his test was negative, okay? He'll know what it's all about."

"Negative test," I said, as if writing it down. "Okay," I added, and hung up. "Negative test," I said to Luke, back at my post beside him, our hands plunging in the cool, colorful toppings before us. As I was about to repeat myself for everyone to hear, Luke stopped my left hand with his right, and, putting an onion-dotted finger to my lips, his whiskery chin near my ear, warned me that this might be information best kept to ourselves.

Steve Two was saying, awed as always by the ways of women, "Those nurses and their white panty hoses!"

When I relayed the news to Waldman, the following night, he pulled the little speaker buttons from his head and peered at me, his mouth open.

"Say what?" he said.

"You had a message that your test was negative," I told him, trying to remain discreet, having stopped him before he entered the kitchen. HIV, I had decided, though it could have been anything.

He shook, like someone chilled, from his hips to his hair. Like someone who'd been given back his life. "Thanks," he told me, the only thing I remember him ever saying to me. I had nothing to do with his good news, but the pleasure I had in being its bearer carried me for days.

Even though we lasted only a summer, Goodfellows managed to attract regulars, a few of them. There were the guys from the 7-Eleven around the corner, the women from the Laundromat two stores over, a few families in the neighborhood who ate salad bar once or twice a week. The most faithful regular was an older bag lady who stopped by to have coffee every evening around five. She wore dense glasses like twin magnifying lenses, her eyes behind them big and runny as two raw eggs. Mrs. Crow. Some evenings she brought her grandson Donny, who was also a regular. With her he was always well-behaved and humiliated, but later, when he returned with his friends, he revealed himself as a ten-year-old thug. The graffiti on the mall walls was undoubtedly his and his friends', and Marvin's generous policy of providing free soda refills had bought us a clean storefront.

Donny had bad eyes, like his grandmother, but he worked around his disability rather than wear glasses. Not that he had any call to read anything though his Asteroids game seemed hindered by his having to put his nose to the screen. Over the course of the summer, Marvin and Luke had tried to tutor Donny without his catching on. This included thinly-veiled lessons in the solar system using pepperonies and Canadian bacon on a twenty-four-inch circular heaven of tomato sauce, or more complicated three-dimensional structures involving toothpicks and pineapple chunks to illustrate the construction of a molecule or floating suspension bridge. Donny liked Luke and Marvin. He was smart enough, and young enough, to give in to their foolishness. His grandmother couldn't keep him away from his friends, and his friends wouldn't let him quit being their leader. The cleverest part of Marvin and Luke's teaching was really the simplest: they let him hang around. Steve Two would have been the boy's idol under other circumstances, but because he was quick enough to see that Luke and Marvin did not entirely approve of Steve, the boy held his esteem in check.

Donny's interest in me had to do with my breasts. He made no secret of his fascination, constantly staring in his unfocused way at my chest.

"Just slap him around," Luke suggested.

Marvin illustrated. "*Fa-thwack, thwack,*" he said, flipping his hands.

"But be kind," Luke said. "Gentle. He's our mascot, after all."

I suspected Donny of stealing from us, but that was probably because I myself had been taking a few things. For example, I loved those old-fashioned shakers we had filled with Parmesan cheese and what looked like crayon shavings, red pepper flakes. Filling the flakes jars made me sneeze, and suffering was the excuse I used for taking a shaker home in my purse. Sometimes, more than a few times, I balled a twenty-dollar bill in my palm and stuffed it in my jeans pocket. The price of a medium pizza was $19.98, so I'd just punch NO SALE and refund two cents, hanging on to the twenty. I felt I deserved a little bonus now and then.

We talked a lot about where our money would go. It's not an unusual topic anywhere, what you'd do if you won the lottery. Marvin was saving money for school; so was Luke. Annette wanted to own her own beauty salon, but I don't think she really thought she'd ever do it. Steve Two saw himself operating his own Goodfellows someday, though of course it wouldn't be in Wichita, and he'd get rid of a couple of things, like the self-serve aspect of it and the jukebox. "But really," he began backpedaling, "I love Bob Dylan."

Annette snorted. "That man's the biggest crybaby I ever heard, all that whining around like a car stuck in second gear. '*Buck*-ets of rain, *buck*-ets of tears,'" she imitated, badly, then added, "Needs a fuckin' bucket to carry the tune." Marvin and Luke plugged their ears. Somber Steve One never talked about what he did with his money or what he'd do with more of it—but he was the only one of us with a family, the only one with a baby on the way. I myself was being sent to college by my parents in the fall; paychecks were supposed to be for luxuries, but I had already purchased some antiques on layaway at the junk store across the parking lot. The day I made the final payment on my first piece I had the store owner deliver my rosewood and crushed velvet chaise longue to Goodfellows, where Cherie and Wild Man and Steve One came out to stare at it beside the cigarette machine, bewildered.

Cherie sat down on it and said, "Kind of uncomfortable."

Steve One just turned around and went back to work in the hot kitchen, swiping at his forehead with his hanky. But Luke thought my purchase funky and amusing. He and Marvin approved. Later, during our break, Luke and I sat on it and observed our empty parking lot. Still later that night, he followed me home in his truck to deliver it to my parents' living room. My fifteen-year-old niece Lydia, visiting from San Diego, was still awake watching television. When I introduced her to Luke, he bowed a few times and started backing out the front door.

"What a dweeb," she said when he was gone. "And *why* did you buy *that*?" The chaise sat in the middle of the rug like an old red swaybacked horse.

"I don't know. I've always wanted a chaise longue."

She laughed, invoking the family joke for strays. "Yes, but does it eat much?" In my bedroom I set it beneath my window, and after work at night, when everyone else slept, I would sit on the rough nap smelling the unknown past that had infiltrated the cushion. I looked at the neighborhood I'd grown up in, through the tree leaves that had always trembled between me and it, working on my future nostalgia for the view. At these times my aloneness would come at me, like sad music, like heartache, like the dim knowledge of death, and I would welcome my own pale version of despair.

A few weeks later when I arrived at work there was a police car out front. My heart went banging: my thefts were discovered. Inside, up in Marvin's office above the kitchen, I could see a menacing black-uniformed officer through the curtained window. Luke was at the front counter, watching my feet as I walked in.

"What's this?" I asked.

"Money's been disappearing," he said, shrugging. He stared at me, but how was I to take it?

"How much?" I said, coming around the counter, waiting to hear footsteps on the ceiling, waiting to hear Marvin summon me by my alias to his office.

"About five hundred," he said. "Cherie's been making off with our lunch rush, such as it is."

I sighed, shivering the way Waldman had to hear his life was safe. "Five hundred?"

Luke nodded, wiggling his eyebrows.

"How did she get caught?" I asked, afraid suddenly there might be more arrests.

"Steve Two," Luke said. This made sense; Steve Two had a fervent crusading attitude toward Goodfellows. Whenever I'd taken money, I'd made sure he was nowhere in sight.

"What do you call those?" He pointed at my feet.

"Clogs?" I said.

"Clogs," he said thoughtfully, leaving me at the front. Later Cherie went away with the cop, her boyfriend conspicuously absent. Marvin hated having to have her arrested. "If it was up to me," he said as we shared a Sprite at the counter, "I would have just let her go, but once the Steves were involved . . ."

"It's a drag," I said. Cherie had been saving her money for a waterbed. My purchasing furniture had reminded her of her own goal. She told me she was getting a king-size one with a heater and a black lacquer headboard with bookcases and built-in reading lights. I'd lied and said that sounded cool.

Steve One's wife gave birth in August during a tornado warning. Everyone in the store except me was outside looking for funnels. I was honor bound by my real parents to behave in a levelheaded manner and keep away from windows. Acts of God were not dalliances.

So I was there to take the news. Steve One gave me an earful: his wife's thirty-two-hour labor, the baby's inability to move into the birth canal, the C-section that had resulted, "Apgar!" he kept insisting, some test his baby had failed. I tried to make encouraging noises at the right moments though I was sitting on the floor stretching the phone cord under the front counter to avoid taking glass slivers in the face should our enormous window implode.

"Congratulations," I said without thinking, sitting on the sticky floor, noticing the greasy filth accumulating behind the soda canisters, the pennies permanently adhered to the linoleum.

"Her name is Ashley Cristolyn Damascus," he reported proudly. I almost asked, "Damascus?" before remembering he had a name other than Steve One.

"Congratulations," I repeated.

"Thanks, Jane," he said, and I could picture him wiping that earnest sweat from his brow with his handkerchief, then folding the hanky twice and returning it to his rear pocket where its white corner would hang like a tag. From outside I heard the all-clear sound. "Man, I'm tired," said Steve One from St. Joe's maternity ward.

"Tell your wife congratulations," I said.

"I'll see you guys right soon."

We hung up as everybody came back in, all of them disappointed at seeing nothing. I gave them Steve's news. We baked a celebratory pizza with the baby's first name spelled out in green pepper slices. Nobody else was in the mood for Goodfellows that night—bad weather, plus our novelty had worn off, our prices were still high, and the walls of the mall had been spray painted with skulls and crossbones and phalluses, which seemed to discourage business.

School was scheduled to start. Goodfellows was clearly about to end. My fun there was almost over; my dorm room in Lawrence at the University of Kansas, three hours away, waited for me. On the last night I was to work, Marvin and Annette came in together, holding hands, Marvin not only not embarrassed but silly with happiness. I was stunned. Annette told me they'd spent the day together in bed. She went to work like it was nothing, filling beer pitchers, slapping orders through the window, running toothpicks along the crevices to collect gray scum with which she threatened to top somebody's pizza. I listened to Marvin and Luke with profound disillusion, wondering what Annette's conquest really meant. Was Marvin using her? Was this possibility worse than the other one, that he actually liked her? It made me unusually forgetful and incompetent that night. Somehow the restaurant seemed dirtier, less like home and more like a failing business in a strip mall.

Then the phone rang and we got the news that Steve One's baby wasn't expected to live. Things had not been going well, but we'd all thought they were normal baby dilemmas, jaundice and colic. None of the rest of us had children; I know I hadn't given the baby's illness more than passing consideration. Now it was "extreme failure to thrive." On the telephone—Marvin talking in the back, me listening in the front—Steve One told us from the hospital he wouldn't be in to check our percentages this night.

I was eighteen. I said to Steve One, the father of a baby about to die, "Maybe it was her smoking," meaning his wife's. She'd not quit during her pregnancy. It was perhaps conceivable this *was* the reason the baby would die, but so what? I was eighteen. I had no idea what I was saying. The line went quiet, the two men waiting for me to hang up. I did, burning in shame, in anger, happy to be leaving this life behind me.

At closing, Steve One appeared at the glass front door, his head lowered as he searched his heavy ring for the right key. I held my ubiquitous damp diaper, recalling as usual the young woman who'd stood there earlier in the summer bleeding. When Steve One entered everyone clustered near him. His daughter had died two hours earlier. His wife was drugged. Having nowhere else to go, he'd come to Goodfellows wearing his saggy pants and company shirt. When I tried to apologize for my previous insensitivity, he merely shook his head, forgiving me in his uncomplicated way. He had no reason to care what in the world I ever thought or did. Hundreds of waitresses would pass this way; I would be replaced, superseded, forgotten.

After we closed I went home with Luke and spent the night at his apartment, sitting on the couch watching his fish aquarium and letting him read rhymed couplets to me. Why wasn't he touching me? Why weren't we kissing? His apartment was unexceptional, except that it was his. I drank it in from the lumpy fake-leather couch. The support system was shot, so we'd slid close to each other. Luke smelled of scorched cornmeal pizza crust and cigarette butts, though we'd separated those two trash categories as we cleaned up, leaving the edible in Goodfellows boxes out by the Dumpster, as we did every night. This was at Luke and Marvin's insistence. It seemed to me that everyone I knew, *everyone*, was better than I. When Steve Two heard the baby had died, he went directly to Steve One and gave him a hug, laying his round Charlie Brown head on Steve One's chest. Annette had burst into tears. Where had this come from, I wondered? Where was it in me? The only time I'd ever cried at Goodfellows was chopping onions.

Luke's poetry was unfathomable, his apartment still and stuffy. We sat together so long not touching that by daybreak I was rigid with nerves, my face sore from wearing an interested expression all night. When it became abundantly clear that he wasn't going to do anything, when the sky outside his dirty shades started to go purple with daybreak, I finally stood to leave. Instead of a kiss, he gave me a Xeroxed sheaf of sonnets written by a manic-depressive friend of his in Wyoming. I thanked him and left, sleepy, edgy, dissatisfied.

My role in the Goodfellows family meant that I hovered uncertainly, watching it fall apart, unable to do a thing except abandon it the minute I drove out of the parking lot. Luke wrote to me but I only skimmed his letters and didn't respond, my shame—of him, of myself—thereby confined to a place and time I'd put away. I never saw any of those people again, not even accidentally, though Goodfellows could have been the proving ground for my next job, my next little family, and the next one, and the next, and all the others that were to come.

1994

Questions

1. Is the narrator's interview for Goodfellows typical for such a position?
2. How would you describe the narrator? What do we come to know about her? Were you surprised by her theft? Did it change your opinion of her?
3. What is family-like about the relationship of the coworkers in Goodfellows? How did the employees, for instance, seem like a family when they responded to the injured girl pounding on the windows? Did they respond as a family to first the birth and then the death of Steve One's child? Refer to other scenes and specific characters when answering this question.
4. Compare the family at Goodfellows with the narrator's work family in T. C. Boyle's "The Lie."
5. Do you think that coworkers often form a kind of second family? Refer to your own experiences, observations, and discussions with others in your answer.
6. Why does Goodfellows close? What should the franchise owners have done differently?
7. Is the narrator correct when she says that "you inevitably choose someone to love" on your job? Refer to your own experiences, observations, and discussions with others in your answer.
8. What did the narrator learn about work from her summer at Goodfellows? Are the lessons typical of those learned from a first job?
9. What did the narrator learn about life from working at Goodfellows? Are the lessons typical of those learned from a first job?
10. How do the minor characters contribute to the narrator's education?

Daniel Orozco (b. 1957)

A native of San Francisco, Daniel Orozco studied at the University of Washington, where he earned an MFA, and at Stanford University, where he was a Scowcroft Fellow in Creative Writing and a L'Heureux Fellow in Fiction, and a Jones Lecturer in Fiction in the Creative Writing Program. His short stories have been published in prestigious collections such as *The Best American Short Stories*, *The Best American Mystery Stories*, the *Pushcart Prize Anthology* (2005), and *Harper's Magazine*, among others. His essay "Shakers" appeared in *The Best American Essays* (2006). Currently, he teaches creative writing at the University of Idaho.

"Orientation" first appeared in *The Seattle Review* and was later published in *The Best American Short Stories* (1995). Orozco commented in the *Superstition Review*, "I've worked in offices for about eleven years, mostly in Human Resources, and I've also worked as a temp. So 'Orientation' reflects a kind of life lived in offices."

ORIENTATION

Those are the offices and these are the cubicles. That's my cubicle there, and this is your cubicle. This is your phone. Never answer your phone. Let the Voicemail System answer it. This is your Voicemail System Manual. There are no personal phone calls allowed. We do, however, allow for emergencies. If you must make an emergency phone call, ask your supervisor first. If you can't find your supervisor, ask Phillip Spiers, who sits over there. He'll check with Clarissa Nicks, who sits over there. If you make an emergency phone call without asking, you may be let go.

These are your IN and OUT boxes. All the forms in your IN box must be logged in by the date shown in the upper left-hand corner, initialed by you in the upper right-hand corner, and distributed to the Processing Analyst whose name is numerically coded in the lower left-hand corner. The lower right-hand corner is left blank. Here's your Processing Analyst Numerical Code Index. And here's your Forms Processing Procedures Manual.

You must pace your work. What do I mean? I'm glad you asked that. We pace our work according to the eight-hour workday. If you have twelve hours of work in your IN box, for example, you must compress that work into the eight-hour day. If you have one hour of work in your IN box, you must expand that work to fill the eight hour day. That was a good question. Feel free to ask questions. Ask too many questions, however, and you may be let go.

That is our receptionist. She is a temp. We go through receptionists here. They quit with alarming frequency. Be polite and civil to the temps. Learn their names, and invite them to lunch occasionally. But don't get close to them, as it only makes it more difficult when they leave. And they always leave. You can be sure of that.

5   The men's room is over there. The women's room is over there. John LaFountaine, who sits over there, uses the women's room occasionally. He says it is accidental. We know better, but we let it pass. John LaFountaine is harmless, his forays into the forbidden territory of the women's room simply a benign thrill, a faint blip on the dull flat line of his life.

Russell Nash, who sits in the cubicle to your left, is in love with Amanda Pierce, who sits in the cubicle to your right. They ride the same bus together after work. For Amanda Pierce, it is just a tedious bus ride made less tedious by the idle nattering of Russell Nash. But for Russell Nash, it is the highlight of his day. It is the highlight of his life. Russell Nash has put on forty pounds, and grows fatter with each passing month, nibbling on chips and cookies while peeking glumly over the partitions at Amanda Pierce, and gorging himself at home on cold pizza and ice cream while watching adult videos on TV.

Amanda Pierce, in the cubicle to your right, has a six-year-old son named Jamie, who is autistic. Her cubicle is plastered from top to bottom with the boy's crayon artwork—sheet after sheet of precisely drawn concentric circles and ellipses, in black and yellow. She rotates them every other Friday. Be sure to comment on them. Amanda Pierce also has a husband, who is a lawyer. He subjects her to an escalating array of painful and humiliating sex games, to which Amanda Pierce reluctantly submits. She comes to work exhausted and freshly wounded each morning, wincing from the abrasions on her breasts, or the bruises on her abdomen, or the second-degree burns on the backs of her thighs.

But we're not supposed to know any of this. Do not let on. If you let on, you may be let go.

Amanda Pierce, who tolerates Russell Nash, is in love with Albert Bosch, whose office is over there. Albert Bosch, who only dimly registers Amanda Pierce's existence, has eyes only for Ellie Tapper, who sits over there. Ellie Tapper, who hates Albert Bosch, would walk through fire for Curtis Lance. But Curtis Lance hates Ellie Tapper. Isn't the world a funny place? Not in the ha-ha sense, of course.

10   Anika Bloom sits in that cubicle. Last year, while reviewing quarterly reports in a meeting with Barry Hacker, Anika Bloom's left palm began to bleed. She fell into a trance, stared into her hand, and told Barry Hacker when and how his wife would die. We laughed it off. She was, after all, a new employee.

But Barry Hacker's wife is dead. So unless you want to know exactly when and how you'll die, never talk to Anika Bloom.

Cohn Heavey sits in that cubicle over there. He was new once, just like you. We warned him about Anika Bloom. But at last year's Christmas Potluck, he felt sorry for her when he saw that no one was talking to her. Cohn Heavey brought her a drink. He hasn't been himself since. Cohn Heavey is doomed. There's nothing he can do about it, and we are powerless to help him. Stay away from Cohn Heavey. Never give any of your work to him. If he asks to do something, tell him you have to check with me. If he asks again, tell him I haven't gotten back to you.

This is the Fire Exit. There are several on this floor, and they are marked accordingly. We have a Floor Evacuation Review every three months, and an Escape Route Quiz once a month. We have our Biannual Fire Drill twice a year, and our Annual Earthquake Drill once a year. These are precautions only. These things never happen.

For your information, we have a comprehensive health plan. Any catastrophic illness, any unforeseen tragedy is completely covered. All dependents are completely covered. Larry Bagdikian, who sits over there, has six daughters. If anything were to happen to any of his girls, or to all of them, if all six were to simultaneously fall victim to illness or injury—stricken with a hideous degenerative muscle disease or some rare toxic blood disorder, sprayed with semiautomatic gunfire while on a class field trip, or attacked in their bunk beds by some prowling nocturnal lunatic—if any of this were to pass, Larry's girls would all be taken care of. Larry Bagdikian would not have to pay one dime. He would have nothing to worry about.

We also have a generous vacation and sick leave policy. We have an excellent disability insurance plan. We have a stable and profitable pension fund. We get group discounts for the symphony, and block seating at the ballpark. We get commuter ticket books for the bridge. We have Direct Deposit. We are all members of Costco.

This is our kitchenette. And this, this is our Mr. Coffee. We have a coffee 15 pool, into which we each pay two dollars a week for coffee, filters, sugar, and CoffeeMate. If you prefer Cremora or half-and-half to CoffeeMate, there is a special pool for three dollars a week. If you prefer Sweet'n Low to sugar, there is a special pool for two-fifty a week. We do not do decaf. You are allowed to join the coffee pool of your choice, but you are not allowed to touch the Mr. Coffee.

This is the microwave oven. You are allowed to heat food in the microwave oven. You are not, however, allowed to cook food in the microwave oven.

We get one hour for lunch. We also get one fifteen-minute break in the morning, and one fifteen-minute break in the afternoon. Always take your breaks, if you skip a break, it is gone forever. For your information, your break is a privilege, not a right. If you abuse the break policy, we are authorized to rescind your breaks. Lunch, however, is a right, not a privilege. If you abuse the lunch policy, our hands will be tied, and we will be forced to look the other way. We will not enjoy that.

This is the refrigerator. You may put your lunch in it. Barry Hacker, who sits over there, steals food from this refrigerator. His petty theft is an outlet for his grief. Last New Year's Eve, while kissing his wife, a blood vessel burst in her brain. Barry Hacker's wife was two months pregnant at the time, and lingered in a coma for half a year before dying. It was a tragic loss for Barry Hacker. He hasn't been himself since. Barry Hacker's wife was a beautiful woman. She was also completely covered. Barry Hacker did not have to pay one dime. But his dead wife haunts him. She haunts all of us. We have seen her, reflected in the monitors of our computers, moving past our cubicles. We have seen the dim shadow of her face in our photocopies. She pencils herself in in the reception-ist's appointment book, with the notation: To see Barry Hacker. She has left messages in the receptionist's Voicemail box, messages garbled by the electronic chirrups and buzzes in the phone line, her voice echoing from an immense distance within the ambient hum. But the voice is hers. And beneath her voice, beneath the tidal whoosh of static and hiss, the gurgling and crying of a baby can be heard.

In any case, if you bring a lunch, put a little something extra in the bag for Barry Hacker. We have four Barrys in this office. Isn't that a coincidence?

20   This is Matthew Payne's office. He is our Unit Manager, and his door is always closed. We have never seen him, and you will never see him. But he is here. You can be sure of that. He is all around us.

This is the Custodian's Closet. You have no business in the Custodian's Closet.

And this, this is our Supplies Cabinet. If you need supplies, see Curtis Lance. He will log you in on the Supplies Cabinet Authorization Log, then give you a Supplies Authorization Slip. Present your pink copy of the Supplies Authorization Slip to Ellie Tapper. She will log you in on the Supplies Cabinet Key Log, then give you the key. Because the Supplies Cabinet is located outside the Unit Manager's office, you must be very quiet. Gather your supplies quietly. The Supplies Cabinet is divided into four sections. Section One contains letter-head stationery, blank paper and envelopes, memo and note pads, and so on. Section Two contains pens and pencils and typewriter and printer ribbons, and the like. In Section Three we have erasers, correction fluids, transparent tapes, glue sticks, et cetera. And in Section Four we have paper clips and push pins and scissors and razor blades. And here are the spare blades for the shredder. Do not touch the shredder, which is located over there. The shredder is of no concern to you.

Gwendolyn Stich sits in that office there. She is crazy about penguins, and collects penguin knickknacks: penguin posters and coffee mugs and stationery, penguin stuffed animals, penguin jewelry, penguin sweaters and T-shirts and socks. She has a pair of penguin fuzzy slippers she wears when working late at the office. She has a tape cassette of penguin sounds which she listens to for re-laxation. Her favorite colors are black and white. She has personalized license plates that read PEN GWEN. Every morning, she passes through all the cubicles to wish each of us a good morning. She brings Danish on Wednesdays for Hump Day morning break, and doughnuts on Fridays for TGIF afternoon break. She organizes the Annual Christmas Potluck, and is in charge of the Birthday List. Gwendolyn Stich's door is always open to all of us. She will always lend an ear, and put in a good word for you; she will always give you a hand, or the shirt off her back, or a shoulder to cry on. Because her door is always open, she hides and cries in a stall in the women's room. And John LaFountaine—who, enthralled when a woman enters, sits quietly in his stall with his knees to his chest—John LaFountaine has heard her vomiting in there. We have come upon Gwendolyn Stich huddled in the stairwell, shivering in the updraft, sipping a Diet Mr. Pibb and hugging her knees. She does not let any of this interfere with her work. If it interfered with her work, she might have to be let go.

Kevin Howard sits in that cubicle over there. He is a serial killer, the one they call the Carpet Cutter, responsible for the mutilations across town. We're not supposed to know that, so do not let on. Don't worry. His compulsion inflicts itself on strangers only, and the routine established is elaborate and unwavering. The victim must be a white male, a young adult no older than thirty, heavyset, with dark hair and eyes, and the like. The victim must be chosen at random, before sunset, from a public place; the victim is followed home, and must put up a struggle; et cetera. The carnage inflicted is precise: the angle and direction of the incisions; the layering of skin and muscle tissue; the rearrangement of the visceral organs; and so on. Kevin Howard does not let any of this interfere with his work. He is, in fact, our fastest typist. He types as if he were on fire. He has a secret crush on Gwendolyn Stich, and leaves a red-foil-wrapped Hershey's Kiss on her desk every afternoon. But he hates Anika Bloom, and keeps well away from her. In his presence, she has uncontrollable fits of shaking and trembling. Her left palm does not stop bleeding.

In any case, when Kevin Howard gets caught, act surprised. Say that he 25 seemed like a nice person, a bit of a loner, perhaps, but always quiet and polite.

This is the photocopier room. And this, this is our view. It faces southwest. West is down there, toward the water. North is back there. Because we are on the seventeenth floor, we are afforded a magnificent view. Isn't it beautiful? It overlooks the park, where the tops of those trees are. You can see a segment of the bay between those two buildings there. You can see the sun set in the gap between those two buildings over there. You can see this building reflected in the glass panels of that building across the way. There. See? That's you, waving. And look there. There's Anika Bloom in the kitchenette, waving back.

Enjoy this view while photocopying. If you have problems with the photocopier, see Russell Nash. If you have any questions, ask your supervisor. If you can't find your supervisor, ask Phillip Spiers. He sits over there. He'll check with Clarissa Nicks. She sits over there. If you can't find them, feel free to ask me. That's my cubicle. I sit in there.

1994

Questions

1. What is the situation in the story? Who is talking? Do you think that he is always truthful or is he sometimes playful?

2. Who is the listener? What do you think is going through the listener's mind? Why does he not ask questions of the speaker?

3. Did you find the story amusing? Does the delivery of the information contribute to the humor? How would you characterize the speaker's delivery?

4. Orozco used to conduct office orientations: "I'd done employee training and orientations during my office work days, and I kind of liked showing people the ropes, answering questions, initiating the uninitiated." How do you think Orozco's experiences influenced the story and its speaker?

5. Orozco said that "the drama is large in an office, huge and momentous, and manifested in the most mundane things—the jammed photocopier, the misplaced (or, stolen!) stapler, the yen for a longer job title on your nameplate." How do the speaker's comments reflect this statement?

6. "You hear a little bit about everybody in an office—more than you ever want to know," said Orozco. "And if you work there long enough, you can know everything about somebody, without ever meeting their family or being invited to their home, without ever seeing what they wear when they're not at work. That's the paradox of intimacy in office life—knowing so much about people you don't know at all." Do you agree with Orozco? Refer to your own experiences, observations, and discussions with others in your answer.

7. If you were in the position of the listener in the story, how would you conduct yourself in the office during the days ahead?

PART III

HARD WORK AND HARD TIMES: THE WORKING POOR

Introduction

In this section, we hear from blue-collar or low-wage earners, voices too often underrepresented in cultures throughout the world. These readings will focus largely on their daily struggles and concerns, which are often more basic and far different from even the middle class. The second selection, Carl Sandburg's "Chicago," is as much a tribute to the common laborer as it is to the city, both of which Sandburg mythologizes.

In several selections, workers keep themselves motivated through hope, even if the hope is distant or vague. In Hamlin Garland's "Under the Lion's Paw," the Haskins move westward in hopes of rebuilding their lives, and in "Washerwoman," Sandburg's protagonist clings to her faith in a better afterlife. For many, however, hope is muted as their focus is fully on the here and now, which is to say, survival. In the excerpt from *Nickel and Dimed: On (Not) Getting by in America*, Barbara Ehrenreich and coworkers struggle to cover the most basic expenses.

Most of the individuals depicted in this section have few job, let alone career, options. Often, to survive either the humiliation or boredom of their work, they create strategies of evasion. Consider, for instance, the dancer in Claude McKay's "Harlem Dancer" and the worker in Tom Wayman's "Factory Time." It can be a daily struggle for many of the laborers, like Ehrenreich and her coworkers or Dolores Dante in Studs Terkel's *Working: People Talk About What They Do All Day and How They Feel About What They Do*, to maintain self-worth and dignity in a world of abusive bosses, mean-spirited customers, and images of elusive grandeur in the media. Consider, too, Jim Daniels's Digger as he waits on the unemployment line. Rage will often build, but it must be contained— see the waiter in Kraft Rompf's "Waiting Table." Rap artist Cam'ron speaks for several of the characters in this section with "I Hate My Job."

Others persevere with the hope that their children will have a better life. This might have been the motivation of the father in Robert Hayden's "Those Winter Sundays," who seems to endure a punishing job and a bad marriage for the sake of his son—a son who looks back at his father's sacrifice with appreciation, admiration, and regret.

Too often the individuals represented in this section feel exploited and marginalized, cut off from the possibilities promised by the American Dream. As you read these selections, consider the relevancy to these individuals of the pragmatism of Benjamin Franklin in "The Way to Wealth" and the idealism of Henry David Thoreau in "Life without Principle." Have the individuals represented in this section had ample opportunity to achieve their dreams or their potential?

Hamlin Garland (1860-1940)

Born in Wisconsin, Hamlin Garland grew up on a succession of midwestern farms. In 1884, he moved to Boston in order to take a teaching position and to begin his literary career. After revisiting the Midwest in 1887 and again in 1889, he decided to write about the hardships and toil of the farmer, especially after having seen his mother suffer a paralytic stroke after years of farm labor. Garland's first success came in 1891 with *Main-Travelled Roads*, a collection of short stories about farm life and from which "Under the Lion's Paw" is taken. Garland's work sounds a sympathetic voice for farming families and their struggle against natural elements, illness, and a capitalist culture that often seems to undermine their efforts.

A prolific writer who also lived in Chicago, New York City, and Hollywood, Garland, among other works, published a biography on Ulysses S. Grant, a chronicle on the Klondike Gold Rush, several stories on the American Indian, two books on psychic phenomena, and a series of memoirs, one of which, *A Daughter of the Middle Border*, earned him the Pulitzer Prize for biography in 1922.

UNDER THE LION'S PAW[1]

I

It was the last of autumn and first day of winter coming together. All day long the ploughmen on their prairie farms had moved to and fro in their wide level fields through the falling snow, which melted as it fell, wetting them to the skin—all day, notwithstanding the frequent squalls of snow, the dripping, desolate clouds, and the muck of the furrows, black and tenacious as tar.

Under their dripping harness the horses swung to and fro silently, with that marvellous uncomplaining patience which marks the horse.

---

[1]First printed in *Harper's Weekly*, September 7. 1889, and collected as one of the six stories in the first edition of *Main-Travelled Roads* (1891; six more stories were added in 1893). "Under the Lion's Paw" was intended as propaganda and served Garland frequently as a text in his lectures on the need for social and economic reform.

All day the wild geese, honking wildly, as they sprawled sidewise down the wind, seemed to be fleeing from an enemy behind, and with neck outthrust and wings extended, sailed down the wind, soon lost to sight.

Yet the ploughman behind his plough, though the snow lay on his ragged greatcoat, and the cold clinging mud rose on his heavy boots, fettering him like gyves, whistled in the very beard of the gale. As day passed, the snow, ceasing to melt, lay along the ploughed land, and lodged in the depth of the stubble, till on each slow round the last furrow stood out black and shining as jet between the ploughed land and the gray stubble.

When night began to fall, and the geese, flying low, began to alight invisibly in the near corn-field, Stephen Council was still at work "finishing a land." He rode on his sulky plough when going with the wind, but walked when facing it. Sitting bent and cold but cheery under his slouch hat, he talked encouragingly to his four-in-hand.

"Come round there, boys!—Round agin! We got t' finish this land. Come in there, Dan! *Stiddy*, Kate,—stiddy! None o'y'r tantrums, Kittie. It's purty tuff, but got a be did. *Tchk! tchk!* Step along, Pete! Don't let Kate git y'r single-tree on the wheel. *Once* more!"

They seemed to know what he meant, and that this was the last round, for they worked with greater vigor than before.

"Once more, boys, an' then, sez I, oats an' a nice warm stall, an' sleep f'r all."

By the time the last furrow was turned on the land it was too dark to see the house, and the snow was changing to rain again. The tired and hungry man could see the light from the kitchen shining through the leafless hedge, and he lifted a great shout, "Supper f'r a half a dozen!"

It was nearly eight o'clock by the time he had finished his chores and started for supper. He was picking his way carefully through the mud, when the tall form of a man loomed up before him with a premonitory cough.

"Waddy ye want?" was the rather startled question of the farmer.

"Well, ye see," began the stranger, in a deprecating tone, "we'd like t' git in f'r the night. We've tried every house f'r the last two miles, but they hadn't any room f'r us. My wife's jest about sick, 'n' the children are cold and hungry—"

"Oh, y' want'o stay all night, eh?"

"Yes, sir; it 'ud be a great accom—"

"Waal, I don't make it a practice t' turn anybuddy way hungry, not on sech nights as this. Drive right in. We ain't got much, but sech as it is—"

But the stranger had disappeared. And soon his steaming, weary team, with drooping heads and swinging single-trees, moved past the well to the block beside the path. Council stood at the side of the "schooner" and helped the children out—two little half-sleeping children—and then a small woman with a babe in her arms.

"There ye go!" he shouted jovially, to the children. "*Now* we're all right! Run right along to the house there, an' tell Mam' Council you wants sumpthin' t' eat. Right this way, Mis'—keep right off t' the right there. I'll go an' git a lantern. Come," he said to the dazed and silent group at his side.

"Mother," he shouted, as he neared the fragrant and warmly lighted kitchen, "here are some wayfarers an' folks who need sumpthin' t' eat an' a place t' snooze." He ended by pushing them all in.

Mrs. Council, a large, jolly, rather coarse-looking woman, took the children in her arms. "Come right in, you little rabbits. 'Most asleep, hey? Now here's a drink o' milk f'r each o' ye. I'll have s'm tea in a minute. Take off y'r things and set up t' the fire."

While she set the children to drinking milk, Council got out his lantern and went out to the barn to help the stranger about his team, where his loud, hearty voice could be heard as it came and went between the haymow and the stalls.

The woman came to light as a small, timid, and discouraged-looking woman, but still pretty, in a thin and sorrowful way.

"Land sakes! An' you've travelled all the way from Clear Lake t'-day in this mud! Waal! waal! No wonder you're all tired out. Don't wait f'r the men, Mis'—" She hesitated, waiting for the name.

"Haskins."

"Mis' Haskins, set right up to the table an' take a good swig o' tea whilst I make y' s'm toast. It's green tea, an' it's good. I tell Council as I git older I don't seem to enjoy Young Hyson n'r Gunpowder. I want the reel green tea, jest as it comes off'n the vines. Seems r' have more heart in it, some way. Don't s'pose it has. Council says it's all in m' eye."

Going on in this easy way, she soon had the children filled with bread and milk and the woman thoroughly at home, eating some toast and sweet-melon pickles, and sipping the tea.

"See the little rats!" she laughed at the children. "They're full as they can stick now, and they want to go to bed. Now, don't git up, Mis' Haskins; set right where you are an' let me look after 'em. I know all about young ones, though I'm all alone now. Jane went an' married last fall. But, as I tell Council, it's lucky we keep our health. Set right there, Mis' Haskins; I won't have you stir a finger."

It was an unmeasured pleasure to sit there in the warm, homely kitchen, the jovial chatter of the housewife driving out and holding at bay the growl of the impotent, cheated wind.

The little woman's eyes filled with tears which fell down upon the sleeping baby in her arms. The world was not so desolate and cold and hopeless, after all.

"Now I hope Council won't stop out there and talk politics all night. He's the greatest man to talk politics an' read the *Tribune*—How old is it?"

She broke off and peered down at the face of the babe.

"Two months 'n' five days," said the mother, with a mother's exactness.

"Ye don't say! I want 'o know! The dear little pudzy-wudzy!" she went on, stirring it up in the neighborhood of the ribs with her fat forefinger.

"Pooty tough on 'oo to go gallivant'n' 'cross lots this way—"

"Yes, that's so; a man can't lift a mountain," said Council, entering the door. "Mother, this is Mr. Haskins, from Kansas. He's been eat up 'n' drove out by grasshoppers."

"Glad t' see yeh!—Pa, empty that wash-basin 'n' give him a chance t' wash."

Haskins was a tall man, with a thin, gloomy face. His hair was a reddish brown, like his coat, and seemed equally faded by the wind and sun, and his sallow face, though hard and set, was pathetic somehow. You would have felt that he had suffered much by the line of his mouth showing under his thin, yellow mustache.

"Hain't Ike got home yet, Sairy?"

"Hain't seen 'im."

"W-a-a-l, set right up, Mr. Haskins; wade right into what we've got; 'tain't much, but we manage to live on it—she gits fat on it," laughed Council, pointing his thumb at his wife.

After supper, while the women put the children to bed, Haskins and Council talked on, seated near the huge cooking-stove, the steam rising from their wet clothing. In the Western fashion Council told as much of his own life as he drew from his guest. He asked but few questions, but by and by the story of Haskins' struggles and defeat come out. The story was a terrible one, but he told it quietly, seated with his elbows on his knees, gazing most of the time at the hearth.

"I didn't like the looks of the country, anyhow," Haskins said, partly rising and glancing at his wife. "I was ust t' northern Ingyannie, where we have lots o' timber 'n' lots o' rain, 'n' I didn't like the looks o' that dry prairie. What galled me the worst was goin' s' far away acrosst so much fine land layin' all through here vacant."

"And the hoppers eat ye four years, hand runnin', did they?"

"Eat! They wiped us out. They chawed everything that was green. They jest set around waitin' f'r us to die t' eat us, too. My God! I ust t' dream of 'em sittin' 'round on the bedpost, six feet long, workin' their jaws. They eet the fork-handles. They got worse 'n' worse till they jest rolled on one another, piled up like snow in winter. Well, it ain't no use. If I was t' talk all winter I couldn't tell nawthin'. But all the while I couldn't help thinkin' of all that land back here that nobuddy was usin' that I ought 'o had 'stead o' bein' out there in that cussed country."

"Waal, why didn't ye stop an' settle here?" asked Ike, who had come in and was eating his supper.

"Fer the simple reason that you fellers wantid ten 'r fifteen dollars an acre fer the bare land, and I hadn't no money fer that kind o' thing."

"Yes, I do my own work," Mrs. Council was heard to say in the pause which followed. "I'm a gettin' purty heavy t' be on m' laigs all day, but we can't afford t' hire, so I keep rackin' around somehow, like a foundered horse. S' lame—I tell Council he can't tell how lame I am, f'r I'm jest as lame in one laig as t' other." And the good soul laughed at the joke on herself as she took a handful of flour and dusted the biscuit-board to keep the dough from sticking.

"Well, I hain't *never* been very strong," said Mrs. Haskins. "Our folks was Canadians an' small-boned, and then since my last child I hain't got up again fairly. I don't like t' complain. Tim has about all he can bear now—but they was days this week when I jest wanted to lay right down an' die."

"Waal, now, I'll tell ye," said Council, from his side of the stove, silencing everybody with his good-natured roar, "I'd go down and *see* Butler, *anyway*, if I was you. I guess he'd let you have his place purty cheap; the farm's all run down. He's ben anxious t' let t' some-buddy next year. It 'ud be a good chance fer you. Anyhow, you go to bed and sleep like a babe. I've got some ploughin' t' do, anyhow, an' we'll see if somethin' can't be done about your case. Ike, you go out an' see if the horses is all right, an' I'll show the folks t' bed."

When the tired husband and wife were lying under the generous quilts of the spare bed, Haskins listened a moment to the wind in the eaves, and then said, with a slow and solemn tone,

"There are people in this world who are good enough t' be angels, an' only haff t' die to *be* angels."

II

Jim Butler was one of those men called in the West "land poor." Early in the history of Rock River he had come into the town and started in the grocery business in a small way, occupying a small building in a mean part of the town. At this period of his life he earned all he got, and was up early and late sorting beans, working over butter, and carting his goods to and from the station. But a change came over him at the end of the second year, when he sold a lot of land for four times what he paid for it. From that time forward he believed in land speculation as the surest way of getting rich. Every cent he could save or spare from his trade he put into land at forced sale, or mortgages on land, which were "just as good as the wheat," he was accustomed to say.

Farm after farm fell into his hands, until he was recognized as one of the leading landowners of the county. His mortgages were scattered all over Cedar County, and as they slowly but surely fell in he sought usually to retain the former owner as tenant.

He was not ready to foreclose; indeed, he had the name of being one of the "easiest" men in the town. He let the debtor off again and again, extending the time whenever possible.

"I don't want y'r land," he said. "All I'm after is the int'rest on my money— that's all. Now. if y' want 'o stay on the farm, why, I'll give y' a good chance. I can't have the land layin' vacant." And in many cases the owner remained as tenant.

In the meantime he had sold his store; he couldn't spend time in it; he was mainly occupied now with sitting around town on rainy days smoking and "gassin' with the boys," or in riding to and from his farms. In fishing-time he fished a good deal. Doc Grimes, Ben Ashley, and Cal Cheatham were his cronies on these fishing excursions or hunting trips in the time of chickens or partridges. In winter they went to Northern Wisconsin to shoot deer.

In spite of all these signs of easy life Butler persisted in saying he "hadn't enough money to pay taxes on his land," and was careful to convey the impression that he was poor in spite of his twenty farms. At one time he was said to be worth fifty thousand dollars, but land had been a little slow of sale of late, so that he was not worth so much.

A fine farm, known as the Higley place, had fallen into his hands in the usual way the previous year, and he had not been able to find a tenant for it. Poor Higley, after working himself nearly to death on it in the attempt to lift the mortgage, had gone off to Dakota, leaving the farm and his curse to Butler.

This was the farm which Council advised Haskins to apply for; and the next day Council hitched up his team and drove down town to see Butler.

"You jest let *me* do the talkin'," he said. "We'll find him wearin' out his pants on some salt barrel somew'ers; and if he thought you *wanted* a place he'd sock it to you hot and heavy. You jest keep quiet; I'll fix 'im."

Butler was seated in Ben Ashley's store telling fish yarns when Council sauntered in casually.

"Hello, But; lyin' agin, hey?"

"Hello, Stevel how goes it?"

"Oh, so-so. Too dang much rain these days. I thought it was goin' t' freeze up f'r good last night. Tight squeak if I get m' ploughin' done. How's farmin' with *you* these days?"

"Bad. Ploughin' ain't half done."

"It 'ud be a religious idee f'r you t' go out an' take a hand y'rself."

"I don't haff to," said Butler, with a wink.

"Got anybody on the Higley place?"

"No. Know of anybody?"

"Waal, no; not eggsackly. I've got a relation back t' Michigan who's ben hot an' cold on the idee o' comin' West f'r some time. *Might* come if he could get a good lay-out. What do you talk on the farm?"

"Well, I d' know. I'll rent it on shares or I'll rent it money rent."

"Waal, how much money, say?"

"Well, say ten per cent, on the price—two-fifty."

"Waal, that ain't bad. Wait on 'im till 'e thrashes?"

Haskins listened eagerly to this important question, but Council was coolly eating a dried apple which he had speared out of a barrel with his knife. Butler studied him carefully.

"Well, knocks me out of twenty-five dollars interest."

"My relation'll need all he's got t' git his crops in," said Council, in the safe, indifferent way.

"Well, all right; *say* wait," concluded Butler.

"All right; this is the man. Haskins, this is Mr. Butler—no relation to Ben— the hardest-working man in Cedar County."

On the way home Haskins said: "I ain't much better off. I'd like that farm; it's a good farm, but it's all run down, an' so 'm I. I could make a good farm of it if I had half a show. But I can't stock it n'r seed it."

"Waal, now, don't you worry," roared Council in his ear. "We'll pull y' through somehow till next harvest. He's agreed t' hire it ploughed, an' you can earn a hundred dollars ploughin' an' y' c'n git the seed o' me, an' pay me back when y' can."

Haskins was silent with emotion, but at last he said, "I ain't got nothin' t' live on."

"Now, don't you worry 'bout that. You jest make your headquarters at ol' Steve Council's. Mother'll take a pile o' comfort in havin' y'r wife an' children 'round. Y' see, Jane's married off lately, an' Ike's away a good 'eal, so we'll be darn glad t' have y' stop with us this winter. Nex' spring we'll see if y' can't git a start agin." And he chirruped to the team, which sprang forward with the rumbling, clattering wagon.

"Say, looky here, Council, you can't do this. I never saw—" shouted Haskins in his neighbor's ear.

Council moved about uneasily in his seat and stopped his stammering gratitude by saying: "Hold on, now; don't make such a fuss over a little thing. When I see a man down, an' things all on top of 'm, I jest like t' kick 'em off an' help 'm up. That's the kind of religion I got, an' it's about the *only* kind."

They rode the rest of the way home in silence. And when the red light of the lamp shone out into the darkness of the cold and windy night, and he thought of this refuge for his children and wife, Haskins could have put his arm around, the neck of his burly companion and squeezed him like a lover. But he contented himself with saying, "Steve Council, you'll git y'r pay f'r this some day."

"Don't want any pay. My religion ain't run on such business principles."

The wind was growing colder, and the ground was covered with a white frost, as they turned into the gate of the Council farm, and the children came rushing out, shouting, "Papa's come!" They hardly looked like the same children who had sat at the table the night before. Their torpidity, under the influence of sunshine and Mother Council, had given way to a sort of spasmodic cheerfulness, as insects in winter revive when laid on the hearth.

III

Haskins worked like a fiend, and his wife, like the heroic woman that she was, bore also uncomplainingly the most terrible burdens. They rose early and toiled without intermission till the darkness fell on the plain, then tumbled into bed, every bone and muscle aching with fatigue, to rise with the sun next morning to the same round of the same ferocity of labor.

The eldest boy drove a team all through the spring, ploughing and seeding, milked the cows, and did chores innumerable, in most ways taking the place of a man.

An infinitely pathetic but common figure—this boy on the American farm, where mere is no law against child labor. To see him in his coarse clothing, his huge boots, and his ragged cap, as he staggered with a pail of water from the well, or trudged in the cold and cheerless dawn out into the frosty field behind his team, gave the city-bred visitor a sharp pang of sympathetic pain. Yet Haskins loved his boy, and would have saved him from this if he could, but he could not.

By June the first year the result of such Herculean toil began to show on the farm. The yard was cleaned up and sown to grass, the garden ploughed and planted, and the house mended.

Council had given them four of his cows.

"Take 'em an' run 'em on shares. I don't want 'o milk s' many. Ike's away s' much now, Sat'd'ys an' Sund'ys. I can't stand the bother anyhow."

Other men, seeing the confidence of Council in the newcomer, had sold him tools on time; and as he was really an able farmer, he soon had round him many evidences of his care and thrift. At the advice of Council he had taken the farm for three years, with the privilege of re-renting or buying at the end of the term.

"It's a good bargain, an' y' want 'o nail it," said Council. "If you have any kind ov a crop, you c'n pay y'r debts, an' keep seed an' bread."

The new hope which now sprang up in the heart of Haskins and his wife grew great almost as a pain by the time the wide field of wheat began to wave and rustle and swirl in the winds of July. Day after day he would snatch a few moments after supper to go and look at it.

"Have ye seen the wheat t'-day, Nettie?" he asked one night as he rose from supper.

"No, Tim, I ain't had time."

"Well, take time now. Le's go look at it."

She threw an old hat on her head—Tommy's hat—and looking almost pretty in her thin, sad way, went out with her husband to the hedge.

"Ain't it grand, Nettie? Just look at it."

It was grand. Level, russet here and there, heavy-headed, wide as a lake, and full of multitudinous whispers and gleams of wealth, it stretched away before the gazers like the fabled field of the cloth of gold.

"Oh, I think—I *hope* we'll have a good crop, Tim; and oh, how good the people have been to us!"

"Yes; I don't know where we'd be t'-day if it hadn't ben f'r Council and his wife."

"They're the best people in the world," said the little woman, with a great sob of gratitude.

"We'll be in the field on Monday, sure," said Haskins, gripping the rail on the fence as if already at the work of the harvest.

The harvest came, bounteous, glorious, but the winds came and blew it into tangles, and the rain matted it here and there close to the ground, increasing the work of gathering it threefold.

Oh, how they toiled in those glorious days! Clothing dripping with sweat, arms aching, filled with briers, fingers raw and bleeding, backs broken with the weight of heavy bundles, Haskins and his man toiled on. Tommy drove the harvester, while his father and a hired man bound on the machine. In this way they cut ten acres every day, and almost every night after supper, when the hand went to bed, Haskins returned to the field shocking the bound grain in the light of the moon. Many a night he worked till his anxious wife came out at ten o'clock to call him in to rest and lunch.

At the same time she cooked for the men, took care of the children, washed and ironed, milked the cows at night, made the butter, and sometimes fed the horses and watered them while her husband kept at the shocking.

No slave in the Roman galleys could have toiled so frightfully and lived, for this man thought himself a free man, and that he was working for his wife and babes.

When he sank into his bed with a deep groan of relief, too tired to change his grimy, dripping clothing, he felt that he was getting nearer and nearer to a home of his own, and pushing the wolf of want a little farther from his door.

There is no despair so deep as the despair of a homeless man or woman. To roam the roads of the country or the streets of the city, to feel there is no rood of ground on which the feet can rest, to halt weary and hungry outside lighted windows and hear laughter and song within,—these are the hungers and rebellions that drive men to crime and women to shame.

It was the memory of this homelessness, and the fear of its coming again, that spurred Timothy Haskins and Nettie, his wife, to such ferocious labor during that first year.

IV

" 'M, yes; 'm, yes; first-rate," said Butler, as his eye took in the neat garden, the pig-pen, and the well filled barnyard. "You're gitt'n' quite a stock around yeh. Done well, eh?"

Haskins was showing Butler around the place. He had not seen it for a year, having spent the year in Washington and Boston with Ashley, his brother-in-law, who had been elected to Congress.

"Yes, I've laid out a good deal of money durin' the last three years. I've paid out three hundred dollars f'r fencin'."

"Um—h'm! I see, I see," said Butler, while Haskins went on:

"The kitchen there cost two hundred; the barn ain't cost much in money, but I've put a lot o' time on it. I've dug a new well, and I—"

"Yes, yes, I see. You've done well. Stock worth a thousand dollars," said Butler, picking his teeth with a straw.

"About that," said Haskins, modestly. "We begin to feel's if we was gitt'n' a home f'r ourselves; but we've worked hard. I tell you we begin to feel it, Mr. Butler, and we're goin' t' begin to ease up purty soon. We've been kind o' plannin' a trip back t' *her* folks after the fall ploughin's done."

"*Eggs*-actly!" said Butler, who was evidently thinking of something else. "I suppose you've kind o' eale'lated on stayin' here three years more?"

"Well, yes. Fact is, I think I c'n buy the farm this fall, if you'll give me a reasonable show."

"Um—m! What do you call a reasonable show?"

"Well, say a quarter down and three years' time."

Butler looked at the huge stacks of wheat, which filled the yard, over which the chickens were fluttering and crawling, catching grasshoppers, and out of which the crickets were singing innumerably. He smiled in a peculiar way as he said, "Oh, I won't be hard on yeh. But what did you expect to pay f'r the place?"

"Why, about what you offered it for before, two thousand five hundred, or *possibly* three thousand dollars," he added quickly, as he saw the owner shake his head.

"This farm is worth five thousand and five hundred dollars," said Butler, in a careless and decided voice.

"*What!*" almost shrieked the astounded Haskins. "What's that? Five thousand? Why, that's double what you offered it for three years ago."

"Of course, and it's worth it. It was all run down then; now it's in good shape. You've laid out fifteen hundred dollars in improvements, according to your own story."

"But *you* had nothin't' do about that. It's my work an' my money."

"You bet it was; but it's my land."

"But what's to pay me for all my -"

"Ain't *you* had the use of 'em?" replied Butler, smiling calmly into his face.

Haskins was like a man struck on the head with a sandbag; he couldn't think: he stammered as he tried to say: "But I never'd git the use—You'd rob me! More'n that: you agreed you promised that I could buy or rent at the end of three years at—"

"That's all right. But I didn't say I'd let you carry off the improvements, nor that I'd go on renting the farm at two-fifty. The land is doubled in value, it don't matter how; it don't enter into the question: an' now you can pay me five hundred dollars a year rent, or take it on your own terms at fifty-five hundred, or— git out."

He was turning away when Haskins, the sweat pouring from his face, fronted him, saying again:

"But *you've* done nothing to make it so. You hain't added a cent. I put it all there myself, expectin' to buy. I worked an' sweat to improve it. I was workin' for myself an' babes—"

"Well, why didn't you buy when I offered to sell? What y' kickin' about?"

"I'm kickin' about payin' you twice f'r my own things,—my own fences, my own kitchen, my own garden."

Butler laughed. "You're too green t' eat, young feller. *Your* improvements! The law will sing another tune."

"But I trusted your word."

"Never trust anybody, my friend. Besides, I didn't promise not to do this thing. Why, man, don't look at me like that. Don't take me for a thief. It's the law. The reg'lar thing. Everybody does it."

"I don't care if they do. It's stealin' jest the same. You take three thousand dollars of my money—the work o' my hands and my wife's." He broke down at this point. He was not a strong man mentally. He could face hardship, ceaseless toil, but he could not face the cold and sneering face of Butler.

"But I don't take it," said Butler, coolly. "All you've got to do is to go on jest as you've been a-doin', or give me a thousand dollars down, and a mortgage at ten per cent on the rest.

Haskins sat down blindly on a bundle of oats near by, and with staring eyes and drooping head went over the situation. He was under the lion's paw. He felt a horrible numbness in his heart and limbs. He was hid in a mist, and there was no path out.

Butler walked about, looking at the huge stacks of grain, and pulling now and again a few handfuls out, shelling the heads in his hands and blowing the chaff away. He hummed a little tune as he did so. He had an accommodating air of waiting.

Haskins was in the midst of the terrible toil of the last year. He was walking again in the rain and the mud behind his plough; he felt the dust and dirt of the threshing. The ferocious husking-time, with its cutting wind and biting, clinging snows, lay hard upon him. Then he thought of his wife, how she had cheerfully cooked and baked, without holiday and without rest.

"Well, what do you think of it?" inquired the cool, mocking, insinuating voice of Butler.

"I think you're a thief and a liar!" shouted Haskins, leaping up. "A black-hearted houn'!" Butler's smile maddened him; with a sudden leap he caught a fork in his hands, and whirled it in the air. "You'll never rob another man, damn ye!" he grated through his teeth, a look of pitiless ferocity in his accusing eyes.

Butler shrank and quivered, expecting the blow; stood, held hypnotized by the eyes of the man he had a moment before despised—a man transformed into an avenging demon. But in the deadly hush between the lift of the weapon and its fall there came a gush of faint, childish laughter and then across the range of his vision, far away and dim, he saw the sun-bright head of his baby girl, as with the pretty, tottering run of a two-year-old, she moved across the grass of the dooryard. His hands relaxed; the fork fell to the ground; his head lowered.

"Make out y'r deed an' mor'gage, an' git off'n my land, an' don't ye never cross my line agin; if y' do, I'll kill ye."

Butler backed away from the man in wild haste, and climbing into his buggy with trembling limbs drove off down the road, leaving Haskins seated dumbly on the sunny pile of sheaves, his head sunk into his hands.

1891

Questions

1. Discuss the relationships among the farming families, especially the Councils and the Haskins. What do the relationships reveal about midwestern farming conditions and the necessity of helping one another? Are the families both friends and competitors?
2. Consider the division of labor within the farming family. Which responsibilities fall on the men and which on the women? What part do the children play in this division of labor?
3. The narrator writes that "on the American farm . . . there is no law against child labor." Does Garland suggest that there should be such laws? Are the parents at fault for requiring children to work long hours on the family farm?

4. What is your impression of Stephen Council when we first see him? Consider the narrator's initial description of him as with the cold and snow "fettering him like gyves," Council ploughed the land, "whistled in the very beard of the gale," and spoke "encouragingly" to his team of horses who "seemed to know what he meant."

5. What is your initial impression of Jim Butler when we meet him at the beginning of the second section?

6. Who triumphs at the end of the story? Does Butler triumph because he got his price or does Haskins because he got the land? What is the significance of the baby's cry as Haskins raises the fork to murder Butler?

7. Are the characters in "Under the Lion's Paw" individuals or types? Does Garland use character for political purposes? Explain your answer.

8. Prominent author and critic William Dean Howells promoted Garland and said that "Under the Lion's Paw" was "a lesson in political economy, as well as tragedy of the darkest cast." Do you agree with Howell's consideration of the tale as a tragedy?

9. What is the significance of the title?

10. What is the significance of Council's evoking religion when Haskins states that he will repay him some day? "Don't want any pay," says Council. "My religion ain't run on such business principles."

11. Do Council and Haskins achieve a higher degree of job satisfaction and fulfillment than other individuals and characters in this collection? Compare them, for example, with the workers in the engine room of O'Neill's *The Hairy Ape* or Mike LeFevre and Dolores Dante from Terkel's *Working.*

Carl Sandburg (1878–1967)

C arl Sandburg was born to Swedish immigrants living in Galesburg, Illinois. At thirteen years of age, he dropped out of school to help support his family. He worked at various jobs, including as a farm laborer, milkman, dishwasher, stagehand, brick layer, sign painter, salesman, and house painter, and he served in the Spanish–American War of 1898, all before he enrolled at Lombard College, where he excelled in basketball and had a good academic record although he left before graduating. He worked as a newspaper reporter for several years before becoming a secretary to the mayor of Milwaukee for two years. He wrote poetry, but not with the concentration of subsequent years.

Sandburg's first real poetic recognition came when "Chicago" was published in the prestigious *Poetry: A Magazine of Verse* in 1914. He published *Chicago Poems*, his first collection, in 1916, followed by *Cornhuskers* in 1918. By 1920, he was at the height of his poetic powers and with *Smoke and Steel* he became known as the poet of the common people. His popularity grew through the years. He is also known for his children's books and his classic biography, *Abraham Lincoln: The Prairie Years* (1926), which won a Pulitzer Prize. His *Complete Poems*, published in 1950, earned him a Pulitzer for poetry.

CHICAGO

Hog Butcher for the World,
Tool Maker, Stacker of Wheat,
Player with Railroads and the Nation's Freight Handler;
Stormy, husky, brawling,
City of the Big Shoulders:

They tell me you are wicked and I believe them, for I have seen your painted women under the gas lamps luring the farm boys.
And they tell me you are crooked and I answer: Yes, it is true I have seen the gunman kill and go free to kill again.

And they tell me you are brutal and my reply is: On the faces of women and children I have seen the marks of wanton hunger.

And having answered so I turn once more to those who sneer at this my city, and I give them back the sneer and say to them:

Come and show me another city with lifted head singing so proud to be alive and coarse and strong and cunning.

Flinging magnetic curses amid the toil of piling job on job, here is a tall bold slugger set vivid against the little soft cities;

Fierce as a dog with tongue lapping for action, cunning as a savage pitted against the wilderness,

Bareheaded,
Shoveling,
Wrecking,
Planning,
Building, breaking, rebuilding,

Under the smoke, dust all over his mouth, laughing with white teeth,
Under the terrible burden of destiny laughing as a young man laughs,
Laughing even as an ignorant fighter laughs who has never lost a battle,
Bragging and laughing that under his wrist is the pulse, and under his ribs the heart of the people,
Laughing!
Laughing the stormy, husky, brawling laughter of Youth, half-naked, sweating, proud to be Hog Butcher, Tool Maker, Stacker of Wheat, Player with Railroads and Freight Handler to the Nation.

1916

Questions

1. What portrait of Chicago emerges from the poem? Consider the visual and action-oriented images when answering this question.
2. Describe the form of the poem. What does the form suggest about the city?
3. What does the poem suggest about the city's laborers?
4. Why do you think that Sandburg capitalizes the catalogue of workers in the closing lines?

Washerwoman

WASHERWOMAN

The washerwoman is a member of the Salvation Army.
And over the tub of suds rubbing underwear clean
She sings that Jesus will wash her sins away
And the red wrongs she has done God and man
Shall be white as driven snow.
Rubbing underwear she sings of the Last Great Washday.

1916

Questions

1. What portrait of the washerwoman emerges from the poem?
2. Sandburg was a long-standing socialist. How do his socialist beliefs inform the poem?

Claude McKay (1890–1948)

Claude McKay worked briefly as a police constable in his native Jamaica. After publishing two volumes of verse, he left the island in 1912 to study at Tuskegee Institute, where he remained only briefly, and then at Kansas State University, where he studied agriculture for two years. In 1914, he moved to New York to establish himself as a writer. He traveled to England in 1919 and returned to Harlem to publish *Harlem Shadows*, a collection of poems that had an enormous impact on the Harlem Renaissance. McKay's leftist politics took him to Russia in 1923, after which he settled in France for several years, where he wrote his first novel, *Home to Harlem* (1928). After a dozen years in Europe and North Africa, he returned to Harlem and eventually settled in Chicago.

HARLEM DANCER

Applauding youths laughed with young prostitutes
And watched her perfect, half-clothed body sway;
Her voice was like the sound of blended flutes
Blown by black players upon a picnic day.
5   She sang and danced on gracefully and calm,
The light gauze hanging loose about her form;
To me she seemed a proudly-swaying palm
Grown lovelier for passing through a storm.
Upon her swarthy neck black shiny curls
10   Luxuriant fell; and tossing coins in praise,
The wine-flushed, bold-eyed boys, and even the girls,
Devoured her shape with eager, passionate gaze;
But looking at her falsely-smiling face,
I knew her self was not in that strange place.

1917

Questions

1. Paraphrase the scene described in the poem.
2. Does the dancer enjoy her work? Why or why not?
3. Does McKay sympathize with the dancer?

Studs Terkel (1912–2008)

L ouis "Studs" Terkel was born to Russian–Jewish parents in New York City. When he was eleven years old, his family moved to Chicago, where Terkel lived most of his life. Although he graduated from the University of Chicago Law School, he never pursued a career in law. Instead, he acted, hosted a radio show, and wrote. He had his own television show called *Studs' Place*, in which he played himself as a restaurant owner. The contract for the show was cancelled when Terkel refused to testify against other left-wing activists to Senator Joseph McCarthy and the House Un-American Activities Committee. His popular radio show remained on air in Chicago from 1952 to 1997.

Terkel gained a national audience, however, through his books, especially his oral histories. In *Hard Times: An Oral History of the Great Depression* (1970), he documents the struggle through the memories of those who endured the Depression. In 1985, he won a Pulitzer Prize for *"The Good War": An Oral History of World War II*. The selections in this text come from *Working: People Talk about What They Do All Day and How They Feel about What They Do* (1974), which was transformed into a Broadway musical and a Public Broadcasting Service special. These and Terkel's other books helped to establish oral history as a serious genre.

From *WORKING*, DOLORES DANTE, WAITRESS

Dolores Dante

She has been a waitress in the same restaurant for twenty-three years. Many of its patrons are credit card carriers on an expense account— conventioneers, politicians, labor leaders, agency people. Her hours are from 5:00 P.M. to 2:00 A.M. six days a week. She arrives earlier "to get things ready, the silverware, the butter. When people come in and ask for you, you would like to be in a position to handle them all, because that means more money for you."

"I became a waitress because I needed money fast and you don't get it in an office. My husband and I broke up and he left me with debts

and three children. My baby was six months. The fast buck, your tips. The first ten-dollar bill that I got as a tip, a Viking guy gave to me. He was a very robust, terrific atheist. Made very good conversation for us, 'cause I am too."

"Everyone says all waitresses have broken homes. What they don't realize is when people have broken homes they need to make money fast, and do this work. They don't have broken homes because they're waitresses."

I have to be a waitress. How else can I learn about people? How else does the world come to me? I can't go to everyone. So they have to come to me. Everyone wants to eat, everyone has hunger. And I serve them. If they've had a bad day, I nurse them, cajole them. Maybe with coffee I give them a little philosophy. They have cocktails, I give them political science.

I'll say things that bug me. If they manufacture soap, I say what I think about pollution. If it's automobiles, I say what I think about them. If I pour water I'll say, "Would you like your quota of mercury today?" If I serve cream, I say, "Here is your substitute. I think you're drinking plastic." I just can't keep quiet. I have an opinion on every single subject there is. In the beginning it was theology, and my bosses didn't like it. Now I am a political and my bosses don't like it. I speak *sotto voce*. But if I get heated, then I don't give a damn. I speak like an Italian speaks. I can't be servile. I give service. There is a difference.

I'm called by my first name. I like my name. I hate to be called Miss. Even when I serve a lady, a strange woman, I will not say madam. I hate ma'am. I always say milady. In the American language there is no word to address a woman, to indicate whether she's married or unmarried. So I say milady. And sometimes I playfully say to the man milord.

It would be very tiring if I had to say, "Would you like a cocktail?" and say that over and over. So I come out different for my own enjoyment. I would say, "What's exciting at the bar that I can offer?" I can't say, "Do you want coffee?" Maybe I'll say, "Are you in the mood for coffee?" Or, "The coffee sounds exciting." Just rephrase it enough to make it interesting for me. That would make them take an interest. It becomes theatrical and I feel like Mata Hari and it intoxicates me.

People imagine a waitress couldn't possibly think or have any kind of aspiration other than to serve food. When somebody says to me, "You're great, how come you're *just* a waitress?" *Just* a waitress. I'd say, "Why, don't you think you deserve to be served by me?" It's implying that he's not worthy, not that I'm not worthy. It makes me irate. I don't feel lowly at all. I myself feel sure. I don't want to change the job. I love it.

Tips? I feel like Carmen. It's like a gypsy holding out a tambourine and they throw the coin. (Laughs.) If you like people, you're not thinking of the tips. I never count my money at night. I always wait till morning. If I thought about my tips I'd be uptight. I never look at a tip. You pick it up fast. I would do my bookkeeping in the morning. It would be very dull for me to know I was making so much and no more. I do like challenge. And it isn't demeaning, not for me.

There might be occasions when the customers might intend to make it demeaning—the man about town, the conventioneer. When the time comes to pay the check, he would do little things, "How much should I give you?" He might make an issue about it. I did say to one, "Don't play God with me. Do what you want." Then it really didn't matter whether I got a tip or not. I would spit it out, my resentment—that he dares make me feel I'm operating only for a tip.

He'd ask for his check. Maybe he's going to sign it. He'd take a very long time and he'd make me stand there, "Let's see now, what do you think I ought to give you?" He would not let go of that moment. And you knew it. You know he meant to demean you. He's holding the change in his hand, or if he'd sign, he'd flourish the pen and wait. These are the times I really get angry. I'm not reticent. Something would come out. Then I really didn't care. "Goddamn, keep your money!"

There are conventioneers, who leave their lovely wives or their bad wives. They approach you and say, "Are there any hot spots?" "Where can I find girls?" It is, of course, first directed at you. I don't mean that as a compliment, 'cause all they're looking for is females. They're not looking for companionship or conversation. I am quite adept at understanding this. I think I'm interesting enough that someone may just want to talk to me. But I would philosophize that way. After all, what is left after you talk? The hours have gone by and I could be home resting or reading or studying guitar, which I do on occasion. I would say, "What are you going to offer me? Drinks?" And I'd point to the bar, "I have it all here." He'd look blank and then I'd say, "A man? If I need a man, wouldn't you think I'd have one of my own? Must I wait for you?"

Life doesn't frighten me any more. There are only two things that relegate us—the bathroom and the grave. Either I'm gonna have to go to the bathroom now or I'm gonna die now. I go to the bathroom.

And I don't have a high opinion of bosses. The more popular you are, the more the boss holds it over your head. You're bringing them business, but he knows you're getting good tips and you won't leave. You have to worry not to overplay it, because the boss becomes resentful and he uses this as a club over your head.

If you become too good a waitress, there's jealousy. They don't come in and say, "Where's the boss?" They'll ask for Dolores. It doesn't make a hit. That makes it rough. Sometimes you say. Aw hell, why am I trying so hard? I did get an ulcer. Maybe the things I kept to myself were twisting me.

It's not the customers, never the customers. It's injustice. My dad came from Italy and I think of his broken English—*injoost*. He hated injustice. If you hate injustice for the world, you hate more than anything injustice toward you. Loyalty is never appreciated, particularly if you're the type who doesn't like small talk and are not the type who makes reports on your fellow worker. The boss wants to find out what is going on surreptitiously. In our society today you have informers everywhere. They've informed on cooks, on coworkers. "Oh, someone wasted this." They would say I'm talking to all the customers. "I saw her carry such-and-such out. See if she wrote that on her check." "The salad looked like it was a double salad." I don't give anything away. I just give myself. Informers will manufacture things in order to make their job worth-while. They're not sure of themselves as workers. There's always someone who wants your station, who would be pretender to the crown. In life there is always someone who wants somebody's job.

I'd get intoxicated with giving service. People would ask for me and I didn't have enough tables. Some of the girls are standing and don't have cus-tomers. There is resentment. I feel self-conscious. I feel a sense of guilt. It cramps my style. I would like to say to the customer, "Go to so-and-so." But you can't do that, because you feel a sense of loyalty. So you would rush, get to your customers quickly. Some don't care to drink and still they wait for you. That's a compliment.

There is plenty of tension. If the cook isn't good, you fight to see that the customers get what you know they like. You have to use diplomacy with cooks, who are always dangerous. (Laughs.) They're madmen. (Laughs.) You have to be their friend. They better like you. And your bartender better like you too, be-cause he may do something to the drink. If your bartender doesn't like you, your cook doesn't like you, your boss doesn't like you, the other girls don't like you, you're in trouble.

And there will be customers who are hypochondriacs, who feel they can't eat, and I coax them. Then I hope I can get it just the right way from the cook. I may mix the salad myself, just the way they want it.

Maybe there's a party of ten. Big shots, and they'd say, "Dolores, I have special clients, do your best tonight." You just hope you have the right cook be-hind the broiler. You really want to pleasure your guests. He's selling some-thing, he wants things right, too. You're giving your all. How does the steak look? If you cut his steak, you look at it surreptitiously. How's it going?

Carrying dishes is a problem. We do have accidents. I spilled a tray once with steaks for seven on it. It was a big, gigantic T-bone, all sliced.

But when that tray fell, I went with it, and never made a sound, dish and all (softly) never made a sound. It took about an hour and a half to cook that steak. How would I explain this thing? That steak was salvaged. (Laughs.)

Some don't care. When the plate is down you can hear the sound. I try not to have that sound. I want my hands to be right when I serve. I pick up a glass, I want it to be just right. I get to be almost Oriental in the serving. I like it to look nice all the way. To be a waitress, it's an art. I feel like a ballerina, too. I have to go between those tables, between those chairs . . . Maybe that's the reason I always stayed slim. It is a certain way I can go through a chair no one else can do. I do it with an air. If I drop a fork, there is a certain way I pick it up. I know they can see how delicately I do it. I'm on stage.

I tell everyone I'm a waitress and I'm proud. If a nurse gives service, I say, "You're a professional." Whatever you do, be professional. I always compliment people.

I like to have my station looking nice. I like to see there's enough ash trays when they're having their coffee and cigarettes. I don't like ash trays so loaded that people are not enjoying the moment. It offends me. I don't do it be-cause I think that's gonna make a better tip. It offends me as a person.

People say, "No one does good work any more." I don't believe it. You know who's saying that? The man at the top, who says the people beneath him are not doing a good job. He's the one who always said, "You're nothing." The housewife who has all the money, she believed housework was demeaning, 'cause she hired someone else to do it. If it weren't so demeaning, why didn't *she* do it? So anyone who did her housework was a person to be demeaned. The maid who did all the housework said, "Well hell, if this is the way you feel about it, I won't do your housework. You tell me I'm no good. I'm nobody. Well, maybe I'll go out and be somebody." They're only mad because they can't find someone to do it now. The fault is not in the people who did the—quote—lowly work.

Just a waitress. At the end of the night I feel drained. I think a lot of waitresses become alcoholics because of that. In most cases, a waiter or a waitress doesn't eat. They handle food, they don't have time. You'll pick at something in the kitchen, maybe a piece of bread. You'll have a cracker, a little bit of soup. You go back and take a teaspoonful of something. Then maybe sit down afterwards and have a drink, maybe three, four, five. And bartenders, too. most of them are alcoholics. They'd go out in a group. There are after-hour places. You've got to go release your tension. So they go out before they go to bed. Some of them stay out all night.

It's tiring, it's nerve-racking. We don't ever sit down. We're on stage and the bosses are watching. If you get the wrong shoes and you get the wrong stitch in that shoe, that does bother you. Your feet hurt, your body aches. If you come out in anger at things that were done to you, it would only make you feel cheapened. Really I've been keeping it to myself. But of late. I'm beginning to spew it out. It's almost as though I sensed my body and soul had had quite enough.

It builds and builds and builds in your guts. Near crying. I can think about it . . . (She cries softly.) Cause you're tired. When the night is done, you're tired. You've had so much, there's so much going . . . You had to get it done. The dread that something wouldn't be right, because you want to please. You hope everyone is satisfied. The night's done, you've done your act. The curtains close.

The next morning is pleasant again. I take out my budget book, write down how much I made, what my bills are. I'm managing. I won't give up this job as long as I'm able to do it. I feel out of contact if I just sit at home. At work they all consider me a kook. (Laughs.) That's okay. No matter where I'd be, I would make a rough road for me. It's just me, and I can't keep still. It hurts, and what hurts has to come out.

POSTSCRIPT: *After sixteen years—that was seven years ago—I took a trip to Hawaii and the Caribbean for two weeks. Went with a lover. The kids saw it—they're all married now. (Laughs.) One of my daughters said, "Act your age." I said, "Honey, if I were acting my age, I wouldn't be walking. My bones would ache. You don't want to hear about my arthritis. Aren't you glad I'm happy?"*

1972

Questions

1. According to Dante, how do employers and customers perceive waiters and waitresses?
2. What does Dante think of her bosses and customers?
3. Why does the boss not like when a customer requests a specific member of the wait staff?
4. What does Dante like and dislike about her work?
5. Why is it important to Dante not to count her earnings until the next morning?
6. Why does she say that "[I] sense my body and soul had had quite enough"?
7. Overall, how does her job make her feel about herself?
8. Why do her coworkers think that she is a "kook"?
9. Compare Dante with the speaker in Rompf's "Waiting Table," the wait staff in Ehrenreich's *Nickel and Dimed*, and the dancer in McKay's "Harlem Dancer."

Robert Hayden (1913–1980)

Born Asa Bundy Sheffey, Robert Hayden had a difficult childhood in a poor neighborhood in Detroit, Michigan. He lived on and off with his warring parents and in the home of a foster family, who lived next door. Because of his small stature and impaired vision, he had difficulty getting along with his peers. He spent much of his time reading. After graduating from high school, he attended Detroit City College (later Wayne State University) and then the University of Michigan.

Hayden's first collection of poetry, *Heart-Shape in the Dust*, appeared in 1940, but he gained widespread acclaim with the publication of his *Selected Poems* in 1966, the same year in which he won the Grand Prize for Poetry at the First World Festival of Negro Arts held in Senegal. His poetry is informed by his deep knowledge of African–American history and his adherence to the Bahá'í Faith, a monotheistic Middle Eastern religion. He was a professor at Fisk University for twenty-three years before finishing his teaching career with eleven years at the University of Michigan.

THOSE WINTER SUNDAYS

Sundays too my father got up early
and put his clothes on in the blueblack cold,
then with cracked hands that ached
from labor in the weekday weather made
5 banked fires blaze. No one ever thanked him.

I'd wake and hear the cold splintering, breaking,
When the rooms were warm, he'd call,
and slowly I would rise and dress,
fearing the chronic angers of that house,

10 Speaking indifferently to him,
who had driven out the cold
and polished my good shoes as well.
What did I know, what did I know
of love's austere and lonely offices?

1962

Questions

1. What do you think prompted the speaker to write this poem?
2. What does the speaker most recall about his father?
3. How do work and family duty define the father? How does he seem to carry out both responsibilities in the same way?
4. What was the atmosphere like in the speaker's home?

Kraft Rompf (b. 1948)

K raft Rompf, a professor of English at the Community College of Baltimore County, Essex, Maryland, was born in Hamburg, Germany, and is a graduate of the Writing Seminars at The Johns Hopkins University. He is a coeditor of *The McGraw–Hill Book of Poetry* and *The McGraw–Hill Book of Fiction* (with Robert DiYanni), and the author of two volumes of poetry—*Skunk Missal* and *Five Fingers*. His poetry has appeared in *Poetry Now, The New York Quarterly, The Falcon, Exquisite Corpse,* and *The Bitter Oleander.* He has read and discussed his poetry on National Public Radio; at the Folger Shakespeare Library; and at various colleges, bars, and coffeehouses in and near New York City, Baltimore, and Washington, DC.

WAITING TABLE

To serve, I wait and pluck
the rose, brush crumbs, carry

madly trays of oysters and
Bloody Marys, Swinging through

5   doors, I hear them: mouths
open, eyes bugging, choking;

they beat a white clothed
table for caffeine piping

hot and sweet, sweet sugar
10   Oh, I should pour it in

their eyes! And set their
tongues afire, How the chef

understands when I order
tartare and shout, "Let them

eat it raw!" Oh I would stuff
15   their noses with garlic

and the house pianist
could play the Hammer March

on their toes, But for a
tip—for a tip, for a tip   20

I would work so very, very
hard, and so gladly let

them shine into my soul,
and bow to them and laugh

with them and sing, I would   25
gladly give them everything.

1978

Questions

1. Describe the speaker and his attitude toward his job.
2. Do you think that the speaker's attitude toward his customers is justified? Why or why not?
3. What career advice would you offer the speaker in this poem?
4. What does the structure of the poem reveal about the emotional expression of the speaker?
5. Compare the perspective of the speaker in this poem with that of Dolores Dante from Terkel's *Working*.
6. Read the poem in light of Barbara Ehrenreich's waitressing experiences in *Nickel and Dimed*, paragraphs 43–44 ("the perfect storm"). Does doing so perhaps cause you to reconsider your first impression of the speaker?

Jim Daniels (b. 1956)

Born in Detroit, Michigan, Jim Daniels has published eleven volumes of poetry and three collections of short fiction. Educated at Alman College and Bowling Green State University, he has won numerous awards for his poetry, including the Brittingham Prize in Poetry awarded by the University of Wisconsin. He is currently the Thomas Stockman Baker Professor of English at Carnegie Mellon University, where he directs the Creative Writing program. He is best known for his working-class poetry in which he articulates the concerns of those often ignored or without a medium for expression.

DIGGER LAID OFF

Right years since
the last time. Never thought
it would happen again.

You thought your seniority
5 was a hole you were digging—
the deeper you dug, the safer
you felt.

At the unemployment office
you shuftle in line with the rest,
10 shufting from foot to foot,
wobbling like a bowling pin.
Angry, but you don't know
at who or what.

When you were a kid, you waited
15 in line for football physicals.
Naked, nowhere to hide.
You can't pick your eyes up
off the floor. If they ask you,
you will cough.

2002

Questions

1. Explain the emotions that Digger feels as he waits in the unemployment line.
2. Digger is not sure with whom or with what he is angry. Why doesn't he know? With whom or with what do you think he is angry?
3. Consider his images of digging a hole, of "wobbling like a bowling pin," and of being "naked." What do they suggest about Digger?

Tom Wayman (b. 1945)

Tom Wayman lived his first seven years in Hawkesbury, Ontario, Canada, a pulp mill town on the Ottawa River, before his father, a pulp mill chemist, moved his family to Prince Rupert, British Columbia, a fishing and pulp mill town just south of Alaska. When he was fourteen years old, his family moved to Vancouver, British Columbia. Wayman graduated from the University of British Columbia and then earned an MFA at the University of California, Irvine. He has worked at various manual and academic jobs in the Canadian provinces of Alberta and Ontario, and in Colorado and Michigan. He has been writer-in-residence at several universities, including the University of Winnipeg, the University of Toronto, and, currently, the University of Calgary.

Best known for his poetry, Wayman has published seventeen volumes of poetry, as well as collections of essays and short fiction while editing several anthologies, including *Paperwork*, a collection of contemporary poems about daily work life. As a writer and an editor, Wayman has frequently focused on workplace experiences and the effect of work on individuals at and away from the workplace. "Factory Time" is from *Did I Miss Anything?: Selected Poems 1973–1993*.

FACTORY TIME

The day divides neatly into four parts
marked off by the breaks. The first quarter
is a full two hours, 7:30 to 9:30, but that's okay
in theory, because I'm supposed to be fresh, but in fact
after some evenings it's a long first two hours.
Then, a ten-minute break. Which is good
another way, too: the second quarter
thus has ten minutes knocked off, 9:40 to 11:30
which is only 110 minutes, or
to put it another way, if I look at my watch
and it says 11:10
I can cheer up because if I had still been in the first
quarter
and had worked for 90 minutes there would be

30 minutes to go, but now there is only
20. If it had been the first quarter, I could expect
the same feeling at 9 o'clock as here I have
when it is already ten minutes after 11.

Then it's lunch: a stretch, and maybe a little walk around.
And at 12 sharp the endless quarter begins:
a full two afternoon hours. And it's only the start
of the afternoon. Nothing to hope for the whole time.
Come to think of it, today
is probably only Tuesday. Or worse, Monday,
with the week barely begun and the day
only just half over, four hours down
and 36 to go this week
(if the foreman doesn't come padding by about 3
some afternoon and ask us all to work overtime)
Now while I'm trying to get through this early Tuesday
afternoon
maybe this is a good place to say
Wednesday, Thursday and Friday have their personalities too.
As a matter of fact, Wednesday after lunch
I could be almost happy
because when that 12 noon hooter blast goes
the week is precisely and officially half over.
All downhill from here: Thursday, as you know
is the day before Friday
which means a little celebrating Thursday night
—perhaps a few rounds in the pub after supper—
won't do me any harm. If I don't get much sleep
Thursday night, so what? I can sleep in Saturday.
And Friday right after lunch Mike the foreman appears
with the long cheques dripping out of his hands
and he is so polite to each of us as he passes them over
just like they taught him in foreman school.
After that, not too much gets done.
People go away into a corner and add and subtract like crazy
trying to catch the Company in a mistake
or figuring out what incredible percentage the government
has taken this week, or what the money will actually mean
in terms of savings or payments—and me, too.

But wait. It's still Tuesday afternoon.
And only the first half of that: all the minutes
until 2—which comes at last
and everyone drops what they are doing
if they hadn't already been drifting toward

their lunchboxes, or edging between the parts-racks
in the direction of the caterer's carts
which always appear a few minutes before the hooter
and may be taken on good authority as incontrovertible proof
that 2 o'clock is actually going to arrive.

And this last ten minute break of the day
is when I finally empty my lunchbox and the thermos inside
and put the now lightweight container back on its shelf
and dive into the day's fourth quarter: only 110 minutes.
Also, 20 to 30 minutes before the end I stop
and push a broom around, or just fiddle with something
or maybe fill up various parts-trays with washers
and bolts, or talk to the partsman, climb out of my
coveralls, and genrally slack off.
Until the 4 p.m. hooter of hooters
when I dash to the timeclock, a little shoving and pushing
in line, and I'm done. Whew.

But even when I quit
the numbers of the minutes and hours from this shift
stick with me: I can look at a clock some morning
months afterwards, and see it is 20 minutes to 9
—that is, if I'm ever out of bed that early—
and the automatic computer in my head
starts to type out: *20 minutes to 9, that means
30 minutes to work after 9: you are
50 minutes from the break; 50 minutes
of work, and it is only morning, and it is only
Monday, you poor dumb bastard. . . .*

And that's how it goes, round the clock, until a new time
from another job bores its way into my brain.

                                                                                1993

Questions

1. What does the speaker think about while he works? What does this tell you about the kind of work that he does?
2. Consider the rhythm and tone of the poem. How do they reflect his work and his attitude toward his work?
3. Is the speaker in danger of becoming dehumanized? Why or why not?
4. How do you think that this speaker would respond to Thoreau's statement from "Life without Principle": "The ways by which you may get money almost without exception lead downward. To have done anything by which you earned money merely is to have been truly idle or worse." Does the poem reflect this sentiment?

5. Do you sympathize with the speaker? Why or why not?

6. Suppose the speaker came to you for career advice. What would you tell him? From the poem, what do you think are his strengths and weaknesses?

7. Have you had or do you know someone who has had a similar work experience as the speaker's? If you know someone else who has had a similar experience, ask for his or her reaction to the poem. Did he or she have feelings similar to those of the speaker?

8. Compare the speaker with Digger in Daniels's "Digger Laid Off" and the workers in Shu Ting's "Assembly Line."

9. Compare the speaker with Mike LeFevre in Terkel's "Who Built the Pyramids?"

Barbara Ehrenreich (b. 1941)

Born in Butte, Montana, Barbara Ehrenreich earned a degree in physics from Reed College and went on to earn a PhD in cell biology from Rockefeller University. Instead of a scientific career, however, Ehrenreich decided to make social and political activism her life's work. She has been a featured columnist in *The New York Times*, *The Atlantic Monthly*, *The Progressive*, and *Salon.com*, and she has written twenty books, including *Bait and Switch: The (Futile) Pursuit of the American Dream* (2005) and *This Land Is Their Land: Reports from a Divided Nation* (2008), which addresses the economic divide between rich and poor in America.

This selection, originally published in *Harper's Magazine*, was included in *Nickel and Dimed: On (Not) Getting By in America*, her 2001 best seller, in which Ehrenreich went undercover to study the realities of life for low-wage earners.

From *NICKEL AND DIMED: ON (NOT) GETTING BY IN AMERICA*

Nickel-and-Dimed

At the beginning of June 1998 I leave behind everything that normally soothes the ego and sustains the body—home, career, companion, reputation, ATM card—for a plunge into the low-wage workforce. There, I become another, occupationally much diminished "Barbara Ehrenreich"—depicted on job-application forms as a divorced homemaker whose sole work experience consists of housekeeping in a few private homes. I am terrified, at the beginning, of being unmasked for what I am: a middle-class journalist setting out to explore the world that welfare mothers are entering, at the rate of approximately 50,000 a month, as welfare reform kicks in. Happily, though, my fears turn out to be entirely unwarranted: during a month of poverty and toil, my name goes unnoticed and for the most part unuttered. In this parallel universe where my father never got out of the mines and I never got through college, I am "baby," "honey," "blondie," and, most commonly, "girl."

My first task is to find a place to live. I figure that if I can earn $7 an hour—which, from the want ads, seems doable—I can afford to spend $500 on rent, or maybe, with severe economies, $600. In the Key West area, where I live, this pretty much confines me to flophouses and trailer homes—like the one, a pleasing fifteen-minute drive from town, that has no air-conditioning, no screens, no fans, no television, and, by way of diversion, only the challenge of evading the landlord's Doberman pinscher. The big problem with this place, though, is the rent, which at $675 a month is well beyond my reach. All right, Key West is expensive. But so is New York City, or the Bay Area, or Jackson Hole, or Telluride, or Boston, or any other place where tourists and the wealthy compete for living space with the people who clean their toilets and fry their hash browns.[1] Still, it is a shock to realize that "trailer trash" has become, for me, a demographic category to aspire to.

So I decide to make the common trade-off between affordability and convenience, and go for a $500-a-month efficiency thirty miles up a two-lane highway from the employment opportunities of Key West, meaning forty-five minutes if there's no road construction and I don't get caught behind some sundazed Canadian tourists. I hate the drive, along a roadside studded with white crosses commemorating the more effective head-on collisions, but it's a sweet little place—a cabin, more or less, set in the swampy back yard of the converted mobile home where my landlord, an affable TV repairman, lives with his bartender girlfriend. Anthropologically speaking, a bustling trailer park would be preferable, but here I have a gleaming white floor and a firm mattress, and the few resident bugs are easily vanquished.

Besides, I am not doing this for the anthropology. My aim is nothing so mistily subjective as to "experience poverty" or find out how it "really feels" to be a long-term low-wage worker. I've had enough unchosen encounters with poverty and the world of low-wage work to know it's not a place you want to visit for touristic purposes; it just smells too much like fear. And with all my real-life assets—bank account, IRA, health insurance, multiroom home—waiting indulgently in the background, I am, of course, thoroughly insulated from the terrors that afflict the genuinely poor.

No, this is a purely objective, scientific sort of mission. The humanitarian rationale for welfare reform—as opposed to the more punitive and stingy impulses that may actually have motivated it—is that work will lift poor women out of poverty while simultaneously inflating their self-esteem and hence their future value in the labor market. Thus, whatever the hassles involved in finding child care, transportation, etc., the transition from welfare to work will end happily, in greater prosperity for all. Now there are many problems with this comforting prediction, such as the fact that the economy will inevitably undergo a downturn, eliminating many jobs. Even without a downturn, the influx of a million former welfare recipients into the low-wage labor market could depress

---

[1]According to the Department of Housing and Urban Development, the "fair-market rent" for an efficiency is $551 here in Monroe County, Florida. A comparable rent in the five boroughs of New York City is $704; in San Francisco, $713; and in the heart of Silicon Valley, $808. The fair-market rent for an area is defined as the amount that would be needed to pay rent plus utilities for "privately owned, decent, safe, and sanitary rental housing of a modest (non-luxury) nature with suitable amenities." [Author's note]

wages by as much as 11.9 percent, according to the Economic Policy Institute (EPI) in Washington, D.C.

But is it really possible to make a living on the kinds of jobs currently available to unskilled people? Mathematically, the answer is no, as can be shown by taking $6 to $7 an hour, perhaps subtracting a dollar or two an hour for child care, multiplying by 160 hours a month, and comparing the result to the prevailing rents. According to the National Coalition for the Homeless, for example, in 1998 it took, on average nationwide, an hourly wage of $8.89 to afford a one-bedroom apartment, and the Preamble Center for Public Policy estimates that the odds against a typical welfare recipient's landing a job at such a "living wage" are about 97 to 1. If these numbers are right, low-wage work is not a solution to poverty and possibly not even to homelessness.

It may seem excessive to put this proposition to an experimental test. As certain family members keep unhelpfully reminding me, the viability of low-wage work could be tested, after a fashion, without ever leaving my study. I could just pay myself $7 an hour for eight hours a day, charge myself for room and board, and total up the numbers after a month. Why leave the people and work that I love? But I am an experimental scientist by training. In that business, you don't just sit at a desk and theorize; you plunge into the everyday chaos of nature, where surprises lurk in the most mundane measurements. Maybe, when I got into it, I would discover some hidden economies in the world of the low-wage worker. After all, if 30 percent of the workforce toils for less than $8 an hour, according to the EPI, they may have found some tricks as yet unknown to me. Maybe—who knows?—I would even to able to detect in myself the bracing psychological effects of getting out of the house, as promised by the welfare wonks at places like the Heritage Foundation. Or, on the other hand, maybe there would be unexpected costs—physical, mental, or financial—to throw off all my calculations. Ideally, I should do this with two small children in tow, that being the welfare average, but mine are grown and no one is willing to lend me theirs for a month-long vacation in penury. So this is not the perfect experiment, just a test of the best possible case: an unencumbered woman, smart and even strong, attempting to live more or less off the land.

On the morning of my first full day of job searching, I take a red pen to the want ads, which are auspiciously numerous. Everyone in Key West's booming "hospitality industry" seems to be looking for someone like me—trainable, flexible, and with suitably humble expectations as to pay. I know I possess certain traits that might be advantageous—I'm white and, I like to think, well-spoken and poised—but I decide on two rules: One, I cannot use any skills derived from my education or usual work—not that there are a lot of want ads for satirical essayists anyway. Two, I have to take the best-paid job that is offered me and of course do my best to hold it; no Marxist rants or sneaking off to read novels in the ladies' room. In addition, I rule out various occupations for one reason or another. Hotel front-desk clerk, for example, which to my surprise is regarded as unskilled and pays around $7 an hour, gets eliminated because it involves standing in one spot for eight hours a day. Waitressing is similarly something I'd like to avoid, because I remember it leaving me bone tired when

I was eighteen, and I'm decades of varicosities and back pain beyond that now. Telemarketing, one of the first refuges of the suddenly indigent, can be dismissed on grounds of personality. This leaves certain supermarket jobs, such as deli clerk, or housekeeping in Key West's thousands of hotel and guest rooms. Housekeeping is especially appealing, for reasons both atavistic and practical: it's what my mother did before I came along, and it can't be too different from what I've been doing part-time, in my own home, all my life.

So I put on what I take to be a respectful-looking outfit of ironed Bermuda shorts and scooped-neck T-shirt and set out for a tour of the local hotels and supermarkets. Best Western, Econo Lodge, and HoJo's all let me fill out application forms, and these are, to my relief, interested in little more than whether I am a legal resident of the United States and have committed any felonies. My next step is Winn-Dixie, the supermarket, which turns out to have a particularly onerous application process, featuring a fifteen-minute "interview" by computer since, apparently, no human on the premises is deemed capable of representing the corporate point of view. I am conducted to a large room decorated with posters illustrating how to look "professional" (it helps to be white and, if female, permed) and warning of the slick promises that union organizers might try to tempt me with. The interview is multiple choice: Do I have anything, such as child-care problems, that might make it hard for me to get to work on time? Do I think safety on the job is the responsibility of management? Then, popping up cunningly out of the blue: How many dollars' worth of stolen goods have I purchased in the last year? Would I turn in a fellow employee if I caught him stealing? Finally, "Are you an honest person?"

Apparently, I ace the interview, because I am told that all I have to do is show up in some doctor's office tomorrow for a urine test. This seems to be a fairly general rule: if you want to stack Cheerio boxes or vacuum hotel rooms in chemically fascist America, you have to be willing to squat down and pee in front of some health worker (who has no doubt had to do the same thing herself). The wages Winn-Dixie is offering—$6 and a couple of dimes to start with—are not enough, I decide, to compensate for this indignity.[2]

I lunch at Wendy's, where $4.99 gets you unlimited refills at the Mexican part of the Superbar, a comforting surfeit of refried beans and "cheese sauce." A teenage employee, seeing me studying the want ads, kindly offers me an application form, which I fill out, though here, too, the pay is just $6 and change an hour. Then it's off for a round of the locally owned inns and guest-houses. At "The Palms," let's call it, a bouncy manager actually takes me around to see the rooms and meet the existing housekeepers, who, I note with satisfaction, look

---

[2]According to the *Monthly Labor Review* (November 1996), 28 percent of work sites surveyed in the service industry conduct drug tests (corporate workplaces have much higher rates), and the incidence of testing has risen markedly since the Eighties. The rate of testing is highest in the South (56 percent of work sites polled), with the Midwest in second place (50 percent). The drug most likely to be detected—marijuana, which can be detected in urine for weeks—is also the most innocuous, while heroin and cocaine are generally undetectable three days after use. Prospective employees sometimes try to cheat the tests by consuming excessive amounts of liquids and taking diuretics and even masking substances available through the Internet. [Author's note]

pretty much like me—faded ex-hippie types in shorts with long hair pulled back in braids. Mostly, though, no one speaks to me or even looks at me except to proffer an application form. At my last stop, a palatial B&B, I wait twenty minutes to meet "Max," only to be told that there are no jobs now but there should be one soon, since "nobody lasts more than a couple weeks." (Because none of the people I talked to knew I was a reporter, I have changed their names to protect their privacy and, in some cases perhaps, their jobs.)

Three days go by like this, and, to my chagrin, no one out of the approximately twenty places I've applied calls me for an interview. I had been vain enough to worry about coming across as too educated for the jobs I sought, but no one even seems interested in finding out how overqualified I am. Only later will I realize that the want ads are not a reliable measure of the actual jobs available at any particular time. They are, as I should have guessed from Max's comment, the employers' insurance policy against the relentless turnover of the low-wage workforce. Most of the big hotels run ads almost continually, just to build a supply of applicants to replace the current workers as they drift away or are fired, so finding a job is just a matter of being at the right place at the right time and flexible enough to take whatever is being offered that day. This finally happens to me at one of the big discount hotel chains, where I go, as usual, for housekeeping and am sent, instead, to try out as a waitress at the attached "family restaurant," a dismal spot with a counter and about thirty tables that looks out on a parking garage and features such tempting fare as "Pollish [sic] sausage and BBQ sauce" on 95-degree days. Phillip, the dapper young West Indian who introduces himself as the manager, interviews me with about as much enthusiasm as if he were a clerk processing me for Medicare, the principal questions being what shifts can I work and when can I start. I mutter something about being woefully out of practice as a waitress, but he's already on to the uniform: I'm to show up tomorrow wearing black slacks and black shoes; he'll provide the rust-colored polo shirt with HEARTHSIDE embroidered on it, though I might want to wear my own shirt to get to work, ha ha. At the word "tomorrow," something between fear and indignation rises in my chest. I want to say, "Thank you for your time, sir, but this is just an experiment, you know, not my actual life."

So begins my career at the Hearthside, I shall call it, one small profit center within a global discount hotel chain, where for two weeks I work from 2:00 till 10:00 P.M. for $2.43 an hour plus tips.[3] In some futile bid for gentility, the management has barred employees from using the front door, so my first day I enter through the kitchen, where a red-faced man with shoulder-length blond hair is throwing frozen steaks against the wall and yelling, "Fuck this shit!" "That's just Jack," explains Gail, the wiry middle-aged waitress who is assigned

---

[3]According to the Fair Labor Standards Act, employers are not required to pay "tipped employees," such as restaurant servers, more than $2.13 an hour in direct wages. However, if the sum of tips plus $2.13 an hour falls below the minimum wage, or $5.15 an hour, the employer is required to make up the difference. This fact was not mentioned by managers or otherwise publicized at either of the restaurants where I worked. [Author's note]

to train me. "He's on the rag again"—a condition occasioned, in this instance, by the fact that the cook on the morning shift had forgotten to thaw out the steaks. For the next eight hours, I run after the agile Gail, absorbing bits of instruction along with fragments of personal tragedy. All food must be trayed, and the reason she's so tired today is that she woke up in a cold sweat thinking of her boyfriend, who killed himself recently in an upstate prison. No refills on lemonade. And the reason he was in prison is that a few DUIs caught up with him, that's all, could have happened to anyone. Carry the creamers to the table in a monkey bowl, never in your hand. And after he was gone she spent several months living in her truck, peeing in a plastic pee bottle and reading by candlelight at night, but you can't live in a truck in the summer, since you need to have the windows down, which means anything can get in, from mosquitoes on up.

At least Gail puts to rest any fears I had of appearing overqualified. From the first day on, I find that of all the things I have left behind, such as home and identity, what I miss the most is competence. Not that I have ever felt utterly competent in the writing business, in which one day's success augurs nothing at all for the next. But in my writing life, I at least have some notion of procedure: do the research, make the outline, rough out a draft, etc. As a server, though, I am beset by requests like bees: more iced tea here, ketchup over there, a to-go box for table fourteen, and where are the high chairs, anyway? Of the twenty-seven tables, up to six are usually mine at any time, though on slow afternoons or if Gail is off, I sometimes have the whole place to myself. There is the touch-screen computer-ordering system to master, which is, I suppose, meant to minimize server-cook contact, but in practice requires constant verbal fine-tuning: "That's gravy on the mashed, okay? None on the meatloaf," and so forth—while the cook scowls as if I were inventing these refinements just to torment him. Plus, something I had forgotten in the years since I was eighteen: about a third of a server's job is "side work" that's invisible to customers—sweeping, scrubbing, slicing, refilling, and restocking. If it isn't all done, every little bit of it, you're going to face the 6:00 P.M. dinner rush defenseless and probably go down in flames. I screw up dozens of times at the beginning, sustained in my shame entirely by Gail's support—"It's okay, baby, everyone does that sometimes"—because, to my total surprise and despite the scientific detachment I am doing my best to maintain, I care.

The whole thing would be a lot easier if I could just skate through it as Lily Tomlin in one of her waitress skits, but I was raised by the absurd Booker T. Washingtonian precept that says: If you're going to do something, do it well. In fact, "well" isn't good enough by half. Do it better than anyone has ever done it before. Or so said my father, who must have known what he was talking about because he managed to pull himself, and us with him, up from the mile-deep copper mines of Butte to the leafy suburbs of the Northeast, ascending from boilermakers to martinis before booze beat out ambition. As in most endeavors I have encountered in my life, doing it "better than anyone" is not a reasonable goal. Still, when I wake up at 4:00 A.M. in my own cold sweat, I am not thinking about the writing deadlines I'm neglecting; I'm thinking about the table whose order I screwed up so that one of the boys didn't get his kiddie meal until the rest of the family had moved on to their Key Lime pies. That's the other powerful motivation I hadn't expected—the customers, or "patients," as I can't help thinking of them on account of the mysterious vulnerability that seems to have left them temporarily unable to feed themselves. After a few days at the Hearthside, I feel the service ethic kick in like a shot of oxytocin, the nurturance hormone. The plurality of my customers are hard-working locals—truck drivers, construction workers, even housekeepers from the attached hotel—and I want them to have the closest to a "fine dining experience that the grubby circumstances will allow. No "you guys" for me; everyone over twelve is "sir" or "ma'am." I ply them with iced tea and coffee refills; I return, mid-meal, to inquire how everything is; I doll up their salads with chopped raw mushrooms, summer squash slices, or whatever bits of produce I can find that have survived their sojourn in the cold-storage room mold-free.

There is Benny, for example, a short, tight-muscled sewer repairman, who cannot even think of eating until he has absorbed a half hour of air-conditioning and ice water. We chat about hyperthermia and electrolytes until he is ready to order some finicky combination like soup of the day, garden salad, and a side of grits. There are the German tourists who are so touched by my pidgin "Willkommen" and "Ist alles gut?" that they actually tip. (Europeans, spoiled by their trade-union-ridden, high-wage welfare states, generally do not know that they are supposed to tip. Some restaurants, the Hearthside included, allow servers to "grat" their foreign customers, or add a tip to the bill. Since this amount is added before the customers have a chance to tip or not tip, the practice amounts to an automatic penalty for imperfect English.) There are the two dirt-smudged lesbians, just off their construction shift, who are impressed enough by my suave handling of the fly in the piña colada that they take the time to praise me to Stu, the assistant manager. There's Sam, the kindly retired cop, who has to plug up his tracheotomy hole with one finger in order to force the cigarette smoke into his lungs.

Sometimes I play with the fantasy that I am a princess who, in penance for some tiny transgression, has undertaken to feed each of her subjects by hand. But the non-princesses working with me are just as indulgent, even when this means flouting management rules—concerning, for example, the number of croutons that can go on a salad (six). "Put on all you want," Gail whispers, "as long as Stu isn't looking." She dips into her own tip money to buy biscuits and gravy for an out-of-work mechanic who's used up all his money on dental surgery, inspiring me to pick up the tab for his milk and pie. Maybe the same high levels of agape can be found throughout the "hospitality industry." I remember the poster decorating one of the apartments I looked at which said "If you seek happiness for yourself you will never find it. Only when you seek happiness for others will it come to you," or words to that effect—an odd sentiment, it seemed to me at the time, to find in the dank one room basement apartment of a bellhop at the Best Western. At the Hearthside, we utilize whatever bits of autonomy we have to ply our customers with the illicit calories that signal our love. It is our job as servers to assemble the salads and desserts, pouring the dressings and squirting the whipped cream. We also control the number of butter patties our customers get and the amount of sour cream on their baked potatoes. So if you wonder why Americans are so obese, consider the fact that waitresses both express their humanity and earn their tips through the covert distribution of fats.

Ten days into it, this is beginning to look like a livable lifestyle. I like Gail, who is "looking at fifty" but moves so fast she can alight in one place and then, another without apparently being anywhere between them. I clown around with Lionel, the teenage Haitian busboy, and catch a few fragments of conversation with Joan, the svelte fortyish hostess and militant feminist who is the only one of us who dares to tell Jack to shut the fuck up. I even warm up to Jack when, on a slow night and to make up for a particularly unwarranted attack on my abilities, or so I imagine, he tells me about his glory days as a young man at "coronary school"—or do you say "culinary"?—in Brooklyn, where he dated a knock-out Puerto Rican chick and learned everything there is to know about food. I finish up at 10:00 or 10:30, depending on how much side work I've been able to get done during the shift, and cruise home to the tapes I snatched up at random when I left my real home—Marianne Faithfull, Tracy Chapman, Enigma, King Sunny Ade, the Violent Femmes—just drained enough for the music to set my cranium resonating but hardly dead. Midnight snack is Wheat Thins and Monterey Jack, accompanied by cheap white wine on ice and whatever AMC has to offer. To bed by 1:30 or 2:00, up at 9:00 or 10:00, read for an hour while my uniform whirls around in the landlord's washing machine, and then it's another eight hours spent following Mao's central instruction, as laid out in the Little Red Book, which was: Serve the people.

I could drift along like this, in some dreamy proletarian idyll, except for two things. One is management. If I have kept this subject on the margins thus far it is because I still flinch to think that I spent all those weeks under the surveillance of men (and later women) whose job it was to monitor my behavior for signs of sloth, theft, drug abuse, or worse. Not that managers and especially "assistant managers" in low-wage settings like this are exactly the class enemy. In the restaurant business, they are mostly former cooks or servers, still capable of pinch-hitting in the kitchen or on the floor, just as in hotels they are likely to be former clerks, and paid a salary of only about $400 a week. But everyone knows they have crossed over to the other side, which is, crudely put, corporate as opposed to human. Cooks want to prepare tasty meals; servers want to serve them graciously; but managers are there for only one reason—to make sure that money is made for some theoretical entity that exists far away in Chicago or New York, if a corporation can be said to have a physical existence at all. Reflecting on her career, Gail tells me ruefully that she had sworn, years ago, never to work for a corporation again. "They don't cut you no slack. You give and you give, and they take."

Managers can sit—for hours at a time if they want—but it's their job to see that no one else ever does, even when there's nothing to do, and this is why, for servers, slow times can be as exhausting as rushes. You start dragging out each little chore, because if the manager on duty catches you in an idle moment, he will give you something far nastier to do. So I wipe, I clean, I consolidate ketchup bottles and recheck the cheesecake supply, even tour the tables to make sure the customer evaluation forms are all standing perkily in their places—wondering all the time how many calories I burn in these strictly theatrical exercises. When, on a particularly dead afternoon, Stu finds me glancing at a *USA Today* a customer has left behind, he assigns me to vacuum the entire floor with the broken vacuum cleaner that has a handle only two feet long, and the only way to do that without incurring orthopedic damage is to proceed from spot to spot on your knees.

On my first Friday at the Hearthside there is a "mandatory meeting for all restaurant employees," which I attend, eager for insight into our overall marketing strategy and the niche (your basic Ohio cuisine with a tropical twist?) we aim to inhabit. But there is no "we" at this meeting. Phillip, our top manager except for an occasional "consultant" sent out by corporate headquarters, opens it with a sneer: "The break room—it's disgusting. Butts in the ashtrays, newspapers lying around, crumbs." This windowless little room, which also houses the time clock for the entire hotel, is where we stash our bags and civilian clothes and take our half-hour meal breaks. But a break room is not a right, he tells us. It can be taken away. We should also know that the lockers in the break room and whatever is in them can be searched at any time. Then comes gossip; there has been gossip; gossip (which seems to mean employees talking among themselves) must stop. Off-duty employees are henceforth barred from eating at the restaurant, because "other servers gather around them and gossip." When Phillip has exhausted his agenda of rebukes, Joan complains about the condition of the ladies' room and I throw in my two bits about the vacuum cleaner. But I don't see any backup coming from my fellow servers, each of whom has subsided into her own personal funk; Gail, my role model, stares sorrowfully at a point six inches from her nose. The meeting ends when Andy, one of the cooks, gets up, muttering about breaking up his day off for this almighty bullshit.

Just four days later we are suddenly summoned into the kitchen at 3:30 P.M., even though there are live tables on the floor. We all—about ten of us—stand around Phillip, who announces grimly that there has been a report of some "drug activity" on the night shift and that, as a result, we are now to be a "drug-free" workplace, meaning that all new hires will be tested, as will possibly current employees on a random basis. I am glad that this part of the kitchen is so dark, because I find myself blushing as hard as if I had been caught toking up in the ladies' room myself: I haven't been treated this way—lined up in the corridor, threatened with locker searches, peppered with carelessly aimed accusations— since junior high school. Back on the floor, Joan cracks, "Next they'll be telling us we can't have sex on the job." When I ask Stu what happened to inspire the crackdown, he just mutters about "management decisions" and takes the opportunity to upbraid Gail and me for being too generous with the rolls. From now on there's to be only one per customer, and it goes out with the dinner, not with the salad. He's also been riding the cooks, prompting Andy to come out of the kitchen and observe—with the serenity of a man whose customary implement is a butcher knife—that "Stu has a death wish today."

Later in the evening, the gossip crystallizes around the theory that Stu is himself the drug culprit, that he uses the restaurant phone to order up marijuana and sends one of the late servers out to fetch it for him. The server was caught, and she may have ratted Stu out or at least said enough to cast some suspicion on him, thus accounting for his pissy behavior. Who knows? Lionel, the busboy, entertains us for the rest of the shift by standing just behind Stu's back and sucking deliriously on an imaginary joint.

The other problem, in addition to the less-than-nurturing management style, is that this job shows no sign of being financially viable. You might imagine, from a comfortable distance, that people who live, year in and year out, on $6 to $10 an hour have discovered some survival stratagems unknown to the middle class. But no. It's not hard to get my co-workers to talk about their living situations, because housing, in almost every case, is the principal source of disruption in their lives, the first thing they fill you in on when they arrive for their shifts. After a week, I have compiled the following survey:

- Gail is sharing a room in a well-known downtown flophouse for which she and a roommate pay about $250 a week. Her roommate, a male friend, has begun hitting on her, driving her nuts, but the rent would be impossible alone.
- Claude, the Haitian cook, is desperate to get out of the two-room apartment he shares with his girlfriend and two other, unrelated, people. As far as I can determine, the other Haitian men (most of whom only speak Creole) live in similarly crowded situations.
- Annette, a twenty-year-old server who is six months pregnant and has been abandoned by her boyfriend, lives with her mother, a postal clerk.
- Marianne and her boyfriend are paying $170 a week for a one-person trailer.
- Jack, who is, at $10 an hour, the wealthiest of us, lives in a trailer he owns, paying only the $400-a-month lot fee.
- The other white cook, Andy, lives on his dry-docked boat, which, as far as I can tell from his loving descriptions, can't be more than twenty feet long. He offers to take me out on it, once it's repaired, but the offer comes with inquiries as to my marital status, so I do not follow up on it.
- Tina and her husband are paying $60 a night for a double room in a Days Inn. This is because they have no car and the Days Inn is within walking distance of the Hearthside. When Marianne, one of the breakfast servers, is tossed out of her trailer for subletting (which is against the trailer-park rules), she leaves her boyfriend and moves in with Tina and her husband.
- Joan, who had fooled me with her numerous and tasteful outfits (hostesses wear their own clothes), lives in a van she parks behind a shopping center at night and showers in Tina's motel room. The clothes are from thrift shops.[4]

---

[4] I could find no statistics on the number of employed people living in cars or vans, but according to the National Coalition for the Homeless's 1997 report, "Myths and Facts About Homelessness," nearly one in five homeless people (in twenty-nine cities across the nation) is employed in a full- or part-time job. [Author's note]

It strikes me, in my middle-class solipsism, that there is gross improvi-dence in some of these arrangements. When Gail and I are wrapping silverware in napkins—the only task for which we are permitted to sit—she tells me she is thinking of escaping from her roommate by moving into the Days Inn herself. I am astounded: How can she even think of paying between $40 and $60 a day? But if I was afraid of sounding like a social worker, I come out just sounding like a fool. She squints at me in disbelief, "And where am I supposed to get a month's rent and a month's deposit for an apartment?" I'd been feeling pretty smug about my $500 efficiency, but of course it was made possible only by the $1,300 I had allotted myself for start-up costs when I began my low-wage life: $1,000 for the first month's rent and deposit, $100 for initial groceries and cash in my pocket, $200 stuffed away for emergencies. In poverty, as in certain propositions in physics, starting conditions are everything.

There are no secret economies that nourish the poor; on the contrary, there are a host of special costs. If you can't put up the two months' rent you need to secure an apartment, you end up paying through the nose for a room by the week. If you have only a room, with a hot plate at best, you can't save by cooking up huge lentil stews that can be frozen for the week ahead. You eat fast food, or the hot dogs and styrofoam cups of soup that can be microwaved in a convenience store. If you have no money for health insurance—and the Hearthside's niggardly plan kicks in only after three months—you go without routine care or prescription drugs and end up paying the price. Gail, for exam-ple, was fine until she ran out of money for estrogen pills. She is supposed to be on the company plan by now, but they claim to have lost her application form and need to begin the paperwork all over again. So she spends $9 per mi-graine pill to control the headaches she wouldn't have, she insists, if her estro-gen supplements were covered. Similarly, Marianne's boyfriend lost his job as a roofer because he missed so much time after getting a cut on his foot for which he couldn't afford the prescribed antibiotic.

My own situation, when I sit down to assess it after two weeks of work, would not be much better if this were my actual life. The seductive thing about waitressing is that you don't have to wait for payday to feel a few bills in your pocket, and my tips usually cover meals and gas, plus something left over to stuff into the kitchen drawer I use as a bank. But as the tourist business slows in the summer heat, I sometimes leave work with only $20 in tips (the gross is higher, but servers share about 15 percent of their tips with the bus-boys and bartenders). With wages included, this amounts to about the minimum wage of $5.15 an hour. Although the sum in the drawer is piling up, at the present rate of accumulation it will be more than a hundred dollars short of my rent when the end of the month comes around. Nor can I see any expenses to cut. True, I haven't gone the lentil-stew route yet, but that's because I don't have a large cooking pot, pot holders, or a ladle to stir with (which cost about $30 at Kmart, less at thrift stores), not to mention onions, carrots, and the indispensable bay leaf. I do make my lunch almost every day—usually some slow-burning, high-protein combo like frozen chicken patties with melted cheese on top and canned pinto beans on the side. Dinner is at the Hearthside, which offers its employees a choice of BLT, fish sandwich, or hamburger for only $2. The burger lasts longest, especially if it's heaped with gut-puckering jalapeños, but by midnight my stomach is growling again.

So unless I want to start using my car as a residence, I have to find a second, or alternative, job. I call all the hotels where I filled out housekeeping applications weeks ago—the Hyatt, Holiday Inn, Econo Lodge, Hojo's, Best Western, plus a half dozen or so locally run guesthouses. Nothing. Then I start making the rounds again, wasting whole mornings waiting for some assistant manager to show up, even dipping into places so creepy that the front-desk clerk greets you from behind bulletproof glass and sells pints of liquor over the counter. But either someone has exposed my real-life housekeeping habits—which are, shall we say, mellow—or I am at the wrong end of some infallible ethnic equation: most, but by no means all, of the working housekeepers I see on my job searches are African Americans, Spanish-speaking, or immigrants from the Central European post-Communist world, whereas servers are almost invariably white and monolingually English-speaking. When I finally get a positive response, I have been identified once again as server material. Jerry's, which is part of a well-known national family restaurant chain and physically attached here to another budget hotel chain, is ready to use me at once. The prospect is both exciting and terrifying, because, with about the same number of tables and counter seats, Jerry's attracts three or four times the volume of customers as the gloomy old Hearthside.

I start out with the beautiful, heroic idea of handling the two jobs at once, and for two days I almost do it: the breakfast/lunch shift at Jerry's, which goes till 2:00, arriving at the Hearthside at 2:10, and attempting to hold out until 10:00. In the ten minutes between jobs, I pick up a spicy chicken sandwich at the Wendy's drive-through window, gobble it down in the car, and change from khaki slacks to black, from Hawaiian to rust polo. There is a problem, though. When during the 3:00 to 4:00 P.M. dead time I finally sit down to wrap silver, my flesh seems to bond to the seat. I try to refuel with a purloined cup of soup, as I've seen Gail and Joan do dozens of times, but a manager catches me and hisses "No eating!" though there's not a customer around to be offended by the sight of food making contact with a server's lips. So I tell Gail I'm going to quit, and she hugs me and says she might just follow me to Jerry's herself.

But the chances of this are miniscule. She has left the flophouse and her 30 annoying roommate and is back to living in her beat-up old truck. But guess what? she reports to me excitedly later that evening: Phillip has given her permission to park overnight in the hotel parking lot, as long as she keeps out of sight, and the parking lot should be totally safe, since it's patrolled by a hotel security guard! With the Hearthside offering benefits like that, how could anyone think of leaving?

True, I take occasional breaks from this life, going home now and then to catch up on e-mail and for conjugal visits (though I am careful to "pay" for anything I eat there), seeing *The Truman Show* with friends and letting them buy my ticket. And I still have those what-am-I-doing-here moments at work, when I get so homesick for the printed word that I obsessively reread the six-page menu. But as the days go by, my old life is beginning to look exceedingly strange. The e-mails and phone messages addressed to my former self come from a distant race of people with exotic concerns and far too much time on their hands. The neighborly market I used to cruise for produce now looks forbiddingly like a Manhattan yuppie emporium. And when I sit down one morning in my real home to pay bills from my past life, I am dazzled at the two-and three-figure sums owed to outfits like Club BodyTech and Amazon.com.

Management at Jerry's is generally calmer and more "professional" than at the Hearthside, with two exceptions. One is Joy, a plump, blowsy woman in her early thirties, who once kindly devoted several minutes to instructing me in the correct one-handed method of carrying trays but whose moods change disconcertingly from shift to shift and even within one. Then there's B.J., a.k.a. B.J.-the-bitch, whose contribution is to stand by the kitchen counter and yell, "Nita, your order's up, move it!" or, "Barbara, didn't you see you've got another table out there? Come on, girl!" Among other things, she is hated for having replaced the whipped-cream squirt cans with big plastic whipped-cream-filled baggies that have to be squeezed with both hands—because, reportedly, she saw or thought she saw employees trying to inhale the propellant gas from the squirt cans, in the hope that it might be nitrous oxide. On my third night, she pulls me aside abruptly and brings her face so close that it looks as if she's planning to butt me with her forehead. But instead of saying, "You're fired," she says, "You're doing fine." The only trouble is I'm spending time chatting with customers: "That's how they're getting you." Furthermore I am letting them "run me," which means harassment by sequential demands: you bring the ketchup and they decide they want extra Thousand Island; you bring that and they announce they now need a side of fries; and so on into distraction. Finally she tells me not to take her wrong. She tries to say things in a nice way, but you get into a mode, you know, because everything has to move so fast.[5]

I mumble thanks for the advice, feeling like I've just been stripped naked by the crazed enforcer of some ancient sumptuary law: No chatting for you, girl. No fancy service ethic allowed for the serfs. Chatting with customers is for the beautiful young college-educated servers in the downtown carpaccio joints, the kids who can make $70 to $100 a night. What had I been thinking? My job is to move orders from tables to kitchen and then trays from kitchen to tables. Customers are, in fact, the major obstacle to the smooth transformation of information into food and food into money—they are, in short, the enemy. And the painful thing is that I'm beginning to see it this way myself. There are the traditional asshole types—frat boys who down multiple Buds and then make a fuss because the steaks are so emaciated and the fries so sparse—as well as the variously impaired—due to age, diabetes, or literacy issues—who require patient nutritional counseling.

---

[5]In *Workers in a Lean World: Unions in the International Economy* (Verso, 1997), Kim Moody cites studies finding an increase in stress-related workplace injuries and illness between the mid-1980s and the early 1990s. He argues that rising stress levels reflect a new system of "management by stress," in which workers in a variety of industries are being squeezed to extract maximum productivity, to the detriment of their health. [Author's note]

I make friends, over time, with the other "girls" who work my shift: Nita, the tattooed twenty-something who taunts us by going around saying brightly, "Have we started making money yet?" Ellen, whose teenage son cooks on the graveyard shift and who once managed a restaurant in Massachusetts but won't try out for management here because she prefers being a "common worker" and not "ordering people around." Easy-going fiftyish Lucy, with the raucous laugh, who limps toward the end of the shift because of something that has gone wrong with her leg, the exact nature of which cannot be determined without health insurance. We talk about the usual girl things—men, children, and the sinister allure of Jerry's chocolate peanut-butter cream pie—though no one, I notice, ever brings up anything potentially expensive, like shopping or movies. As at the Hearthside, the only recreation ever referred to is partying, which requires little more than some beer, a joint, and a few close friends. Still, no one here is homeless, or cops to it anyway, thanks usually to a working husband or boyfriend. All in all, we form a reliable mutual-support group: If one of us is feeling sick or overwhelmed, another one will "bev" a table or even carry trays for her. If one of us is off sneaking a cigarette or a pee,[6] the others will do their best to conceal her absence from the enforcers of corporate rationality.

But my saving human connection—my oxytocin receptor, as it were— 35 George, the nineteen-year-old, fresh-off-the-boat Czech dishwasher. We get to talking when he asks me, tortuously, how much cigarettes cost at Jerry's. I do my best to explain that they cost over a dollar more here than at a regular store and suggest that he just take one from the half-filled packs that are always lying around on the break table. But that would be unthinkable. Except for the one tiny earring signaling his allegiance to some vaguely alternative point of view, George is a perfect straight arrow—crew-cut, hardworking, and hungry for eye contact. "Czech Republic," I ask, "or Slovakia?" and he seems delighted that I know the difference. "Václav Havel," I try. "Velvet Revolution, Frank Zappa?" "Yes, yes, 1989," he says, and I realize we are talking about history.

My project is to teach George English. "How are you today, George?" I say at the start of each shift. "I am good, and how are you today, Barbara?" I learn that he is not paid by Jerry's but by the "agent" who shipped him over—$5 an hour, with the agent getting the dollar or so difference between that and what Jerry's pays dishwashers. I learn also that he shares an apartment with a crowd of other Czech "dishers," as he calls them, and that he cannot sleep until one of them goes off for his shift, leaving a vacant bed. We are having one of our ESL

---

[6]Until April 1998, there was no federally mandated right to bathroom breaks. According to Marc Linder and Ingrid Nygaard, authors of *Void Where Prohibited: Rest Breaks and the Right to Urinate on Company Time* (Cornell University Press, 1997), "The right to rest and void at work is not high on the list of social or political causes supported by professional or executive employees, who enjoy personal workplace liberties that millions of factory workers can only daydream about. . . . While we were dismayed to discover that workers lacked an acknowledged legal right to void at work, (the workers) were amazed by outsiders' naïve belief that their employers would permit them to perform this basic bodily function when necessary. . . . A factory worker, not allowed a break for six-hour stretches, voided into pads worn inside her uniform; and a kindergarten teacher in a school without aides had to take all twenty children with her to the bathroom and line them up outside the stall door when she voided." [Author's note]

sessions late one afternoon when B.J. catches us at it and orders "Joseph" to take up the rubber mats on the floor near the dishwashing sinks and mop underneath. "I thought your name was George," I say loud enough for B.J. to hear as she strides off back to the counter. Is she embarrassed? Maybe a little, because she greets me back at the counter with "George, Joseph—there are so many of them!" I say nothing, neither nodding nor smiling, and for this I am punished later when I think I am ready to go and she announces that I need to roll fifty more sets of silverware and isn't it time I mixed up a fresh four-gallon batch of blue-cheese dressing? May you grow old in this place, B.J., is the curse I beam out at her when I am finally permitted to leave. May the syrup spills glue your feet to the floor.

I make the decision to move closer to Key West. First, because of the drive. Second and third, also because of the drive: gas is eating up $4 to $5 a day, and although Jerry's is as high-volume as you can get, the tips average only 10 percent, and not just for a newbie like me. Between the base pay of $2.15 an hour and the obligation to share tips with the busboys and dishwashers, we're averaging only about $7.50 an hour. Then there is the $30 I had to spend on the regulation tan slacks worn by Jerry's servers—a setback it could take weeks to absorb. (I had combed the town's two downscale department stores hoping for something cheaper but decided in the end that these marked-down Dockers, originally $49, were more likely to survive a daily washing.) Of my fellow servers, everyone who lacks a working husband or boyfriend seems to have a second job: Nita does something at a computer eight hours a day; another welds. Without the forty-five-minute commute, I can picture myself working two jobs and having the time to shower between them.

So I take the $500 deposit I have coming from my landlord, the $400 I have earned toward the next month's rent, plus the $200 reserved for emergencies, and use the $1,100 to pay the rent and deposit on trailer number 46 in the Overseas Trailer Park, a mile from the cluster of budget hotels that constitute Key West's version of an industrial park. Number 46 is about eight feet in width and shaped like a barbell inside, with a narrow region—because of the sink and the stove—separating the bedroom from what might optimistically be called the "living" area, with its two-person table and half-sized couch. The bathroom is so small my knees rub against the shower stall when I sit on the toilet, and you can't just leap out of the bed, you have to climb down to the foot of it in order to find a patch of floor space to stand on. Outside, I am within a few yards of a liquor store, a bar that advertises "free beer tomorrow," a convenience store, and a Burger King—but no supermarket or, alas, laundromat. By reputation, the Overseas park is a nest of crime and crack, and I am hoping at least for some vibrant, multicultural street life. But desolation rules night and day, except for a thin stream of pedestrian traffic heading for their jobs at the Sheraton or 7-Eleven. There are not exactly people here but what amounts to canned labor, being preserved from the heat between shifts.

In line with my reduced living conditions, a new form of ugliness arises at Jerry's. First we are confronted—via an announcement on the computers through which we input orders—with the new rule that the hotel bar is henceforth off-limits to restaurant employees. The culprit, I learn through the grapevine, is the ultra-efficient gal who trained me—another trailer-home dweller and a mother of three. Something had set her off one morning, so she slipped out for a nip and returned to the floor impaired. This mostly hurts Ellen, whose habit it is to free her hair from its rubber band and drop by the bar for a couple of Zins before heading home at the end of the shift, but all of us feel the chill. Then the next day, when I go for straws, for the first time I find the dry-storage room locked. Ted, the portly assistant manager who opens it for me, explains that he caught one of the dishwashers attempting to steal something, and, unfortunately, the miscreant will be with us until a replacement can be found—hence the locked door. I neglect to ask what he had been trying to steal, but Ted tells me who he is—the kid with the buzz cut and the earring. You know, he's back there right now.

I wish I could say I rushed back and confronted George to get his side of 40 the story. I wish I could say I stood up to Ted and insisted that George be given a translator and allowed to defend himself, or announced that I'd find a lawyer who'd handle the case pro bono. The mystery to me is that there's not much worth stealing in the dry-storage room, at least not in any fence-able quantity: "Is Gyorgi here, and am having 200—maybe 250—ketchup packets. What do you say?" My guess is that he had taken—if he had taken anything at all—some Saltines or a can of cherry-pie mix, and that the motive for taking it was hunger.

So why didn't I intervene? Certainly not because I was held back by the kind of moral paralysis that can pass as journalistic objectivity. On the contrary, something new—something loathsome and servile—had infected me, along with the kitchen odors that I could still sniff on my bra when I finally undressed at night. In real life I am moderately brave, but plenty of brave people shed their courage in concentration camps, and maybe something similar goes on in the infinitely more congenial milieu of the low-wage American workplace. Maybe, in a month or two more at Jerry's, I might have regained my crusading spirit. Then again, in a month or two I might have turned into a different person altogether—say, the kind of person who would have turned George in. But this is not something I am slated to find out.

I can do this two-job thing, is my theory, if I can drink enough caffeine and avoid getting distracted by George's ever more obvious suffering.[7] The first few days after being caught he seemed not to understand the trouble he was in, and our chirpy little conversations had continued. But the last couple of shifts he's been listless and unshaven, and tonight he looks like the ghost we all know him to be, with dark half-moons hanging from his eyes. At one point, when I am briefly immobilized by the task of filling little paper cups with sour cream for baked potatoes, he comes over and looks as if he'd like to explore

---

[7]In 1996, the number of persons holding two or more jobs averaged 7.8 million, or 6.2 percent of the workforce. It was about the same rate for men and for women (6.1 versus 6.2), though the kinds of jobs differ by gender. About two thirds of multiple jobholders work one job full-time and the other part-time. Only a heroic minority—4 percent of men and 2 percent of women—work two full-time jobs simultaneously. (From John F. Stinson Jr., "New Data on Multiple Jobholding Available from the CPS," in the *Monthly Labor Review*. March 1997.) [Author's note]

the limits of our shared vocabulary, but I am called to the floor for a table. I resolve to give him all my tips that night and to hell with the experiment in low-wage money management. At eight, Ellen and I grab a snack together standing at the mephitic end of the kitchen counter, but I can only manage two or three mozzarella sticks and lunch had been a mere handful of McNuggets. I am not tired at all, I assure myself, though it may be that there is simply no more "I" left to do the tiredness monitoring. What I would see, if I were more alert to the situation, is that the forces of destruction are already massing against me. There is only one cook on duty, a young man names Jesus ("Hay-Sue," that is) and he is new to the job. And there is Joy, who shows up to take over in the middle of the shift, wearing high heels and a long, clingy white dress and fuming as if she'd just been stood up in some cocktail bar.

Then it comes, the perfect storm. Four of my tables fill up at once. Four tables is nothing for me now, but only so long as they are obligingly staggered. As I bev table 27, tables 25, 28, and 24 are watching enviously. As I bev 25, 24 glowers because their bevs haven't even been ordered. Twenty-eight is four yuppyish types, meaning everything on the side and agonizing instructions as to the chicken Caesars. Twenty-five is a middle-aged black couple, who complain, with some justice, that the iced tea isn't fresh and the tabletop is sticky. But table 24 is the meteorological event of the century: ten British tourists who seem to have made the decision to absorb the American experience entirely by mouth. Here everyone has at least two drinks—iced tea and milk shake, Michelob and water (with lemon slice, please)—and a huge promiscuous orgy of breakfast specials, mozz sticks, chicken strips, quesadillas; burgers with cheese and without, sides of hash browns with cheddar, with onions, with gravy, seasoned fries, plain fries, banana splits. Poor Jesus! Poor me! Because when I arrive with their first tray of food—after three prior trips just to refill bevs—Princess Di refuses to eat her chicken strips with her pancake-and-sausage special, since, as she now reveals, the strips were meant to be an appetizer. Maybe the others would have accepted their meals, but Di, who is deep into her third Michelob, insists that everything else go back while they work on their "starters." Meanwhile, the yuppies are waving me down for more decaf and the black couple looks ready to summon the NAACP.

Much of what happened next is lost in the fog of war. Jesus starts going under. The little printer on the counter in front of him is spewing out orders faster than he can rip them off, much less produce the meals. Even the invincible Ellen is ashen from stress. I bring table 24 their reheated main courses, which they immediately reject as either too cold or fossilized by the microwave. When I return to the kitchen with their trays (three trays in three trips), Joy confronts me with arms akimbo: "What is this?" She means the food—the plates of rejected pancäkes, hash browns in assorted flavors, toasts, burgers, sausages, eggs. "Uh, scrambled with cheddar," I try, "and that's . . ." "NO," she screams in my face. "Is it a traditional, a super-scramble, an eye-opener?" I pretend to study my check for a clue, but entropy has been up to its tricks, not only on the plates but in my head, and I have to admit that the original order is beyond reconstruction. "You don't know an eye-opener from a traditional?" she demands in outrage. All I know, in fact, is that my legs have lost interest in the current venture and have announced their intention to fold. I am saved by a yuppie (mercifully not one of mine) who chooses this moment to charge into the kitchen to bellow that his food is twenty-five minutes late. Joy screams at him to get the hell out of her kitchen, please, and then turns on Jesus in a fury, hurling an empty tray across the room for emphasis.

I leave. I don't walk out, I just leave. I don't finish my side work or pick up my credit-card tips, if any, at the cash register or, of course, ask Joy's permission to go. And the surprising thing is that you *can* walk out without permission, that the door opens, that the thick tropical night air parts to let me pass, that my car is still parked where I left it. There is no vindication in this exit, no fuck-you surge of relief, just an overwhelming, dank sense of failure pressing down on me and the entire parking lot. I had gone into this venture in the spirit of science, to test a mathematical proposition, but somewhere along the line, in the tunnel vision imposed by long shifts and relentless concentration, it became a test of myself, and clearly I have failed. Not only had I flamed out as a housekeeper/server, I had even forgotten to give George my tips, and, for reasons perhaps best known to hardworking, generous people like Gail and Ellen, this hurts. I don't cry, but I am in a position to realize, for the first time in many years, that the tear ducts are still there, and still capable of doing their job.

When I moved out of the trailer park, I gave the key to number 46 to Gail and arranged for my deposit to be transferred to her. She told me that Joan is still living in her van and that Stu had been fired from the Hearthside. I never found out what happened to George.

In one month, I had earned approximately $1,040 and spent $517 on food, gas, toiletries, laundry, phone, and utilities. If I had remained in my $500 efficiency, I would have been able to pay the rent and have $22 left over (which is $78 less than the cash I had in my pocket at the start of the month). During this time I bought no clothing except for the required slacks and no prescription drugs or medical care (I did finally buy some vitamin B to compensate for the lack of vegetables in my diet). Perhaps I could have saved a little on food if I had gotten to a supermarket more often, instead of convenience stores, but it should be noted that I lost almost four pounds in four weeks, on a diet weighted heavily toward burgers and fries.

How former welfare recipients and single mothers will (and do) survive in the low-wage workforce, I cannot imagine. Maybe they will figure out how to condense their lives—including child-raising, laundry, romance, and meals—into the couple of hours between full-time jobs. Maybe they will take up residence in their vehicles, if they have one. All I know is that I couldn't hold two jobs and I couldn't make enough money to live on with one. And I had advantages unthinkable to many of the long-term poor—health, stamina, a working car, and no children to care for and support. Certainly nothing in my experience contradicts the conclusion of Kathryn Edin and Laura Lein, in their recent book *Making Ends Meet: How Single Mothers Survive Welfare and Low-Wage Work*, that low-wage work actually involves more hardship and deprivation than life at the mercy of the welfare state. In the coming months and years, economic conditions for the working poor are bound to worsen, even without the almost inevitable recession. As mentioned earlier, the influx of former welfare recipients into the low-skilled workforce will have a depressing effect on both wages and the number of jobs available. A general economic downturn will only enhance these effects and the working poor will of course be facing it without the slight, but nonetheless often saving, protection of welfare as a backup.

The thinking behind welfare reform was that even the humblest jobs are morally uplifting and psychologically buoying. In reality they are likely to be fraught with insult and stress. But I did discover one redeeming feature of the most abject low-wage work—the camaraderie of people who are in almost all cases, far too smart and funny and caring for the work they do and the wages they're paid. The hope, of course, is that someday these people will come to know what they're worth, and take appropriate action.

1999

Questions

1. Why does Ehrenreich say that her experiment is not perfect, but "a test of the best possible case"? Does her statement affect your reading of the excerpt? Do you find her experience to be credible?

2. What are the choices that Ehrenreich has to make in order to survive on her low wages? Do any of her choices surprise you more than others?

3. What are the greatest obstacles, financial and otherwise, that the low-wage earners face? Are any of these obstacles degrading?

4. What do you think is the long-term impact of the obstacles that you cited above on low-wage earners and their families? Why is it difficult for low-wage earners to move into the middle class?

5. How do you think that Ehrenreich's experience would have been different if she were an actual worker, a single parent, and/or a member of a minority?

6. What does her interview (paragraphs 9–10) reveal about employer–employee relationships in low-wage jobs? Did the questions seem fair? Surprising? Have you experienced similar interviews? Explain your answer.

7. Which actions of her fellow employees surprise Ehrenreich?

8. Ehrenreich conducted her experiment from 1998–2000, a time of economic growth and prosperity. How would her experiences have been different in a less prosperous time or during an economic recession?

9. Compare what Ehrenreich learns after her first week at Hearthside (paragraphs 21–25) with the speaker's comments about his coworkers in Orozco's "Orientation."

10. Did your perceptions of blue-collar Americans change as a result of this selection? Why or why not?

11. What is the lowest-paying job that you have ever had? What would it be like to live on that wage? If it were a part-time job, project the wage to a full-time salary or 40 hours a week.

Cam'ron (b. 1976)

Cameron Giles, better known by his stage name Cam'ron, was born in Harlem. He began rapping in the early 1990s with Big L, Mase, and his cousin Bloodshed in Children of the Corn. Cam'ron left the group to pursue a basketball career. His big break as a rapper came when Mase introduced him to Notorious B. I. G., who, in turn, introduced him to Lance "Un" Rivera, who immediately signed Cam'ron to his Untertainment label. Cam'ron's first solo release was *Confessions of Fire* in 1998. Since then, he has released several albums and appeared in several films. His most recent release is *Crime Pays* (2009), which includes "I Hate My Job."

I HATE MY JOB

Yo, I hate my boss
Dude think he know it all
And I know I know it all
But I follow protocol
Hope he sit in a casket   5
Got me sittin' in traffic
It's 7 a.m. (sheesh)
And I woke up late
Didn't even have a shower
Lunch break? Give me a break   10
A damn half-an-hour
All this bullshit for twelve bucks an hour
Plug me to Chuck D, wanna fight the power
Instead I light the sour before I go in the office
Being here eight hours sure will get you nauseous   15
Lady across from me telling me her problems
I'm looking at her like yo
How the fuck I'm gone solve 'em
You know our ethnicity
Car note, rent, don't forget electricity   20
Internet, cable and the phone all connected
Food, gas, tolls oh now it's getting hectic
Brand new clothes

25   Nah, you'd rather see me naked
      Yo check it, I got my check
      Now I'm feelin' disrespected
      Why am I workin' here
      It ain't workin' here,
      It ain't worth it here
30   I'm never gone persevere
      Ain't no money for new shoes or purses here
      I should've done my first career, huh
      Nursin' yeah
      Now I'm sittin' here thinkin' bout the work I put in
35   This verse from the everyday working woman

      I put on my pants, put on my shoes
      I pray to God, paid all my dues
      I'm tryin to win, seem like I was born to lose
      All I can say is (yeah, yeah, yeah, yeah)
40   I say let me through
      But they don't let me through
      You wanna quit, goddamn I'm ready to
      Lifestyle I'm livin' ain't steady boo
      All I could say (yeah, yeah, yeah, yeah)

45   Hey yo I'm lookin' for a job
      Ain't nobody hiring
      Then I asked the boss
      When y'all doing firing
      You I'm admiring
50   Nice job, family man, car and
      Lookin' in these want ads are tiring
      Could've been a fireman, learned to do wiring
      Then get retirement, I blame my environment
55   I'm on an interview, for delivery
      Locked up, felony, now the dude quizzin' me
      I'm workin' on my future
      Why you need to know my history
      All he did was Google me, no big mystery
60   He ain't diggin' me
      Politely he was dissin' me
      No we're not hiring
      But thanks for the visit, please
      He ain't want me, my grandmother warned me
      Them goddamn felonies would haunt me, taught me
65   No second chance, back to the same block
      Go home my baby's mom done changed locks
      This a game, huh, okay the game's on

Then she opened the door with the chain on
Said she been reaching out for several days
I ain't helpin' out, we need to go our separate ways   70
I was just amazed, wanna go another route
Let me get my clothes
Said she took 'em to my mother's house
She was pissed off, yeah P.O.'ed
And said go head and wild out   75
I'll call your P.O.

I put on my pants, put on my shoes
I pray to God, paid all my dues
I'm tryin to win, seem like I was born to lose
All I can say is (yeah, yeah, yeah, yeah)   80
I say let me through
But they don't let me through
You wanna quit, goddamn I'm ready to
Lifestyle I'm livin' ain't steady boo
All I could say (yeah, yeah, yeah, yeah)   85

2009

Questions

1. According to the lyrics, what are the daily problems confronted by the working class?
2. What is the tone of the song? What does the tone reveal about working-class life?
3. Watch Cam'ron's video for "I Hate My Job" on YouTube. How do the video and the music add to the lyrics?
4. How does the singer in "I Hate My Job" compare with the workers in Ehrenreich's *Nickel and Dimed* and the narrators of Tillie Olsen's "I Stand Here Ironing" and T. C. Boyle's "The Lie"?
5. What other authors and characters in this text might express similar feelings to that of Cam'ron's speaker?

PART IV

THE IMMIGRANT EXPERIENCE

Introduction

America has always relied on the arrival of impoverished immigrants to populate and develop its lands. In the early 1600s, in *The General History of Virginia, New England, and the Summer Isles, The Sixth Book*, John Smith tried to rally the disadvantaged, "the fatherless children of thirteen or fourteen years of age, or young married people that have small wealth to live on," to come to America to "recreate themselves before their own doors in their own boats upon the sea," promising that "here by their labor [they] may live exceeding well." Thus, the American Dream was articulated and at work from the very start.

At the time of the American Revolution, a French immigrant, Jean de Crèvecoeur, was awestruck by the American experiment and its potential: "Here individuals of all nations are melted into a new race of men, whose labours and posterity will one day cause great changes in the world." Then, assuming the voice of America, he addressed the immigrant: "If thou wilt work, I have bread for thee; if thou wilt be honest, sober, and industrious, I have greater rewards to confer on thee—ease and independence. I will give thee fields to feed and clothe thee; a comfortable fireside to sit by, and tell thy children by what means thou hast prospered" (*Letters from an American Farmer*, third letter). Does America still hold out the same promise to immigrants?

In 1886, the Statue of Liberty was dedicated in New York Harbor. On its base is "The New Colossus," a sonnet by Emma Lazarus, bearing the often-quoted closing lines:

> . . . Give me your tired, your poor,
> Your huddled masses yearning to breathe free,
> The wretched refuse of your teeming shore.
> Send these, the homeless, tempest-tossed to me,
> I lift my lamp beside the golden door!

These firm and unequivocal words of welcome express the ideal of America. As the above quotations remind us, America has long relied on immigrants to infuse America with new ideas and new cultures that keep the American experiment dynamic. After all, immigrants do much more than reinforce a cheap workforce.

When you read the works in this section, compare the ideal and the promises of America with the expressions of immigrant reality. Note, for instance, the lament of Woody Guthrie in "Plane Wreck at Los Gatos (Deportee)," in which America demonstrates no mourning over a plane crash that claims the lives of deported migrant workers, and the hostility toward immigrants that Jimmy Santiago Baca voices in his poem, "So Mexicans Are Taking Jobs from Americans." Consider, too, the irony in Martín Espada's "Jorge the Church Janitor Finally Quits" as the author questions America's sensitivity and receptiveness to immigrants.

In "El Olor de Cansansio (The Smell of Fatigue)," Melida Rodas recalls the long hours and struggle of her father who left a respected white-collar job in his politically oppressive native land to work in the steamy kitchens of Jersey City. While John Smith correctly sees America as a land of opportunity and regeneration, he does not foresee the struggle with identity and self-esteem that often accompanies the new immigrant. These issues, however, are explored in Jamaica Kincaid's "Mariah," in which a confused young immigrant is uncertain as to what American culture expects of her.

The selections in "The Immigrant Experience" raise many questions about America's self-definition and identity. Consider the works in this section in the context of the brief excerpts above from Smith, Crèvecoeur, and Lazarus. Has America kept its implicit promise to immigrants? Has America lived up to its ideals? Do you think that we appreciate immigrants more or less today? Are the concerns of immigrants sufficiently voiced in our culture? Is the immigrant experience easier today than in the past? Why or why not? The answers to these questions are perhaps various and certainly complex.

Upton Sinclair
(1878-1968)

Born in Baltimore and raised in New York City, Upton Sinclair attended the City College of New York and Columbia University. By the age of twenty, he had begun his writing career by publishing juvenile fiction in magazines and newspapers. After a number of early novels, Sinclair began to hit his stride in 1904 with *Manassas*, a Civil War novel. Shortly after the book was published, he joined the Socialist Party of America whose politics would inform the rest of his life and his writing. Sinclair ran for political office several times as either a socialist or a Democrat espousing socialist principles.

In 1904, Fred Warren, the editor of *Appeal to Reason*, a socialist journal, commissioned Sinclair to write a novel about contemporary wage slavery and the working conditions in the stockyards of Chicago. The challenge led to Sinclair's most important work, *The Jungle* (1906), from which the following selections are excerpted. The novel tells the story of Jurgis Rudkus, a Lithuanian immigrant who is brutally exploited in his quest to achieve the American Dream. After years of struggle, homelessness, and the deaths of his wife and son, Rudkus finds renewal at the end of the novel in the socialist cause. *The Jungle's* impact was immediate. President Theodore Roosevelt invited Sinclair to the White House and ordered an investigation of the meatpacking industry. Although regulations were passed and reforms were initiated, Sinclair was disappointed that his socialist message went largely unheeded. Throughout his long career, which included more than fifty novels and twenty books of nonfiction, Sinclair remained a critic of the capitalist system with what he saw as its too often unchecked greed and inequities.

From *THE JUNGLE*

JURGIS talked lightly about work, because he was young. They told him stories about the breaking down of men, there in the stockyards of Chicago, and of what had happened to them afterwards—stories to make your flesh creep, but Jurgis would only laugh. He had only been there four months, and he was young, and a giant besides. There was too much health in him. He could not even imagine how it would feel to be beaten. "That is well enough for men like you," he would say "szilpnas[1], puny fellows—but my back is broad."

Jurgis was like a boy, a boy from the country. He was the sort of man the bosses like to get hold of, the sort they make it a grievance they cannot get hold of. When he was told to go to a certain place he would go there on the run. When he had nothing to do for the moment he would stand round fidgeting, dancing, with the overflow of energy that was in him. If he were working in a line of men the line always moved too slowly for him, and you could pick him out by his impatience and restlessness. That was why he had been picked out on one important occasion; for Jurgis had stood outside of Smith and Company's "General Time Station" not more than half an hour, the second day of his arrival in Chicago, before he had been beckoned by one of the bosses. Of this he was very proud, and it made him more disposed than ever to laugh at the pessimists. In vain would they all tell him that there were men in that crowd from which he had been chosen who had stood there a month—yes, many months—and not been chosen yet. "Yes," he would say, "but what sort of men? broken-down tramps and good-for-nothings, fellows who have spent all their money drinking, and want to get more for it. Do not tell me, there is always work for a man! Do you want me to believe that with these arms"—and he would clench his fists and hold them up in the air, so that you might see the rolling muscles—"that with these arms people will ever let me starve?"

The men upon the killing-floor felt also the effects of the slump which had turned Marija[2] out; but they felt it in a different way, and a way which made Jurgis understand at last all the bitterness of the men. The big packers did not turn their hands off and close down, like the canning-factories; but they began to run for shorter and shorter hours. If they had wished to set forth the fact that all their employees together were of less importance to them than a single one of the animals they killed, they could not have managed the thing differently than they did.

They had always required the men to be on the killing-floor and ready for work at seven o'clock although there was almost never any work to be done till the buyers out in the yards had gotten to work, and some cattle had come over the chutes. That would often be ten or eleven o'clock, which was bad enough, in all conscience; but now, in the slack season, they would perhaps not have a thing for their men to do till late in the afternoon—and still every mother's son of them had to be on the killing-floor at seven o'clock in the morning! And there they would have to loaf around, in a place where the thermometer might be twenty degrees below zero! At first one would see them running about, or skylarking with each other, trying to keep warm, but before the day was over they would become quite chilled through and exhausted, and when the cattle finally came, so near frozen that to move was an agony. And then suddenly the place would spring into activity, and the merciless "speeding-up" would begin!

---

[1] *szilpnas*: weak or frail (Lithuanian)
[2] Marija is the cousin of Rudkus's wife.

There were weeks at a time when Jurgis went home after such a day as this with not more than two hours' work to his credit—which meant about thirty-five cents. There were many days when the total was less than half an hour, and others when there was none at all. Not half a dozen times in the whole long agony of that winter was there work early enough in the morning to justify their coming before daylight. The general average was about six hours a day, which meant for Jurgis about six dollars a week, and this six hours of work would be done after standing on the killing-floor till one o'clock, or perhaps even three or four o'clock in the afternoon. It would be done all in one heart-breaking rush, without allowing a single instant for rest. Like as not there would come a rush of cattle at the very end of the day, which the men would have to dispose of before they went home, often working by electric-light till nine or ten, or even twelve or one o'clock, and without a single instant for a bite of supper. Jurgis tried hard to find out the reason for all this, but the men did not understand it, except vaguely. They knew that they were at the mercy of the cattle. Perhaps the buyers would be holding off for better prices; if they could scare the shippers into thinking that they meant to buy nothing that day, they could get their own terms.

A time of peril on the killing-floor was when a steer broke loose. In the killing of the cattle at Anderson's they had, of course, no thought save of speed. In the slaughter-houses of Europe, where there are laws, they fit over the head of the animal a leather cap having a nail in it; then, provided the knocker has only skill enough to hit the nail with a big mallet, he cannot fail to kill the animal. But they never stopped for things like that in the yards—the knockers would lean over the pens and slap away at the creatures with a pointed hammer, and if they did not kill at the first blow, they had only to try again. So now and then you might see one banging away for a full minute, with the steer plunging and bellowing in agony and terror. That was nothing—only sometimes, in the haste of speeding-up, they would dump the animal out on the floor before it was fully stunned, and it would get upon its feet and run amuck. Then there would be a yell of warning—the men would drop everything, and dash for the nearest pillar, slipping here and there on the slimy floor, and tumbling head over heels over each other. This was bad enough in the summer, when a man could see; in winter time it was enough to make your hair stand up, for the room would be so full of steam that you could not see five feet in front of you. To be sure, the steer was generally blind and frantic, and not especially bent on hurting anyone; but think of the chances of running upon a knife, while two men out of three had one in his hand! And then the floor boss would come rushing up with a rifle and begin blazing away! Jurgis had seen times when as many as eight shots had to be fired, in a room with hundreds of men in it.

It was in one of these melees that Jurgis fell into his trap. That is the very word to describe it—it was so cruel, and so utterly not to be foreseen. At first he hardly noticed it, it was such a slight accident—simply that in leaping out of the way he turned his ankle. There was a twinge of pain, but Jurgis was used to pain, and did not coddle himself. When he came to walk home, however, he realized that it was hurting him a great deal; and in the morning his ankle was swollen out nearly double its size, and he could not get his foot into his shoe. Still, even then, he did nothing more than swear a little, and wrapped his foot in old rags, and hobbled out to take the car. It chanced to be a rush day at Anderson's, and all the long morning he limped about with his aching foot; by noon-time the pain was so great that it made him faint, and after a couple of hours in the afternoon he was fairly beaten, and had to tell the boss. They sent for the company doctor, and he examined the foot and told Jurgis to go home to bed, adding that he had probably laid himself up for months by his folly. The injury was not one that Anderson and Company could be held responsible for, and so that was all there was to it, so far as the doctor was concerned.

Jurgis got home somehow, scarcely able to see for the pain, and with an awful terror in his soul. Elzbieta[3] helped him into bed and bandaged his injured foot with cold water, and tried hard not to let him see her dismay; when the rest came home at night she met them outside and told them, and they, too, put on a cheerful face, saying it would only be for a week or two, and that they would pull him through.

When they had gotten him to sleep, however, they sat by the kitchen fire and talked it over in frightened whispers. They were in for a siege, that was plainly to be seen. Jurgis had only about sixty dollars in the bank, and the slack season was upon them. Both Jonas[4] and Marija might soon be earning no more than enough to pay their board, and besides that there was only the wages of Ona[5], and the little pittance of the boy. There was the rent to pay, and still some on the furniture; there was the insurance just due, and every month there was sack after sack of coal. It was January, mid-winter, an awful time to have to face privation. Deep snows would come again; and who would carry Ona to her work now? She might lose her place—she was almost certain to lose it. And then little Stanislovas[6] began to whimper—who would take care of him?

It was dreadful that an accident of this sort, that no man can help, and that is quite certain to happen to a workingman now and then in his life, should have meant such suffering.

FOR THREE weeks after his injury Jurgis never got up from bed. It was a very obstinate sprain; the swelling would not go down, and the pain still continued. At the end of that time, however, he could contain himself no longer, and began trying to walk a little every day, laboring to persuade himself that he was better. No arguments could stop him, and three or four days later he declared that he was going back to work. He limped to the cars and got to Smith's, where he found that the boss had kept his place—that is, was willing to turn out into the snow the poor devil he had hired in the meantime. Every now and then the pain would force Jurgis to stop work, but he stuck it out till nearly an hour before closing. Then he was forced to acknowledge that he

---

[3]Elzbieta is a strong and nurturing mother of six and the stepmother of Rudkus's wife.
[4]Elzbieta's brother, Jonas, encouraged the family to immigrate to America.
[5]Kind and hopeful, Ona is Rudkus's wife. Later, she is raped by her boss.
[6]Stanislovas, about fourteen years old, is one of Elzbieta's children and is afraid of frostbite.

could not go on without fainting; it almost broke his heart to do it, and he stood leaning against a pillar and weeping like a child. Two of the men had to help him to the car, and when he got out he had to sit down and wait in the snow till some one came along.

So they put him to bed again, and sent for the doctor, as they ought to have done in the beginning. It transpired that he had twisted a tendon out of place, and could never have gotten well without attention. Then he gripped the sides of the bed, and shut his teeth together and turned white with agony, while the doctor pulled and wrenched away at his swollen ankle. When finally the doctor left, he told him that he would have to lie quiet for two months, and that if he went to work before that time he might lame himself for life.

The latter part of April Jurgis went to see the doctor, and was given a bandage to lace about his ankle, and told that he might go back to work. It needed more than the permission of the doctor, however, for when he showed up on the killing-floor of Smith's he was told by the foreman that it had not been possible to keep his job for him. Jurgis knew what this meant, simply that the foreman had found some one else to do the work as well, and did not want to bother to make a change. He stood in the doorway, looking mournfully on, seeing his friends and companions at work, and feeling like an outcast. Then he went out and took his place with the mob of the unemployed.

This time, however, Jurgis did not have the same fine confidence, nor the same reason for it. He was no longer the finest-looking man in the throng, and the bosses no longer made for him; he was thin and haggard, and his clothes were seedy, and he looked miserable. And there were hundreds who looked and felt just like him, and who had been wandering about Packingtown for months begging for work. This was a critical time in Jurgis's life, and if he had been a weaker man he would have gone the way the rest did. Those out of-work wretches would stand about the packing-houses every morning till the police drove them away, and then they would scatter among the saloons. . .

The peculiar bitterness of all this was that Jurgis saw so plainly the meaning of it. In the beginning he had been fresh and strong, and he had gotten a job the first day; but now he was second-hand, so to speak, and they did not want him. He was a damaged article, to put it exactly. And yet it was in their service that he had been damaged! They had got the best out of him, there was the truth—they had worn him out, with their speeding up and their damned carelessness, and now they had thrown him away! And Jurgis would make the acquaintance of some of these unemployed men; he would stroll away with them, and perhaps sit in a saloon and talk a while with them; and he found that they had all had the same experience. . . .

All this time that he was seeking for work, there was a dark shadow hanging over Jurgis; as if a savage beast were lurking somewhere in the pathway of his life, and he knew it, and yet could not help approaching. There are all stages of being out of work, and he faced in dread the prospect of reaching the lowest. There is a place in Packingtown that waits for the lowest man—the fertilizer plant! . . .

It was to this building that Jurgis came daily, as if dragged by an unseen hand.

His labor took him about one minute to learn. Before him was one of the vents of the mill in which the fertilizer was being ground; it came out in a great brown river, with a spray of the finest dust flung forth in clouds. Jurgis was given a shovel, and along with half a dozen others it was his task to shovel this fertilizer into cars. That others were at work, he knew by the sound, and by the fact that he sometimes collided with them; otherwise they might as well not have been there, for in the blinding clouds of dust a man could not see six feet in front of his face. When he had filled one cart he had to grope around him until another came, and if there was none on hand he continued to grope until one arrived. In five minutes he was, of course, a mass of fertilizer from head to feet; they gave him a sponge to tie over his mouth, so that he could breathe, but the sponge did not prevent his lips and eyelids from caking up with it, and his ears from filling solid. He looked like a brown ghost at twilight—from hair to shoes he became the color of the building, and of everything in it, and for that matter a hundred yards outside it. The building had to be left open, and when a wind blew, Anderson and Company lost a great deal of fertilizer; doubtless, however, they had figured it out, and found that they would lose more in extra wages than they would have saved in fertilizer, had they closed it up tight. As it was, it was hard to retain—not common laborers, for these were always to be had in droves—but bosses and trusty men to take charge; in the month of November, 1900, there was one week when one hundred and twenty-six men were employed and only six were able to continue.

It was possible for Jurgis to conquer his revulsion from the odor of the fertilizer, but he could not prevent his body from rebelling. Working in his shirtsleeves and with the thermometer at over a hundred, the phosphates soaked in through every pore of his skin, and in five minutes he had a headache, and in fifteen was almost dazed. The blood was pounding in his brain like an engine's throbbing; there was a frightful pain in the top of his skull, and he could hardly control his hands. Still, with the memory of his four months' siege behind him, he fought on, in a frenzy of determination; and half an hour later he began to vomit—he vomited until it seemed as if his insides must be torn to shreds. A man could get used to the fertilizer-mill, the boss had said, if he would only make up his mind to it; but Jurgis now began to see that it was a question of making up his stomach.

At the end of that day of horror, he could scarcely stand. He had to catch himself now and then, and lean against a building and get his bearings. Most of the men, when they came out, made straight for a saloon—they seemed to place fertilizer and rattle-snake poison in one class. But Jurgis was too ill to think of drinking—he could only make his way to the street and stagger onto a car. He had a sense of humor, and later on, when he became an old hand, he used to think it fun to get on a street car and see what happened. Now, however, he was too ill to see it—how the people in the car began to gasp and sputter, to put their handkerchiefs to their noses, and transfix him with furious glances. Jurgis only knew that a man in front of him immediately got up and gave him a seat; and that half a minute later the two people on each side of him got up; and that in a full minute the crowded car was nearly empty—

those passengers who could not get room on the platform having gotten out to walk.

Of course, Jurgis had made his home a miniature fertilizer-mill a minute after entering. The stuff was half an inch deep in his skin—his whole system was full of it, and it would have taken a week, not merely of scrubbing, but of vigorous exercise, to get it out of him. As it was, he could be compared with nothing known to men, save that newest discovery of the savants, a substance which emits energy in large quantities and for unlimited time, without being itself in the least diminished in power. Jurgis smelt so that he made all the food at the table taste, and set the whole family to vomiting; for himself, it was three days before he could keep anything upon his stomach—he might wash his hands and use a knife and fork, but were not his mouth and throat filled with the poison?

And still Jurgis stuck it out! In spite of splitting headaches he would stagger down to the plant and take his stand once more, and begin to shovel in the blinding clouds of dust. And so at the end of the week he was a fertilizer-man for life—he was able to eat again, and though his head never stopped aching, it ceased to be so bad that he could not work. Every man who worked in the fertilizer plant was dying slowly of deadly diseases; but so long as the process was slow enough, it did not trouble them much—the men outside were dying more rapidly still.

1906

Questions

1. Describe the physical and psychological deterioration of young Rudkus. Do you hold anyone or anything responsible for his deterioration?
2. Describe the working conditions on the killing floor. Is Sinclair suggesting anything by his selection of detail? Why does Sinclair allude to the slaughterhouses of Europe?
3. Does the killing of animals seem efficient and humane?
4. Characterize how Rudkus's employer treats him after his injury. As part of your answer, discuss why the company sends a doctor to examine Rudkus's injured foot. Should the company be held responsible for this injury? What, if anything, should the company do for the injured Rudkus and to prevent such accidents in the future?
5. Describe the conditions in the fertilizer plant. Given the era, do you think that the company did all it could to protect its workers and to make working conditions as safe as possible?
6. How does Rudkus's work in the slaughterhouse and in the fertilizer plant affect both him and his family?
7. What is the significance of the title?
8. Today, many low-wage earners live one paycheck from homelessness. How does Rudkus's story illustrate this very real threat to many members of the working class?
9. Compare and contrast the working conditions that Rudkus endures with those of the men in the engine room in O'Neill's *The Hairy Ape*.

10. Compare and contrast the political implications and statements in *The Jungle* and *The Hairy Ape.*

11. Consider the following statement made by Sinclair in 1951 when discussing his California gubernatorial bids:

> The American People will take Socialism, but they won't take the label. I certainly proved it in the case of EPIC [End Poverty in California]. Running on the Socialist ticket [in 1926] I got 60,000 votes, and running on the slogan to "End Poverty in California" [in 1934 on the Democratic ticket] I got 879,000 [losing by some 250,000 votes]. I think we simply have to recognize the fact that our enemies have succeeded in spreading the Big Lie. There is no use attacking it by a front attack, it is much better to out-flank them.

What is socialism? Do you agree with Sinclair's statement? Before answering, consider the economic climate of 1926 (the Roaring Twenties) and 1934 (The Great Depression).

12. Compare and contrast the immigrant experience of Rudkus with that of the father in Rodas's "El Olor de Cansansio (The Smell of Fatigue)."

13. Investigate the conditions of factory workers in the United States and around the world. Are the conditions much different today from what Sinclair depicts in *The Jungle?*

Woody Guthrie
(1912–1967)

Born in Okemah, Oklahoma, Woodrow Wilson Guthrie developed into perhaps America's most important folk singer. His early years were marked by hardship and tragedy, including the accidental death of a sister, the family's financial ruin, and the institutionalization of his mother. He left Okemah in 1931 and married for the first time in 1933. As heavy dust storms descended on the Midwest in the 1930s, Guthrie, like many "dustbowl refugees," headed to California, where he eventually performed traditional and original songs on KFVD radio in Los Angeles. As his leftist principles began to develop, he attacked corrupt officials, insensitive landowners and employers, and governmental neglect of the needy while advocating the humanist principles of Jesus Christ and union organization.

Upon arrival in New York City in 1940, Guthrie had his own radio show, but quickly grew disillusioned by its politics and commercialism, and recorded his classic collection of songs, *Dust Bowl Ballads*. His constant traveling, performing, and radical politics ended his first marriage, and, in 1945, he remarried. His autobiographical novel, *Bound for Glory*, was published in 1943 to critical acclaim. Serving in the United States Army and the Merchant Marines, Guthrie was a zealous spokesperson against Hitler and fascism. After the war, he settled in Coney Island, Brooklyn, from which he continued to perform and travel until the effects of Huntington's chorea, a hereditary and degenerative disease, became too debilitating. By the time of his death, he was a hero to a new generation of musicians, including Bob Dylan, Joan Baez, and others. In more recent years, his songs have been recorded by rock bands such as the Dropkick Murphys, Anti-Flag, and Wilco. Guthrie's best know song is "This Land Is Your Land."

PLANE WRECK AT LOS GATOS (DEPORTEE)

Woody Guthrie wrote these lyrics after reading a newspaper account of a plane crash that killed twenty-eight deported Mexican migrant workers near Coalinga, California, on January 28, 1948. Martin Hoffman wrote the music.

The crops are all in and the peaches are rott'ning,
The oranges piled in their creosote dumps;

They're flying 'em back to the Mexican border
To pay all their money to wade back again

Goodbye to my Juan, goodbye, Rosalita,
Adios mis amigos, Jesus y Maria;
You won't have your names when you ride the big airplane,
All they will call you will be "deportees"

My father's own father, he waded that river,
They took all the money he made in his life;
My brothers and sisters come working the fruit trees,
And they rode the truck till they took down and died.

Some of us are illegal, and some are not wanted,
Our work contract's out and we have to move on;
Six hundred miles to that Mexican border,
They chase us like outlaws, like rustlers, like thieves.

We died in your hills, we died in your deserts,
We died in your valleys and died on your plains.
We died 'neath your trees and we died in your bushes,
Both sides of the river, we died just the same.

The sky plane caught fire over Los Gatos Canyon,
A fireball of lightning, and shook all our hills,
Who are all these friends, all scattered like dry leaves?
The radio says, "They are just deportees"

Is this the best way we can grow our big orchards?
Is this the best way we can grow our good fruit?
To fall like dry leaves to rot on my topsoil
And be called by no name except "deportees"?

1948

Questions

1. What is suggested by the detail that oranges are allowed to rot?
2. What does the song suggest about the treatment of Mexican migrant workers in the United States?
3. Why does Guthrie place *deportees* in quotation marks? What is implicit in Guthrie's use of *deportees*?
4. How do you identify the singer? Be sure to consider the third stanza.
5. Who is represented by the following pronouns: *they* and *you* (first and second stanzas), *they* (third and fourth), *your* (fifth), and *we* (seventh).
6. What is Guthrie's intent with the series of questions that conclude the song? What does he want the listener to consider?
7. How does the song appeal to our sense of compassion and justice?

Salvatore La Puma
(1929–2008)

B orn in Bensonhurst, in Brooklyn, New York, La Puma made Santa Barbara, California, his home in 1967. After serving as a medic in the Korean War, La Puma worked in advertising and then real estate, and only began writing fiction when in his fifties. His first collection of short stories, *The Boys from Brooklyn* (1987), earned him the Flannery O'Connor Award for Short Fiction and the American Book Award. His fiction draws heavily on his Italian–American roots.

CAKES

That summer he sweated first from the humidity which in 1940 everyone in Brooklyn sweated from; then he sweated from the hot ovens at Carlo Amato's pastry shop in Bensonhurst four or five nights a week; then he sweated from the hot ovens at a pastry shop Downtown every day of the week except on Sunday, when he usually slept until noon. From Downtown, Giovanni Vitale came home at the end of a workday on the BMT subway to his wife, Lisa, to their three kids, Anna, Steve, and Johnny. After dinner they would all listen to the Philco[1]. Then Giovanni and the eldest kid, Johnny, eleven, walked three long blocks and two short blocks, past the old people who fanned themselves on the stoops, to Carlo's shop on Seventeenth Avenue.

For five dollars extra, that August night's work began with a batch of cannoli. The burned lard once again was ladled from a tall can into a large copper pot which was put on the ring stove with its lone, very big and very hot burner. When the cannoli wrapped on short broomsticks were fried to a crisp, they bobbed up to the surface of the steamy and boiling lard and he scooped them out with a strainer.

"You want some coffee I could give you, or a sandwich?" the shop owner's wife, Martina Amato, asked Giovanni. "How about you, Johnny? You want some ice cream, some soda?" Johnny watched his

---

[1]Philco refers to an early radio.

father as his father watched the woman get the coffee. Carlo Amato, who usually baked the goods sold in his own shop, had nodded from a small marble table without moving from his chair when Giovanni and Johnny came in. Giovanni had nodded back. Carlo wasn't too strong, Giovanni had said to his son, so he helped Carlo out at night, as Johnny helped him out. With Johnny's help, father and son would finish up by eleven instead of after midnight for the father alone. The next morning Johnny would still be sleepy, and his mother would tickle his toes until he climbed out of bed for breakfast with his sister and brother. By then his father would already be on the subway headed again for the pastry shop Downtown.

"Hey, Dad, in the flour here, moving around, are some brown things, you ought to see this." Johnny was at the mixer where he put in a scoop of flour after his previous scoop was worked in by the blade that rotated. "I put in two scoops, but you ought to see this, Dad. I don't think I should put in any more. I see what they are. Bugs. The flour is crawling with bugs. Wow! Look at those bugs."

A Chesterfield was attached to Giovanni's lower lip when he came over with his hands covered with tufts of yellow butter cream, which he whipped by hand in another copper pot, and his cigarette would be ruined if he touched it. "In the flour after a while the eggs hatch," he said. "Insects lay them in the wheat in the field. When we bake the cookies, it won't matter; the bugs will melt. In some countries, they eat things like ants and grasshoppers." The movement of his lip as he spoke caused the long ash at the end of his cigarette to drop into the dough with the insects. Johnny reached in for the ash but he was quickly yanked back by his father. "Never, never do that." The risky things a son could do worried him even though Giovanni was too tired to worry about bugs and cigarette ash in the dough. After Johnny hesitated a moment over his father's easy acceptance of the bugs, he too decided that it was no big deal. Even the cigarette ash in the dough that turned with the blade was forgotten after Johnny covered the ash with another scoop of flour.

Back at the marble-top worktable big enough for two pastrymen, Giovanni would make next a batch of *sfudelle*. Ghostly white, his face and arms covered with flour, he rolled out a sheet of dough until it was thin as cloth and then rolled it up like a thick window shade. With a broad blade, he sliced it like bread, and using his quick and calloused fingers, he then fanned out the slices until half the rings were on top and half were on bottom. Between the dough-hinged halves, he stuffed the yellow butter cream.

The physical work, the heat from the ovens with their wide mouths and black iron doors one above the other in two rows from about the level of his knees to above his head, the long hours for little pay in those times when most other Sicilians too didn't earn enough to buy many cakes—when almost no one was well off—all these conditions left Giovanni little time for anything else but more work; maybe one joke for his own kids, maybe two tender words for Lisa. To keep doing his work, he found pleasure from the batches that looked good and tasted good with nothing wasted or burned or flushed down the toilet where a failed batch was sent. Another pleasure he had was when he told stories about his bachelor days when he ice-skated in Central Park with the rich girls who lived in brownstones off Fifth Avenue nearby and how they brought him presents and behind the bushes he kissed them—but they wouldn't take him home.

"I don't believe you, Giovanni, that you kissed so many girls that you said you kissed," said Martina, at the small table with her husband where they both sipped black coffee with anisette. Her husband's face turned to her and then to Giovanni, but Carlo really looked elsewhere, inside himself or out past the shop to a distant place. Giovanni understood, but there was nothing he could do for Carlo, aside from the cakes he made for his old friend. Martina said, "You should go to bed now, Carlo. It's better you don't stay up so late. I close up the shop myself."

"I'm not so tired," Carlo said. "About Giovanni, for myself, I believe him. I believe he kissed all the girls he said, because he gave them his *biscotti*, from the recipe from his father. Not because he is so handsome. Tell me, who is more handsome, me or Giovanni?"

"You are more handsome, Carlo," his wife said, as she touched his wavy white hair.

"He is," agreed Giovanni. "He still has all his hair while mine is half gone."

Into the center of stars and half moons that would be baked as cookies, Johnny pressed pieces of red or green maraschino cherries. He looked over at his father and then looked at Carlo and thought that his father was more handsome. There was no doubt about it. When Johnny had placed the cookies in the pans, his father shuffled the pans like oversized playing cards into the ovens. The anise biscuits that his father had just taken out of the ovens Johnny carried to the front shop where he would stack them up. While out there he also had a slice of spumoni and soda-jerked a soda for himself that was mostly chocolate syrup. At that late hour no customers had come into the front shop, which had white walls and white floor tiles and white fluorescents. All that white helped Johnny to keep his eyes open.

Quietly the boy sat behind the counter and worked there, and when Carlo later came by and suggested that Johnny also sample the tortoni which were in the freezer, Johnny took a tortoni too. Carlo went out the door and up to the apartment over the shop. In the ceiling Johnny could hear Carlo's footsteps and wondered if Carlo would be all right. Then he went to the back shop to ask his father if he would like to have a tortoni.

With the ricotta cream, his father stuffed the fresh cannoli skins he had just made. At the small table with her forehead on her arm, Martina cried softly to herself: at this late hour she could no longer pretend that Carlo's illness was just a bad dream; if she could drain her tears, then she too could go upstairs and hold Carlo as if her arms could keep him here.

"Sure, bring me a tortoni, please," his father said. "And bring me a glass of soda water, plain."

Then Johnny carried the pans of baked stars and half-moons out to the front shop where he dusted them with a large shaker of powdered sugar, and also now and then dusted his own tongue. Between yawns, he built the cookies up in trays decorated with doilies. To stay awake he tried to think about the Harley he intended to have someday, but when he put his head down for two seconds, he dropped off. The old couple who came in minutes later for lemon ice startled him. He went to get Martina who came out to serve them, and after they left she stayed there while Johnny tried again to build up the cookies. His head nodded more than once and he had to jerk himself awake. So Martina seated herself beside him, put her arms around him, and before he knew what happened his eyes closed and his face went down on her breast where he was held like that. For half an hour he slept there until his father finished up and came out to the front shop where he half filled a sack with cookies and biscuits to take home to the family.

"You have to wake up now," Giovanni said as he shook the boy.

As his eyes snapped open, Johnny said, "I'm wide awake."

1987

Questions

1. What is Giovanni Vitale's schedule?
2. Does Vitale enjoy his work? What gives him satisfaction besides the pay?
3. What is your reaction to Vitale's seeming lack of concern about bugs and cigarette ashes in the dough?
4. Why do you think that Vitale insists that his son Johnny help him at Carlo's? What values does Vitale pass on to his son during these evenings?
5. How is "Cakes" a story about the immigrant experience? How do immigrants in this story help one another? How do they maintain their culture and values? How do the behavior and comments of Vitale's son suggest that he has become assimilated into American culture?
6. Compare and contrast the fathers in "Cakes" and Rodas's "El Olor de Cansansio (The Smell of Fatigue)."

Jamaica Kincaid
(b. 1949)

Born Elaine Cynthia Potter Richardson on the island of Antigua, Jamaica Kincaid immigrated to New York to work as an *au pair* at seventeen years of age. She earned a high school diploma in night school and attended college at the New School for Social Research and Franconia College in New Hampshire. She returned to Manhattan to begin her career as a writer and took a position as a staff writer on *The New Yorker*. Throughout her work, Kincaid explores the problems of colonialism (Antigua was a British colony until 1967) and family relationships, particularly between mothers and daughters. Her works include the novels *Lucy* (1990) and *The Autobiography of My Mother* (1995), the memoir *My Brother* (1997) about her youngest brother's AIDS-related death, the collection of short stories *At the Bottom of the River* (1983), and a travelogue *Among Flowers: A Walk in the Himalayas* (2005). "Mariah" was first published in *The New Yorker* and, later, as part of the novel *Lucy*.

MARIAH

One morning in early March, Mariah said to me, "You have never seen spring, have you?" And she did not have to await an answer, for she already knew. She said the word "spring" as if spring were a close friend, a friend who had dared to go away for a long time and soon would reappear for their passionate reunion. She said, "Have you ever seen daffodils pushing their way up out of the ground? And when they're in bloom and all massed together, a breeze comes along and makes them do a curtsy to the lawn stretching out in front of them. Have you ever seen that? When I see that, I feel so glad to be alive." And I thought, So Mariah is made to feel alive by some flowers bending in the breeze. How does a person get to be that way?

I remembered an old poem[1] I had been made to memorize when I was ten years old and a pupil at Queen Victoria Girls' School. I had been made to memorize it, verse after verse, and then had recited the whole poem to an auditorium full of parents, teachers, and my fellow pupils. After I was done, everybody stood up and applauded with an

---

[1] William Wordsworth's "I Wandered Lonely as a Cloud"

enthusiasm that surprised me, and later they told me how nicely I had pronounced every word, how I had placed just the right amount of special emphasis in places where that was needed, and how proud the poet, now long dead, would have been to hear his words ringing out of my mouth. I was then at the height of my two-facedness: that is, outside I seemed one way, inside I was another; outside false, inside true. And so I made pleasant little noises that showed both modesty and appreciation, but inside I was making a vow to erase from my mind, line by line, every word of that poem. That night after I had recited the poem, I dreamt, continuously it seemed, that I was being chased down a narrow cobbled street by bunches and bunches of those same daffodils that I had vowed to forget, and when finally I fell down from exhaustion they all piled on top of me, until I was buried deep underneath them and was never seen again. I had forgotten all of this until Mariah mentioned daffodils, and now I told it to her with such an amount of anger I surprised both of us. We were standing quite close to each other, but as soon as I had finished speaking, without a second of deliberation we both stepped back. It was only one step that was made, but to me it felt as if something that I had not been aware of had been checked.

Mariah reached out to me and, rubbing her hand against my cheek, said, "What a history you have." I thought there was a little bit of envy in her voice, and so I said, "You are welcome to it if you like."

After that, each day, Mariah began by saying, "As soon as spring comes," and so many plans would follow that I could not see how one little spring could contain them. She said we would leave the city and go to the house on one of the Great Lakes, the house where she spent her summers when she was a girl. We would visit some great gardens. We would visit the zoo—a nice thing to do in springtime; the children would love that. We would have a picnic in the park as soon as the first unexpected and unusually warm day arrived. An early-evening walk in the spring air—that was something she really wanted to do with me, to show me the magic of a spring sky.

On the very day it turned spring, a big snowstorm came, and more snow fell on that day than had fallen all winter. Mariah looked at me and shrugged her shoulders. "How typical," she said, giving the impression that she had just experienced a personal betrayal. I laughed at her, but I was really wondering, How do you get to be a person who is made miserable because the weather changed its mind, because the weather doesn't live up to your expectations? How do you get to be that way?

While the weather sorted itself out in various degrees of coldness, I walked around with letters from my family and friends scorching my breasts. I had placed these letters inside my brassiere, and carried them around with me wherever I went. It was not from feelings of love and longing that I did this; quite the contrary. It was from a feeling of hatred. There was nothing so strange about this, for isn't it so that love and hate exist side by side? Each letter was a letter from someone I had loved at one time without reservation. Not too long before, out of politeness, I had written my mother a very nice letter, I thought, telling her about the first ride I had taken in an underground train. She wrote back to me, and after I read her letter, I was afraid to even put my face outside the door. The letter was filled with detail after detail of horrible and vicious things she had read or heard about that had taken place on those very same underground trains on which I traveled. Only the other day, she wrote, she had read of an immigrant girl, someone my age exactly, who had had her throat cut while she was a passenger on perhaps the very same train I was riding.

But, of course, I had already known real fear. I had known a girl, a schoolmate of mine, whose father had dealings with the Devil. Once, out of curiosity, she had gone into a room where her father did his business, and she had looked into things that she should not have, and she became possessed. She took sick, and we, my other schoolmates and I, used to stand in the street outside her house on our way home from school and hear her being beaten by what possessed her, and hear her as she cried out from the beatings. Eventually she had to cross the sea, where the Devil couldn't follow her, because the Devil cannot walk over water. I thought of this as I felt the sharp corners of the letters cutting into the skin over my heart. I thought, On the one hand there was a girl being beaten by a man she could not see; on the other there was a girl getting her throat cut by a man she could see. In this great big world, why should my life be reduced to these two possibilities?

When the snow fell, it came down in thick, heavy glops, and hung on the trees like decorations ordered for a special occasion—a celebration no one had heard of, for everybody complained. In all the months that I had lived in this place, snowstorms had come and gone and I had never paid any attention, except to feel that snow was an annoyance when I had to make my way through the mounds of it that lay on the sidewalk. My parents used to go every Christmas Eve to a film[2] that had Bing Crosby standing waist-deep in snow and singing a song at the top of his voice. My mother once told me that seeing this film was among the first things they did when they were getting to know each other, and at the time she told me this I felt strongly how much I no longer liked even the way she spoke; and so I said, barely concealing my scorn, "What a religious experience that must have been." I walked away quickly, for my thirteen-year-old heart couldn't bear to see her face when I had caused her pain, but I couldn't stop myself.

In any case, this time when the snow fell, even I could see that there was something to it—it had a certain kind of beauty; not a beauty you would wish for every day of your life, but a beauty you could appreciate if you had an excess of beauty to begin with. The days were longer now, the sun set later, the evening sky seemed lower than usual, and the snow was the color and texture of a half-cooked egg white, making the world seem soft and lovely and—unexpectedly, to me—nourishing. That the world I was in could be soft, lovely, and nourishing was more than I could bear, and so I stood there and wept, for I didn't want to love one more thing in my life, didn't want one more thing that could make my heart break into a million little pieces at my feet. But all the same, there it was,

---

[2]*Holiday Inn* (1942), a movie starring Bing Crosby and Fred Astaire

and I could not do much about it; for even I could see that I was too young for real bitterness, real regret, real hard-heartedness.

The snow came and went more quickly than usual. Mariah said that the way the snow vanished, as if some hungry being were invisibly swallowing it up, was quire normal for that time of year. Everything that had seemed so brittle in the cold of winter—sidewalks, buildings, trees, the people themselves—seemed to slacken and sag a bit at the seams. I could now look back at the winter. It was my past, so to speak, my first real past—a past that was my own and over which I had the final word. I had just lived through a bleak and cold rime, and it is not to the weather outside that I refer. I had lived through this time, and as the weather changed from cold to warm it did not bring me along with it. Something settled inside me, something heavy and hard. It stayed there, and I could not think of one thing to make it go away. I thought, So this must be living, this must be the beginning of the time people later refer to as "years ago, when I was young."

My mother had a friendship with a woman—a friendship she did not advertise, for this woman had spent time in jail. Her name was Sylvie; she had a scar on her right cheek, a human-teeth bite. It was as if her cheek were a half-ripe fruit and someone had bitten into it, meaning to eat it, but then realized it wasn't ripe enough. She had gotten into a big quarrel with another woman over this: which of the two of them a man they both loved should live with. Apparently Sylvie said something that was unforgivable, and the other woman flew into an even deeper rage and grabbed Sylvie in an embrace, only it was not an embrace of love but an embrace of hatred, and she left Sylvie with the marked cheek. Both women were sent to jail for public misconduct, and going to jail was something that for the rest of their lives no one would let them forget. It was because of this that I was not allowed to speak to Sylvie, that she was not allowed to visit us when my father was at home, and that my mother's friendship with her. was supposed to be a secret. I used to observe Sylvie, and I noticed that whenever she stopped to speak, even in the briefest conversation, immediately her hand would go up to her face and caress her little rosette (before I knew what it was, I was sure that the mark on her face was a rose she had put there on purpose because she loved the beauty of roses so much she wanted to wear one on her face), and it was as if the mark on her face bound her to something much deeper than its reality, something that she could not put into words. One day, outside my mother's presence, she admired the way my corkscrew plaits fell around my neck, and then she said something that I did not hear, for she began by saying, "Years ago when I was young," and she pinched up her scarred cheek with her fingers and twisted it until I thought it would fall off like a dark, purple plum in the middle of her pink palm, and her voice became heavy and hard, even though she was laughing all the time she spoke. That is how I came to think that heavy and hard was the beginning of living, real living; and though I might not end up with a mark on my cheek, I had no doubt that I would end up with a mark somewhere.

I was standing in front of the kitchen sink one day, my thoughts centered, naturally, on myself, when Mariah came in—danced in, actually—singing an old song, a song that was popular when her mother was a young woman, a song she herself most certainly would have disliked when she was a young woman and so she now sang it with an exaggerated tremor in her voice to show how ridiculous she still found it. She twirled herself wildly around the room and came to a sharp stop without knocking over anything, even though many things were in her path.

She said, "I have always wanted four children, four girl children. I love my children." She said this clearly and sincerely. She said this without doubt on the one hand or confidence on the other. Mariah was beyond doubt or confidence. I thought, Things must have always gone her way, and not just for her but for everybody she has ever known from eternity; she has never had to doubt, and so she has never had to grow confident; the right thing always happens to her; the thing she wants to happen happens. Again I thought, How does a person get to be that way?

Mariah said to me, "I love you." And again she said it clearly and sincerely, without confidence or doubt. I believed her, for if anyone could love a young woman who had come from halfway around the world to help her take care of her children, it was Mariah. She looked so beautiful standing there in the middle of the kitchen. The yellow light from the sun came in through a window and fell on the pale-yellow linoleum tiles of the floor, and on the walls of the kitchen, which were painted yet another shade of pale yellow, and Mariah, with her pale-yellow skin and yellow hair, stood still in this almost celestial light, and she looked blessed, no blemish or mark of any kind on her cheek or anywhere else, as if she had never quarreled with anyone over a man or over anything, would never have to quarrel at all, had never done anything wrong and had never been to jail, had never had to leave anywhere for any reason other than a feeling that had come over her. She had washed her hair that morning and from where I stood I could smell the residue of the perfume from the shampoo in her hair. Then underneath that I could smell Mariah herself. The smell of Mariah was pleasant. Just that—pleasant. And I thought, But that's the trouble with Mariah—she smells pleasant. By then I already knew that I wanted to have a powerful odor and would not care if it gave offense.

On a day on which it was clear that there was no turning back as far as the weather was concerned, that the winter season was over and its return would be a noteworthy event, Mariah said that we should prepare to go and spend some time at the house on the shore of one of the Great Lakes. Lewis would not accompany us. Lewis would stay in town and take advantage of our absence, doing things that she and the children would not enjoy doing with him. What these things were I could not imagine. Mariah said we would take a train, for she wanted me to experience spending the night on a train and waking up to breakfast on the train as it moved through freshly plowed fields. She made so many arrangements—I had not known that just leaving your house for a short time could be so complicated.

Early that afternoon, because the children, my charges, would not return home from school until three, Mariah took me to a garden, a place she described as among her favorites in the world. She covered my eyes with a handkerchief, and then, holding me by the hand, she walked me to a spot in a clearing. Then she removed the handkerchief and said, "Now, look at this." I looked. It was a big area with lots of thick-trunked, tall trees along winding paths. Along the paths and underneath the trees were many, many yellow flowers the size and shape of play teacups, or fairy skirts. They looked like something to eat and something to wear at the same time; they looked beautiful; they looked simple, as if made to erase a complicated and unnecessary idea. I did not know what these flowers were, and so it was a mystery to me why I wanted to kill them. Just like that. I wanted to kill them. I wished that I had an enormous scythe; I would just walk down the path, dragging it alongside me, and I would cut these flowers down at the place where they emerged from the ground.

Mariah said, "These are daffodils. I'm sorry about the poem, but I'm hoping you'll find them lovely all the same."

There was such joy in her voice as she said this, such a music, how could I explain to her the feeling I had about daffodils—that it wasn't exactly daffodils, but that they would do as well as anything else? Where should I start? Over here or over there? Anywhere would be good enough, but my heart and my thoughts were racing so that every time I tried to talk I stammered and by accident bit my own tongue.

Mariah, mistaking what was happening to me for joy at seeing daffodils for the first time, reached out to hug me, but I moved away, and in doing that I seemed to get my voice back. I said, "Mariah, do you realize that at ten years of age I had to learn by heart a long poem about some flowers I would not see in real life until I was nineteen?"

As soon as I said this, I felt sorry that I had cast her beloved daffodils in a scene she had never considered, a scene of conquered and conquests; a scene of brutes masquerading as angels and angels portrayed as brutes. This woman who hardly knew me loved me, and she wanted me to love this thing—a grove brimming over with daffodils in bloom—that she loved also. Her eyes sank back in her head as if they were protecting themselves, as if they were taking a rest after some unexpected hard work. It wasn't her fault. It wasn't my fault. But nothing could change the fact that where she saw beautiful flowers I saw sorrow and bitterness. The same thing could cause us to shed tears, but those tears would not taste the same. We walked home in silence. I was glad to have at last seen what a wretched daffodil looked like.

When the day came for us to depart to the house on the Great Lake, I was sure that I did not want to go, but at midmorning I received a letter from my mother bringing me up to date on things she thought I would have missed since I left home and would certainly like to know about. "It still has not rained since you left," she wrote. "How fascinating," I said to myself with bitterness. It had not rained once for over a year before I left. I did not care about that any longer. The object of my life now was to put as much distance between myself and the events mentioned in her letter as I could manage. For I felt that if I could put enough miles between me and the place from which that letter came, and if I could put enough events between me and the events mentioned in the letter, would I not be free to take everything just as it came and not see hundreds of years in every gesture, every word spoken, every face?

On the train, we settled ourselves and the children into our compartments—two children with Mariah, two children with me. In one of the few films I had seen in my life so far, some people on a train did this—settled into their compartments. And so I suppose I should have felt excitement at doing something I had never done before and had only seen done in a film. But almost everything I did now was something I had never done before, and so the new was no longer thrilling to me unless it reminded me of the past. We went to the dining car to eat our dinner. We sat at tables—the children by themselves. They had demanded that, and had said to Mariah that they would behave, even though it was well known that they always did. The other people sitting down to eat dinner all looked like Mariah's relatives; the people waiting on them all looked like mine. The people who looked like my relatives were all older men and very dignified, as if they were just emerging from a church after Sunday service. On closer observation, they were not at all like my relatives; they only looked like them. My relatives always gave backchat. Mariah did not seem to notice what she had in common with the other diners, or what I had in common with the waiters. She acted in her usual way, which was that the world was round and we all agreed on that, when I knew that the world was flat and if I went to the edge I would fall off.

That night on the train was frightening. Every time I tried to sleep; just as it seemed that I had finally done so, I would wake up sure that thousands of people on horseback were following me, chasing me, each of them carrying a cutlass to cut me up into small pieces. Of course, I could tell it was the sound of the wheels on the tracks that inspired this nightmare, but a real explanation made no difference to me. Early that morning, Mariah left her own compartment to come and tell me that we were passing through some of those freshly plowed fields she loved so much. She drew up my blind, and when I saw mile after mile of turned-up earth, I said, a cruel tone to my voice, "Well, thank God I didn't have to do that." I don't know if she understood what I meant, for in that one statement I meant many different things.

When we got to our destination, a man Mariah had known all her life, a man who had always done things for her family, a man who came from Sweden, was waiting for us. His name was Gus, and the way Mariah spoke his name it was as if he belonged to her deeply, like a memory. And, of course, he was a part of her past, her childhood: he was there, apparently, when she took her first steps; she had caught her first fish in a boat with him; they had been in a storm on the lake and their survival was a miracle, and so on. Still, he was a real person, and I thought Mariah should have long separated the person Gus standing in front of her in the present from all the things he had meant to her in the past. I wanted to say to him, "Do you not hate the way she says your name, as if she owns you?" But then I thought about it and could see that a person coming from Sweden was a person altogether different from a person like me.

We drove through miles and miles of country-side, miles and miles of nothing. I was glad not to live in a place like this. The land did not say,

"Welcome. So glad you could come." It was more, "I dare you to stay here." At last we came to a small town. As we drove through it, Mariah became excited; her voice grew low, as if what she was saying only she needed to hear. She would exclaim with happiness or sadness, depending, as things passed before her. In the half a year or so since she had last been there, some things had changed, some things had newly arrived, and some things had vanished completely. As she passed through this town, she seemed to forget she was the wife of Lewis and the mother of four girl children. We left the small town and a silence fell on everybody, and in my own case I felt a kind of despair. I felt sorry for Mariah; I knew what she must have gone through, seeing her past go swiftly by in front of her. What an awful thing that is, as if the ground on which you are standing is being slowly pulled out from under your feet and beneath is nothing, a hole through which you fall forever.

The house in which Mariah had grown up was beautiful, I could immediately see that. It was large, sprawled out, as if rooms had been added onto it when needed, but added on all in the same style. It was modeled on the farmhouse that Mariah's grandfather grew up in, somewhere in Scandinavia. It had a nice veranda in front, a perfect place from which to watch rain fall. The whole house was painted a soothing yellow with white trim, which from afar looked warm and inviting. From my room I could see the lake. I had read of this lake in geography books, had read of its origins and its history, and now to see it up close was odd, for it looked so ordinary, gray, dirty, unfriendly, not a body of water to make up a song about. Mariah came in, and seeing me studying the water she flung her arms around me and said, "Isn't it great?" But I wasn't thinking that at all. I slept peacefully, without any troubling dreams to haunt me; it must have been that knowing there was a body of water outside my window, even though it was not the big blue sea I was used to, brought me some comfort.

Mariah wanted all of us, the children and me, to see things the way she did. She wanted us to enjoy the house, all its nooks and crannies, all its sweet smells, all its charms, just the way she had done as a child. The children were happy to see things her way. They would have had to be four small versions of myself not to fall at her feet in adoration. But I already had a mother who loved me, and I had come to see her love as a burden and had come to view with horror the sense of self-satisfaction it gave my mother to hear other people comment on her great love for me. I had come to feel that my mother's love for me was designed solely to make me into an echo of her; and I didn't know why, but I felt that I would rather be dead than become just an echo of someone. That was not a figure of speech. Those thoughts would have come as a complete surprise to my mother, for in her life she had found that her ways were the best ways to have, and she would have been mystified as to how someone who came from inside her would want to be anyone different from her. I did not have an answer to this myself. But there it was. Thoughts like these had brought me to be sitting on the edge of a Great Lake with a woman who wanted to show me her world and hoped that I would like it, too. Sometimes there is no escape, but often the effort of trying will do quite nicely for a while.

I was sitting on the veranda one day with these thoughts when I saw Mariah come up the path, holding in her hands six grayish-blackish fish. She said "Taa-daah! Trout!" and made a big sweep with her hands, holding the fish up in the light, so that rainbow-like colors shone on their scales. She sang out, "I will make you fishers of men," and danced around me. After she stopped, she said, "Aren't they beautiful? Gus and I went out in my old boat—my very, very old boat—and we caught them. My fish. This is supper. Let's go feed the minions."

It's possible that what she really said was "millions," not "minions." Certainly she said it in jest. But as we were cooking the fish, I was thinking about it. "Minions." A word like that would haunt someone like me; the place where I came from was a dominion of someplace else. I became so taken with the word "dominion" that I told Mariah this story: When I was about five years old or so, I had read to me for the first time the story of Jesus Christ feeding the multitudes with seven loaves and a few fishes. After my mother had finished reading this to me, I said to her, "But how did Jesus serve the fish? boiled or fried?" This made my mother look at me in amazement and shake her head. She then told everybody she met what I had said, and they would shake their heads and say, "What a child!" It wasn't really such an unusual question. In the place where I grew up, many people earned their living by being fishermen. Often, after a fisherman came in from sea and had distributed most of his fish to people with whom he had such an arrangement, he might save some of them, clean and season them, and build a fire, and he and his wife would fry them at the seashore and put them up for sale. It was quite a nice thing to sit on the sand under a tree, seeking refuge from the hot sun, and eat a perfectly fried fish as you took in the view of the beautiful blue sea, former home of the thing you were eating. When I had inquired about the way the fish were served with the loaves, to myself I had thought, Not only would the multitudes be pleased to have something to eat, not only would they marvel at the miracle of turning so little into so much, but they might go on to pass a judgment on the way the food tasted. I know it would have mattered to me. In our house, we all preferred boiled fish. It was a pity that the people who recorded their life with Christ never mentioned this small detail, a detail that would have meant a lot to me.

When I finished telling Mariah this, she looked at me, and her blue eyes (which I would have found beautiful even if I hadn't read millions of books in which blue eyes were always accompanied by the word "beautiful") grew dim as she slowly closed the lids over them, then bright again as she opened them wide and then wider.

A silence fell between us; it was a deep silence, but not too thick and not too black. Through it we could hear the clink of the cooking utensils as we cooked the fish Mariah's way, under flames in the oven, a way I did not like. And we could hear the children in the distance screaming—in pain or pleasure, I could not tell.

Mariah and I were saying good night to each other the way we always did, with a hug and a kiss, but this time we did it as if we both wished we hadn't gotten such a custom started. She was almost out of the room when she turned and said, "I was looking forward to telling you that I have Indian blood, that the reason I'm so good at catching fish and hunting birds and roasting corn and doing all sorts of things is that I have Indian blood. But now, I don't know why, I feel I shouldn't tell you that. I feel you will take it the wrong way."

This really surprised me. What way should I take this? Wrong way? Right way? What could she mean? To look at her, there was nothing remotely like an Indian about her. Why claim a thing like that? I myself had Indian blood in me. My grandmother is a Carib Indian. That makes me one-quarter Carib Indian. But I don't go around saying that I have some Indian blood in me. The Carib Indians were good sailors, but I don't like to be on the sea; I only like to look at it. To me my grandmother is my grandmother, not an Indian. My grandmother is alive; the Indians she came from are all dead. If someone could get away with it, I am sure they would put my grandmother in a museum, as an example of something now extinct in nature, one of a handful still alive. In fact, one of the museums to which Mariah had taken me devoted a whole section to people, all dead, who were more or less related to my grandmother.

Mariah says, "I have Indian blood in me," and underneath everything I could swear she says it as if she were announcing her possession of a trophy. How do you get to be the sort of victor who can claim to be the vanquished also?

I now heard Mariah say, "Well," and she let out a long breath, full of sadness, resignation, even dread. I looked at her; her face was miserable, tormented, ill-looking. She looked at me in a pleading way, as if asking for relief, and I looked back, my face and my eyes hard; no matter what, I would not give it.

I said, "All along I have been wondering how you got to be the way you are. Just how it was that you got to be the way you are."

Even now she couldn't let go, and she reached out, her arms open wide, to give me one of her great hugs. But I stepped out of its path quickly, and she was left holding nothing. I said it again. I said, "How do you get to be that way?" The anguish on her face almost broke my heart, but I would not bend. It was hollow, my triumph, I could feel that, but I held on to it just the same.

1990

Questions

1. Why does the narrator say of Mariah, "How does a person get to be that way?" What is the tone of voice in her question?
2. Describe the narrator. Refer to passages that reveal her search for identity and self-definition.
3. Why does the narrator resent William Wordsworth's poem "I Wandered Lonely as a Cloud"? How do you interpret her dream about daffodils? Why does she react as she does to the daffodils that Mariah shows her?
4. How would you characterize the relationship of the narrator with Mariah? Do you think that it is representative of a typical relationship between a live-in *au pair* and her employer?
5. Why do you think that the narrator can be hostile to Mariah?

6. How would you characterize the relationship of the narrator with her mother?

7. What is the narrator's response to seeing the waiters on the train?

8. What does the narrator mean when she looks at the plowed fields and says, "'Well, thank God I didn't have to do that.' . . . in that one statement I meant many different things"?

9. Explain the narrator's hollow triumph at the end of the story.

10. How is "Mariah" a story about the immigrant experience? Which of the narrator's reflections and feelings do you think are typical of an immigrant? Which are atypical?

Jimmy Santiago Baca
(b. 1952)

Born in New Mexico of Indio–Mexican descent, Jimmy Santiago Baca was abandoned by his parents at two years of age. He was taken in by his grandmother before being sent to an orphanage, from which he ran away at thirteen years of age. At twenty-one years of age, Baca began serving six and a half years in prison, including time in isolation and on death row. In prison, however, he developed a passion for poetry that turned his life around. His first career break came when poet Denise Levertov, an editor at *Mother Jones*, accepted three of his poems for publication. These poems were included in his first volume, *Immigrants in Our Own Land*, published in 1979, the year he was released from prison. That same year, he passed the General Educational Development (GED®) tests, and, in 1984, he graduated from the University of New Mexico. In 1987, he gained international fame when his semi-autobiographical novel in verse, *Martin and Meditations on the South Valley*, received the American Book Award for poetry. His central themes include life in the American Southwest barrios and the struggles of the impoverished, the exploited, and the marginalized. Baca conducts writing workshops at prisons, libraries, and community centers, and, in 2005, he created Cedar Tree, a nonprofit foundation that provides opportunities for those in need to improve their lives. In addition to poetry, Baca has written memoirs, novels, short fiction, essays, and a screenplay.

SO MEXICANS ARE TAKING JOBS FROM AMERICANS

O Yes? Do they come on horses
with rifles, and say,
Ese gringo, gimmee your job?
And do you, gringo, take off your ring,
5   drop your wallet into a blanket
spread over the ground, and walk away?
I hear Mexicans are taking your jobs away.
Do they sneak into town at night,

and as you're walking home with a whore,
do they mug you, a knife at your throat,   10
saying, I want your job?
Even on TV, an asthmatic leader
crawls turtle heavy, leaning on an assistant,
and from a nest of wrinkles on his face,
a tongue paddles through flashing waves   15
of lightbulbs, of cameramen, rasping
"They're taking our jobs away."
Well, I've gone about trying to find them,
asking just where the hell are these fighters.
The rifles I hear sound in the night   20
are white farmers shooting blacks and browns
whose ribs I see jutting out
and starving children,
I see the poor marching for a little work,
I see small white farmers selling out   25
to clean-suited farmers living in New York,
who've never been on a farm,
don't know the look of a hoof or the smell
of a woman's body bending all day long in fields.
I see this, and I hear only a few people   30
got all the money in this world, the rest
count their pennies to buy bread and butter.
Below that cool green sea of money,
millions and millions of people fight to live,
search for pearls in the darkest depths   35
of their dreams, hold their breath for years
trying to cross poverty to just having something.
The children are dead already. We are killing them,
that is what America should be saying;
on TV, in the streets, in offices, should be saying,   40
"We aren't giving the children a chance to live."
Mexicans are taking our jobs, they say instead.
What they really say is, let them die,
and the children too.

1982

Questions

1. What is the tone of the poem? Does the tone shift?
2. Compare and contrast the depiction of Mexicans and whites in the poem. Where do the author's sympathies lie?

3. According to the author, are Mexicans or immigrants taking jobs from Americans? Summarize the poem's argument. Be sure to interpret the last two lines of the poem as part of your answer.
4. Do you think that Mexicans and immigrants are taking jobs from Americans? Why or why not?
5. Read "So Mexicans Are Taking Jobs from Americans" and Rodas's "El Olor de Cansansio (The Smell of Fatigue)." How do the arguments of Baca and Rodas complement one another?

Martín Espada
(b. 1957)

B orn in Brooklyn, New York, Espada attended the University of
Wisconsin and Northeastern University. He has held a variety of
jobs, from bouncer to journalist in Nicaragua, all of which in-
form his poetry. Currently, he works as a tenant lawyer in Boston. He
writes frequently of the struggle of the underclass and the immigrant.
Among his several collections of poetry are *The Immigrant Iceboy's
Bolero* (1982), *Trumpets from the Islands of Their Eviction* (1987),
Imagine the Angels of Bread (1996), and *Zapata's Disciple* (1998).
"Jorge the Church Janitor Finally Quits" is from his collection *Rebellion
is the Circle of a Lover's Hands* (1990).

JORGE THE CHURCH JANITOR
FINALLY QUITS

No one asks
where I am from,
I must be
from the country of janitors,
I have always mopped this floor.   5
Honduras, you are a squatter's camp
outside the city
of their understanding.

No one can speak

my name,   10
I host the fiesta
of the bathroom,
stirring the toilet
like a punchbowl.
The Spanish music of my name   15
is lost
when the guests complain
about toilet paper.

What they say

20   must be true:
       I am smart,
       but I have a bad attitude.

       No one knows

       that I quit tonight,
25   maybe the mop
       will push on without me,
       Sniffing along the floor
       like a crazy squid
       with stringy gray tentacles.
30   They will call it Jorge.

1990

Questions

1. How is this poem about lost identity?
2. Why does Jorge quit his job?
3. Why is it significant that he works for the church?
4. What is the significance of the last line?
5. What in the immigrant experience and in low-prestige jobs can lead to low self-esteem? Refer to the poem when answering this question.
6. Compare Jorge with the waiter in Kraft Rompf's "Waiting Table" and the workers in O'Neil's *The Hairy Ape.*"
7. Compare Jorge with the speaker in Shu Ting's "Assembly Line."

Melida Rodas
(b. 1972)

Born in Guatemala, Melida Rodas came to the United States when she was seven years of age. Her father, escaping the political and economic oppression of his native land, left his white-collar job and moved to America six months ahead of his family. In New Jersey, he labored in restaurants and delis; upon arrival, his wife worked in a rug factory. Rodas, inspired by Mayan art, the oral story-telling tradition, and religious icons, was encouraged to pursue her interest in art and poetry. Active in the artistic life of Jersey City, Rodas has been a featured artist in galleries and public spaces throughout New Jersey and has read her poetry in various forums, including New Jersey City University, New York University, and Marist College. As a student at New Jersey City University, Rodas developed an interest in writing memoirs. In writing "El Olor de Cansansio (The Smell of Fatigue)," she was inspired by her father.

EL OLOR DE CANSANSIO
(THE SMELL OF FATIGUE)

My father hangs up the phone. He puts away our colorful new kite. He puts away his smile and his Tuesday clothes as he prepares for a new battle. I watch him put on the white shirt. The checkered pants. The boots. He folds a crisp white apron and places it in the pocket of his jacket. I admire the fresh white shirt, the crisp crease that runs down his black-and-white pants. Smelling like soap and shaving cream, he returns to the restaurant where he has been slaving ever since we moved to New Jersey from Guatemala in 1979.

I see him walk slowly, tired. Another cook has left. Another dishonorable discharge, I suppose. My father is brought in to hold down the fort on his day off. The way he always does, like a respectable soldier.

Each day I see my father's hair get grayer. It won't be long before it's silver, like the buttons on a new cadet's jacket, silver like water in the sun. His hands are small. Always callused. Always pink. He holds my face like a moon before he says good-bye. "Next week," he promises, as he points to the drawer that keeps our kite. I wish that he would stay. I try to keep my eyes from telling him as he holds my face. His hands feel so strong. Strong from carrying pots of heavy soup. Strong from fighting the ambush of dinner specials, lunch specials, breakfast specials with eggs, home fries, bacon, silver dollar pancakes, California cheeseburgers, Caesar salads, BLTs, mashed potatoes, French fries with gravy, toast with marmalade, jelly, butter, cream cheese.

My father has always worked hard. Ever since the age of seven when he sold peanuts, which he carried in small bags on a cardboard box. Ever since he shared the streets with the other children who sold Chicklets and shined shoes. With the blind man who sold tickets *de lotteria* and the *viejita* who begged for money outside El Palacio National. He's worked hard ever since his toes were small and wrinkled in the rain because the leather from his shoes had finally surrendered.

Life has always been as hard as the soles of my father's feet. Like the callused hand my face melts into. He holds it like the cantaloupe before a fruit salad. Like life before America. Before it's sliced, devoured, consumed. Guatemala feels like a memory, just a memory. A humble memory that moves slowly and peacefully. It is a place not so gray with buildings. It is a landscape with green mountains, blue skies, and sweet air. It is a place where you don't fear the *Migra*. The force. The clan that comes to take you away. They search in kitchens and factories for their victims. They send them back with suitcases full of postcards of the Statue of Liberty that never got sent, subway tokens, wrinkled letters with Spanish writing decorated with exotic pressed flowers, stamped with colorful postage, smelling like perfume and crayon. Everyone who is here on borrowed time, with expired visas and false documentation, fears the *Migra*. Because it doesn't matter that you have spent all your *centavos* to buy a piece of the American pie. So what if you risked your life crossing the desert with a *coyote*, the man who guides you through the desert and river to the American border? Once you reach the line, once you dodge the bullets that the border patrol has fired at you, once you say *El Salve Maria*, you crawl to American soil. *Mojado. Indocumentado.* No visa. Your wet clothes stick to your tired back. Pictures of your children, of your family, stick to your almost empty wallet.

We come to America by bus. It takes us five days to reach *Los Estados.* We leave our colorful beautiful Guatemala for gray buildings and a promise that here we will have a better life. Here my father doesn't wear a suit and tie to work. Here there is no garden, no fruit trees, no space. Here we live in an apartment. People don't smile. People don't say hello, except for the Puerto Rican lady my mother calls Donna Ortega. She's the only one who is friendly with us when we first arrive. Americans don't want to know us. Not even the children. Patrick, who lives next door, calls me a spic. One day he spits on my face on the way home from school.

Today my father leaves our apartment for the restaurant. The awful place that fatigues him. His shoulders are small and round. His feet are heavy. The image is familiar. I realize that I've seen it before. It is the picture of a wounded soldier who returns to the battle. I feel a large *jocote* in my throat as I try to imagine the number of potatoes my father has peeled. Oh, the difficulty of surviving an infantry of dishes, a Sunday morning rush! And the heat of August days. The sweat on his brow, the napkin he wraps around his forehead to prevent it from blinding him. How do you endure the battles, such battles, Father, with pans and pots as your only allies? Vegetables, meats, oil as your weapons? When is it time to surrender the ladle, the whisk, the spoon?

My father's boots. They alone tell the story of the war. With their greasy suede and vegetable pulp trapped underneath them. When he enters our home, he sheds the boots on the floor, as if never wanting to see them again. A reminder of the American Dream gone sour. Of times that don't get better, just get harder. Every day I've seen life take the years from my father. Years taken with unsympathetic conviction. As I walk past restaurant alleys, I remember the smell of my father's clothes when he comes home.

Sometimes the hours are so hard and so long that he asks me to take off his heavy boots. Proudly, I reach for his feet and try to give him a sense of home and gratitude. I untie the hardened laces. I dispose of the fragments of lettuce and tomato caught between them. I remove his boots like a heavy cast. His feet give off the heat of labor and *cansansio*. His socks I peel off with the delicate care of an archeologist revealing precious Mayan fossils. His pale feet wait to be freed from their torture. I squeeze fatigue away from his toes. I rejuvenate his ankles. I make his beautiful rough heels feel like they can carry him to the front line again tomorrow.

My father leaves our small apartment when the sky is still purple. He leaves when the newspapers outside the candy store are still wrapped with string and the bakery rolls are still warm in large paper bags. He leaves when the chill of Aurora glues me to a poncho my *abuelo* has sent. My father leaves when the house doesn't yet smell like tea, syrup, and eggs. When the only one who hears his footsteps is my mother, as she tries to keep the warmth he has left in their bed.

My father returns when the sky is purple again. When the first stars are saying hello. He comes home when homework is done. When you've brushed your teeth. When dishes have been used, washed, dried, and put away. My father comes home when others have taken off their ties or panty hose, have eaten dinner, paid their bills, and read their favorite book. When the day has simmered and night begins. When the enemy has ceased fire. My father comes home when you grow tired of waiting. When you surrender to the weight of your eyelids and you wish you could have told him that you made honor roll again today.

2000

Questions

1. How does Rodas describe the illegal immigrant's journey to America? What upsets her about that journey?
2. Describe the portrait of the father that emerges from this selection. Do you think that his story is more or less like that of most immigrants, whether legal or not?

3. What is the tone of this selection? Consider how sentence structure contributes to tone.

4. According to this selection, what is the reaction of Americans to immigrants? Do you think that Rodas's perspective is limited and perhaps not representative? Explain your answer.

5. What does this memoir suggest about the American Dream?

6. Read "El Olor de Cansansio" and Baca's "So Mexicans Are Taking Jobs from Americans." How do the arguments of Rodas and Baca complement one another?

7. Compare and contrast the fathers in "El Olor de Cansansio" and La Puma's "Cakes."

PART V

CLASS STRUGGLE AND THE DYNAMICS OF POWER

Introduction

The readings in this section focus on workers in the underclasses and their struggle to live and work with dignity in a workplace and culture that too often devalues them and their contributions.

In William Blake's poems, which open the section, young children are victimized by being forced to clean chimneys, a job that is not just dirty, but also dangerous, and that claimed the lives of many children. Blake points the finger at those responsible, including irresponsible parents, orphanages, the church, and the government; in short, Blake exposes a systemic abuse, which was tolerated for years in England and perpetrated on the country's most vulnerable citizens.

However, is this systemic abuse in nineteenth-century England much different from that practiced in more contemporary cultures with regard to some laborers? Consider Butch Weldy, a character from Edgar Lee Masters's *Spoon River Anthology*. Weldy reforms himself and maintains a job for presumably several years until he suffers an on-the-job injury, leaving him with two broken legs and blind. Weldy's employer, however, refuses to pay him compensation. Weldy is left astonished and confused when the court upholds his employer's decision.

Similarly, in *The Hairy Ape*, Eugene O'Neill's characters work under brutal and treacherous conditions, which, over time, disillusion and dehumanize them. Yet ship owners, who are more concerned with profits than fairness, and government officials, who are concerned with their careers, prevent these laborers from unionizing and earning an appropriate salary in a safer, more dignified environment.

For many, the indignity of the labor and egotistical, mean-spirited bosses can be overwhelming. In James Joyce's "Counterparts," Farrington at first responds to his boss with patience, but by the end of the story, he addresses Mr. Alleyne with sarcasm and fails to complete the day's task. Farrington's frustration with his work is deep, and he carries home his feelings of powerlessness, which lead him to abuse his family. But Mike LeFevre, equally frustrated by his mechanical work, finds comfort and hope in his family, which provides him with a reason to report to the steel mill each day.

In a sense, all of these characters wage the same battle as John Henry, the enduring folk hero. Like John Henry, the characters struggle for dignity, self-worth, appreciation, and job preservation. With each ring of his hammer, Henry strikes a blow for the rights of the working-class laborer, a blow that resonates with most of the voices in this section.

William Blake
(1757–1827)

Born in London, William Blake became an apprentice to an engraver at fourteen years of age. Later, he entered the Royal Academy of Arts as an engraving student but left over artistic differences. An early Romantic, Blake was a radical thinker and artist, who published his poems accompanied by engravings and watercolors, on which he worked with his wife. His works include *Songs of Innocence* (1789), *Songs of Experience* (1794), and the prophetic *Marriage of Heaven and Hell* (1790).

His *Songs of Innocence* is filled with hope and "the sense of wonder and a directness of spiritual apprehension" that the innocent child can feel. Blake celebrates the spontaneous, unreserved, and loving impulses of childhood as he creates a world without fear or repression, not unlike Eden. However, in his *Songs of Experience*, he explores a world of ambiguity and inequities, one in which childhood innocence is corrupted by adult vice and society's institutions. Blake expresses his moral indignation and outrage throughout *Experience*. In these two versions of "The Chimney Sweeper," Blake attacks the abuse of child labor.

From *SONGS OF INNOCENCE*, THE CHIMNEY SWEEPER

William Blake [*1757–1827*]

> When my mother died I was very young,
> And my father sold me while yet my tongue
> Could scarcely cry "'weep! 'weep! 'weep! 'weep!"
> So your chimneys I sweep, and in soot I sleep.
>
> There's little Tom Dacre, who cried when his head,
> That curled like a lamb's back, was shaved: so I said
> "Hush, Tom! never mind it, for when your head's bare
> You know that the soot cannot spoil your white hair."
>
> And so he was quiet, and that very night,
> As Tom was a-sleeping, he had such a sight!

That thousands of sweepers, Dick, Joe, Ned, and Jack,
Were all of them locked up in coffins of black.

And by came an Angel who had a bright key,
And he opened the coffins and set them all free;
Then down a green plain leaping, laughing, they run,
And wash in a river, and shine in the sun.

Then naked and white, all their bags left behind,
They rise upon clouds and sport in the wind;
And the Angel told Tom, if he'd be a good boy,
He'd have God for his father, and never want° joy.

And so Tom awoke; and we rose in the dark,
And got with our bags and our brushes to work.
Though the morning was cold, Tom was happy and warm;
So if all do their duty they need not fear harm.

1789

Questions

1. Why did the speaker become a chimney sweeper?
2. What is suggested by the use of *"weep 'weep! 'weep!'*?
3. How does Tom Dacre's dream help the chimney sweepers rise above their grueling reality? What do the "coffins of black" represent?
4. Why do you think Blake capitalizes *S* in *Sun* in line 16? Is he suggesting a pun?
5. How is the tone of the poem ironic? How does the irony reinforce both childhood innocence and systemic abuse?
6. How does the speaker find comfort? Is he much like Sandburg's "Washerwoman"?

From *SONGS OF EXPERIENCE*, THE CHIMNEY SWEEPER

A little black thing among the snow:
Crying "weep, 'weep,' in notes of woe!
"Where are thy father & mother? say?"
They are both gone up to the church to pray.

"Because I was happy upon the hearth,
And smil'd among the winters snow:
They clothed me in the clothes of death,
And taught me to sing the notes of woe.
"And because I am happy & dance & sing,

They think they have done me no injury:
And are gone to praise God & his Priest & King
Who make up a heaven of our misery."

1794

Questions

1. How is the speaker in the *Experience* version of the poem more experienced, more aware of his situation?
2. What is the tone of the poem?
3. Who does Blake suggest is at fault for the chimney sweepers' lives?
4. How do both versions of "The Chimney Sweeper" take a stand against unfair and abusive labor practices?
5. Research chimney sweepers in England during Blake's lifetime. From what you can discover, does Blake present the situation accurately? When were laws enacted in England and the United States to regulate child labor?

"John Henry"

With approximately 200 renditions, "John Henry" is the most recorded folk song in American history. There are many, many different versions of the song. In fact, it is difficult to find any two recorded lyrics that are exactly the same. In almost all versions of the story, however, John Henry is a black man who serves as a folk hero for the American working class as he proves that a worker is superior to a machine. The song, with its origins in the mid-nineteenth century, has been sung by work gangs, in prisons, in union halls, and in concert halls, and has been recorded by a diverse range of artists, including Harry Belafonte, Joe Bonamassa, Big Bill Broonzy, Johnny Cash, Lonnie Donegan, Roberta Flack, Woody Guthrie, Burl Ives, Lead Belly, Jerry Lee Lewis, Van Morrison, Odetta, Paul Robeson, Pete Seeger, Bruce Springsteen, Merle Travis, and Doc Watson.

JOHN HENRY

John Henry was a little baby
Sittin' on his Mammy's knee
He picked up a hammer and a little piece of steel
Said, "Hammer's gonna be the death of me
Hammer's gonna be the death of me."

John Henry went up on the mountain
Came down on the other side
The mountain was so tall, John Henry was so small
He laid down his hammer and he cried,
Laid down his hammer and he cried

John Henry was a railroad man
He worked from six till five
"Raise 'em up bullies and let 'em drop down,
I'll beat you to the bottom or die
I'll beat you to the bottom or die."

John Henry had a little woman
Her name was Polly Ann

John Henry took sick and had to go to bed
Polly Ann drove steel like a man
Polly Ann drove steel like a man

The Captain said to John Henry
"Gonna bring that steam drill 'round
Gonna bring that steam drill out on the job
Gonna whop that steel on down
Whop that steel on down."

John Henry told his captain
"A man ain't nothin' but a man
Before I let your steam drill beat me down
I'll die with this hammer in my hand
I'll die with this hammer in my hand."

They placed John Henry on the right hand side
The steam drill on the left
He said "Before I let that steam drill beat me down
I'll hammer my fool self to death
I'll hammer my fool self to death."

John Henry told his shaker[1]
"Shaker you had better pray
For if I miss this six-foot steel
Tomorrow will be your buryin' day
Tomorrow will be your buryin' day."

The man that invented that steam drill
Thought he was mighty fine
John Henry sunk her fourteen feet
And the steam drill only made nine
Steam drill only made nine

Sun shine hot an' burnin',
Weren't no breeze at all
Sweat ran down like water down a hill
The day John Henry let his hammer fall
Day John Henry let his hammer fall

John Henry was lyin' on his death bed,
He turned over on his side
And these were the last words John Henry said

---

[1]The shaker worked as a team with the hammer man. The shaker shifted the drill between blows to clear away bits of broken rock and to improve the bite.

"Bring me a cool drink of water 'fore I die
Cool drink of water 'fore I die."

John Henry's woman heard he was dead
She could not rest on her bed
She got up at midnight, caught that No. 4 train,
"I'm goin' where John Henry fell dead
Goin' where John Henry fell dead."

John Henry had a little woman
The dress she wore was blue
She went down the track and never looked back
Saying "Johnny I been true to you
Johnny I been true to you."

They took John Henry to the white house[2]
And buried him in the sand
And every locomotive come roarin' by
Says, "There lays that steel-drivin' man
There lays that steel-drivin' man."

Questions

1. Summarize the story of John Henry according to this version.
2. Describe John Henry. How does the song at once humanize and mythologize John Henry?
3. What do you think John Henry represents to the blue-collar worker?
4. Consult other versions of the John Henry story. How are they similar and different from the one in this text?

---

[2]Refers to the Virginia Penitentiary, which was built using white stone and which had its own burial grounds. Some interpret this reference to suggest that John Henry was a prisoner who was forced to work on the railroad.

James Joyce
(1882-1941)

Irish author James Joyce is widely regarded as one of the most important literary figures of the twentieth century. Raised in a respectable but financially unstable middle-class family, Joyce was educated in a series of rigorous Jesuit schools. In 1902, he left Ireland and lived the remainder of his life in Europe. Yet his clash with Ireland—its values, religion, and culture—would remain the topic of his fiction. He considered Dublin to be "the centre of paralysis" and hoped that when the Irish took "one good look at themselves in my nicely polished looking-glass" he would have introduced "the first step in the spiritual liberation of my country."

Joyce can be a difficult writer, particularly in his novels *Ulysses* (1922) and *Finnegans Wake* (1939), in which he develops his "stream of consciousness" technique, along with a complex system of symbols and allusions. His earlier, shorter fiction is more accessible. "Counterparts" is from his classic collection of stories, *Dubliners* (1914).

COUNTERPARTS

The bell rang furiously and, when Miss Parker went to the tube, a furious voice called out in a piercing north of Ireland accent:

—Send Farrington here!

Miss Parker returned to her machine, saying to a man who was writing at a desk:

—Mr Alleyne wants you upstairs.

The man muttered *Blast him!* under his breath and pushed back his chair to stand up. When he stood up he was tall and of great bulk. He had a hanging face, dark winecoloured with fair eyebrows and moustache; his eyes bulged forward slightly and the whites of them were dirty. He lifted up the counter and, passing by the clients, went out of the office with a heavy step.

He went heavily upstairs until he came to the second landing where a door bore a brass plate with the inscription *Mr Alleyne*. Here he halted puffing with labour and vexation and knocked. The shrill voice cried:

—Come in!

The man entered Mr Alleyne's room. Simultaneously Mr Alleyne, a little man wearing goldrimmed glasses on a clean-shaven face, shot his head up over a pile of documents. The head itself was so pink and hairless that it seemed like a large egg reposing on the papers. Mr Alleyne did not lose a moment:

—Farrington? What is the meaning of this? Why have I always to complain of you? May I ask you why you haven't made a copy of that contract between Bodley and Kirwan? I told you it must be ready by four o'clock.

—But Mr Shelley said, sir, ...

—*Mr Shelley said, sir.* . . . . . Kindly attend to what I say and not to what *Mr Shelley says, sir.* You have always some excuse or another for shirking work. Let me tell you that if the contract is not copied before this evening I'll lay the matter before Mr Crosbie. . . . Do you hear me now?

—Yes, sir.

—Do you hear me now? . . . . Aye and another little matter! I might as well be talking to the wall as talking to you. Understand once for all that you get a half an hour for your lunch and not an hour and a half. How many courses do you want, I'd like to know? . . . Do you mind me, now?

—Yes, sir.

Mr Alleyne bent his head again upon his pile of papers. The man stared fixedly at the polished skull which directed the affairs of Crosbie and Alleyne, gauging its fragility. A spasm of rage gripped his throat for a few moments and then passed, leaving after it a sharp sensation of thirst. The man recognised the sensation and felt that he must have a good night's drinking. The middle of the month was post and, if he could get the copy done in time, Mr Alleyne might give him an order on the cashier. He stood still, gazing fixedly at the head upon the pile of papers. Suddenly Mr Alleyne began to upset all the papers, searching for something. Then, as if he had been unaware of the man's presence till that moment, he shot up his head again, saying:

—Eh! Are you going to stand there all the day? Upon my word, Farrington, you take things easy!

—I was waiting to see. . . .

—Very good, you needn't wait to see. Go downstairs and do your work.

The man walked heavily towards the door and as he went out of the room he heard Mr Alleyne cry after him that if the contract was not copied by evening Mr Crosbie would hear of the matter.

He returned to his desk in the lower office and counted the sheets which remained to be copied. He took up his pen and dipped it in the ink but he continued to stare stupidly at the last words he had written: *In no case shall the said Bernard Bodley be.* . . . . . . The evening was falling and in a few minutes they would be lighting the gas: then he could write. He felt that he must slake the thirst in his throat. He stood up from his desk and, lifting the counter as before, passed out of the office. As he was passing out the chief clerk looked at him inquiringly.

—It's all right, Mr Shelley, said the man pointing with his finger to indicate the objective of his journey.

The chief clerk glanced at the hatrack but, seeing the row complete, offered no remark. As soon as he was on the landing the man pulled a shepherd's plaid cap out of his pocket, put it on his head and ran quickly down the rickety stairs. From the street door he walked on furtively on the inner side of the path towards the corner and all at once dived into a doorway. He was now safe in the dark snug of O'Neill's shop and, filling up the little window that looked into the bar with his inflamed face, the colour of dark wine or dark meat, he called out:

—Here, Pat, give us a g.p., like a good fellow!

The curate brought him a glass of plain porter. The man drank it at a gulp and asked for a caraway seed. He put his penny on the counter and, leaving the curate to grope for it in the gloom, retreated out of the snug as furtively as he had entered it.

Darkness, accompanied by a thick fog, was gaining upon the dusk of February and the lamps in Eustace Street had been lit. The man went up by the houses until he reached the door of the office, wondering whether he could finish his copy in time. On the stairs a moist pungent odour of perfumes saluted his nose: evidently Miss Delacour had come while he was out in O'Neill's. He crammed his cap back again into his pocket and reentered the office, assuming an air of absentmindedness.

—Mr Alleyne has been calling for you, said the chief clerk severely. Where were you?

The man glanced at the two clients who were standing at the counter as if to intimate that their presence prevented him from answering. As the clients were both male the chief clerk allowed himself a laugh:

—I know that game, he said. Five times in one day is a little bit. . . . Well, you better look sharp and get a copy of our correspondence in the Delacour case for Mr Alleyne.

This address in the presence of the public, his run upstairs and the porter he had gulped down so hastily confused the man and, as he sat down at his desk to get what was required, he realised how hopeless was the task of finishing his copy of the contract before half past five. The dark damp night was coming and he longed to spend it in the bars, drinking with his friends amid the glare of gas and the clatter of glasses. He got out the Delacour correspondence and passed out of the office. He hoped Mr Alleyne would not discover that the last two letters were missing.

The moist pungent perfume lay all the way up to Mr Alleyne's room. Miss Delacour was a middleaged woman of Jewish appearance. Mr Alleyne was said to be sweet on her or on her money. She came to the office often and stayed a long time when she came. She was sitting beside his desk now in an aroma of perfumes, smoothing the handle of her umbrella and nodding the great black feather in her hat. Mr Alleyne had swivelled his chair round to face her and thrown his right foot jauntily upon his left knee. The man put the correspondence on the desk and bowed respectfully but neither Mr Alleyne nor Miss Delacour took any notice of his bow. Mr Alleyne tapped a finger on the correspondence and then flicked it towards him as if to say *That's all right: you can go.*

The man returned to the lower office and sat down again at his desk. He stared intently at the incomplete phrase *In no case shall the said Bernard Bodley be.* . . . and thought how strange it was that the last three words began with the same letter. The chief clerk began to hurry Miss Parker, saying she would never have the letters typed in time for post. The man listened to the clicking of the machine for a few minutes and then set to work to finish his copy. But his head was not clear and his mind wandered away to the glare and rattle of the publichouse. It was a night for hot punches. He struggled on with his copy but when the clock struck five he had still fourteen pages to write. Blast it! He couldn't finish it in time. He longed to execrate aloud, to bring his fist down on something violently. He was so enraged that he wrote *Bernard Bernard* instead of *Bernard Bodley* and had to begin again on a clean sheet.

He felt strong enough to clear out the whole office single-handed. His body ached to do something, to rush out and revel in violence. All the indignities of his life enraged him. . . . Could he ask the cashier privately for an advance? No, the cashier was no good, no damn good: he wouldn't give an advance. . . . He knew where he would meet the boys: Leonard and O'Halloran and Nosey Flynn. The barometer of his emotional nature was set for a spell of riot.

His imagination had so abstracted him that his name was called twice before he answered. Mr Alleyne and Miss Delacour were standing outside the counter and all the clerks had turned round in anticipation of something. The man got up from his desk. Mr Alleyne began a tirade of abuse, saying that two letters were missing. The man answered that he knew nothing about them, that he had made a faithful copy. The tirade continued: it was so bitter and violent that the man could hardly restrain his fist from descending upon the head of the manikin before him:

—I know nothing about any other two letters, he said stupidly.

—*You—know—nothing.* Of course you know nothing, said Mr Alleyne. Tell me, he added, glancing first for approval to the lady beside him, do you take me for a fool? Do you think me an utter fool?

The man glanced from the lady's face to the little eggshaped head and back again: and almost before he was aware of it his tongue had found a felicitous moment:

—I don't think, sir, he said, that that's a fair question to put to me.

There was a pause in the very breathing of the clerks. Everyone was astounded (the author of the witticism no less than his neighbours) and Miss Delacour, who was a stout amiable person, began to smile broadly. Mr Alleyne flushed to the hue of a wild rose and his mouth twitched with a dwarf's passion. He shook his fist in the man's face till it seemed to vibrate like the knob of some electric machine:

—You impertinent ruffian! You impertinent ruffian! I'll make short work of you! Wait till you see! You'll apologise to me for your impertinence or you'll quit the office instanter! You'll quit this, I'm telling you, or you'll apologise to me!

He stood in a doorway opposite the offices watching to see if the cashier would come out alone. All the clerks passed and finally the cashier came out with the chief clerk. It was no use trying to say a word to him when he was with the chief clerk. The man felt that his position was bad enough. He had been obliged to offer an abject apology to Mr Alleyne for his impertinence but he knew what a hornet's nest the office would be for him. He could remember the way in which Mr Alleyne had hounded little Peake out of the office in order to make room for his own nephew. He felt savage and thirsty and revengeful, annoyed with himself and with everyone else. Mr Alleyne would never give him an hour's rest: his life would be a hell to him. He had made a proper fool of himself this time. Could he not keep his tongue in his cheek? But they had never pulled together from the first, he and Mr Alleyne, ever since the day Mr Alleyne had overheard him mimicking his north of Ireland accent to amuse Higgins and Miss Parker: that had been the beginning of it. He might have tried Higgins for the money but sure Higgins never had anything for himself. A man with two establishments to keep up, of course he couldn't.

He felt his great body again aching for the comfort of the publichouse. The fog had begun to chill him and he wondered could he touch Pat in O'Neill's. He could not touch him for more than a bob—and a bob was no use. Yet he must get money somewhere or other: he had spent his last penny for the g.p. and soon it would be too late for getting money anywhere. Suddenly, as he was fingering his watchchain, he thought of Terry Kelly's pawnoffice in Fleet Street. That was the dart! Why didn't he think of it sooner?

He went through the narrow alley of Temple Bar quickly, muttering to himself that they could all go to hell because he was going to have a good night of it. The clerk in Terry Kelly's said *A crown!* but the consignor held out for six shillings and in the end the six shillings was allowed him literally. He came out of the pawnoffice joyfully, making a little cylinder of the coins between his thumb and fingers. In Westmoreland Street the footpaths were crowded with young men and women returning from business and ragged urchins ran here and there yelling out the names of the evening editions. The man passed through the crowd, looking on the spectacle generally with proud satisfaction and staring masterfully at the officegirls. His head was full of the noises of tramgongs and swishing trolleys and his nose already sniffed the curling fumes of punch. As he walked on he preconsidered the terms in which he would narrate the incident to the boys:

—So, I just looked at him—coolly, you know— and looked at her. Then I looked back at him again—taking my time, you know. *I don't think that that's a fair question to put to me,* says I.

Nosey Flynn was sitting up in his usual corner of Davy Byrne's and when he heard the story he stood Farrington a half-one, saying it was as smart a thing as ever he heard. Farrington stood a drink in his turn. After a while O'Halloran and Paddy Leonard came in and the story was repeated to them. O'Halloran stood tailors of malt, hot, all round and told the story of the retort he had made to the chief clerk when he was in Callan's of Fownes's Street; but, as the retort was after the manner of the liberal shepherds in the eclogues, he had to admit that it was not so clever as Farrington's retort. At this Farrington told the boys to polish off that and have another.

Just as they were naming their poisons who should come in but Higgins! Of course he had to join in with the others. The men asked him to give his version of it and he did so with great vivacity for the sight of five small hot whiskies was very exhilarating. Everyone roared laughing when he showed the way in which Mr Alleyne shook his fist in Farrington's face. Then he imitated Farrington, saying *And here was my nabs, as cool as you please*, while Farrington looked at the company out of his heavy dirty eyes, smiling and at times drawing forth stray drops of liquor from his moustache with the aid of his lower lip.

When that round was over there was a pause. O'Halloran had money but neither of the other two seemed to have any so the whole party left the shop somewhat regretfully. At the corner of Duke Street Higgins and Nosey Flynn bevelled off to the left while the other three turned back towards the city. Rain was drizzling down on the cold streets and when they reached the Ballast Office, Farrington suggested the Scotch House. The bar was full of men and loud with the noise of tongues and glasses. The three men pushed past the whining matchsellers at the door and formed a little party at the corner of the counter. They began to exchange stories. Leonard introduced them to a young fellow named Weathers who was performing at the Tivoli as an acrobat and knockabout *artiste*. Farrington stood a drink all round. Weathers said he would take a small Irish and Apollinaris. Farrington, who had definite notions of what was what, asked the boys would they have an Apollinaris too: but the boys told Tim to make theirs hot. The talk became theatrical. O'Halloran stood a round and then Farrington stood another round, Weathers protesting that the hospitality was too Irish. He promised to get them in behind the scenes and introduce them to some nice girls. O'Halloran said that he and Leonard would go, but that Farrington wouldn't go because he was a married man and Farrington's heavy dirty eyes leered at the company in token that when he understood when he was being chaffed. Weathers made them all have just one little tincture at his expense and promised to meet them later on at Mulligan's in Poolbeg Street.

When the Scotch House closed they went round to Mulligan's. They went into the parlour at the back and O'Halloran ordered small hot specials all round. They were all beginning to feel mellow. Farrington was just standing another round when Weathers came back. Much to Farrington's relief he drank a glass of bitter this time. Funds were running low but they had enough to keep them going. Presently two young women with big hats and a young man in a check suit came in and sat at a table close by. Weathers saluted them and told the company that they were out of the Tivoli. Farrington's eyes wandered at every moment in the direction of one of the young women. There was something striking in her appearance. An immense scarf of peacockblue muslin was wound round her hat and knotted in a great bow under her chin; and she wore bright yellow gloves reaching to the elbow. Farrington gazed admiringly at the plump arm which she moved very often and with much grace; and, when after a little time she answered his gaze, he admired still more her large dark brown eyes. The oblique staring expression in them fascinated him. She glanced at him once or twice and, when the party was leaving the room, she brushed against his chair and said *O, pardon!* in a London accent. He watched her leave the room in the hope that she would look back at him but he was disappointed. He cursed his want of money and cursed all the rounds he had stood, particularly all the whiskies and Apollinaris which he had stood to Weathers. If there was one thing that he hated it was a sponge. He was so angry that he lost count of the conversation of his friends.

When Paddy Leonard called him he found that they were talking about feats of strength. Weathers was showing his biceps muscle to the company and boasting so much that the other two had called on Farrington to uphold the national honour. Farrington pulled up his sleeve accordingly and showed his biceps muscle to the company. The two arms were examined and compared and finally it was agreed to have a trial of strength. The table was cleared and the two men rested their elbows on it, clasping hands. When Paddy Leonard said *Go!* each was to try to bring down the other's hand on to the table. Farrington looked very serious and determined.

The trial began. After about thirty seconds Weathers brought his opponent's hand slowly down on to the table. Farrington's dark winecoloured face flushed darker still with anger and humiliation at having been defeated by such a stripling.

—You're not to put the weight of your body behind it. Play fair, he said.

—Who's not playing fair? said the other.

—Come on again. The two best out of three.

The trial began again. The veins stood out on Farrington's forehead and the pallor of Weathers' complexion changed to peony. Their hands and arms trembled under the stress. After a long struggle Weathers again brought his opponent's hand slowly on to the table. There was a murmur of applause from the spectators. The curate, who was standing beside the table, nodded his red head towards the victor and said with loutish familiarity:

—Ah! that's the knack!

—What the hell do you know about it? said Farrington fiercely, turning on the man. What do you put in your gab for?

—'Sh, 'sh! said O'Halloran, observing the violent expression of Farrington's face. Pony up, boys. We'll have just one little smahan more and then we'll be off!

A very sullenfaced man stood at the corner of O'Connell Bridge waiting for the little Sandymount tram to take him home. He was full of smouldering anger and revengefulness. He felt humiliated and discontented: he did not even feel drunk and he had only twopence in his pocket. He cursed everything. He had done for himself in the office, pawned his watch, spent all his money; and he had not even got drunk. He began to feel thirsty again and he longed to be back again in the hot reeking publichouse. He had lost his reputation as a strong man, having been defeated twice by a mere boy. His heart swelled with fury and when he thought of the woman in the big hat who had brushed against him and said *Pardon!* his fury nearly choked him.

His tram let him down at Shelbourne Road and he steered his great body along in the shadow of the wall of the barracks. He loathed returning to his home. When he went in by the sidedoor he found the kitchen empty and the kitchen fire nearly out. He bawled upstairs:

—Ada! Ada!

His wife was a little sharpfaced woman who bullied her husband when he was sober and was bullied by him when he was drunk. They had five children. A little boy came running down the stairs.

—Who is that? said the man peering through the darkness.

—Me, pa.

—Who are you? Charlie?

—No, pa. Tom.

—Where's your mother?

—She's out at the chapel.

—That's right. . . . Did she think of leaving any dinner for me?

—Yes, pa. I . . .

—Light the lamp. What do you mean by having the place in darkness? Are the other children in bed?

The man sat down heavily on one of the chairs while the little boy lit the lamp. He began to mimick his son's flat accent, saying half to himself: *At the chapel. At the chapel, if you please!* When the lamp was lit he banged his fist on the table and shouted:

—What's for my dinner?

—I'm . . . going to cook it, pa, said the little boy.

The man jumped up furiously and pointed to the fire:

—On that fire! You let the fire out! By God, I'll teach you to do that again!

He took a step to the door and seized the walking stick which was standing behind it:

—I'll teach you to let the fire out! he said, rolling up his sleeve in order to give his arm free play.

The little boy cried *O, pa!* and ran whimpering round the table but the man followed him and caught him by the coat. The little boy looked about him wildly but, seeing no way of escape, fell upon his knees.

—Now, you'll let the fire out the next time! said the man, striking at him viciously with the stick. Take that, you little whelp!

The boy uttered a squeal of pain as the stick cut his thigh. He clasped his hands together in the air and his voice shook with fright.

—O, pa! he cried. Don't beat me, pa! And I'll . . . I'll say a *Hail Mary* for you. . . . I'll say a *Hail Mary* for you, pa, if you don't beat me. . . . I'll say a *Hail Mary*. . . .

1914

Questions

1. How would you characterize the first exchange between Farrington and his supervisor, Mr. Alleyne? Does it seem as though Farrington might have a good explanation? Describe Alleyne as a supervisor.

2. Characterize the second exchange between Farrington and Alleyne. Do you think that Farrington's response is justifiable? Why or why not?

3. Have you or anyone you know worked for a similar supervisor? Comment on your or your acquaintance's experiences. Even without a personal or vicarious experience, how would you recommend dealing with such a supervisor?

4. How would you describe Farrington as a worker? Do you sympathize with him?

5. In the pub, do you think that Farrington delivers an accurate rendition of his exchange with Alleyne? Why does he tell his friends about the incident?

6. What does Farrington's response to his loss at arm wrestling reveal about his self-image?

7. As Farrington returns home, why is he so full of anger, revengefulness, humiliation, and discontent?

8. How would you characterize Farrington as a husband and a father? How does his work affect his behavior in these roles?

9. Joyce created Farrington approximately one hundred years ago, yet individuals like him still exist. Compare Farrington with an actual individual whom you know or one from fiction or film whom you have encountered.

10. How is Farrington similar to the men whom Sojourner Truth warns women about in "Colored Women and Work."

Edgar Lee Masters
(1868-1950)

Edgar Lee Masters was born in Kansas, but grew up in Illinois, near Spoon River, the setting for his most accomplished work. At sixteen years of age, Masters set type for a newspaper, and at Knox College, he published a few poems in the literary journal. After college, he practiced law for thirty years in Chicago, often representing the poor and needy. For five of those years, he had a partnership with Clarence Darrow, a leading member of the American Civil Liberties Union. In 1915, he published *Spoon River Anthology*, a series of epitaphs in verse form on fictional residents in the Spoon River cemetery. This often satirical volume was met with critical and commercial success. A second volume, *The New Spoon River* (1924), did not do nearly as well. In 1921, Masters quit practicing law and devoted himself to a literary career. He went on to publish fifty books—fiction, autobiography, biography, literary criticism, and volumes of poetry—but none has endured like his *Spoon River Anthology*, from which come " 'Butch' Weldy" and "Editor Whedon" (page 283).

'BUTCH' WELDY

After I got religion and steadied down
They gave me a job in the canning works,
And every morning I had to fill
The tank in the yard with gasoline,
That fed the blow-fires in the sheds
To heat the soldering irons.
And I mounted a rickety ladder to do it,
Carrying buckets full of the stuff.
One morning, as I stood there pouring,
The air grew still and seemed to heave,
And I shot up as the tank exploded,
And down I came with both legs broken
And my eyes burned crisp as a couple of eggs,
For someone left a blow-fire going,
And something sucked the flame in the tank.
The Circuit Judge said whoever did it

Was a fellow-servant of mine, and so
Old Rhodes' son didn't have to pay me.
And I sat on the witness stand as blind
As Jack the Fiddler, saying over and over,
"I didn't know him at all."

1915

Questions

1. What is the implication of the opening line and Butch Weldy's reference to getting religion?
2. What happened to Butch Weldy?
3. Why was he in court? What was the judge's decision?
4. Who is "Old Rhodes' son"? What is the implication of *old* and *son*?
5. What is the significance of the last line? What does it reveal about Weldy's character and his response to the judgment?
6. Does the poem make a subtle statement on behalf of labor organizations or unions? Why or why not?

Eugene O'Neill
(1888-1953)

Eugene Gladstone O'Neill, America's first world-class dramatist, was born in a Broadway hotel. As a child, he was educated by private tutors as he traveled on tour with his mother and father, the famous actor James O'Neill. He attended Princeton University in 1906, but was expelled the following year for a drunken prank. He worked as a seaman, which led him to unsuccessful gold prospecting in Honduras and a life of destitution in Buenos Aires. His secret marriage in 1909 ended in divorce three years later. His life from the time of his expulsion from Princeton to his 1912 suicide attempt is marked by depression, alcoholism, decadence, and an utter lack of direction.

The turning point for O'Neill came when he was diagnosed with tuberculosis in 1912. During his recovery, he began reading the works of the great dramatists of the world. In 1914, he attended George Pierce Baker's famous dramatic workshop at Harvard University. In 1916, the Provincetown Players presented O'Neill's first play, *Bound East for Cardiff*. In 1920, O'Neill's *Beyond the Horizon* opened on Broadway to positive reviews and a long run. Within five years, O'Neill's *The Emperor Jones, Anna Christie, The Hairy Ape, All God's Chillun Got Wings*, and *Desire under the Elms* all appeared on Broadway. By bringing ambitious plays to the forefront of the American theatrical scene, O'Neill revolutionized American drama as he inspired other playwrights and authors to write serious and challenging scripts for the stage. His other important works include *Strange Interlude* (1928), *Mourning Becomes Electra* (1931), *The Iceman Cometh* (1939), and the piercingly autobiographical *Long Day's Journey into Night* (1956). In addition to winning the Pulitzer Prize four times (still more times than any other dramatist), he was awarded the Nobel Prize for Literature in 1936—the only American playwright to be so honored. O'Neill's influence on American theater cannot be overstated.

THE HAIRY APE

Characters

Robert Smith, "Yank"	Her Aunt
Paddy	Second Engineer
Long	A Guard

Mildred Douglas   A Secretary of an Organization.

Stokers, Ladies, Gentlemen, etc.

Scenes

SCENE I: The firemen's forecastle of an ocean liner—an hour after sailing from
New York.
SCENE II: Section of promenade deck, two days out—morning.
SCENE III: The stokehole. A few minutes later.
SCENE IV: Same as Scene I. Half an hour later.
SCENE V: Fifth Avenue, New York. Three weeks later.
SCENE VI: An island near the city. The next night.
SCENE VII: In the city. About a month later.
SCENE VIII: In the city. Twilight of the next day.

Scene I

SCENE: *The fireman's forecastle of a transatlantic liner an hour after sailing from
New York for the voyage across. Tiers of narrow, steel bunks, three deep, on all
sides. An entrance in rear. Benches on the floor before the bunks. The room is
crowded with men, shouting, cursing, laughing, singing—a confused, inchoate
uproar swelling into a sort of unity, a meaning—the bewildered, furious, baffled defiance of a beast in a cage. Nearly all the men are drunk. Many bottles
are passed from hand to hand. All are dressed in dungaree pants, heavy ugly
shoes. Some wear singlets, but the majority are stripped to the waist.*

*The treatment of this scene, or of any other scene in the play, should by no
means be naturalistic. The effect sought after is a cramped space in the bowels of
a ship, imprisoned by white steel. The lines of bunks, the uprights supporting
them, cross each other like the steel framework of a cage. The ceiling crushes
down upon the men's heads. They cannot stand upright. This accentuates the
natural stooping posture which shoveling coal and the resultant over-development
of back and shoulder muscles have given them. The men themselves should
resemble those pictures in which the appearance of Neanderthal Man is guessed
at. All are hairy-chested, with long arms of tremendous power, and low, reced-
ing brows above their small, fierce, resentful eyes. All the civilized white races
are represented, but except for the slight differentiation in color of hair, skin,
eyes, all these men are alike.*

The curtain rises on a tumult of sound, YANK *is seated in the foreground.
He seems broader, fiercer, more truculent, more powerful, more sure of himself
than the rest. They respect his superior strength—the grudging respect of fear.
Then, too, he represents to them a self-expression, the very last word in what they
are, their most highly developed individual.*

VOICES. Gif me trink dere, you!
'Ave a wet!
Salute!
Gesundheit!

Skoal!
Drunk as a lord, God stiffen you!
Here's how!
Luck!
Pass back that bottle, damn you!
Pourin' it down his neck!
Ho, Froggy! Where the devil have you been?
La Touraine.
I hit him smash in *yaw*, py Gott!
Jenkins—the First—he's a rotten swine—
And the coppers nabbed him—and I run—
I like peer better. It don't pig head gif you.
A slut, I'm sayin'! She robbed me aslape—
To hell with 'em all!
You're a bloody liar!
Say dot again!

[*Commotion. Two men about to fight are pulled apart.*]
No scrappin' now!
To-night—
See who's the best man!
Bloody Dutchman!
To-night on the for'ard square.
I'll bet on Dutchy.
He packa da wallop, I tella you!
Shut up, Wop!
No fightin', maties. We're nil chums, ain't we?

[*A voice starts bawling a song.*]
"Beer, beer, glorious beer!
Fill yourselves right up to here."

YANK. [*For the first time seeming to take notice of the uproar about him, turns around threateningly—in a tone of contemptuous authority.*] Choke off dat noise! Where d'you get dat beer stuff? Beer, hell! Beer's for goils— and Dutchmen. Me for somep'n wit a kick to it! Gimme a drink, one of youse guys. [*Several bottles are eagerly offered. He takes a tremendous gulp at one of them; then, keeping the bottle in his hands, glares belligerently at the owner, who hastens to acquiesce in this robbery by saying.*] All righto, Yank. Keep it and have another. [*YANK contemptuously turns his back on the crowd again. For a second there is an embarrassed silence. Then—*]

VOICES. We must be passing the Hook.[3]
She's beginning to roll to it.
Six days in hell—and then Southampton.

---

[3]Sandy Hook, New Jersey

Py Yesus, I vish somepody take my first vatch for me!
Gittin' seasick, Square-head?
Drink up and forget it!
What's in your bottle?
Gin.
Dot's nigger trink.
Absinthe? It's doped. You'll go off your chump, Froggy!
Cochon!
Whisky, that's the ticket!
Where's Paddy?
Going asleep.
Sing us that whisky song, Paddy.

[*They all turn to an old, wizened Irishman who is dozing, very drunk, on the benches forward. His face is extremely monkey-like with all the sad, patient pathos of that animal in his small eyes.*]

Singa da song, Caruso Pat!
He's gettin' old. The drink is too much for him.
He's too drunk.

PADDY. [*Blinking about him, starts to his feet resentfully, swaying, holding on to the edge of a bunk.*] I'm never too drunk to sing. 'Tis only when I'm dead to the world I'd be wishful to sing at all. [*With a sort of sad contempt.*] "Whisky Johnny," ye want? A chanty, ye want? Now that's a queer wish from the ugly like of you, God help you. But no matter. [*He starts to sing in a thin, nasal, doleful tone.*]

Oh, whiskey is the life of man!
 Whiskey! O Johnny! [*They all join in on this.*]
Oh, whiskey is the life of man!
 Whiskey for my Johnny! [*Again chorus.*]
Oh, whiskey drove my old man mad!
 Whiskey! O Johnny!
Oh, whiskey drove my old man mad!
 Whiskey for my Johnny!

YANK. [*Again turning around scornfully.*] Aw hell! Nix on dat old sailing ship stuff! All dat bull's dead, see? And you're dead, too, yuh damned old Harp, on'y yuh don't know it. Take it easy, see? Give us a rest. Nix on de loud noise. [*With a cynical grin.*] Can't youse see I'm tryin' to t'ink?

ALL. [*Repeating the word after him as one with the same cynical amused mockery.*] Think! [*The chorused word has a brazen metallic quality as if their throats were phonograph horns. It is followed by a general uproar of hard, barking laughter.*]

VOICES. Don't be cracking your head wit ut, Yank.
You gat headache, py yingo!
One thing about it—it rhymes with drink!
Ha, ha, ha!

Drink, don't think!
Drink, don't think!
Drink, don't think!

[*A whole chorus of voices has taken up this refrain, stamping on the floor, pounding on the benches with fists.*]

YANK. [*Taking a gulp from his bottle—good-naturedly.*] Aw right. Can de noise. I get yuh de foist time.

[*The uproar subsides. A very drunken sentimental tenor begins to sing.*]

"Far away in Canada,
    Far across the sea,
There's a lass who fondly waits
    Making a home for me—"

YANK. [*Fiercely contemptuous.*] Shut up, yuh lousy boob! Where d'yuh get dat tripe? Home? Home, hell! I'll make a home for yuh! I'll knock yuh dead. Home! T'hell wit home! Where d'yuh get dat tripe? Dis is home, see? What d'yuh want wit home? [*Proudly.*] I runned away from mine when I was a kid. On'y too glad to beat it, dat was me. Home was lickings for me, dat's all. But yuh can bet your shoit no one ain't never licked me since! Wanter try it, any of youse? Huh! I guess not. [*In a more placated but still contemptuous tone.*] Goils waitin' for you, huh? Aw, hell! Dat's all tripe. Dey don't wait for no one. Dey'd doublecross yuh for a nickel. Dey're all tarts, get me? Treat 'em rough, dat's me. To hell wit'em. Tarts, dat's what, de whole bunch of 'em.

LONG. [*Very drunk, jumps on a bench excitedly, gesticulating with a bottle in his hand.*] Listen 'ere, Comrades! Yank 'ere is right. 'E says this 'ere stinkin' ship is our 'ome. And 'e says as 'ome is 'ell. And 'e's right! This is 'ell. We lives in 'ell, Comrades—and right enough we'll die in it. [*Raging.*] And who's ter blame, I arsks yer? We ain't. We wasn't born this rotten way. All men is borne free and ekal. That's in the bleedin' Bible, maties. But what d'they care for the Bible—them lazy, bloated swine what travels first cabin? Them's the ones. They dragged us down 'til we're on'y wage slaves in the bowels of a bloody ship, sweatin', burnin' up, eatin' coal dust! Hit's them's ter blame—the damned Capitalist clarss!

[*There had been a gradual murmur of contemptuous resentment rising among the men until now he is interrupted by a storm of catcalls, hisses, boos, hard laughter.*]

VOICES. Turn it off!
    Shut up!
    Sit down!
    Closa da face!
    Tamn fool! [*Etc.*]

YANK. [*Standing up and glaring at* LONG.] Sit down before I knock yuh down! [LONG *makes haste to efface himself.* YANK *goes on contemptuously.*]

De Bible, huh? De Cap'tlist class, huh? Aw nix on dat Salvation Army-Socialist bull. Git a soapbox! Hire a hall! Come and be saved, huh? Jerk us to Jesus, huh? Aw g'wan! I've listened to lots of guys like you, see. Yuh're all wrong. Wanter know what I t'ink? Yuh ain't no good for no one. Yuh're de bunk. Yuh ain't got no noive, get me? Yuh're yellow, dat's what. Yellow, dat's you. Say! What's dem slobs in de foist cabin got to do wit us? We're better men dan dey are, ain't we? Sure! One of us guys could clean up de whole mob wit one mit. Put one of 'em down here for one watch in de stokehole, what'd happen? Dey'd carry him off on a stretcher. Dem boids don't amount to nothin'. Dey're just baggage. Who makes dis old tub run? Ain't it us guys? Well den, we belong, don't we? We belong and dey don't. Dat's all. [*A loud chorus of approval.* YANK *goes on.*] As for dis bein' hell—aw, nuts! Yuh lost your noive, dat's what. Dis is a man's job, get me? It belongs. It runs dis tub. No stiffs need apply. But yuh're a stiff, see? Yuh're yellow, dat's you.

VOICES. [*With a great hard pride in them.*]
   Righto!
   A man's job!
   Talk is cheap, Long.
   He never could hold up his end.
   Divil take him!
   Yank's right. We make it go.
   Py Gott, Yank say right ting!
   We don't need no one cryin' over us.
   Makin' speeches.
   Throw him out!
   Yellow!
   Chuck him overboard!
   I'll break his jaw for him!

[*They crowd around* LONG *threateningly.*]

YANK. [*Half good-natured again—contemptuously.*] Aw, take it easy. Leave him alone. He ain't woith a punch. Drink up. Here's how, whoever owns dis. [*He takes a long swallow from his bottle. All drink with him. In a flash all is hilarious amiability again, backslapping, loud talk, etc.*]

PADDY. [*Who has been sitting in a blinking, melancholy daze—suddenly cries out in a voice full of old sorrow.*] We belong to this, you're saying? We make the ship to go, you're saying? Yerra[4] then, that Almighty God have pity on us! [*His voice runs into the wail of a keen,[5] he rocks back and forth on his bench. The men stare at him, startled and impressed in spite of themselves.*] Oh, to be back in the fine days of my youth, ochone![6] Oh, there was fine beautiful ships them days—clippers wid tall masts

[4]truly
[5]a lament for the dead
[6]*ochone:* alas (Irish)

touching the sky—fine strong men in them—men that was sons of the sea as if 'twas the mother that bore them. Oh, the clean skins of them, and the clear eyes, the straight backs and full chests of them! Brave men they was, and bold men surely! We'd be sailing out, bound down round the Horn maybe. We'd be making sail in the dawn, with a fair breeze, singing a chanty song wid no care to it. And astern the land would be sinking low and dying out, but we'd give it no heed but a laugh, and never a look behind. For the day that was, was enough, for we was free men—and I'm thinking 'tis only slaves do be giving heed to the day that's gone or the day to come—until they're old like me. [*With a sort of religious exaltation.*] Oh, to be scudding south again wid the power of the Trade Wind driving her on steady through the nights and the days! Full sail on her! Nights and days! Nights when the foam of the wake would be flaming wid fire, when the sky'd be blazing and winking wid stars. Or the full of the moon maybe. Then you'd see her driving through the gray night, her sails stretching aloft all silver and white, not a sound on the deck, the lot of us dreaming dreams, till you'd believe 'twas no real ship at all you was on but a ghost ship like the *Flying Dutchman* they say does be roaming the seas forevermore without touching a port. And these was the days, too. A warm sun on the clean decks. Sun warming the blood of you, and wind over the miles of shiny green ocean like strong drink to your lungs. Work—aye, hard work—but who'd mind that at all? Sure, you worked under the sky and 'twas work wid skill and daring to it. And wid the day done, in the dog watch, smoking me pipe at ease, the lookout would be raising land maybe, and we'd see the mountains of South Americy wid the red fire of the setting sun painting their white tops and the clouds floating by them! [*His tone of exaltation ceases. He goes on mournfully.*] Yerra, what's the use of talking? 'Tis a dead man's whisper. [*To* YANK *resentfully.*] 'Twas them days men belonged to ships, not now. 'Twas them days a ship was part of the sea, and a man was part of a ship, and the sea joined all together and made it one. [*Scornfully.*] Is it one wid this you'd be, Yank—black smoke from the funnels smudging the sea, smudging the decks—the bloody engines pounding and throbbing and shaking—wid divil a sight of sun or a breath of clean air—choking our lungs wid coal dust—breaking our backs and hearts in the hell of the stokehole—feeding the bloody furnace—feeding our lives along wid the coal, I'm thinking—caged in by steel from a sight of the sky like bloody apes in the Zoo! [*With a harsh laugh.*] Ho-ho, divil mend you! Is it to belong to that you're wishing? Is it a flesh and blood wheel of the engines you'd be?

YANK. [*Who has been listening with a contemptuous sneer, barks out the answer.*] Sure ting! Dat's me. What about it?

PADDY. [*As if to himself—with great sorrow.*] Me time is past due. That a great wave wid sun in the heart of it may sweep me over the side sometime I'd be dreaming of the days that's gone!

YANK. Aw, yuh crazy Mick! [*He springs to his feet and advances on* PADDY *threateningly—then stops, fighting some queer struggle within himself— lets his hands fall to his sides—contemptuously.*] Aw, take it easy. Yuh're aw right at dat. Yuh're bugs, dat's all—nutty as a cuckoo. All dat tripe yuh been pullin'—Aw, dat's all right. On'y it's dead, get me? Yuh don't belong no more, see. Yuh don't get de stuff. Yuh're too old. [*Disgustedly.*] But aw say, come up for air onct in a while, can't yuh? See what's happened since yuh croaked. [*He suddenly bursts forth vehemently, growing more and more excited.*] Say! Sure! Sure I meant it! What de hell—Say, lemme talk! Hey! Hey, you old Harp! Hey, youse guys! Say, listen to me—wait a moment—I gotter talk, see. I belong and he don't. He's dead but I'm livin'. Listen to me! Sure, I'm part of de engines! Why de hell not! Dey move, don't dey? Dey're speed, ain't dey! Dey smash trou, don't dey? Twenty-five knots a hour! Dat's goin' some! Dat's new stuff! Dat belongs! But him, he's too old. He gets dizzy. Say, listen. All dat crazy tripe about nights and days; all dat crazy tripe about stars and moons; all dat crazy tripe about suns and winds, fresh air and de rest of it—Aw hell, dat's all a dope dream! Hittin' de pipe of de past, dat's what he's doin'. He's old and don't belong no more. But me, I'm young! I'm in de pink! I move wit it! It, get me! I mean de ting dat's de guts of all dis. It ploughs trou all de tripe he's been sayin'. It blows dat up! It knocks dat dead! It slams dat offen de face of de oith; It, get me! De engines and de coal and de smoke and all de rest of it! He can't breathe and swallow coal dust, but I kin, see? Dat's fresh air for me! Dat's food for me! I'm new, get me? Hell in de stokehole? Sure! It takes a man to work in hell. Hell, sure, dat's my fav'rite climate. I eat it up! I git fat on it! It's me makes it hot! It's me makes it roar! It's me makes it move! Sure, on'y for me everyting stops. It all goes dead, get me? De noise and smoke and all de engines movin' de woild, dey stop. Dere ain't nothin' no more! Dat's what I'm sayin'. Everyting else dat makes de woild move, somep'n makes it move. It can't move witout somep'n else, see? Den yuh get down to me. I'm at de bottom, get me! Dere ain't nothin' foither. I'm de end! I'm de start! I start somep'n and de woild moves! It—dat's me!—de new dat's moiderin' de old! I'm de ting in coal dat makes it boin; I'm steam and oil for de engines; I'm de ting in noise dat makes yuh hear it; I'm smoke and express trains and steamers and factory whistles; I'm de ting in gold dat makes it money! And I'm what makes iron into steel! Steel, dat stands for de whole ting! And I'm steel—steel—steel! I'm de muscles in steel, de punch behind it! [*As he says this he pounds with his fist against the steel bunks. All the men, roused to a pitch of frenzied self-glorification by his speech, do likewise. There is a deafening metallic roar, through which* YANK's *voice can be heard bellowing.*] Slaves, hell! We run de whole woiks. All de rich guys dat tink dey're somep'n, dey ain't nothin'! Dey don't belong. But us guys, we're in de move, we're at de bottom, de whole ting is us! [PADDY *from the start of* YANK's *speech has been taking one gulp after another from his bottle, at first frightenedly, as if he were afraid to listen, then desperately, as if to drown his senses, but finally has achieved complete indifferent, even amused, drunkenness.* YANK *sees his lips moving. He quells the uproar with a shout.*] Hey, youse guys, take it easy! Wait a moment! De nutty Harp is sayin' somep'n.

PADDY. [*Is heard now—throws his head back with a mocking burst of laughter.*] Ho-ho-ho-ho-ho—

YANK. [*Drawing back his fist, with a snarl.*] Aw! Look out who yuh're givin' the bark!

PADDY. [*Begins to sing the "Miller of Dee" with enormous good nature.*]

> "I care for nobody, no, not I,
> And nobody cares for me."

YANK. [*Good-natured himself in a flash, interrupts* PADDY *with a slap on the bare back like a report.*] Dat's de stuff! Now yuh're gettin' wise to somep'n. Care for nobody, dat's de dope! To hell wit 'em all! And nix on nobody else carin'. I kin care for myself, get me! [*Eight bells sound, muffled, vibrating through the steel walls as if some enormous brazen gong were imbedded in the heart of the ship. All the men jump up mechanically, file through the door silently close upon each other's heels in what is very like a prisoners' lockstep.* YANK *slaps* PADDY *on the back.*] Our watch, yuh old Harp! [*Mockingly.*] Come on down in hell. Eat up de coal dust. Drink in de heat. It's it, see! Act like yuh liked it, yuh better—or croak yuhself.

PADDY. [*With jovial defiance.*] To the divil wid it! I'll not report this watch. Let thim log me and be damned. I'm no slave the like of you. I'll be sittin' here at me ease, and drinking, and thinking, and dreaming dreams.

YANK. [*Contemptuously.*] Tinkin' and dreamin', what'll that get yuh? What's tinkin' got to do with it? We move, don't we? Speed, ain't it? Fog, dat's all you stand for. But we drive trou dat, don't we? We split dat up and smash trou—twenty-five knots a hour! [*Turns his back on* PADDY *scornfully.*] Aw, yuh make me sick! Yuh don't belong! [*He strikes out the door in rear.* PADDY *hums to himself, blinking drowsily.*]

[*Curtain.*]

Scene II

SCENE: *Two days out. A section of the promenade deck.* MILDRED DOUGLAS *and her* AUNT *are discovered reclining in deck chairs. The former is a girl of twenty, slender, delicate, with a pale, pretty face marred by a self-conscious expression of disdainful superiority. She looks fretful, nervous, and discontented, bored by her own anemia. Her* AUNT *is a pompous and proud—and fat—old lady. She is a type even to the point of double chin and lorgnette. She is dressed pretentiously, as if afraid her face alone would never indicate her position in life.* MILDRED *is dressed all in white.*

The impression to be conveyed by this scene is one of the beautiful, vivid life of the sea all about—sunshine on the deck in a great flood, the fresh sea wind blowing across it. In the midst of this, these two incongruous, artificial figures, inert and disharmonious, the elder like a gray lump of dough touched up with rouge, the younger looking as if the vitality of her stock had been sapped before she was conceived, so that she is the expression not of its life energy but merely of the artificialities that energy had won for itself in the spending.

MILDRED. [*Looking up with affected dreaminess.*] How the black smoke swirls back against the sky! Is it not beautiful?

AUNT. [*Without looking up.*] I dislike smoke of any kind.

MILDRED. My great-grandmother smoked a pipe—a clay pipe.

AUNT. [*Ruffling.*] Vulgar.

MILDRED. She was too distant a relative to be vulgar. Time mellows pipes.

AUNT. [*Pretending boredom but irritated.*] Did the sociology you took up at college teach, you that—to play the ghoul on every possible occasion, excavating old bones? Why not let your great-grandmother rest in her grave?

MILDRED. [*Dreamily.*] With her pipe beside her—puffing in Paradise.

AUNT. [*With spite.*] Yes, you are a natural born ghoul. You are even getting to look like one, my dear.

MILDRED. [*In a passionless tone.*] I detest you, Aunt. [*Looking at her critically.*] Do you know what you remind me of? Of a cold pork pudding against a background of linoleum tablecloth in the kitchen of a—but the possibilities are wearisome. [*She closes her eyes.*]

AUNT. [*With a bitter laugh.*] Merci for your candor. But since I am and must be your chaperon—in appearance, at least—let us patch up some sort of armed truce. For my part you are quite free to indulge any pose of eccentricity that beguiles you—as long as you observe the amenities—

MILDRED. [*Drawling.*] The inanities?

AUNT. [*Going on as if she hadn't heard.*] After exhausting the morbid thrills of social service work on New York's East Side—how they must have hated you, by the way, the poor that you made so much poorer in their own eyes!—you are now bent on making your slumming international. Well, I hope Whitechapel[7] will provide the needed nerve tonic. Do not ask me to chaperon you there, however. I told your father I would not. I loathe deformity. We will hire an army of detectives and you may investigate everything—they allow you to see.

MILDRED. [*Protesting with a trace of genuine earnestness.*] Please do not mock at my attempts to discover how the other half lives. Give me credit for some sort of groping sincerity in that at least. I would like to help

---

[7]a poor district in London.

them. I would like to be some use in the world. Is it my fault I don't know how? I would like to be sincere, to touch life somewhere. [*With weary bitterness.*] But I'm afraid I have neither the vitality nor integrity. All that was burnt out in our stock before I was born. Grandfather's blast furnaces, flaming to the sky, melting steel, making millions—then father keeping those home fires burning, making more millions—and little me at the tail-end of it all. I'm a waste product in the Bessemer process—like the millions. Or rather, I inherit the acquired trait of the by-product, wealth, but none of the energy, none of the strength of the steel that made it. I am sired by gold and damned by it, as they say at the race track—damned in more ways than one. [*She laughs mirthlessly.*]

AUNT. [*Unimpressed—superciliously.*] You seem to be going in for sincerity to-day. It isn't becoming to you, really—except as an obvious pose. Be as artificial as you are, I advise. There's a sort of sincerity in that, you know. And, after all, you must confess you like that better.

MILDRED. [*Again affected and bored.*] Yes, I suppose I do. Pardon me for my outburst. When a leopard complains of its spots, it must sound rather grotesque. [*In a mocking tone.*] Purr, little leopard. Purr, scratch, tear, kill, gorge yourself and be happy—only stay in the jungle where your spots are camouflage. In a cage they make you conspicuous.

AUNT. I don't know what you are talking about.

Mildred. It would be rude to talk about anything to you. Let's just talk. [*She looks at her wrist watch.*] Well, thank goodness, it's about time for them to come for me. That ought to give me a new thrill, Aunt.

AUNT. [*Affectedly troubled.*] You don't mean to say you're really going? The dirt—the heat must be frightful—

MILDRED. Grandfather started as a puddler. I should have inherited an immunity to heat that would make a salamander shiver. It will be fun to put it to the test.

AUNT. But don't you have to have the captain's—or someone's—permission to visit the stokehole?

MILDRED. [*With a triumphant smile.*] I have it—both his and the chief engineer's. Oh, they didn't want to at first, in spite of my social service credentials. They didn't seem a bit anxious that I should investigate how the other half lives and works on a ship. So I had to tell them that my father, the president of Nazareth Steel, chairman of the board of directors of this line, had told me it would be all right.

AUNT. He didn't.

MILDRED. How naïve age makes one! But I said he did, Aunt. I even said he had given me a letter to them—which I had lost. And they were afraid to take the chance that I might be lying. [*Excitedly.*] So it's ho! for the stokehole. The second engineer is to escort me. [*Looking at her watch again.*] It's time. And here he comes, I think. [*The* SECOND ENGINEER *enters. He is a husky, fine-looking man of thirty-five or so. He stops before the two and tips his cap, visibly embarrassed and ill-at-ease.*]

SECOND ENGINEER. Miss Douglas?

MILDRED. Yes. [*Throwing off her rugs and getting to her feet.*] Are we all ready to start?

SECOND ENGINEER. In just a second, ma'am. I'm waiting for the Fourth. He's coming along.

MILDRED. [*With a scornful smile.*] You don't care to shoulder this responsibility alone, is that it?

SECOND ENGINEER. [*Forcing a smile.*] Two are better than one. [*Disturbed by her eyes, glances out to sea—blurts out.*] A fine day we're having.

MILDRED. Is it?

SECOND ENGINEER. A nice warm breeze—

MILDRED. It feels cold to me.

SECOND ENGINEER. But it's hot enough in the sun—

MILDRED. Not hot enough for me. I don't like Nature. I was never athletic.

SECOND ENGINEER. [*Forcing a smile.*] Well, you'll find it hot enough where you're going.

MILDRED. Do you mean hell?

SECOND ENGINEER. [*Flabbergasted, decides to laugh.*] Ho-ho! No, I mean the stokehole.

MILDRED. My grandfather was a puddler. He played with boiling steel.

SECOND ENGINEER. [*All at sea—uneasily.*] Is that so? Hum, you'll excuse me, ma'am, but are you intending to wear that dress?

MILDRED. Why not?

SECOND ENGINEER. You'll likely rub against oil and dirt. It can't be helped.

MILDRED. It doesn't matter. I have lots of white dresses.

SECOND ENGINEER. I have an old coat you might throw over—

MILDRED. I have fifty dresses like this. I will throw this one into the sea when I come back. That ought to wash it clean, don't you think?

SECOND ENGINEER. [*Doggedly.*] There's ladders to climb down that are none too clean—and dark alleyways—

MILDRED. I will wear this very dress and none other.

SECOND ENGINEER. No offense meant. It's none of my business. I was only warning you—

MILDRED. Warning? That sounds thrilling.

SECOND ENGINEER. [*Looking down the deck—with a sigh of relief.*] There's the Fourth now. He's waiting for us. If you'll come—

MILDRED. Go on. I'll follow you. [*He goes.* MILDRED *turns a mocking smile on her aunt.*] An oaf—but a handsome, virile oaf.

AUNT. [*Scornfully.*] Poser!

MILDRED. Take care. He said there were dark alleyways—

AUNT. [*In the same tone.*] Poser!

MILDRED. [*Biting her lips angrily.*] You are right. But would that my millions were not so anemically chaste!

AUNT. Yes, for a fresh pose I have no doubt you would drag the name of Douglas in the gutter!

MILDRED. From which it sprang. Goodby, Aunt. Don't pray too hard that I may fall into the fiery furnace.

AUNT. Poser!

MILDRED. [*Viciously.*] Old hag! [*She slaps her* AUNT *insultingly across the face and walks off, laughing gayly.*]

AUNT. [*Screams after her.*] I said poser!
    [*Curtain.*]

Scene III

SCENE: *The stokehole. In the rear, the dimly-outlined bulks of the furnaces and boilers. High overhead one hanging electric bulb sheds just enough light through the murky air laden with coal dust to pile up masses of shadows everywhere. A line of men, stripped to the waist, is before the furnace doors. They bend over, looking neither to right nor left, handling their shovels as if they were part of their bodies, with a strange, awkward, swinging rhythm. They use the shovels to throw open the furnace doors. Then from these fiery round holes in the black a flood of terrific light and heat pours full upon the men who are outlined in silhouette in the crouching, inhuman attitudes of chained gorillas. The men shovel with a rhythmic motion, swinging as on a pivot from the coal which lies in heaps on the floor behind to hurl it into the flaming mouths before them. There is a tumult of noise—the brazen clang of the furnace doors as they are flung open or slammed shut, the grating, teeth-gritting grind of steel against steel, of crunching coal. This clash of sounds stuns one's ears with its rending dissonance. But there is order in it, rhythm, a mechanical regulated recurrence, a tempo. And rising above all, making the air hum with the quiver of liberated energy, the roar of leaping flames in the furnaces, the monotonous throbbing beat of the engines.*

As the curtain rises, the furnace doors are shut. The men are taking a breathing spell. One or two are arranging the coal behind them, pulling it into more accessible heaps. The others can be dimly made out leaning on their shovels in relaxed attitudes of exhaustion.

PADDY. [*From somewhere in the line—plaintively.*] Yerra, will this divil's own watch nivir end? Me back is broke. I'm destroyed entirely.

YANK. [*From the center of the line—with exuberant scorn.*] Aw, yuh make me sick! Lie down and croak, why don't yuh? Always beefin', dat's you!

Say, dis is a cinch! Dis was made for me! It's my meat, get me! [*A whistle is blown—a thin, shrill note from somewhere overhead in the darkness,* YANK *curses without resentment.*] Dere's de damn engineer crackin' de whip. He tinks we're loafin'.

PADDY. [*Vindictively.*] God stiffen him!

YANK. [*In an exultant tone of command.*] Come on, youse guys! Git into de game! She's gittin' hungry! Pile some grub in her. Trow it into her belly! Come on now, all of youse! Open her up!

[*At this last all the men, who have followed his movements of getting into position, throw open their furnace doors with a deafening clang. The fiery light floods over their shoulders as they bend round for the coal. Rivulets of sooty sweat have traced maps on their backs. The enlarged muscles form bunches of high light and shadow.*]

YANK. [*Chanting a count as he shovels without seeming effort.*] One—two—tree—[*His voice rising exultantly in the joy of battle.*] Dat's de stuff! Let her have it! All togedder now! Sling it into her! Let her ride! Shoot de piece now! Call de toin on her! Drive her into it! Feel her move! Watch her smoke! Speed, dat's her middle name! Give her coal, youse guys! Coal, dat's her booze! Drink it up, baby! Let's see yuh sprint! Dig in and gain a lap! Dere she go-o-e-s. [*This last in the chanting formula of the gallery gods at the six-day bike race. He slams his furnace door shut. The others do likewise with as much unison as their wearied bodies will permit. The effect is of one fiery eye after another being blotted out with a series of accompanying bangs.*]

PADDY. [*Groaning.*] Me back is broke. I'm bate out—bate—

[*There is a pause. Then the inexorable whistle sounds again from the dim regions above the electric light. There is a growl of cursing rage from all sides.*]

YANK. [*Shaking his fist upward—contemptuously.*] Take it easy dere, you! Who d'yuh tinks runnin' dis game, me or you? When I git ready, we move. Not before! When I git ready, get me!

VOICES. [*Approvingly.*] That's the stuff!
　　　Yank tal him, py golly!
　　　Yank ain't afeerd.
　　　Goot poy, Yank!
　　　Give him hell!
　　　Tell 'im 'e's a bloody swine!
　　　Bloody slave-driver!

YANK. [*Contemptuously.*] He ain't got no noive. He's yellow, get me? All de engineers is yellow. Dey got streaks a mile wide. Aw, to hell wit him! Let's move, youse guys. We had a rest. Come on, she needs it! Give her pep! It ain't for him. Him and his whistle, dey don't belong. But we belong, see! We gotter feed de baby! Come on! [*He turns and flings his furnace door open. They all follow his lead. At this instant the* SECOND *and* FOURTH ENGINEERS *enter from the darkness on the left with* MILDRED *between them. She starts, turns paler, her pose is crumbling, she shivers with fright in spite of the blazing heat, but forces herself to leave the* ENGINEERS *and take a few steps nearer the men. She is right behind* YANK. *All this happens quickly while the men have their backs turned.*]

YANK. Come on, youse guys! [*He is turning to get coal when the whistle sounds again in a peremptory, irritating note. This drives* YANK *into a sudden fury. While the other men have turned full around and stopped dumfounded by the spectacle of* MILDRED *standing there in her white dress,* YANK *does not turn far enough to see her. Besides, his head is thrown back, he blinks upward through the murk trying to find the owner of the whistle, he brandishes his shovel murderously over his head in one hand, pounding on his chest, gorilla-like, with the other, shouting.*] Toin off dat whistle! Come down outa dere, yuh yellow, brass-buttoned, Belfast bum, yuh! Come down and I'll knock yer brains out! Yuh lousy, stinkin', yellow mut of a Catholic-moiderin' bastard! Come down and I'll moider yuh! Pullin' dat whistle on me, huh? I'll show yuh! I'll crash yer skull in! I'll drive yer teet' down yer troat! I'll slam yer nose trou de back of yer head! I'll cut yer guts out for a nickel, yuh lousy boob, yuh dirty, crummy, muck-eatin' son of a—[*Suddenly he becomes conscious of all the other men staring at something directly behind his back. He whirls defensively with a snarling, murderous growl, crouching to spring, his lips drawn back over his teeth, his small eyes gleaming ferociously. He sees* MILDRED, *like a white apparition in the full light from the open furnace doors. He glares into her eyes, turned to stone. As for her, during his speech she has listened, paralyzed with horror, terror, her whole personality crushed, beaten in, collapsed, by the terrific impact of this unknown, abysmal brutality, naked and shameless. As she looks at his gorilla face, and his eyes bore into hers, she utters a low, choking cry and shrinks away from him, putting both hands up before her eyes to shut out the sight of his face, to protect her own. This startles* YANK *to a reaction. His mouth falls open, his eyes grow bewildered.*]

MILDRED. [*About to faint—to the* ENGINEERS, *who now have her one by each arm—whimperingly.*] Take me away! Oh, the filthy beast! [*She faints. They carry her quickly back, disappearing in the darkness at the left, rear. An iron door clangs shut. Rage and bewildered fury rush back on* YANK. *He feels himself insulted in some unknown fashion in the very heart of his pride. He roars.*] God damn yuh! [*And hurls his shovel after them at the door which has just closed. It hits the steel bulkhead with a clang and falls clattering on the steel floor. From overhead the whistle sounds again in a long, angry, insistent command.*]

[*Curtain.*]

Scene IV

SCENE: *The firemen's forecastle.* YANK'S *watch has just come off duty and had dinner. Their faces and bodies shine from a soap and water scrubbing but around their eyes, where a hasty dousing does not touch, the coal dust sticks like black makeup, giving them a queer, sinister expression.* YANK *has not washed either face or body. He stands out in contrast to them, a blackened, brooding figure. He is seated forward on a bench in the exact attitude of Rodin's "The Thinker."*[8] *The others, most of them smoking pipes, are staring at* YANK *half-apprehensively, as if fearing an outburst; half-amusedly, as if they saw a joke somewhere that tickled them.*

> VOICES. He ain't ate nothin'.
>> Py golly, a fallar gat to gat grub in him.
>> Divil a lie.
>> Yank feeda da fire, no feeda da face.
>> Ha-ha.
>> He ain't even washed hisself.
>> He's forgot.
>> Hey, Yank, you forgot to wash.

> YANK. [*Sullenly.*] Forgot nothin'! To hell wit washin'.

> VOICES. It'll stick to you.
>> It'll get under your skin.
>> Give yer the bleedin' itch, that's wot.
>> It makes spots on you—like a leopard.
>> Like a piebald nigger, you mean.
>> Better wash up, Yank.
>> You sleep better.
>> Wash up, Yank.
>> Wash up! Wash up!

> YANK. [*Resentfully.*] Aw say, youse guys. Lemme alone. Can't youse see I'm tryin' to tink?

> ALL. [*Repeating the word after him as one with cynical mockery.*] Think! [*The word has a brazen, metallic quality as if their throats were phonograph horns. It is followed by a chorus of hard, barking laughter.*]

> YANK. [*Springing to his feet and glaring at them belligerently.*] Yes, tink! Tink, dat's what I said. What about it? [*They are silent, puzzled by his sudden resentment at what used to be one of his jokes,* YANK *sits down again in the same attitude of "The Thinker."*]

> VOICES. Leave him alone.
>> He's got a grouch on.
>> Why wouldn't he?

---

[8]Auguste Rodin (1840–1917), a French sculptor whose creation, *The Thinker*, sits in deep contemplation.

PADDY. [*With a wink at the others.*] Sure I know what's the matther. 'Tis aisy to see. He's fallen in love, I'm telling you.

ALL. [*Repeating the word after him as one with cynical mockery.*] Love! [*The word has a brazen, metallic quality as if their throats were phonograph horns. It is followed by a chorus of hard, barking laughter.*]

YANK. [*With a contemptuous snort.*] Love, hell! Hate, dat's what. I've fallen in hate, get me?

PADDY. [*Philosophically.*] 'Twould take a wise man to tell one from the other. [*With a bitter, ironical scorn, increasing as he goes on.*] But I'm telling you it's love that's in it. Sure what else but love for us poor bastes in the stokehole would be bringing a fine lady, dressed like a white quane, down a mile of ladders and steps to be havin' a look at us?

[*A growl of anger goes up from all sides.*]

LONG. [*Jumping on a bench—hectically.*] Hinsultin' us! Hinsultin' us, the bloody cow! And them bloody engineers! What right 'as they got to be exhibitin' us 's if we was bleedin' monkeys in a menagerie? Did we sign for hinsults to our dignity as 'onest workers? Is that in the ship's articles? You kin bloody well bet it ain't! But I knows why they done it. I arsked a deck steward 'o she was and 'e told me. 'Er old man's a bleedin' millionaire, a bloody Capitalist! 'E's got enuf bloody gold to sink this bleedin' ship! 'E makes arf the bloody steel in the world! 'E owns this bloody boat! And you and me, Comrades, we're 'is slaves! And the skipper and mates and engineers, they're 'is slaves, too! And she's 'is bloody daughter and we're all 'er slaves, too! And she gives 'er orders as 'ow she wants to see the bloody animals below decks and down they takes 'er!

[*There is a roar of rage from all sides.*]

YANK. [*Blinking at him bewilderedly.*] Say! Wait a moment! Is all dat straight goods?

LONG. Straight as string! The bleedin' steward as waits on 'em, 'e told me about 'er. And what're we goin' ter do, I arsks yer? 'Ave we got ter swaller 'er hinsults like dogs? It ain't in the ship's articles. I tell yer we got a case. We kin go to law—

YANK. [*With abysmal contempt.*] Hell! Law!

ALL. [*Repeating the word after him as one with cynical mockery.*] Law! [*The word has a brazen metallic quality as if their throats were phonograph horns. It is followed by a chorus of hard, barking laughter.*]

LONG. [*Feeling the ground slipping from under his feet—desperately.*] As voters and citizens we kin force the bloody governments—

YANK. [*With abysmal contempt.*] Hell! Governments!

ALL. [*Repeating the word after him as one with cynical mockery.*] Governments! [*The word has a brazen metallic quality as if their throats were phonograph horns. It is followed by a chorus of hard, barking laughter.*]

LONG. [*Hysterically.*] We're free and equal in the sight of God—

YANK. [*With abysmal contempt.*] Hell! God!

ALL. [*Repeating the word after him as one with cynical mockery.*] God! [*The word has a brazen metallic quality as if their throats were phonograph horns. It is followed by a chorus of hard, barking laughter.*]

YANK. [*Witheringly.*] Aw, join de Salvation Army!

ALL. Sit down! Shut up! Damn fool! Sea-lawyer!

[LONG *slinks back out of sight.*]

PADDY. [*Continuing the trend of his thoughts as if he had never been interrupted—bitterly.*] And there she was standing behind us, and the Second pointing at us like a man you'd hear in a circus would be saying: In this cage is a queerer kind of baboon than ever you'd find in darkest Africy. We roast them in their own sweat—and be damned if you won't hear some of thim saying they like it! [*He glances scornfully at* YANK.]

YANK. [*With a bewildered uncertain growl.*] Aw!

PADDY. And there was Yank roarin' curses and turning round wid his shovel to brain her—and she looked at him, and him at her—

YANK. [*Slowly.*] She was all white. I thought she was a ghost. Sure.

PADDY. [*With heavy, biting sarcasm.*] 'Twas love at first sight, divil a doubt of it! If you'd seen the endearin' look on her pale mug when she shriveled away with her hands over her eyes to shut out the sight of him! Sure, 'twas as if she'd seen a great hairy ape escaped from the Zoo!

YANK. [*Stung—with a growl of rage.*] Aw!

PADDY. And the loving way Yank heaved his shovel at the skull of her, only she was out the door! [*A grin breaking over his face.*] 'Twas touching, I'm telling you! It put the touch of home, swate home in the stokehole.

[*There is a roar of laughter from all.*]

YANK. [*Glaring at* PADDY *menacingly.*] Aw, choke dat off, see!

PADDY. [*Not heeding him—to the others.*] And her grabbin' at the Second's arm for protection. [*With a grotesque imitation of a woman's voice.*] Kiss me, Engineer dear, for it's dark down here and me old man's in Wall Street making money! Hug me tight, darlin', for I'm afeerd in the dark and me mother's on deck makin' eyes at the skipper!

[*Another roar of laughter.*]

YANK. [*Threateningly.*] Say! What yuh tryin' to do, kid me, yuh old Harp?

PADDY. Divil a bit! Ain't I wishin' myself you'd brained her?

YANK. [*Fiercely.*] I'll brain her! I'll brain her yet, wait 'n' see! [*Coming over to* PADDY—*slowly.*] Say, is dat what she called me—a hairy ape?

PADDY. She looked it at you if she didn't say the word itself.

YANK. [*Grinning horribly.*] Hairy ape, huh? Sure! Dat's de way she looked at me, aw right. Hairy ape! So dat's me, huh? [*Bursting into rage—as if she were still in front of him.*] Yuh skinny tart! Yuh whitefaced bum, yuh! I'll show yuh who's a ape! [*Turning to the others, bewilderment seizing him again.*] Say, youse guys. I was bawlin' him out for pullin' de whistle on us. You heard me. And den I seen youse lookin' at somep'n and I thought he'd sneaked down to come up in back of me, and I hopped around to knock him dead wit de shovel. And dere she was wit de light on her! Christ, yuh coulda pushed me over with a finger! I was scared, get me? Sure! I thought she was a ghost, see? She was all in white like dey wrap around stiffs. You seen her. Kin yuh blame me? She didn't belong, dat's what. And den when I come to and seen it was a real skoit and seen de way she was lookin' at me—like Paddy said—Christ, I was sore, get me? I don't stand for dat stuff from nobody. And I flung de shovel—on'y she'd bear it. [*Furiously.*] I wished it'd banged her! I wished it'd knocked her block off!

LONG. And be 'anged for murder or 'lectrocuted? She ain't bleedin' well worth it.

YANK. I don't give a damn what! I'd be square wit her, wouldn't I? Tink I wanter let her put somep'n over on me? Tink I'm goin' to let her git away wit dat stuff? Yuh don't know me! No one ain't never put nothin' over on me and got away wit it, see!—not dat kind of stuff—no guy and no skoit neither! I'll fix her! Maybe she'll come down again—

VOICE. No chance, Yank. You scared her out of a year's growth.

YANK. I scared her? Why de hell should I scare her? Who de hell is she? Ain't she de same as me? Hairy ape, huh? [*With his old confident bravado.*] I'll show her I'm better'n her, if she on'y knew it. I belong and she don't, see! I move and she's dead! Twenty-five knots a hour, dat's me! Dat carries her but I make dat. She's on'y baggage. Sure! [*Again bewilderedly.*] But, Christ, she was funny lookin'! Did yuh pipe her hands? White and skinny. Yuh could see de bones trough 'em. And her mush,[9] dat was dead white, too. And her eyes, dey was like dey'd seen a ghost. Me, dat was! Sure! Hairy ape! Ghost, huh? Look at dat arm! [*He extends his right arm, swelling out the great muscles.*] I coulda took her wit dat, wit just my little finger even, and broke her in two. [*Again bewilderedly.*] Say, who is dat skoit, huh? What is she? What's she come from? Who made her? Who give her de noive to look at me like dat? Dis ting's got my goat right. I don't get her. She's new to me. What does a skoit like her mean, huh? She don't belong, get me! I can't see her. [*With growing anger.*] But one ting I'm wise to, aw right, aw right! Youse all kin bet your shoits I'll get even wit her. I'll show her if she tinks she—She grinds de organ and I'm on de string, huh? I'll fix her! Let her come down again and I'll fling her in de furnace! She'll move

---

[9]face

den! She won't shiver at nothin', den! Speed, dat'll be her! She'll belong den! [*He grins horribly.*]

PADDY. She'll never come. She's had her belly-full, I'm telling you. She'll be in bed now, I'm thinking, wid ten doctors and nurses feedin' her salts to clean the fear out of her.

YANK. [*Enraged.*] Yuh tink I made her sick, too, do yuh? Just lookin' at me, huh? Hairy ape, huh? [*In a frenzy of rage.*] I'll fix her! I'll tell her where to git off! She'll git down on her knees and take it back or I'll burst de face offen her! [*Shaking one fist upward and beating on his chest with the other.*] I'll find yuh! I'm comin', d'yuh hear? I'll fix yuh, God damn yuh! [*He makes a rush for the door.*]

VOICES. Stop him!
He'll get shot!
He'll murder her!
Trip him up!
Hold him!
He's gone crazy!
Gott, he's strong!
Hold him down!
Look out for a kick!
Pin his arms!

[*They have all piled on him and, after a fierce struggle, by sheer weight of numbers have borne him to the floor just inside the door.*]

PADDY. [*Who has remained detached.*] Kape him down till he's cooled off. [*Scornfully.*] Yerra, Yank, you're a great fool. Is it payin' attention at all you are to the like of that skinny sow widout one drop of rale blood in her?

YANK. [*Frenziedly, from the bottom of the heap.*] She done me doit! She done me doit, didn't she? I'll git square wit her! I'll get her some way! Git offen me, youse guys! Lemme up! I'll show her who's a ape!
[*Curtain.*]

Scene V

SCENE: *Three weeks later. A corner of Fifth Avenue in the Fifties on a fine Sunday morning. A general atmosphere of clean, well-tidied, wide street; a flood of mellow, tempered sunshine; gentle, genteel breezes. In the rear, the show windows of two shops, a jewelry establishment on the corner, a furrier's next to it. Here the adornments of extreme wealth are tantalizingly displayed. The jeweler's window is gaudy with glittering diamonds, emeralds, rubies, pearls, etc., fashioned in ornate tiaras, crowns, necklaces, collars, etc. From each piece hangs an enormous tag from which a dollar sign and numerals in intermittent electric lights wink out the incredible prices. The same in the furrier's. Rich furs of all varieties hang there bathed in a downpour of artificial light. The general effect is of a background of magnificence cheapened and made grotesque by commercialism, a background in tawdry disharmony with the clear light and sunshine on the street itself.*

Up the side street YANK *and* LONG *come swaggering.* LONG *is dressed in shore clothes, wears a black Windsor tie, cloth cap.* YANK *is in his dirty dungarees. A fireman's cap with black peak is cocked defiantly on the side of his head. He has not shaved for days and around his fierce, resentful eyes—as around those of* LONG *to a lesser degree—the black smudge of coal dust still sticks like make-up. They hesitate and stand together at the corner, swaggering, looking about them with a forced, defiant contempt.*

LONG. [*Indicating it all with an oratorical gesture.*] Well, 'ere we are. Fif' Avenoo. This 'ere's their bleedin' private lane, as yer might say. [*Bitterly.*] We're trespassers 'ere. Proletarians keep orf the grass!

YANK. [*Dully.*] I don't see no grass, yuh boob. [*Staring at the sidewalk.*] Clean, ain't it? Yuh could eat a fried egg offen it. The white wings[10] got some job sweepin' dis up. [*Looking up and down the avenue—surlily.*] Where's all de white-collar stiffs yuh said was here—and de skoits—*her* kind?

LONG. In church, blarst 'em! Arskin' Jesus to give 'em more money.

YANK. Choich, huh? I useter go to choich onct—sure—when I was a kid. Me old man and woman, dey made me. Dey never went demselves, dough. Always got too big a head on Sunday mornin', dat was dem. [*With a grin.*] Dey was scrappers for fair, bot' of dem. On Satiday nights when dey bot' got a skinful dey could put up a bout oughter been staged at de Garden. When dey got trough dere wasn't a chair or table wit a leg under it. Or else dey bot' jumped on me for somep'n. Dat was where I loined to take punishment. [*With a grin and a swagger.*] I'm a chip offen de old block, get me?

LONG. Did yer old man follow the sea?

YANK. Naw. Worked along shore. I runned away when me old lady croaked wit de tremens. I helped at truckin' and in de market. Den I shipped in de stokehole. Sure. Dat belongs. De rest was nothin'. [*Looking around him.*] I ain't never seen dis before. De Brooklyn waterfront, dat was where I was dragged up. [*Taking a deep breath.*] Dis ain't so bad at dat, huh?

LONG. Not bad? Well, we pays for it wiv our bloody sweat, if yer wants to know!

YANK. [*With sudden angry disgust.*] Aw, hell! I don't see no one, see—like her. All dis gives me a pain. It don't belong. Say, ain't dere a back room around dis dump? Let's go shoot a ball. All dis is too clean and quiet and dolled-up, get me! It gives me a pain.

LONG. Wait and yer'll bloody well see—

---

[10]a term for street cleaners who wore white uniforms

YANK. I don't wait for no one. I keep on de move. Say, what yuh drag me up here for, anyway? Tryin' to kid me, yuh simp, yuh?

LONG. Yer wants to get back at 'er, don't yer? That's what yer been sayin' every bloomin' hour since she hinsulted yer.

YANK. [*Vehemently.*] Sure thing I do! Didn't I try to get even with her in Southampton? Didn't I sneak on de dock and wait for her by de gang-plank? I was goin' to spit in her pale mug, see! Sure, right in her pop-eyes! Dat woulda made me even, see? But no chanct. Dere was a whole army of plain-clothes bulls around. Dey spotted me and gimme de bum's rush. I never seen her. But I'll git square wit her yet, you watch! [*Furiously.*] De lousy tart! She tinks she kin get away wit moider—but not wit me! I'll fix her! I'll think of a way!

LONG. [*As disgusted as he dares to be.*] Ain't that why I brought yer up 'ere—to show yer? Yer been lookin' at this 'ere 'ole affair wrong. Yer been actin' an' talkin' 's if it was all a bleedin' personal matter between yer and that bloody cow. I wants to convince yer she was on'y a representative of 'er clarss. I wants to awaken yer bloody clarss consciousness. Then yer'll see it's 'er clarss yer've got to fight, not 'er alone. There's a 'ole mob of 'em like 'er, Gawd blind 'em!

YANK. [*Spitting on his hands—belligerently.*] De more de merrier when I gits started. Bring on de gang!

LONG. Yer'll see 'em in arf a mo', when that church lets out. [*He turns and sees the window display in the two stores for the first time.*] Blimey! Look at that, will yer? [*They both walk back and stand looking in the jeweler's.* LONG *flies into a fury.*] Just look at this 'ere bloomin' mess! Just look at it! Look at the bleedin' prices on 'em—more'n our 'ole bloody stokehole makes in ten voyages sweatin' in 'ell! And they—'er and 'er bloody clarss—buys 'em for toys to dangle on 'em! One of these 'ere would buy scoff for a starvin' family for a year!

YANK. Aw, cut de sob stuff! T' hell wit de starvin' family! Yuh'll be passin' de hat to me next. [*With naïve admiration.*] Say, dem tings is pretty, huh? Bet yuh dey'd hock for a piece of change aw right. [*Then turning away, bored.*] But, aw hell, what good are dey? Let her have 'em. Dey don't be-long no more'n she does. [*With a gesture of sweeping the jewelers into oblivion.*] All dat don't count, get me?

LONG. [*Who has moved to the furrier's—indignantly.*] And I s'pose this 'ere don't count neither—skins of poor, 'armless animals slaughtered so as 'er and 'ers can keep their bleedin' noses warm!

YANK. [*Who has been staring at something inside—with queer excitement.*] Take a slant at dat! Give it de once-over! Monkey fur—two t'ousand bucks! [*Bewilderedly.*] Is dat straight goods—monkey fur? What de hell—?

LONG. [*Bitterly.*] It's straight enuf. [*With grim humor.*] They wouldn't bloody well pay that for a 'airy ape's skin—no, nor for the 'ole livin' ape with all 'is 'ead, and body, and soul thrown in!

YANK. [*Clenching his fists, his face growing pale with rage as if the skin in the window were a personal insult.*] Trowin' it up in my face! Christ! I'll fix her!

LONG. [*Excitedly.*] Church is out. 'Ere they come, the bleedin' swine. [*After a glance at* YANK's *lowering face—uneasily.*] Easy goes, Comrade. Keep yer bloomin' temper. Remember force defeats itself. It ain't our weapon. We must impress our demands through peaceful means—the votes of the on-marching proletarians of the bloody world!

YANK. [*With abysmal contempt.*] Votes, hell! Votes is a joke, see. Votes for women! Let dem do it!

LONG. [*Still more uneasily.*] Calm, now. Treat 'em wiv the proper contempt. Observe the bleedin' parasites but 'old yer 'orses.

YANK. [*Angrily.*] Git away from me! Yuh're yellow, dat's what. Force, dat's me! De punch, dat's me every time, see!

[*The crowd from church enter from the right, sauntering slowly and affectedly, their heads held stiffly up, looking neither to right nor left, talking in toneless, simpering voices. The women are rouged, calcimined, dyed, overdressed to the nth degree. The men are in Prince Alberts, high hats, spats, canes, etc. A procession of gaudy marionettes, yet with something of the relentless horror of Frankensteins[3] in their detached, mechanical unawareness.*]

VOICES. Dear Doctor Caiaphas! He is so sincere!
 What was the sermon? I dozed off.
 About the radicals, my dear—and the false doctrines that are being preached.
 We must organize a hundred per cent American bazaar.
 And let everyone contribute one one-hundredth per cent of their income tax.
 What an original idea!
 We can devote the proceeds to rehabilitating the veil of the temple.
 But that has been done so many times.

YANK. [*Glaring from one to the other of them—with an insulting snort of scorn.*] Huh! Huh!

[*Without seeming to see him, they make wide detours to avoid the spot where he stands in the middle of the sidewalk.*]

LONG. [*Frightenedly.*] Keep yer bloomin' mouth shut, I tells yer.

YANK. [*Viciously.*] G'wan! Tell it to Sweeney! [*He swaggers away and deliberately lurches into a top-hatted gentleman, then glares at him pugnaciously.*] Say, who d'yuh tink yuh're bumpin? Tink yuh own de oith?

GENTLEMAN. [*Coldly and affectedly.*] I beg your pardon. [*He has not looked at* YANK *and passes on without a glance, leaving him bewildered.*]

LONG. [*Rushing up and grabbing* YANK's *arm.*] 'Ere! Come away! This wasn't what I meant. Yer'll 'ave the bloody coppers down on us.

YANK. [*Savagely—giving him a push that sends him sprawling.*] G'wan!

LONG. [*Picks himself up—hysterically.*] I'll pop orf then. This ain't what I meant. And whatever 'appens, yer can't blame me. [*He slinks off left.*]

YANK. T' hell wit youse! [*He approaches a lady—with a vicious grin and a smirking wink.*] Hello, Kiddo. How's every little ting? Got anyting on for to-night? I know an old boiler down to de docks we kin crawl into. [*The lady stalks by without a look, without a change of pace.* YANK *turns to others—insultingly.*] Holy smokes, what a mug! Go hide yuhself before de horses shy at yuh. Gee, pipe de heine on dat one! Say, youse, yuh look like de stoin of a ferryboat. Paint and powder! All dolled up to kill! Yuh look like stiffs laid out for de boneyard! Aw, g'wan, de lot of youse! Yuh give me de eye-ache. Yuh don't belong, get me! Look at me, why don't youse dare? I belong, dat's me! [*Pointing to a skyscraper across the street which is in process of construction—with bravado.*] See dat building goin' up dere? See de steel work? Steel, dat's me! Youse guys live on it and tink yuh're somep'n. But I'm *in* it, see! I'm de hoistin' engine dat makes it go up! I'm it—de inside and bottom of it! Sure! I'm steel and steam and smoke and de rest of it! It moves—speed—twenty-five stories up—and me at de top and bottom—movin'! Youse simps don't move. Yuh're on'y dolls I winds up to see 'm spin. Yuh're de garbage, get me—de leavins— de ashes we dump over de side! Now, what 'a' yuh gotta say? [*But as they seem neither to see nor hear him, he flies into a fury.*] Bums! Pigs! Tarts! Bitches! [*He turns in a rage on the men, bumping viciously into them but not jarring them the least bit. Rather it is he who recoils after each collision. He keeps growling.*] Git off de oith! G'wan, yuh bum! Look where yuh're goin', can't yuh? Git outa here! Fight, why don't yuh? Put up yer mits! Don't be a dog! Fight or I'll knock yuh dead! [*But, without seeming to see him, they all answer with mechanical affected politeness.*] I beg your pardon. [*Then at a cry from one of the women, they all scurry to the furrier's window.*]

THE WOMAN. [*Ecstatically, with a gasp of delight.*] Monkey fur! [*The whole crowd of men and women chorus after her in the same tone of affected delight.*] Monkey fur!

YANK. [*With a jerk of his head back on his shoulders, as if he had received a punch full in the face—raging.*] I see yuh, all in white! I see yuh, yuh white-faced tart, yuh! Hairy ape, huh? I'll hairy ape yuh! [*He bends down and grips at the street curbing as if to pluck it out and hurl it. Foiled in this, snarling with passion, he leaps to the lamp-post on the corner and tries to pull it up for a club. Just at that moment a bus is heard rumbling up. A fat, high-hatted, spatted gentleman runs out from the side street. He calls out plaintively.*] Bus! Bus! Stop there! [*And runs full tilt into the bending, straining* YANK, *who is howled off his balance.*]

YANK. [*Seeing a fight—with a roar of joy as he springs to his feet.*] At last! Bus, huh? I'll bust yuh! [*He lets drive a terrific swing, his fist landing full on the fat gentleman's face. But the gentleman stands unmoved as if nothing had happened.*]

GENTLEMAN. I beg your pardon. [*Then irritably.*] You have made me lose my bus. [*He claps his hands and begins to scream:*] Officer! Officer!

[*Many police whistles shrill out on the instant and a whole platoon of policemen rush in on* YANK *from all sides. He tries to fight but is clubbed to the pavement and fallen upon. The crowd at the window have not moved or noticed this disturbance. The clanging gong of the patrol wagon approaches with a clamoring din.*]

    [*Curtain.*]

Scene VI

SCENE: *Night of the following day. A row of cells in the prison on Blackwell's Island. The cells extend back diagonally from right front to left rear. They do not stop, but disappear in the dark background as if they ran on, numberless, into infinity. One electric bulb from the low ceiling of the narrow corridor sheds its light through the heavy steel bars of the cell at the extreme front and reveals part of the interior.* YANK *can be seen within, crouched on the edge of his cot in the attitude of Rodin's "The Thinker." His face is spotted with black and blue bruises. A bloodstained bandage is wrapped around his head.*

YANK. [*Suddenly starting as if awakening from a dream, reaches out and shakes the bars—aloud to himself, wonderingly.*] Steel. Dis is the Zoo, huh? [*A burst of hard, barking laughter comes from the unseen occupants of the cells, runs back down the tier, and abruptly ceases.*]

VOICES. [*Mockingly.*] The Zoo. That's a new name for this coop—a damn good name!

    Steel, eh? You said a mouthful. This is the old iron house.

    Who is that boob talkin'?

    He's the bloke they brung in out of his head. The bulls had beat him up fierce.

YANK. [*Dully.*] I musta been dreamin'. I tought I was in a cage at de Zoo—but de apes don't talk, do dey?

VOICE. [*With mocking laughter.*] You're in a cage aw right.

    A coop!

    A pen!

    A sty!

    A kennel! [*Hard laughter—a pause.*]

    Say, guy! Who are you? No, never mind lying. What are you?

    Yes, tell us your sad story. What's your game?

    What did they jug yuh for?

YANK. [*Dully.*] I was a fireman—stokin' on de liners. [*Then with sudden rage, rattling his cell bars.*] I'm a hairy ape, get me? And I'll bust youse all in de jaw if yuh don't lay off kiddin' me.

VOICES. Huh! You're a hard boiled duck, ain't you!

    When you spit, it bounces! [*Laughter.*]

Aw, can it. He's a regular guy. Ain't you?

What did he say he was—a ape?

YANK. [*Defiantly.*] Sure ting! Ain't dat what youse all are—apes? [*A silence. Then a furious rattling of bars from down the corridor.*]

A VOICE. [*Thick with rage.*] I'll show yuh who's a ape, yuh bum!

VOICES. Ssshh! Nix!

Can de noise!

Piano!

You'll have the guard down on us!

YANK. [*Scornfully.*] De guard? Yuh mean de keeper, don't yuh? [*Angry exclamations from all the cells.*]

VOICE. [*Placatingly.*] Aw, don't pay no attention to him. He's off his nut from the beatin'-up he got. Say, you guy! We're waitin' to hear what they landed you for—or ain't yuh tellin'?

YANK. Sure, I'll tell youse. Sure! Why de hell not? On'y—youse won't get me. Nobody gets me but me, see? I started to tell de Judge and all he says was: "Toity days to tink it over." Tink it over! Christ, dat's all I been doin' for weeks! [*After a pause.*] I was tryin' to get even wit someone, see?—someone dat done me doit.

VOICES. [*Cynically.*] De old stuff, I bet. Your goil, huh?

Give yuh the double-cross, huh?

That's them every time!

Did yuh beat up de odder guy?

YANK. [*Disgustedly.*] Aw, yuh're all wrong! Sure dere was a skoit in it—but not what youse mean, not dat old tripe. Dis was a new kind of skoit. She was dolled up all in white—in de stokehole. I tought she was a ghost. Sure. [*A pause.*]

VOICES. [*Whispering.*] Gee, he's still nutty.

Let him rave. It's fun listenin'.

YANK. [*Unheeding—groping in his thoughts.*] Her hands—dey was skinny and white like dey wasn't real but painted on somep'n. Dere was a million miles from me to her—twenty-five knots a hour. She was like some dead ting de cat brung in. Sure, dat's what. She didn't belong. She belonged in de window of a toy store, or on de top of a garbage can, see! Sure! [*He breaks out angrily.*] But would yuh believe it, she had de noive to do me doit. She lamped me like she was seein' somep'n broke loose from de menagerie. Christ, yuh'd oughter seen her eyes! [*He rattles the bars of his cell furiously.*] But I'll get back at her yet, you watch! And if I can't find her I'll take it out on de gang she runs wit. I'm wise to where dey hangs out now. I'll show her who belongs! I'll show her who's in de move and who ain't. You watch my smoke!

VOICES. [*Serious and joking.*] Dats de talkin'!

Take her for all she's got!

What was this dame, anyway? Who was she, eh?

YANK. I dunno. First cabin stiff. Her old man's a millionaire, dey says—name of Douglas.

VOICES. Douglas? That's the president of the Steel Trust, I bet.
Sure. I seen his mug in de papers.
He's filthy with dough.

VOICE. Hey, feller, take a tip from me. If you want to get back at that dame, you better join the Wobblies. You'll get some action then.

YANK. Wobblies? What de hell's dat?

VOICE. Ain't you ever heard of the I.W.W.?[11]

YANK. Naw. What is it?

VOICE. A gang of blokes—a tough gang. I been readin' about 'em to-day in the paper. The guard give me the *Sunday Times*. There's a long spiel about 'em. It's from a speech made in the Senate by a guy named Senator Queen. [*He is in the cell next to* YANK'S. *There is a rustling of paper.*] Wait'll I see if I got light enough and I'll read you. Listen. [*He reads:*] "There is a menace existing in this country to-day which threatens the vitals of our fair Republic—as foul a menace against the very life-blood of the American Eagle as was the foul conspiracy of Catiline against the eagles of ancient Rome!"[12]

VOICE. [*Disgustedly.*] Aw, hell! Tell him to salt de tail of dat eagle!

VOICE. [*Reading.*] "I refer to that devil's brew of rascals, jailbirds, murderers and cut-throats who libel all honest workingmen by calling themselves the Industrial Workers of the World; but in the light of their nefarious plots, I call them the Industrious *Wreckers* of the World!"

YANK. [*With vengeful satisfaction.*] Wreckers, dat's de right dope! Dat belongs! Me for dem!

VOICE. Ssshh! [*Reading.*] "This fiendish organization is a foul ulcer on the fair body of our Democracy—"

VOICE. Democracy, hell! Give him the boid, fellers—the raspberry! [*They do.*]

VOICE. Ssshh! [*Reading:*] "Like Cato I say to this Senate, the I. W. W. must be destroyed.[13] For they represent an ever-present dagger pointed at the heart of the greatest nation the world has ever known, where all men are born free and equal, with equal opportunities to all, where the Founding Fathers have guaranteed to each one happiness, where Truth, Honor, Liberty, Justice, and the Brotherhood of Man are a religion absorbed with

---

[11]The Industrial Workers of the World is a labor organization that attempted to unite industrial workers.
[12]Lucius Sergius Catilina (ca. 108–62 B.C.E.), a Roman politician, is best known for the Catiline (or Catilinarian) conspiracy, an attempt to overthrow the Roman Republic.
[13]Marcus Porcius Cato (234–149 B.C.E.), a Roman senator, argued for years that Rome should attack Carthage.

one's mother's milk, taught at our father's knee, sealed, signed, and stamped upon in the glorious Constitution of these United States!" [*A perfect storm of hisses, catcalls, boos, and hard laughter.*]

VOICES. [*Scornfully.*] Hurrah for de Fort' of July!
> Pass de hat!
> Liberty!
> Justice!
> Honor!
> Brotherhood!

ALL. [*With abysmal scorn.*] Aw, hell!

VOICE. Give that Queen Senator guy the bark! All togedder now—one—two—tree—[*A terrific chorus of barking and yapping.*]

GUARD. [*From a distance.*] Quiet there, youse—or I'll git the hose. [*The noise subsides.*]

YANK. [*With growling rage.*] I'd like to catch that Senator guy alone for a second. I'd loin him some trute!

VOICE. Ssshh! Here's where he gits down to cases on the Wobblies. [*Reads:*] "They plot with fire in one hand and dynamite in the other. They stop not before murder to gain their ends, nor at the outraging of defenseless womanhood. They would tear down society, put the lowest scum in the seats of the mighty, turn Almighty God's revealed plan for the world topsy-turvy, and make of our sweet and lovely civilization a shambles, a desolation where man, God's masterpiece, would soon degenerate back to the ape!"

VOICE. [*To* YANK.) Hey, you guy. There's your ape stuff again.

YANK. [*With a growl of fury.*] I got him. So dey blow up tings, do dey? Dey turn tings round, do dey? Hey, lend me dat paper, will yuh?

VOICE. Sure. Give it to him. On'y keep it to yourself, see. We don't wanter listen to no more of that slop.

VOICE. Here you are. Hide it under your mattress.

YANK. [*Reaching out.*] Tanks. I can't read much but I kin manage. [*He sits, the paper in the hand at his side, in the attitude of Rodin's "The Thinker." A pause. Several snores from down the corridor. Suddenly* YANK *jumps to his feet with a furious groan as if some appalling thought had crashed on him—bewilderedly.*] Sure—her old man—president of de Steel Trust—makes half de steel in de world—steel—where I tought I belonged—drivin' trou—movin'—in dat—to make* her—*and cage me in for her to spit on! Christ! [*He shakes the bars of his cell door till the whole tier trembles. Irritated, protesting exclamations from those awakened or trying to get to sleep.*] He made dis—dis cage! Steel! It don't belong, dat's what! Cages, cells, locks, bolts, bars—dat's what it means!—holdin' me down wit him at de top! But I'll drive trou! Fire, dat melts it! I'll be fire—under de heap-fire dat never goes out—hot as hell—breakin' out in de night— [*While he has been saying this last he has shaken his cell door to a clanging accompaniment. As he comes to the "breakin' out" he seizes one bar with both hands and, putting his two feet up against the others so that his position is parallel to the floor like a monkey's, he gives a great wrench backwards. The bar bends like a licorice stick under his tremendous strength. Just at this moment the* PRISON GUARD *rushes in, dragging a hose behind him.*]

GUARD. [*Angrily.*] I'll loin youse bums to wake me up! [*Sees* YANK.] Hello, it's you, huh? Got the D. Ts., hey? Well, I'll cure 'em. I'll drown your snakes for yuh! [*Noticing the bar.*] Hell, look at dat bar bended! On'y a bug is strong enough for dat!

YANK. [*Glaring at him.*] Or a hairy ape, yuh big yellow bum! Look out! Here I come! [*He grabs another bar.*]

GUARD. [*Scared now—yelling off left.*] Toin de hose on, Ben!—full pressure! And call de others—and a straitjacket! [*The curtain is falling. As it hides* YANK *from view, there is a splattering smash as the stream of water hits the steel of* YANK's *cell.*]

[*Curtain.*]

Scene VII

SCENE: *Nearly a month later. An I. W. W. local near the waterfront, showing the interior of a front room on the ground floor, and the street outside. Moonlight on the narrow street, buildings massed in black shadow. The interior of the room, which is general assembly room, office, and reading-room, resembles some dingy settlement boys' club. A desk and high stool are in one corner. A table with papers, stacks of pamphlets, chairs about it, is at center. The whole is decidedly cheap, banal, commonplace, and unmysterious as a room could well be. The secretary is perched on the stool making entries in a large ledger. An eye shade casts his face into shadows. Eight or ten men, longshoremen, iron workers, and the like, are grouped about the table. Two are playing checkers. One is writing a letter. Most of them are smoking pipes. A big signboard is on the wall at the rear, "Industrial. Workers of the World—Local No. 57."*

[YANK *comes down the street outside. He is dressed as in Scene Five. He moves cautiously, mysteriously. He comes to a point opposite the door; tiptoes softly up to it, listens, is impressed by the silence within, knocks carefully, as if he were guessing at the password to some secret rite. Listens. No answer. Knocks again a bit louder. No answer. Knocks impatiently, much louder.*]

SECRETARY. [*Turning around on his stool.*] What the hell is that—someone knocking? [*Shouts.*] Come in, why don't you? [*All the men in the room look up.* YANK *opens the door slowly, gingerly, as if afraid of an ambush. He looks around for secret doors, mystery, is taken aback by the commonplaceness of the room and the men in it, thinks he may have gotten in the wrong place, then sees the signboard on the wall and is reassured.*]

YANK. [*Blurts out.*] Hello.

MEN. [*Reservedly.*] Hello.

YANK. [*More easily.*] I tought I'd bumped into de wrong dump.

SECRETARY. [*Scrutinizing him carefully.*] Maybe you have. Are you a member?

YANK. Naw, not yet. Dat's what I come for—to join.

SECRETARY. That's easy. What's your job—longshore?

YANK. Naw. Fireman—stoker on de liners.

SECRETARY. [*With satisfaction.*] Welcome to our city. Glad to know you people are waking up at last. We haven't got many members in your line.

YANK. Naw. Dey're all dead to de woild.

SECRETARY. Well, you can help to wake 'em. What's your name? I'll make out your card.

YANK. [*Confused.*] Name? Lemme tink.

SECRETARY. [*Sharply.*] Don't you know your own name?

YANK. Sure; but I been just Yank for so long—Bob, dat's it—Bob Smith.

SECRETARY. [*Writing.*] Robert Smith. [*Fills out the rest of card.*] Here you are. Cost you half a dollar.

YANK. Is dat all—four bits? Dat's easy. [*Gives the* SECRETARY *the money.*]

SECRETARY. [*Throwing it in drawer.*] Thanks. Well, make yourself at home. No introductions needed. There's literature on the table. Take some of those pamphlets with you to distribute aboard ship. They may bring results. Sow the seed, only go about it right. Don't get caught and fired. We got plenty out of work. What we need is men who can hold their jobs—and work for us at the same time.

YANK. Sure. [*But he still stands, embarrassed and uneasy.*]

SECRETARY. [*Looking at him—curiously.*] What did you knock for? Think we had a coon in uniform to open doors?

YANK. Naw. I tought it was locked—and dat yuh'd wanter give me the once-over trou a peep-hole or somep'n to see if I was right.

SECRETARY. [*Alert and suspicious but with an easy laugh.*] Think we were running a crap game? That door is never locked. What put that in your nut?

YANK. [*With a knowing grin, convinced that this is all camouflage, a part of the secrecy.*] Dis burg is full of bulls, ain't it?

SECRETARY. [*Sharply.*] What have the cops to do with us? We're breaking no laws.

YANK. [*With a knowing wink.*] Sure. Youse wouldn't for woilds. Sure. I'm wise to dat.

SECRETARY. You seem to be wise to a lot of stuff none of us knows about.

YANK. [*With another wink.*] Aw, dat's aw right, see. [*Then made a bit resentful by the suspicious glances from all sides.*] Aw, can it! Youse needn't put me trou de toid degree. Can't youse see I belong? Sure! I'm reg'lar. I'll stick, get me? I'll shoot de woiks for youse. Dat's why I wanted to join in.

SECRETARY. [*Breezily, feeling him out.*] That's the right spirit. Only are you sure you understand what you've joined? It's all plain and above board; still, some guys get a wrong slant on us. [*Sharply.*] What's your notion of the purpose of the I. W. W.?

YANK. Aw, I know all about it.

SECRETARY. [*Sarcastically.*] Well, give us some of your valuable information.

YANK. [*Cunningly.*] I know enough not to speak outa my toin. [*Then, resentfully again.*] Aw, say! I'm reg'lar. I'm wise to de game. I know yuh got to watch your step wit a stranger. For all youse know, I might be a plain-clothes dick, or somep'n, dat's what yuh're tinkin', huh? Aw, forget it! I belong, see? Ask any guy down to de docks if I don't.

SECRETARY. Who said you didn't?

YANK. After I'm 'nitiated, I'll show yuh.

SECRETARY. [*Astounded.*] Initiated? There's no initiation.

YANK. [*Disappointed.*] Ain't there no password—no grip nor nothin'?

SECRETARY. What'd you think this is—the Elks—or the Black Hand?[14]

YANK. De Elks, hell! De Black Hand, dey're a lot of yellow back-stickin' Ginees.[15] Naw. Dis is a man's gang, ain't it?

SECRETARY. You said it! That's why we stand on our two feet in the open. We got no secrets.

YANK. [*Surprised but admiringly.*] Yuh mean to say yuh always run wide open—like dis?

SECRETARY. Exactly.

YANK. Den yuh sure got your noive wit youse!

SECRETARY. [*Sharply.*] Just what was it made you want to join us? Come out with that straight.

YANK. Yuh call me? Well, I got noive, too! Here's my hand. Yuh wanter blow tings up, don't yuh? Well, dat's me! I belong!

SECRETARY. [*With pretended carelessness.*] You mean change the unequal conditions of society by legitimate direct action—or with dynamite?

YANK. Dynamite! Blow it offen de oith—steel—all de cages—all de factories, steamers, buildings, jails—de Steel Trust and all dat makes it go.

---

[14]The Elks is a fraternal organization and the Black Hand was an Italian criminal organization.
[15]Ginees, or Guineas, is a derogatory term for Italians.

SECRETARY. So—that's your idea, eh? And did you have any special job in that line you wanted to propose to us? [*He makes a sign to the men, who get up cautiously one by one and group behind* YANK.]

YANK. [*Boldly.*] Sure, I'll come out wit it. I'll show youse I'm one of de gang. Dere's dat millionaire guy, Douglas—

SECRETARY. President of the Steel Trust, you mean? Do you want to assassinate him?

YANK. Naw, dat don't get you nothin'. I mean blow up de factory, de woiks, where he makes de steel. Dat's what I'm after—to blow up de steel, knock all de steel in de woild up to de moon. Dat'll fix tings! [*Eagerly, with a touch of bravado.*] I'll do it by me lonesome! I'll show yuh! Tell me where his works is, how to git there, all de dope. Gimme de stuff, de old butter—and watch me do de rest! Watch de smoke and see it move! I don't give a damn if dey nab me—as long as it's done! I'll soive life for it—and give 'em de laugh! [*Half to himself.*] And I'll write her a letter and tell her de hairy ape done it. Dat'll square tings.

SECRETARY. [*Stepping away from* YANK.] Very interesting. [*He gives a signal. The men, huskies all, throw themselves on* YANK *and before he knows it they have his legs and arms pinioned. But he is too flabbergasted to make a struggle, anyway. They feel him over for weapons.*]

MAN. No gat, no knife. Shall we give him what's what and put the boots to him?

SECRETARY. No. He isn't worth the trouble we'd get into. He's too stupid. [*He comes closer and laughs mockingly in* YANK's *face.*] Ho ho! By God, this is the biggest joke they've put up on us yet. Hey, you Joke! Who sent you—Burns or Pinkerton?[16] No, by God, you're such a bonehead I'll bet you're in the Secret Service! Well, you dirty spy, you rotten agent provocateur, you can go back and tell whatever skunk is paying you blood-money for betraying your brothers that he's wasting his coin. You couldn't catch a cold. And tell him that all he'll ever get on us, or ever has got, is just his own sneaking plots that he's framed up to put us in jail. We are what our manifesto says we are, neither more nor less—and we'll give him a copy of that any time he calls. And as for you— [*He glares scornfully at* YANK, *who is sunk in an oblivious stupor.*] Oh hell, what's the use of talking? You're a brainless ape.

YANK. [*Aroused by the word to fierce but futile struggles.*] What's dat, yuh Sheeny bum, yuh!

SECRETARY. Throw him out, boys. [*In spite of his struggles, this is done with gusto and éclat. Propelled by several parting kicks,* YANK *lands sprawling in the middle of the narrow cobbled street. With a growl he starts to get up and storm the closed door, but stops bewildered by the confusion in his brain, pathetically impotent. He sits there, brooding,*

---

[16]detective agencies

in as near to the attitude of Rodin's "Thinker" as he can get in his position.]

YANK. [*Bitterly.*] So dem boids don't think I belong, neider. Aw, to hell wit 'em! Dey're in de wrong pew—de same old bull—soap-boxes and Salvation Army—no guts! Cut out an hour offen de job a day and make me happy! Gimme a dollar more a day and make me happy! Tree square a day, and cauliflowers in de front yard—ekal rights—a woman and kids—a lousy vote—and I'm all fixed for Jesus, huh? Aw, hell! What does dat get yuh? Dis ting's in your inside, but it ain't your belly. Feedin' your face—sinkers and coffee—dat don't touch it. It's way down—at de bottom. Yuh can't grab it, and yuh can't stop it. It moves, and everything moves. It stops and de whole woild stops. Dat's me now—I don't tick, see?—I'm a busted Ingersoll,[17] dat's what. Steel was me, and I owned de woild. Now I ain't steel, and de woild owns me. Aw, hell! I can't see—it's all dark, get me? It's all wrong! [*He turns a bitter mocking face up like an ape gibbering at the moon.*] Say, youse up dare, Man in de Moon, yuh look so wise, gimme de answer, huh? Slip me de inside dope, de information right from de stable—where do I get off at, huh?

A POLICEMAN. [*Who has come up the street in time to hear this last—with grim humor.*] You'll get off at the station, you boob, if you don't get up out of that and keep movin'.

YANK. [*Looking up at him—with a hard, bitter laugh.*] Sure! Lock me up! Put me in a cage! Dat's de on'y answer yuh know. G'wan, lock me up!

POLICEMAN. What you been doin'?

YANK. Enuf to gimme life for! I was born, see? Sure, dat's de charge. Write it in de blotter. I was born, get me!

POLICEMAN. [*Jocosely.*] God pity your old woman! [*Then matter-of-fact.*] But I've no time for kidding. You're soused. I'd run you in but it's too long a walk to the station. Come on now, get up, or I'll fan your ears with this club. Beat it now! [*He hauls* YANK *to his feet.*]

YANK. [*In a vague mocking tone.*] Say, where do I go from here?

POLICEMAN. [*Giving him a push—with a grin, indifferently.*] Go to hell.

[*Curtain.*]

Scene VIII

SCENE: *Twilight of the next day. The monkey house at the Zoo. One spot of clear gray light falls on the front of one cage so that the interior can be seen. The other cages are vague, shrouded in shadow from which chatterings pitched in a conversational tone can be heard. On the one cage a sign from which the word "Gorilla" stands out. The gigantic animal himself is seen squatting on his haunches on a bench in much the same attitude as Rodin's "Thinker."* YANK

---

[17]a popular, inexpensive watch

enters from the left. Immediately a chorus of angry chattering and screeching breaks out. The gorilla turns his eyes but makes no sound or move.

YANK. [*With a hard, bitter laugh*]. Welcome to your city, huh? Hail, hail, de gang's all here! [*At the sound of his voice the chattering dies away into an attentive silence.* YANK *walks up to the gorilla's cage and, leaning over the railing, stares in at its occupant, who stares back at him, silent and motionless. There is a pause of dead stillness. Then* YANK *begins to talk in a friendly confidential tone, half-mockingly, but with a deep undercurrent of sympathy.*] Say, yuh're some hard-lookin' guy, ain't yuh? I seen lots of tough nuts dat de gang called gorillas, but yuh're de foist real one I ever seen. Some chest yuh got, and shoulders, and dem arms and mits! I bet yuh got a punch in eider fist dat'd knock 'em all silly! [*This with genuine admiration. The gorilla, as if he understood, stands upright, swelling out his chest and pounding on it with his fist.* YANK *grins sympathetically.*] Sure, I get yuh. Yuh challenge de whole woild, huh? Yuh got what I was sayin' even if yuh muffed de woids. [*Then bitterness creeping in.*] And why wouldn't yuh get me? Ain't we both members of de same club—de Hairy Apes? [*They stare at each other—a pause—then* YANK *goes on slowly and bitterly.*] So yuh're what she seen when she looked at me, de white-faced tart! I was you to her, get me? On'y outa de cage —broke out—free to moider her, see? Sure! Dat's what she tought. She wasn't wise dat I was in a cage, too—worser'n yours—sure—a damn sight— 'cause you got some chanct to bust loose—but me— [*He grows confused.*] Aw, hell! it's all wrong, ain't it? [*A pause.*] I s'pose yuh wanter know what I'm doin' here, huh? I been warmin' a bench down to de Battery—ever since last night. Sure. I seen de sun come up. Dat was pretty, too—all red and pink and green. I was lookin' at de skyscrapers— steel—and all de ships comin' in, sailin' out, all over de oith—and dey was steel, too. De sun was warm, dey wasn't no clouds, and dere was a breeze blowin'. Sure, it was great stuff. I got it aw right—what Paddy said about dat bein' de right dope—on'y I couldn't get *in* it, see? I couldn't belong in dat. It was over my head. And I kept tinkin'—and den I beat it up here to see what youse was like. And I waited till dey was all gone to git yuh alone. Say, how d'yuh feel sittin' in dat pen all de time, havin' to stand for 'em comin' and starin' at yuh—de white-faced, skinny tarts and de boobs what marry 'em—makin' fun of yuh, laughin' at yuh, gittin' scared of yuh—damn 'em! [*He pounds on the rail with his fist. The gorilla rattles the bars of his cage and snarls. All the other monkeys set up an angry chattering in the darkness.* YANK *goes on excitedly.*] Sure! Dat's de way it hits me, too. On'y yuh're lucky, see? Yuh don't belong wit 'em and yuh know it. But me, I belong wit 'em—but I don't, see? Dey don't belong wit me, dat's what. Get me? Tinkin' is hard—[*He passes one hand across his forehead with a painful gesture. The gorilla growls impatiently.* YANK *goes on gropingly.*] It's dis way, what I'm drivin' at. Youse can sit and dope dream in de past, green woods, de jungle and de rest of it. Den yuh

belong and dey don't. Den yuh kin laugh at `em, see? Yuh're de champ
of de woild. But' me—I ain't got no past to tink in, nor nothin' dat's
comin', on'y what's now—and dat don't belong. Sure, you're de best off!
Yuh can't tink, can yuh? Yuh can't talk neider. But I kin make a bluff at
talkin' and tinkin'— a'most get away with it—a'most!—and dat's where
de joker comes in. [*He laughs.*] *I* ain't on oith and I ain't in heaven, get
me? I'm in de middle tryin' to separate 'em, takin' all de woist punches
from bot' of 'em. Maybe dat's what dey call hell, huh? But you, yuh're at
de bottom. You belong! Sure! Yuh're de on'y one in de woild dat does,
yuh lucky stiff! [*The gorilla growls proudly.*] And dat's why dey gotter put
yuh in a cage, see? [*The gorilla roars angrily.*] Sure! Yuh get me. It beats
it when you try to tink it or talk it—it's way down—deep—behind—you
'n' me we feel it. Sure! Bot' members of dis club! [*He laughs—then in a
savage tone.*] What de hell! T' hell wit it! A little action, dat's our meat! Dat
belongs! Knock 'em down and keep bustin' 'em till dey croaks yuh wit a
gat—wit steel! Sure! Are yuh game? Dey've looked at youse, ain't dey—in
a cage? Wanter git even? Wanter wind up like a sport 'stead of croakin'
slow in dere? [*The gorilla roars an emphatic affirmative,* YANK *goes on
with a sort of furious exaltation.*] Sure! Yuh're reg'lar! Yuh'll stick to de
finish! Me 'n' you, huh?—bot' members of this club! We'll put up one last
star bout dat'll knock 'em offen deir seats! Dey'll have to make de cages
stronger after we're trou! [*The gorilla is straining at his bars, growling,
hopping from one foot to the other.* YANK *takes a jimmy from under his
coat and forces the lock on the cage door. He throws this open.*] Pardon
from de governor! Step out and shake hands. I'll take yuh for a walk
down Fif' Avenoo. We'll knock 'em offen de oith and croak wit de band
playin'. Come on, Brother. [*The gorilla scrambles gingerly out of his cage.
Goes to* YANK *and stands looking at him.* YANK *keeps his mocking tone—
holds out his hand.*] Shake—de secret grip of our order. [*Something, the
tone of mockery, perhaps, suddenly enrages the animal. With a spring he
wraps his huge arms around* YANK *in a murderous hug. There is a crackling snap of crushed ribs—a gasping cry, still mocking, from* YANK.] Hey, I
didn't say kiss me! [*The gorilla lets the crushed body slip to the floor,
stands over it uncertainly, considering; then picks it up, throws it in the
cage, shuts the door and shuffles off menacingly into the darkness at left.
A great uproar of frightened chattering and whimpering comes from the
other cages. Then* YANK *moves, groaning, opening his eyes, and there, is
silence. He mutters painfully.*] Say—dey oughter match him—with
Zybszko[18]. He got me, aw right. I'm trou. Even him didn't tink I belonged. [*Then, with sudden passionate despair.*] Christ, where do I get off
at? Where do I fit in? [*Checking himself as suddenly.*] Aw, what de hell! No
squawkin', see! No quittin', get me! Croak wit your boots on! [*He grabs
hold of the bars of the cage and hauls himself painfully to his feet—looks
around him bewilderedly—forces a mocking laugh.*] In de cage, huh? [*In*

---

[18]This is a misspelling of Stanislaus Zbyszko, a popular wrestler of the day.

the strident tones of a circus barker.] Ladies and gents, step forward and take a slant at de one and only—[*His voice weakening.*]—one and original—Hairy Ape from de wilds of—[*He slips in a heap on the floor and dies. The monkeys set up a chattering, whimpering wail. And, perhaps, the Hairy Ape at last belongs.*]
   [Curtain.]

1922

Questions

1. *The Hairy Ape* is not a realistic play, although it deals with themes usually found in working-class or realistic literature. It is, however, an expressionist play. Research the definition of expressionism. How does O'Neill distort the realism of his scenery and characters to emphasis his working-class themes? Consider, for instance, the introduction to Scene I and the robotic movements of the crowd on Fifth Avenue in Scene V. What is O'Neill implying through these distortions?
2. As seen in the play, describe the work and the working conditions aboard the ship. Is the situation fair to the workers?
3. Describe Yank. Why is he so angry? How has his childhood and the industrial culture affected his development?
4. How is Yank's name ironic?
5. List examples of when Yank is likened to an ape. What does O'Neill seem to be suggesting through this imagery?
6. What is the significance of O'Neill's comparing Yank to Rodin's *The Thinker* in Scene IV?
7. Describe Mildred. Is she sincere in her attempt to help the underclasses? Why or why not?
8. What is significant about Mildred's father being the president of Nazareth Steel, which builds cages in which to hold gorillas?
9. Compare and contrast the men in the firemen's forecastle with the crowd on Fifth Avenue in Scene V. Be sure to mention in what ways they are similar. What do you think that O'Neill is suggesting through the similarities and differences?
10. Summarize Long's rhetoric in Scene V. How can we tell whether or not O'Neill is sympathetic with Long's rhetoric?
11. How does the play demonstrate class consciousness? Based on the play, how would you describe O'Neill's class politics?
12. How can *The Hairy Ape* be read as a protest against industrialization?
13. What is the central concern of the Wobblies? How are they depicted by Senator Queen and the newspaper? What do the words and actions of the Wobblies suggest about them and the depictions of Queen and the newspaper?
14. Explain the ending of the play. Does Yank finally gain a sense of belonging?
15. Compare and contrast the workers in *The Hairy Ape* with the folk hero John Henry.

Studs Terkel
(1912–2008)

For biographical information, see page 80.

FROM *WORKING*, WHO BUILT THE PYRAMIDS?: MIKE LEFEVRE

Who built the seven towers of Thebes?
The books are filled with the names of kings.
Was it kings who hauled the craggy blocks of stone? . . .
In the evening when the Chinese wall was finished
Where did the masons go? . . .

—Bertolt Brecht

Mike Lefevre

It is a two-flat dwelling, somewhere in Cicero, on the outskirts of Chicago. He is thirty-seven. He works in a steel mill. On occasion, his wife Carol works as a waitress in a neighborhood restaurant; otherwise, she is at home, caring for their two small children, a girl and a boy.

At the time of my first visit, a sculpted statuette of Mother and Child was on the floor, head severed from body. He laughed softly as he indicated his three-year-old daughter: "She Doctor Spock'd it."[19]

I'm a dying breed. A laborer. Strictly muscle work . . . pick it up, put it down, pick it up, put it down. We handle between forty and fifty thousand pounds of steel a day. (Laughs) I know this is hard to believe—from four hundred pounds to three- and four-pound pieces. It's dying.

You can't take pride any more. You remember when a guy could point to a house he built, how many logs he stacked. He built it and he was proud of it. I don't really think I could be proud if a contractor

[19]Dr. Benjamin Spock (1903–1998) was an American pediatrician whose ideas on child rearing influenced several generations.

built a home for me. I would be tempted to get in there and kick the carpenter in the ass (laughs), and take the saw away from him. 'Cause I would have to be part of it, you know.

It's hard to take pride in a bridge you're never gonna cross, in a door you're never gonna open. You're mass-producing things and you never see the end result of it. (Muses) I worked for a trucker one time. And I got this tiny satisfaction when I loaded a truck. At least I could see the truck depart loaded. In a steel mill, forget it. You don't see where nothing goes

I got chewed out by my foreman once. He said. "Mike, you're a good worker but you have a bad attitude." My attitude is that I don't get excited about my job. I do my work but I don't say whoopee-doo. The day I get excited about my job is the day I go to a head shrinker. How are you gonna get excited about pullin' steel? How are you gonna get excited when you're tired and want to sit down?

It's not just the work. Somebody built the pyramids. Somebody's going to build something. Pyramids. Empire State Building—these things just don't happen. There's hard work behind it. I would like to see a building, say, the Empire State. I would like to see on one side of it a foot-wide strip from top to bottom with the name of every bricklayer, the name of every electrician, with all the names. So when a guy walked by, he could take his son and say, "See, that's me over there on the forty-fifth floor. I put the steel beam in." Picasso can point to a painting. What can I point to? A writer can point to a book. Everybody should have something to point to.

It's the not-recognition by other people. To say a woman is *just* a housewife is degrading, right? Okay. *Just* a housewife. It's also degrading to say *just* a laborer. The difference is that a man goes out and maybe gets smashed.

When I was single. I could quit, just split. I wandered all over the country. You worked just enough to get a poke, money in your pocket. Now I'm married and I got two kids . . . (trails off). I worked on a truck dock one time and I was single. The foreman came over and he grabbed my shoulder, kind of gave me a shove. I punched him and knocked him off the dock. I said, "Leave me alone. I'm doing my work, just stay away from me, just don't give me the with-the-hands business."

Hell, if you whip a damn mule he might kick you. Stay out of my way, that's all. Working is bad enough, don't bug me. I would rather work my ass off for eight hours a day with nobody watching me than five minutes with a guy watching me. Who you gonna sock? You can't sock General Motors, you can't sock anybody in Washington, you can't sock a system.

A mule, an old mule, that's the way I feel. Oh yeah. See. (Shows black and blue marks on arms and legs, burns.) You know what I heard from more than one guy at work? "If my kid wants to work in a factory. I am going to kick the hell out of him." I want my kid to be an effete snob. Yeah, mm-hmm. (Laughs.) I want him to be able to quote Walt Whitman, to be proud of it.

If you can't improve yourself, you improve your posterity. Otherwise life isn't worth nothing. You might as well go back to the cave and stay there. I'm sure the first caveman who went over the hill to see what was on the other side—I don't think he went there wholly out of curiosity. He went there because he wanted to get his son out of the cave. Just the same way I want to send my kid to college.

I work so damn hard and want to come home and sit down and lay around. *But I gotta get it out.* I want to be able to turn around to somebody and say. "Hey, fuck you." You know? (Laughs.) The guy sitting next to me on the bus too. 'Cause all day I wanted to tell my foreman to go fuck himself, but I can't.

So I find a guy in a tavern. To tell him that. And he tells me too. I've been in brawls. He's punching me and I'm punching him, because we actually want to punch somebody else. The most that'll happen is the bartender will bar us from the tavern. But at work, you lose your job.

This one foreman I've got, he's a kid. He's a college graduate. He thinks he's better than everybody else. He was chewing me out and I was saying. "Yeah, yeah, yeah." He said. "What do you mean, yeah, yeah, yeah. Yes, *sir*." I told him. "Who the hell are you. Hitler? What is this "*Yes. sir*" bullshit? I came here to work. I didn't come here to crawl. There's a fuckin' difference." One word led to another and I lost.

I got broke down to a lower grade and lost twenty-five cents an hour, which is a hell of a lot. It amounts to about ten dollars a week. He came over—after breaking me down. The guy comes over and smiles at me. I blow up. He didn't know it, but he was about two seconds and two feet away from a hospital. I said, "Stay the fuck away from me." He was just about to say something and was pointing his finger. I just reached my hand up and just grabbed his finger and I just put it back in his pocket. He walked away. I grabbed his finger because I'm married. If I'd a been single. I'd a grabbed his head. That's the difference.

You're doing this manual labor and you know that technology can do it. (Laughs.) Let's face it, a machine can do the work of a man: otherwise they wouldn't have space probes. Why can we send a rocket ship that's unmanned and yet send a man in a steel mill to do a mule's work?

Automation? Depends how it's applied. It frightens me if it puts me out on the street. It doesn't frighten me if it shortens my work week. You read that little thing: what are you going to do when this computer replaces you? Blow up computers. (Laughs.) Really. Blow up computers. I'll be goddamned if a computer is gonna eat before I do! I want milk for my kids and beer for me. Machines can either liberate man or enclave 'im, because they're pretty neutral. It's man who has the bias to put the thing one place or another.

If I had a twenty-hour workweek. I'd get to know my kids better, my wife better. Some kid invited me to go on a college campus. On a Saturday, I was sometimes. Help, it I have a choice of taking my wife and kids to a picnic or going to a college campus, it's gonaa be the picnic. But if I worked a twenty-hour week, I could do both. Don't you think with that twenty hour people could really expand 'Who's to say'. There are some people in factories just by force of circumstance. I'm just like the colored people. Potential Einsteins don't have to be white. They could be in cotton fields, they could be in factories.

The twenty-hour week is a possibility today. The intellectuals, they always say there are potential Lord Byrons, Walt Whitmans, Roosevelts, Picassos working in construction or steel mills or factories. But I don't think they believe it. I think what they're afraid of is the potential Hitlers and Stalins that are there too. The people in power fear the leisure man. Not just the United States. Russia's the same way.

What do you think would happen in this country if, for one year, they experimented and gave everybody a twenty-hour week? How do they know that the guy who digs Wallace[20] today doesn't try to resurrect Hitler tomorrow? Or the guy who is mildly disturbed at pollution doesn't decide to go to General Motors and shit on the guy's desk? You can become a fanatic if you had the time. The whole thing is time. That is. I think, one reason rich kids tend to be fanatic about politics: they have time. Time, that's the important thing.

It isn't that the average working guy is dumb. He's tired, that's all. I picked up a book on chess one time. That thing laid in the drawer for two or three weeks, you're too tired. During the weekends you want to take your kids out. You don't want to sit there and the kid comes up: "Daddy, can I go to the park?" You got your nose in a book? Forget it.

I know a guy fifty-seven years old. Know what he tells me? "Mike, I'm old and tired *all* the time." The first thing happens at work: when the arms start moving, the brain stops. I punch in about ten minutes to seven in the morning. I say hello to a couple of guys I like, I kid around with them. One guy says good morning to you and you say good morning. To another guy you say fuck you. The guy you say fuck you to is your friend.

I put on my hard hat, change into my safety shoes, put on my safety glasses, go to the bonderizer. It's the thing I work on. They rake the metal, they wash it, they dip it in a paint solution, and we take it off. Put it on, take it off, put it on, take it off, put it on, take it off . . .

I say hello to everybody but my boss. At seven it starts. My arms get tired about the first half-hour. After that, they don't get tired any more until maybe the last half-hour at the end of the day. I work from seven to three thirty. My arms are tired at seven thirty and they're tired at three o'clock. I hope to God I never get broke in, because I always want my arms to be tired at seven thirty and three o'clock. (Laughs.) Cause that's when I know that there's a beginning and there's an end. That I'm not brainwashed. In between. I don't even try to think.

If I were to put you in front of a dock and I pulled up a skid in front of you with fifty hundred-pound sacks of potatoes and there are fifty more skids just like it, and this is what you're gonna do all day, what would you think about—potatoes? Unless a guy's a nut, he never thinks about work or talks about it. Maybe about baseball or about getting drunk the other night or he got laid or he didn't get laid. I'd say one out of a hundred will actually get excited about work.

---

[20]George Corey Wallace (1919–1998) was a four-term governor of Alabama and a presidential candidate who was known especially for his opposition to racial integration. He later apologized for his segregationist views.

Why is it that the communists always say they're for the workingman, and as soon as they set up a country, you got guys singing to tractors? They're singing about how they love the factory. That's where I couldn't buy communism. It's the intellectuals' utopia, not mine. I cannot picture myself singing to a tractor. I just can't. (Laughs.) Or singing to steel. (Singsongs.) Oh whoop-dee-doo. I'm at the bonderizer, oh how I love this heavy steel. No thanks. Never hoppen.

Oh yeah. I daydream. I fantasize about a sexy blonde in Miami who's got my union dues. (Laughs.) I think of the head of the union the way I think of the head of my company. Living it up. I think of February in Miami. Warm weather, a place to lay in. When I hear a college kid say, "I'm oppressed." I don't believe him. You know what I'd like to do for one year? Live like a college kid. Just for one year. I'd love to. Wow! (Whispers) Wow! Sports car! Marijuana! (Laughs.) Wild, sexy broads. I'd love that, hell yes. I would.

Somebody has to do this work. If my kid ever goes to college. I just want him to have a little respect, to realize that his dad is one of those somebodies. This is why even on—(muses) yeah. I guess, sure—on the black thing . . . (Sighs heavily.) I can't really hate the colored fella that's working with me all day. The black intellectual I got no respect for. The white intellectual I got no use for. I got no use for the black militant who's gonna scream three hundred years of slavery to me while I'm busting my ass. You know what I mean? (Laughs.) I have one answer for that guy: go see Rockefeller. See Harriman. Don't bother me. We're in the same cotton field. So just don't bug me. (Laughs.)

After work I usually stop off at a tavern. Cold beer. Cold beer right away. When I was single. I used to go into hillbilly bars, get in a lot of brawls. Just to explode. I got a thing on my arm here (indicates scar). I got slapped with a bicycle chain. Oh, wow! (Softly) Mmm. I'm getting older. (Laughs.) I don't explode as much. You might say I'm broken in. (Quickly) No. I'll never be broken in. (Sighs.) When you get a little older, you exchange the words. When you're younger, you exchange the blows.

When I get home. I argue with my wife a little bit. Turn on TV, get mad at the news. (Laughs.) I don't even watch the news that much. I watch Jackie Gleason. I look for any alternative to the ten o'clock news. I don't want to go to bed angry. Don't hit a man with anything heavy at five o'clock. He just can't be bothered. This is his time to relax. The heaviest thing he wants is what his wife has to tell him.

When I come home, know what I do for the first twenty minutes? Fake it. I put on a smile. I got a kid three years old. Sometimes she says, "Daddy, where've you been?" I say, "Work," I could have told her I'd been in Disneyland. What's work to a three-year-old kid? If I feel bad, I can't take it out on the kids. Kids are born innocent of everything but birth. You can't take it out on your wife either. This is why you go to a tavern. You want to release it there rather than do it at home. What does an actor do when he's got a bad movie? I got a bad movie every day.

I don't even need the alarm clock to get up in the morning. I can go out drinking all night, fall asleep at four, and bam! I'm up at six—no matter what I do. (Laughs.) It's a pseudo-death, more or less. Your whole system is paralyzed and you give all the appearance of death. It's an ingrown clock. It's a thing you just get used to. The hours differ. It depends. Sometimes my wife wants to do something crazy like play five hundred rummy or put a puzzle together. It could be midnight, could be ten o'clock, could be nine thirty.

What do you do weekends?

Drink beer, read a book. See that one? *Violence in America.* It's one of them studies from Washington. One of them committees they're always appointing. A thing like that I read on a weekend. But during the weekdays, gee . . . I just thought about it. I don't do that much reading from Monday through Friday. Unless it's a horny book. I'll read it at work and go home and do my homework. (Laughs.) That's what the guys at the plant call it— homework. (Laughs.) Sometimes my wife works on Saturday and I drink beer at the tavern.

I went out drinking with one guy, oh, a long time ago. A college boy. He was working where I work now. Always preaching to me about how you need violence to change the system and all that garbage. We went into a hillbilly joint. Some guy there, I didn't know him from Adam, he said, "You think you're smart." I said, "What's your pleasure?" (Laughs.) He said, "My pleasure's to kick your ass." I told him I really can't be bothered. He said, "What're you, chicken?" I said, "No, I just don't want to be bothered." He came over and said something to me again. I said, "I don't beat women, drunks, or fools. Now leave me alone."

The guy called his brother over. This college boy that was with me, he came nudging my arm, "Mike, let's get out of here." I said, "What are you worried about?" (Laughs.) This isn't unusual. People will bug you. You fend it off as much as you can with your mouth and when you can't, you punch the guy out.

It was close to closing time and we stayed. We could have left, but when you go into a place to have a beer and a guy challenges you—if you expect to go in that place again, you don't leave. If you have to fight the guy, you fight.

I got just outside the door and one of these guys jumped on me and grabbed me around the neck. I grabbed his arm and flung him against the wall. I grabbed him here (indicates throat), and jiggled his head against the wall quite a few times. He kind of slid down a little bit. This guy who said he was his brother took a swing at me with a garrison belt. He just missed and his the wall. I'm looking around for my junior Stalin (laughs), who loves violence and everything. He's gone. Split. (Laughs.) Next day I see him at work. I couldn't get mad at him, he's a baby.

He saw a book in my back pocket one time and he was amazed. He walked up to me and he said, "You read?" I said, "What do you mean. I read?" He said. "All these dummies read the sports pages around here. What are you doing with a book?" I got pissed off at the kid right away. I said, "What do you mean, all these dummies? Don't knock a man who's paying somebody else's way through college." He was a nineteen-year-old effete snob.

Yet you want your kid to be an effete snob?

Yes. I want my kid to look at me and say. "Dad, you're a nice guy, but you're a fuckin' dummy," Hell yes. I want my kid to tell me that he's not gonna be like me . . .

If I were hiring people to work. I'd try naturally to pay them a decent wage. I'd try to find out their first names, their last names, keep the company as small as possible, so I could personalize the whole thing. All I would ask a man is a handshake, see you in the morning. No applications, nothing. I wouldn't be interested in the guy's past. Nobody ever checks the pedigree on a mule, do they? But they do on a man. Can you picture walking up to a mule and saying. "I'd like to know who his granddaddy was?"

I'd like to run a combination bookstore and tavern. (Laughs.) I would like to have a place where college kids came and a steelworker could sit down and talk. Where a workingman could not be ashamed of Walt Whitman and where a college professor could not be ashamed that he painted his house over the weekend.

If a carpenter built a cabin for poets, I think the least the poets owe the carpenter is just three or four one-liners on the wall. A little plaque: Though we labor with our minds, this place we can relax in was built by someone who can work with his hands. And his work is as noble as ours. I think the poet owes something to the guy who builds the cabin for him.

I don't think of Monday. You know what I'm thinking about on Sunday night? Next Sunday. If you work real hard, you think of a perpetual vacation. Not perpetual sleep . . . What do I think of on a Sunday night? Lord, I wish the fuck I could do something else for a living.

I don't know who the guy is who said there is nothing sweeter than an unfinished symphony. Like an unfinished painting and an unfinished poem. If he creates this thing one day—let's say. Michelangelo's Sistine Chapel. It took him a long time to do this, this beautiful work of art. But what if he had to create this Sistine Chapel a thousand times a year? Don't you think that would even dull Michelangelo's mind? Or if da Vinci had to draw his anatomical charts thirty, forty, fifty, sixty, eighty, ninety, a hundred times a day? Don't you think that would even bore da Vinci?

Way back, you spoke of the guys who built the pyramids, not the pharaohs, the unknowns. You put yourself in their category?

Yes. I want my signature on 'em, too. Sometimes, out of pure meanness, when I make something, I put a little dent in it. I like to do something to make it really unique. Hit it with a hammer. I deliberately fuck it up to see if it'll get by, just so I can say I did it. It could be anything. Let me put it this way: I think God invented the dodo bird so when we get up there we could tell Him. "Don't you ever make mistakes?" and He'd say, "Sure, look." (Laughs.) I'd like to make my imprint. My dodo bird. A mistake, *mine.* Let's say the whole building is nothing but red bricks. I'd like to have just the black one or the white one or the purple one. Deliberately fuck up.

This is gonna sound square, but my kid is my imprint. He's my freedom. There's a line in one of Hemingway's books. I think it's from *For Whom the Bell Tolls.* They're behind the enemy lines, somewhere in Spain, and she's pregnant.

She wants to stay with him. He tells her no. He says, "if you die, I die." knowing he's gonna die. But if you go. I go. Know what I mean? The mystics call it the brass bowl. Continuum. You know what I mean? This is why I work. Every time I see a young guy walk by with a shirt and tie and dressed up real sharp, I'm lookin' at my kid, you know? That's it.

1972

Questions

1. Describe LeFevre's work shift.
2. Why is LeFevre frustrated with his job? How does he relieve his frustration?
3. Why does he no longer have pride in his work? Why did he find loading trucks to be more satisfying than his current work in the steel mill? Consider the title of this passage when answering this question.
4. What does he think about his fellow workers? Consider how he addresses them. How does LeFevre sound a voice against worker stereotypes?
5. What does LeFevre mean when he compares himself to "an old mule."
6. Explain LeFevre's statement: "When the arm starts moving, the brain stops." How is he similar to the speaker in Wayman's "Factory Time"?
7. Which television shows does LeFevre watch and why?
8. What does LeFevre mean by an "effete snob"? Why does he want his children to be "effete snobs"?
9. Compare and contrast LeFevre with Farrington in Joyce's "Counterparts."
10. Where does LeFevre find comfort and hope?
11. LeFevre is concerned with the effects of technology and automation on labor. How are his views similar to those expressed in "John Henry"?
12. Why would LeFevre like to see a twenty-four-hour work week? Is such a work week plausible? Why or why not?
13. Could America do more for its laborers? Compare the benefits of an American worker with those in other countries, perhaps Europe and Asia.
14. LeFevre says that he is "a dying breed. A laborer." Is he accurate? Research America's steel industry. What has happened to America's steel mills?
15. Compare and contrast LeFevre's views on labor with those expressed in O'Neill's *The Hairy Ape*. Is one text more radical than the other?

PART VI

RACE, GENDER, AND THE DYNAMICS OF POWER

Introduction

Racial and gender discrimination have been persistent issues throughout world history. When the American colonies decided to break with Great Britain, many of those active in the new nation's founding pushed gender and racial considerations to the forefront of the debate, seeing the American Revolution as an opportunity to correct centuries of wrongdoing. Most famously, perhaps, Thomas Jefferson included an anti-slavery clause in his draft of the Declaration of Independence. However, the Continental Congress decided to delete the clause from the final document. Even as the Congress planned to meet, Abigail Adams, in a letter dated March 31, 1776, implored her husband, the future president, John Adams, to consider the role of women in the New Republic. "Do not put such unlimited power into the hands of the Husbands," she wrote. "Remember all men would be tyrants if they could." Throughout her life, Abigail Adams petitioned for both equal public education for women and for the emancipation of slaves. While the situation has improved dramatically over time, minorities and women still confront discrimination. The works in this section study that discrimination from a variety of perspectives.

Sojourner Truth, who was born into slavery, first fought for abolition before turning her attention to women's rights. In her 1867 address to the first annual meeting of the American Equal Rights Association, reprinted here, she echoes earlier American feminists such as Adams, Margaret Fuller, Lucretia Mott, and Elizabeth Cady Stanton, and anticipates much later feminists such as Betty Friedan and Gloria Steinem as she challenges the patriarchal power structure in her call for wider career opportunities for women and equal pay for equal work—still an issue today. Like Abigail Adams, particularly, she warns against the tyranny of men.

However, while Truth exudes confidence and force in her words—on the page as she did before an audience—other minorities and women depicted in this section feel voiceless and disempowered. In the excerpt from *Black Boy*, Richard Wright walks a tightrope in the "delicately balanced world" of Memphis in the 1920s. His white supervisors and coworkers in the optical factory feel entitled to intimidate and manipulate him for their own self-aggrandizement, entertainment, and relief from the tedium of the factory. Unable to voice a protest without severe consequences, which could include his death, Wright tries to subvert the humiliation by conspiring with Harrison, the other target of the whites. But despite their having had the opportunity, the conspiracy fails because both black men are so bewildered that neither can trust the other. As a result, their humiliation and self-hatred only deepen. Perhaps, however, no one is this section is as helpless and as silenced as the protagonist of Chitra Banerjee Divakaruni's "Song of the Fisher Wife." In this poem, set in a small village in India, the wife confronts exile and unrelieved humiliation and despair, if not unwarranted guilt, as she is blamed her for her husband's death at sea because of an old superstition. Many of the readings here suggest that the worst effects of discrimination are internal because the victims gradually lose self-worth and self-respect.

Some women and minorities do fight back, or at least contemplate fighting back. The speaker in Linda Pastan's "Marks," for example, is determined not to accept the indignity of her family's grading her as if she were a student. She may be playful, but her threat of "dropping out" is real. But the strongest response to frustration and disempowerment comes from Miss Dent in John Cheever's "The Five-Forty-Eight." Dent, a fragile and unstable woman who has not worked in some time, finds employment with Blake, who, at their initial interview, seems more concerned with her physical appearance than her skills. After work one evening, the boss and his secretary have sex, with the result, that Blake promptly fires her the next day. Dent decides to restore her lost dignity and empower herself through a surprising act of revenge.

By acting out a power fantasy, Dent subverts the usual dynamic of the workplace. Her actions, almost certainly, represent a latent impulse in many of the individuals depicted not just in this section but in this text.

Sojourner Truth
(1797–1893)

Born into slavery as Isabella Baumfree, Sojourner Truth began life in Ulster County, New York. At nine years of age, she was sold to a vicious slaveholder who beat and raped her repeatedly. She would be sold three more times before New York State abolished slavery in 1827. The mother of five children, Baumfree became a devout Christian after gaining her freedom. A fiery orator with a strong voice and a sharp sense of humor, she became a traveling evangelist, and, in 1843, took the name Sojourner Truth.

Never able to read or write, she dictated her autobiography, *The Narrative of Sojourner Truth*, which was published in 1850. She toured the country, advocating an end to slavery and promoting equal rights for women. During the Civil War, she encouraged blacks to fight for the North. In 1864, she moved to Washington, DC, and organized a campaign to allow blacks to sit with whites on trains. Abraham Lincoln was so impressed with Sojourner Truth that he welcomed her to the White House. In addition to advocating against slavery and for women's rights, Truth spoke in favor of prison reform and against capital punishment.

ON COLORED WOMEN AND WORK

Address to the First Annual Meeting of the American Equal Rights Association, delivered by Sojourner Truth on May 9, 1867

New York City, May 9, 1867

My friends, I am rejoiced that you are glad, but I don't know how you will feel when I get through. I come from another field—the country of the slave. They have got their liberty—so much good luck to have slavery partly destroyed; not entirely. I want it root and branch destroyed. Then we will all be free indeed. I feel that if I have to answer for the deeds done in my body just as much as a man, I have a right to have just as much as a man.

There is a great stir about colored men getting their rights, but not a word about the colored women; and if colored men get their rights, and not colored women theirs, you see the colored men will be masters over the women, and it will be just as bad as it was before.

So I am for keeping the thing going while things are stirring; because if we wait till it is still, it will take a great while to get it going again. White women are a great deal smarter, and know more than colored women, while colored women do not know scarcely anything.

They go out washing, which is about as high as a colored woman gets, and their men go about idle, strutting up and down; and when the women come home, they ask for their money and take it all, and then scold because there is no food.

I want you to consider on that, chil'n. I call you chil'n; you are somebody's chil'n, and I am old enough to be mother of all that is here. I want women to have their rights. In the courts women have no right, no voice; nobody speaks for them. I wish woman to have her voice there among the pettifoggers. If it is not a fit place for women, it is unfit for men to be there.

I am above eighty years old; it is about time for me to be going. I have been forty years a slave and forty years free, and would be here forty years more to have equal rights for all. I suppose I am kept here because something remains for me to do; I suppose I am yet to help to break the chain.

I have done a great deal of work; as much as a man, but did not get so much pay. I used to work in the field and bind grain, keeping up with the cradler; but men doing no more, got twice as much pay; so with the German women. They work in the field and do as much work, but do not get the pay.

We do as much, we eat as much, we want as much. I suppose I am about the only colored woman that goes about to speak for the rights of the colored women. I want to keep the thing stirring, now that the ice is cracked.

What we want is a little money. You men know that you get as much again as women when you write, or for what you do. When we get our rights we shall not have to come to you for money, for then we shall have money enough in our own pockets; and may be you will ask us for money. But help us now until we get it. It is a good consolation to know that when we have got this battle once fought we shall not be coming to you any more.

You have been having our rights so long, that you think, like a slaveholder, that you own us. I know that it is hard for one who has held the reins for so long to give up; it cuts like a knife. It will feel all the better when it closes up again. I have been in Washington about three years, seeing about these colored people. Now colored men have the right to vote. There ought to be equal rights now more than ever, since colored people have got their freedom. I am going to talk several times while I am here; so now I will do a little singing. I have not heard any singing since I came here.

Accordingly, suiting the action to the word, Sojourner sang, "We are going home." "There, children," said she, "in heaven we shall rest from all our labors; first do all we have to do here. There I am determined to go, not to stop short of that beautiful place, and I do not mean to stop till I get there, and meet you there, too."

1867

Questions

1. Why does Sojourner Truth say that slavery is only "partly destroyed"? The Civil War ended two years prior to her making that statement.

2. What is her complaint about "colored men"? Is the way that she depicts "colored men" similar to how other working-class men might be depicted? Compare her depiction of "colored men" with Farrington in Joyce's "Counterparts."

3. What is Sojourner Truth's complaint about the court system?

4. What is her complaint about the work and the wages afforded "colored women"?

5. What is Sojourner Truth asking her audience to do?

6. Which parts of this speech remained relevant fifty years after its delivery? One hundred years after? Are parts still relevant today? Explain your answer.

Richard Wright
(1908-1960)

The grandson of slaves, Richard Wright, the son of a tenant farmer, was born near Natchez, Mississippi. His family lived in several southern states as his father struggled to make a living before he eventually abandoned his family when Wright was five years of age. As a boy, Wright worked several jobs in order to help his family survive. In 1ate 1927, he left for Chicago, where he worked as a postal clerk, but his job was eliminated during the Great Depression. In 1932, he began attending meetings at the John Reed Club, an organization dominated by the Communist Party, which Wright joined in 1933. Wright used his literary skills in support of party politics, contributing regularly to left-wing publications such as *The New Masses* and *The Daily Worker*. By the early 1940s, Wright had broken with the Communist Party, and, disillusioned with America, he moved to France in 1946, by which time he had developed an international reputation.

Wright's most important works include the collection of stories *Uncle Tom's Children* (1938), the novels *Native Son* (1940) and *The Outsider* (1953), and the autobiographical *Black Boy* (1945). The excerpt included here is from Chapter XII of *Black Boy*; it relates an incident that Wright experienced while working for the Merry Optical Company in Memphis, Tennessee, in 1926.

From *Black Boy,*
Five Dollar Fight

One summer morning I stood at a sink in the rear of the factory washing a pair of eyeglasses that had just come from the polishing machines whose throbbing shook the floor upon which I stood. At each machine a white man was bent forward, working intently. To my left sunshine poured through a window, lighting up the rouge smears and making the factory look garish, violent, dangerous. It was nearing noon and my mind was drifting toward my daily lunch of a hamburger and a bag of peanuts. It had been a routine day, a day more or less like the other days I had spent on the job as errand boy and washer of eyeglasses. I was at peace with the world, that is, at peace in the only way in which a black boy in the South can be at peace with a world of white men.

Perhaps it was the mere sameness of the day that soon made it different from the other days; maybe the white men who operated the machines felt bored with their dull, automatic tasks and hankered for some kind of excitement. Anyway, I presently heard footsteps behind me and turned my head. At my elbow stood a young white man, Mr. Olin, the immediate foreman under whom I worked. He was smiling and observing me as I cleaned emery dust from the eyeglasses.

"Boy, how's it going?" he asked.

"Oh, fine, sir!" I answered with false heartiness, falling quickly into that nigger-being-a-good-natured-boy-in-the-presence-of-a-white-man pattern, a pattern into which I could now slide easily; although I was wondering if he had any criticism to make of my work.

He continued to hover wordlessly at my side. What did he want? It was unusual for him to stand there and watch me; I wanted to look at him, but was afraid to.

"Say, Richard, do you believe that I'm your friend?" he asked me.

The question was so loaded with danger that I could not reply at once. I scarcely knew Mr. Olin. My relationship to him had been the typical relationship of Negroes to southern whites. He gave me orders and I said, "Yes, sir," and obeyed them. Now, without warning, he was asking me if I thought that he was my friend; and I knew that all southern white men fancied themselves as friends of niggers. While fishing for an answer that would say nothing, I smiled.

"I mean," he persisted, "do you think I'm your friend?"

"Well," I answered, skirting the vast racial chasm between us, "I hope you are."

"I am," he said emphatically.

I continued to work, wondering what motives were prompting him. Already apprehension was rising in me.

"I want to tell you something," he said.

"Yes, sir," I said.

"We don't want you to get hurt," he explained. "We like you round here. You act like a good boy."

"Yes, sir," I said. "What's wrong?"

"You don't deserve to get into trouble," he went on.

"Have I done something that somebody doesn't like?" I asked, my mind frantically sweeping over all my past actions, weighing them in the light of the way southern white men thought Negroes should act.

"Well, I don't know," he said and paused, letting his words sink meaningfully into my mind. He lit a cigarette. "Do you know Harrison?"

He was referring to a Negro boy of about my own age who worked across the street for a rival optical house. Harrison and I knew each other casually, but there had never been the slightest trouble between us.

"Yes, sir," I said. "I know him."

"Well, be careful," Mr. Olin said. "He's after you."

"After me? For what?"

"He's got a terrific grudge against you," the white man explained. "What have you done to him?"

The eyeglasses I was washing were forgotten. My eyes were upon Mr. Olin's face, trying to make out what he meant. Was this something serious? I did not trust the white man, and neither did I trust Harrison. Negroes who worked on jobs in the South were usually loyal to their white bosses; they felt that that was the best way to ensure their jobs. Had Harrison felt that I had in some way jeopardized his job? Who was my friend: the white man or the black boy?

"I haven't done anything to Harrison," I said.

"Well, you better watch that nigger Harrison," Mr. Olin said in a low, confidential tone. "A little while ago I went down to get a Coca-Cola and Harrison was waiting for you at the door of the building with a knife. He asked me when you were coming down. Said he was going to get you. Said you called him a dirty name. Now, we don't want any fighting or bloodshed on the job."

I still doubted the white man, yet thought that perhaps Harrison had really interpreted something I had said as an insult.

"I've got to see that boy and talk to him," I said, thinking out loud.

"No, you'd better not," Mr. Olin said. "You'd better let some of us white boys talk to him."

"But how did this start?" I asked, still doubting but half believing.

"He just told me that he was going to get even with you, going to cut you and teach you a lesson," he said. "But don't you worry. Let me handle this."

He patted my shoulder and went back to his machine. He was an important man in the factory, and I had always respected his word. He had the authority to order me to do this or that. Now, why would he joke with me? White men did not often joke with Negroes; therefore, what he had said was serious. I was upset. We black boys worked long hard hours for what few pennies we earned and we were edgy and tense. Perhaps that crazy Harrison was really after me. My appetite was gone. I had to settle this thing. A white man had walked into my delicately balanced world and had tipped it and I had to right it before I could feel safe. Yes, I would go directly to Harrison and ask what was the matter, what I had said that he resented. Harrison was black and so was I; I would ignore the warning of the white man and talk face to face with a boy of my own color.

At noon I went across the street and found Harrison sitting on a box in the basement. He was eating lunch and reading a pulp magazine. As I approached him, he ran his hands into his pockets and looked at me with cold, watchful eyes.

"Say, Harrison, what's this all about?" I asked, standing cautiously four feet from him.

He looked at me a long time and did not answer.

"I haven't done anything to you," I said. "And I ain't got nothing against you," he mumbled, still watchful. "I don't bother nobody."

"But Mr. Olin said that you came over to the factory this morning, looking for me with a knife."

"Aw, naw," he said, more at ease now. "I ain't been in your factory all day." He had not looked at me as he spoke.

"Then what did Mr. Olin mean?" I asked. "I'm not angry with you."

"Shucks, I thought *you* was looking for me to cut me," Harrison explained. "Mr; Olin, he came over here this morning and said you was going to kill me with a knife the moment you saw me. He said you was mad at me because I had insulted you. But I ain't said nothing about you." He still had not looked at me. He rose.

"And I haven't said anything about you," I said.

Finally he looked at me, and I felt better. We two black boys, each working for ten dollars a week, stood staring at each other, thinking, comparing the motives of the absent white man, each asking himself if he could believe the other.

"But why would Mr. Olin tell me things like that?" I asked.

Harrison dropped his head; he laid his sandwich aside.

"I . . . I . . ." he stammered and pulled from his pocket a long, gleaming knife; it was already open. "I was just waiting to see what you was gonna do to me . . ."

I leaned weakly against a wall, feeling sick, my eyes upon the sharp steel blade of the knife.

"You were going to cut me?" I asked.

"If you had cut me, I was gonna cut you first," he said. "I ain't taking no chances."

"Are you angry with me about something?" I asked.

"Man, I ain't mad at nobody," Harrison said uneasily.

I felt how close I had come to being slashed. Had I come suddenly upon Harrison, he would have thought I was trying to kill him and he would have stabbed me, perhaps killed me. And what did it matter if one nigger killed another?

"Look here," I said. "Don't believe what Mr. Olin says."

"I see now," Harrison said. "He's playing a dirty trick on us."

"He's trying to make us kill each other for nothing."

"How come he wanna do that?" Harrison asked.

I shook my head. Harrison sat, but still played with the open knife. I began to doubt. Was he really angry with me? Was he waiting until I turned my back to stab me? I was in torture.

"I suppose it's fun for white men to see niggers fight," I said, forcing a laugh.

"But you might've killed me," Harrison said.

"To white men we're like dogs or cocks," I said.

"I don't want to cut you," Harrison said.

"And I don't want to cut you," I said.

Standing well out of each other's reach, we discussed the problem and decided that we would keep silent about our conference. We would not let Mr. Olin know that we knew that he was egging us to fight. We agreed to ignore any further provocations. At one o'clock I went back to the factory. Mr. Olin was waiting for me, his manner grave, his face serious.

"Did you see that Harrison nigger?" he asked.

"No, sir," I lied.

"Well, he still has that knife for you," he said.

Hate tightened in me. But I kept a dead face.

"Did you buy a knife yet?" he asked me.

"No, sir," I answered.

"Do you want to use mine?" he asked. "You've got to protect yourself, you know."

"No, sir. I'm not afraid," I said.

"Nigger, you're a fool," he spluttered. "I thought you had some sense! Are you going to just let that nigger cut your heart out? His boss gave *him* a knife to use against *you*! Take this knife, nigger, and stop acting crazy!"

I was afraid to look at him; if I had looked at him I would have had to tell him to leave me alone, that I knew he was lying, that I knew he was no friend of mine, that I knew if anyone had thrust a knife through my heart he would simply have laughed. But I said nothing. He was the boss and he could fire me if he did not like me. He laid an open knife on the edge of his workbench, about a foot from my hand. I had a fleeting urge to pick it up and give it to him, point first into his chest. But I did nothing of the kind. I picked up the knife and put it into my pocket.

"Now, you're acting like a nigger with some sense," he said.

As I worked Mr. Olin watched me from his machine. Later when I passed him he called me.

"Now, look here, boy," he began. "We told that Harrison nigger to stay out of this building and leave you alone, see? But I can't protect you when you go home. If that nigger starts at you when you are on your way home, you stab him before he gets a chance to stab you, see?"

I avoided looking at him and remained silent.

"Suit yourself, nigger," Mr. Olin said. "But don't say I didn't warn you."

I had to make my round of errands to deliver eyeglasses and I stole a few minutes to run across the street to talk to Harrison. Harrison was sullen and bashful, wanting to trust me, but afraid. He told me that Mr. Olin had telephoned his boss and had told him to tell Harrison that I had planned to wait for him at the back entrance of the building at six o'clock and stab him. Harrison and I found it difficult to look at each other; we were upset and distrustful. We were not really angry at each other; we knew that the idea of murder had been planted in each of us by the white men who employed us. We told ourselves again and again that we did not agree with the white men; we urged ourselves to keep faith in each other. Yet there lingered deep down in each of us a suspicion that maybe one of us was trying to kill the other.

"I'm not angry with you, Harrison," I said.

"I don't wanna fight nobody," Harrison said bashfully, but he kept his hand in his pocket on his knife.

Each of us felt the same shame, felt how foolish and weak we were in the face of the domination of the whites.

"I wish they'd leave us alone," I said.

"Me too," Harrison said. "There are a million black boys like us to run errands," I said. "They wouldn't care if we killed each other."

"I know it," Harrison said.

Was he acting? I could not believe in him. We were toying with the idea of death for no reason that stemmed from our own lives, but because the men who ruled us had thrust the idea into our minds. Each of us depended upon the whites for the bread we ate, and we actually trusted the whites more than we did each other. Yet there existed in us a longing to trust men of our own color. Again Harrison and I parted, vowing not to be influenced by what our white boss men said to us.

The game of egging Harrison and me to fight, to cut each other, kept up for a week. We were afraid to tell the white men that we did not believe them, for that would have been tantamount to calling them liars or risking an argument that might have ended in violence being directed against us.

One morning a few days later Mr. Olin and a group of white men came to me and asked me if I was willing to settle my grudge with Harrison with gloves, according to boxing rules. I told them that, though I was not afraid of Harrison, I did not want to fight him and that I did not know how to box. I could feel now that they knew I no longer believed them.

When I left the factory that evening, Harrison yelled at me from down the block. I waited and he ran toward me. Did he want to cut me? I backed away as he approached. We smiled uneasily and sheepishly at each other. We spoke haltingly, weighing our words.

"Did they ask you to fight me with gloves?" Harrison asked.

"Yes," I told him. "But I didn't agree."

Harrison's face became eager.

"They want us to fight four rounds for five dollars apiece," he said. "Man, if I had five dollars, I could pay down on a suit. Five dollars is almost half a week's wages for me."

"I don't want to," I said.

"We won't hurt each other," he said.

"But why do a thing like that for white men?"

"To get that five dollars."

"I don't need five dollars that much."

"Aw, you're a fool," he said. Then he smiled quickly.

"Now, look here," I said. "Maybe you are angry with me . . ."

"Naw, I'm not." He shook his head vigorously.

"I don't want to fight for white men. I'm no dog or rooster."

I was watching Harrison closely and he was watching me closely. Did he really want to fight me for some reason of his own? Or was it the money? Harrison stared at me with puzzled eyes. He stepped toward me and I stepped away. He smiled nervously.

"I need that money," he said.

"Nothing doing," I said.

He walked off wordlessly, with an air of anger. Maybe he will stab me now, I thought. I got to watch that fool . . .

For another week the white men of both factories begged us to fight. They made up stories about what Harrison had said about me; and when they saw Harrison they lied to him in the same way. Harrison and I were wary of each other whenever we met. We smiled and kept out of arm's reach, ashamed of ourselves and of each other.

Again Harrison called to me one evening as I was on my way home.

"Come on and fight," he begged.

"I don't want to and quit asking me," I said in a voice louder and harder than I had intended.

Harrison looked at me and I watched him. Both of us still carried the knives that the white men had given us.

"I wanna make a payment on a suit of clothes with that five dollars," Harrison said.

"But those white men will be looking at us, laughing at us," I said.

"What the hell," Harrison said. "They look at you and laugh at you every day, nigger."

It was true. But I hated him for saying it. I ached to hit him in his mouth, to hurt him.

"What have we got to lose?" Harrison asked.

"I don't suppose we have anything to lose," I said.

"Sure," he said. "Let's get the money. We don't care."

"And now they know that we know what they tried to do to us," I said, hating myself for saying it. "And they hate us for it."

"Sure," Harrison said. "So let's get the money. You can use five dollars can't you?"

"Yes."

"Then let's fight for 'em."

"I'd feel like a dog."

"To them, both of us are dogs," he said.

"Yes," I admitted. But again I wanted to hit him.

"Look, let's fool them white men," Harrison said. "We won't hurt each other. We'll just pretend, see? We'll show 'em we ain't dumb as they think, see?"

"I don't know."

"It's just exercise. Four rounds for five dollars. You scared?"

"No."

"Then come on and fight."

"All right," I said. "It's just exercise. I'll fight."

Harrison was happy. I felt that it was all very foolish. But what the hell. I would go through with it and that would be the end of it. But I still felt a vague anger that would not leave.

When the white men in the factory heard that we had agreed to fight, their excitement knew no bounds. They offered to teach me new punches. Each morning they would tell me in whispers that Harrison was eating raw onions for strength. And—from Harrison—I heard that they told him I was eating raw meat for strength. They offered to buy me my meals each day, but I refused. I grew ashamed of what I had agreed to do and wanted to back out of the fight, but I was afraid that they would be angry if I tried to. I felt that if white men tried to persuade two black boys to stab each other for no reason save their own pleasure, then it would not be difficult for them to aim a wanton blow at a black boy in a fit of anger, in a passing mood of frustration.

The fight took place one Saturday afternoon in the basement of a Main Street building. Each white man who attended the fight dropped his share of the pot into a hat that sat on the concrete floor. Only white men were allowed in the basement; no women or Negroes were admitted. Harrison and I were stripped to the waist. A bright electric bulb glowed above our heads. As the gloves were tied on my hands, I looked at Harrison and saw his eyes watching me. Would he keep his promise? Doubt made me nervous.

We squared off and at once I knew that I had not thought sufficiently about what I had bargained for. I could not pretend to fight. Neither Harrison nor I knew enough about boxing to deceive even a child for a moment. Now shame filled me. The white men were smoking and yelling obscenities at us.

"Crush that nigger's nuts, nigger!"

"Hit that nigger!"

"Aw, fight, you goddamn niggers!"

"Sock 'im in his f-k-g piece!"

"Make 'im bleed!"

I lashed out with a timid left. Harrison landed high on my head and, before I knew it, I had landed a hard right on Harrison's mouth and blood came. Harrison shot a blow to my nose. The fight was on, was on against our will. I felt trapped and ashamed. I lashed out even harder, and the harder I fought the harder Harrison fought. Our plans and promises now meant nothing. We fought four hard rounds, stabbing, slugging, grunting, spitting, cursing, crying, bleeding. The shame and anger we felt for having allowed ourselves to be duped crept into our blows and blood ran into our eyes, half blinding us. The hate we felt for the men whom we had tried to cheat went into the blows we threw at each other. The white men made the rounds last as long as five minutes and each of us was afraid to stop and ask for time for fear of receiving a blow that would knock us out. When we were on the point of collapsing from exhaustion, they pulled us apart.

1945

Questions

1. How would you describe Wright at work? What is his demeanor?
2. What does Wright mean when he says that his world is "delicately balanced"? What are the pitfalls that Wright has to be aware of at work? Refer to scenes that illustrate this delicate balance.
3. Would Wright's experiences at work been different if he were white?
4. Why do the white coworkers arrange the fight between Wright and Harrison? Could there be cultural implications in the men's arrangement and enjoyment of the fight?
5. Compare and contrast Wright and Harrison. Do you think that they handled the situation in the best way possible? Why or why not? What would you have done differently?
6. Why do Wright and Harrison rarely speak after the fight?
7. At the end of the excerpt, why does Wright say that he hates Harrison and he hates himself?

John Cheever
(1912–1982)

John Cheever was born in Quincy, Massachusetts, to a comfortable family who suffered the devastating effects of the stock market crash of 1929. To make ends meet, his mother ran a gift store, which Cheever would later call an "abysmal humiliation" for the family. Cheever, never much interested in school, forced his expulsion from the exclusive prep school, Thayer Academy. He would never graduate from high school, but he began his literary career almost immediately after leaving Thayer. His first work was published in *The New Republic* in 1930, and, at twenty-three years of age, his first short story was published in *The New Yorker*, which would continue to publish most of his short fiction.

Through the years, Cheever would struggle with depression, alcoholism, and abuse of prescription drugs. By the early 1970s, Cheever and his work had hit a low point. Most of his fiction was out of print and his new short stories were met with rejection by *The New Yorker*. After treatment for his alcoholism and depression, he surprised critics and readers with his highly acclaimed novel, *Falconer*, a story of redemption. In 1978, Cheever's reputation was further restored with the publication of *The Stories of John Cheever*, a collection of sixty-one stories that became a bestseller, while earning a Pulitzer Prize and a National Book Critics Circle Award.

Cheever's fiction is sophisticated, urbane, and highly polished. He often writes in a detached, satiric tone as he delves behind the façade of upper–middle-class suburbia and into the emotional turmoil of its residents. Today, Cheever is best known for his short stories and novels, such as the autobiographical *Wapshot Chronicle* (1957, winner of the National Book Award), its sequel *Wapshot Scandal* (1964), and *Bullet Park* (1969).

THE FIVE-FORTY-EIGHT

When Blake stepped out of the elevator, he saw her. A few people, mostly men waiting for girls, stood in the lobby watching the elevator doors. She was among them. As he saw her, her face took on a look of such loathing and purpose that he realized she had been waiting for him. He did not approach her. She had no legitimate business with him. They had nothing to say. He turned and walked toward the glass doors at the end of the lobby, feeling that faint guilt and bewilderment we experience when we bypass some old friend or classmate who seems threadbare, or sick, or miserable in some other way. It was five-eighteen by the clock in the Western Union office. He could catch the express. As he waited his turn at the revolving doors, he saw that it was still raining. It had been raining all day, and he noticed now how much louder the rain made the noises of the street. Outside, he started walking briskly east toward Madison Avenue. Traffic was tied up, and horns were blowing urgently on a crosstown street in the distance. The sidewalk was crowded. He wondered what she had hoped to gain by a glimpse of him coming out of the office building at the end of the day. Then he wondered if she was following him.

Walking in the city, we seldom turn and look back. The habit restrained Blake. He listened for a minute—foolishly—as he walked, as if he could distinguish her footsteps from the worlds of sound in the city at the end of a rainy day. Then he noticed, ahead of him on the other side of the street, a break in the wall of buildings. Something had been torn down; something was being put up, but the steel structure had only just risen above the sidewalk fence and daylight poured through the gap. Blake stopped opposite here and looked into a store window. It was a decorator's or an auctioneer's. The window was arranged like a room in which people live and entertain their friends. There were cups on the coffee table, magazines to read, and flowers in the vases, but the flowers were dead and the cups were empty and the guests had not come. In the plate glass, Blake saw a clear reflection of himself and the crowds that were passing, like shadows, at his back. Then he saw her image—so close to him that it shocked him. She was standing only a foot or two behind him. He could have turned then and asked her what she wanted, but instead of recognizing her, he shied away abruptly from the reflection of her contorted face and went along the street. She might be meaning to do him harm—she might be meaning to kill him.

The suddenness with which he moved when he saw the reflection of her face tipped the water out of his hat brim in such a way that some of it ran down his neck. It felt unpleasantly like the sweat of fear. Then the cold water falling into his face and onto his bare hands, the rancid smell of the wet gutters and paving, the knowledge that his feet were beginning to get wet and that he might catch cold—all the common discomforts of walking in the rain—seemed to heighten the menace of his pursuer and to give him a morbid consciousness of his own physicalness and of the ease with which he could be hurt. He could see ahead of him the corner of Madison Avenue, where the lights were brighter. He felt that if he could get to Madison Avenue he would be all right. At the corner, there was a bakery shop with two entrances, and he went in by the door on the crosstown street, bought a coffee ring[1], like any other commuter, and went out the Madison Avenue door. As he started down Madison Avenue, he saw her waiting for him by a hut where newspapers were sold.

---

[1] a coffeecake with fruits and nuts, often iced

She was not clever. She would be easy to shake. He could get into a taxi by one door and leave by the other. He could speak to a policeman. He could run—although he was afraid that if he did run, it might precipitate the violence he now felt sure she had planned. He was approaching a part of the city that he knew well and where the maze of street-level and underground passages, elevator banks, and crowded lobbies made it easy for a man to lose a pursuer. The thought of this, and a whiff of sugary warmth from the coffee ring, cheered him. It was absurd to imagine being harmed on a crowded street. She was foolish, misled, lonely perhaps—that was all it could amount to. He was an insignificant man, and there was no point in anyone's following him from his office to the station. He knew no secrets of any consequence. The reports in his briefcase had no bearing on war, peace, the dope traffic, the hydrogen bomb, or any of the other international skulduggeries that he associated with pursuers, men in trench coats, and wet sidewalks. Then he saw ahead of him the door of a men's bar. Oh, it was so simple!

He ordered a Gibson[2] and shouldered his way in between two other men at the bar, so that if she should be watching from the window she would lose sight of him. The place was crowded with commuters putting down a drink before the ride home. They had brought in on their clothes—on their shoes and umbrellas—the rancid smell of the wet dusk outside, but Blake began to relax as soon as he tasted his Gibson and looked around at the common, mostly not-young faces that surrounded him and that were worried, if they were worried at all, about tax rates and who would be put in charge of merchandising. He tried to remember her name—Miss Dent, Miss Bent, Miss Lent—and he was surprised to find that he could not remember it, although he was proud of the retentiveness and reach of his memory and it had only been six months ago.

Personnel had sent her up one afternoon—he was looking for a secretary. He saw a dark woman—in her twenties, perhaps—who was slender and shy. Her dress was simple, her figure was not much, one of her stockings was crooked, but her voice was soft and he had been willing to try her out. After she had been working for him a few days, she told him that she had been in the hospital for eight months and that it had been hard after this for her to find work, and she wanted to thank him for giving her a chance. Her hair was dark, her eyes were dark; she left with him a pleasant impression of darkness. As he got to know her better, he felt that she was oversensitive and, as a consequence, lonely. Once, when she was speaking to him of what she imagined his life to be—full of friendships, money, and a large and loving family—he had thought he recognized a peculiar feeling of deprivation. She seemed to imagine the lives of the rest of the world to be more brilliant than they were. Once, she had put a rose on his desk, and he had dropped it into the wastebasket. "I don't like roses," he told her.

She had been competent, punctual, and a good typist, and he had found only one thing in her that he could object to—her handwriting. He could not associate the crudeness of her handwriting with her appearance. He would

---

[2]a dry martini

have expected her to write a rounded backhand, and in her writing there were intermittent traces of this, mixed with clumsy printing. Her writing gave him the feeling that she had been the victim of some inner—some emotional—conflict that had in its violence broken the continuity of the lines she was able to make on paper. When she had been working for him three weeks—no longer—they stayed late one night and he offered, after work, to buy her a drink. "If you really want a drink," she said. "I have some whiskey at my place."

She lived in a room that seemed to him like a closet. There were suit boxes and hatboxes piled in a corner, and although the room seemed hardly big enough to hold the bed, the dresser, and the chair he sat in, there was an upright piano against one wall, with a book of Beethoven sonatas on the rack. She gave him a drink and said that she was going to put on something more comfortable. He urged her to; that was, after all, what he had come for. If he had any qualms, they would have been practical. Her diffidence, the feeling of deprivation in her point of view, promised to protect him from any consequences. Most of the many women he had known had been picked for their lack of self-esteem.

When he put on his clothes again, an hour or so later, she was weeping. He felt too contented and warm and sleepy to worry much about her tears. As he was dressing, he noticed on the dresser a note she had written to a cleaning woman. The only light came from the bathroom— the door was ajar—and in this half light the hideously scrawled letters again seemed entirely wrong for her, and as if they must be the handwriting of some other and very gross woman. The next day, he did what he felt was the only sensible thing. When she was out for lunch, he called personnel and asked them to fire her. Then he took the afternoon off. A few days later, she came to the office, asking to see him. He told the switchboard girl not to let her in. He had not seen her again until this evening.

Blake drank a second Gibson and saw by the clock that he had missed the express. He would get the local—the five-forty-eight. When he left the bar the sky was still light; it was still raining. He looked carefully up and down the street and saw that the poor woman had gone. Once or twice, he looked over his shoulder, walking to the station, but he seemed to be safe. He was still not quite himself, he realized, because he had left his coffee ring at the bar, and he was not a man who forgot things. This lapse of memory pained him.

He bought a paper. The local was only half full when he boarded it, and he got a seat on the river side and took off his raincoat. He was a slender man with brown hair—undistinguished in every way, unless you could have divined in his pallor or his gray eyes his unpleasant tastes. He dressed—like the rest of us—as if he admitted the existence of sumptuary laws.[3] His raincoat was the pale buff color of a mushroom. His hat was dark brown; so was his suit. Except for the few bright threads in his necktie, there was a scrupulous lack of color in his clothing that seemed protective.

---

[3]Sumptuary laws, popular in ancient Greece and Rome but also in other cultures, were intended to regulate extravagance. Cheever ridicules the conformity of business attire.

He looked around the car for neighbors. Mrs. Compton was several seats in front of him, to the right. She smiled, but her smile was fleeting. It died swiftly and horribly. Mr. Watkins was directly in front of Blake. Mr. Watkins needed a haircut, and he had broken the sumptuary laws; he was wearing a corduroy jacket. He and Blake had quarreled, so they did not speak.

The swift death of Mrs. Compton's smile did not affect Blake at all. The Comptons lived in the house next to the Blakes, and Mrs. Compton had never understood the importance of minding her own business. Louise Blake took her troubles to Mrs. Compton, Blake knew, and instead of discouraging her crying jags, Mrs. Compton had come to imagine herself a sort of confessor and had developed a lively curiosity about the Blakes' intimate affairs. She had probably been given an account of their most recent quarrel. Blake had come home one night, overworked and tired, and had found that Louise had done nothing about getting supper. He had gone into the kitchen, followed by Louise, and had pointed out to her that the date was the fifth. He had drawn a circle around the date on the kitchen calendar. "One week is the twelfth," he had said. "Two weeks will be the nineteenth." He drew a circle around the nineteenth. "I'm not going to speak to you for two weeks," he had said. "That will be the nineteenth." She had wept, she had protested, but it had been eight or ten years since she had been able to touch him with her entreaties. Louise had got old. Now the lines in her face were ineradicable, and when she clapped her glasses onto her nose to read the evening paper, she looked to him like an unpleasant stranger. The physical charms that had been her only attraction were gone. It had been nine years since Blake had built a bookshelf in the doorway that connected their rooms and had fitted into the bookshelf wooden doors that could be locked, since he did not want the children to see his books. But their prolonged estrangement didn't seem remarkable to Blake. He had quarreled with his wife, but so did every other man born of woman. It was human nature. In any place where you can hear their voices—a hotel courtyard, an air shaft, a street on a summer evening—you will hear harsh words.

The hard feeling between Blake and Mr. Watkins also had to do with Blake's family, but it was not as serious or as troublesome as what lay behind Mrs. Compton's fleeting smile. The Watkinses rented. Mr. Watkins broke the sumptuary laws day after day—he once went to the eight-fourteen in a pair of sandals—and he made his living as a commercial artist. Blake's oldest son—Charlie was fourteen—had made friends with the Watkins boy. He had spent a lot of time in the sloppy rented house where the Watkinses lived. The friendship had affected his manners and his neatness. Then he had begun to take some meals with the Watkinses, and to spend Saturday nights there. When he had moved most of his possessions over to the Watkinses' and had begun to spend more than half his nights there, Blake had been forced to act. He had spoken not to Charlie but to Mr. Watkins, and had, of necessity, said a number of things that must have sounded critical. Mr. Watkins' long and dirty hair and his corduroy jacket reassured Blake that he had been in the right.

But Mrs. Compton's dying smile and Mr. Watkins' dirty hair did not lessen the pleasure Blake took in setting himself in an uncomfortable seat on the five-forty-eight deep underground. The coach was old and smelled oddly like a bomb shelter in which whole families had spent the night. The light that spread from the ceiling down onto their heads and shoulders was dim. The filth on the window glass was streaked with rain from some other journey, and clouds of rank pipe and cigarette smoke had begun to rise from behind each newspaper, but it was a scene that meant to Blake that he was on a safe path, and after his brush with danger he even felt a little warmth toward Mrs. Compton and Mr. Watkins.

The train traveled up from underground into the weak daylight, and the slums and the city reminded Blake vaguely of the woman who had followed him. To avoid speculation or remorse about her, he turned his attention to the evening paper. Out of the corner of his eye he could see the landscape. It was industrial and, at that hour, sad. There were machine sheds and warehouses, and above these he saw a break in the clouds—a piece of yellow light. "Mr. Blake," someone said. He looked up. It was she. She was standing there holding one hand on the back of the seat to steady herself in the swaying coach. He remembered her name then—Miss Dent. "Hello, Miss Dent," he said.

"Do you mind if I sit here?"

"I guess not."

"Thank you. It's very kind of you. I don't like to inconvenience you like this. I don't want to . . ." He had been frightened when he looked up and saw her, but her timid voice rapidly reassured him. He shifted his hams—that futile and reflexive gesture of hospitality—and she sat down. She sighed. He smelled her wet clothing. She wore a formless black hat with a cheap crest stitched onto it. Her coat was thin cloth, he saw, and she wore gloves and carried a large pocketbook.

"Are you living out in this direction now, Miss Dent?"

"No."

She opened her purse and reached for her handkerchief. She had begun to cry. He turned his head to see if anyone in the car was looking, but no one was. He had sat beside a thousand passengers on the evening train. He had noticed their clothes, the holes in their gloves; and if they fell asleep and mumbled he had wondered what their worries were. He had classified almost all of them briefly before he buried his nose in the paper. He had marked them as rich, poor, brilliant or dull, neighbors or strangers, but no one of the thousand had ever wept. When she opened her purse, he remembered her perfume. It had clung to his skin the night he went to her place for a drink.

"I've been very sick," she said. "This is the first time I've been out of bed in two weeks. I've been terribly sick."

"I'm sorry that you've been sick, Miss Dent," he said in a voice loud enough to be heard by Mr. Watkins and Mrs. Compton. "Where are you working now?"

"What?'

"Where are you working now?"

"Oh, don't make me laugh," she said softly.

"I don't understand."

"You poisoned their minds."

He straightened his neck and braced his shoulders. These wrenching movements expressed a brief—and hopeless—longing to be in some other place. She meant trouble. He took a breath. He looked with deep feeling at the half-filled, half-lighted coach to affirm his sense of actuality, of a world in which there was not very much bad trouble after all. He was conscious of her heavy breathing and the smell of her rain-soaked coat. The train stopped. A nun and a man in overalls got off. When it started again, Blake put on his hat and reached for his raincoat.

"Where are you going?" she said.

"I'm going to the next car."

"Oh, no," she said. "No, no, no." She put her white face so close to his ear that he could feel her warm breath on his cheek. "Don't do that," she whispered. "Don't try and escape me. I have a pistol and I'll have to kill you and I don't want to. All I want to do is to talk with you. Don't move or I'll kill you. Don't, don't, don't!"

Blake sat back abruptly in his seat. If he had wanted to stand and shout for help, he would not have been able to. His tongue had swelled to twice its size, and when he tried to move it, it stuck horribly to the roof of his mouth. His legs were limp. All he could think of to do then was to wait for his heart to stop its hysterical beating, so that he could judge the extent of his danger. She was sitting a little sidewise, and in her pocketbook was the pistol, aimed at his belly.

"You understand me now, don't you?" she said. "You understand that I'm serious?" He tried to speak but he was still mute. He nodded his head. "Now we'll sit quietly for a little while," she said. "I got so excited that my thoughts are all confused. We'll sit quietly for a little while, until I can get my thoughts in order again."

Help would come, Blake thought. It was only a question of minutes. Someone, noticing the look on his face or her peculiar posture, would stop and interfere, and it would all be over. All he had to do was to wait until someone noticed his predicament. Out of the window he saw the river and the sky. The rain clouds were rolling down like a shutter, and while he watched, a streak of orange light on the horizon became brilliant. Its brilliance spread—he could see it move—across the waves until it raked the banks of the river with a dim fire-light. Then it was put out. Help would come in a minute, he thought. Help would come before they stopped again; but the train stopped, there were some comings and goings, and Blake still lived on, at the mercy of the woman beside him. The possibility that help might not come was one that he could not face. The possibility that his predicament was not noticeable, that Mrs. Compton would guess that he was taking a poor relation out to dinner at Shady Hill, was something he would think about later. Then the saliva came back into his mouth and he was able to speak.

"Miss Dent?"

"Yes."

"What do you want?"

"I want to talk to you."

"You can come to my office."

"Oh, no. I went there every day for two weeks."

"You could make an appointment."

"No," she said. "I think we can talk here. I wrote you a letter but I've been too sick to go out and mail it. I've put down all my thoughts. I like to travel. I like trains. One of my troubles has always been that I could never afford to travel. I suppose you see this scenery every night and don't notice it any more, but it's nice for someone who's been in bed a long time. They say that He's not in the river and the hills but I think He is. 'Where shall wisdom be found?' it says. 'Where is the place of understanding? The depth saith it is not in me; the sea saith it is not with me, Destruction and death say we have heard the force with our ears.'"[4]

"Oh, I know what you're thinking," she said. "You're thinking that I'm crazy, and I have been very sick again but I'm going to be better. It's going to make me better to talk with you. I was in the hospital all the time before I came to work for you but they never tried to cure me, they only wanted to take away my self-respect. I haven't had any work now for three months. Even if I did have to kill you, they wouldn't be able to do anything to me except put me back in the hospital, so you see I'm not afraid. But let's sit quietly for a little while longer. I have to be calm."

The train continued its halting progress up the bank of the river, and Blake tried to force himself to make some plans for escape, but the immediate threat to his life made this difficult, and instead of planning sensibly, he thought of the many ways in which he could have avoided her in the first place. As soon as he had felt these regrets, he realized their futility. It was like regretting his lack of suspicion when she first mentioned her months in the hospital. It was like regretting his failure to have been warned by her shyness, her diffidence, and the handwriting that looked like the marks of a claw. There was no way of rectifying his mistakes, and he felt—for perhaps the first time in his mature life—the full force of regret. Out of the window, he saw some men fishing on the nearly dark river, and then a ramshackle boat club that seemed to have been nailed together out of scraps of wood that had been washed up on the shore.

Mr. Watkins had fallen asleep. He was snoring. Mrs. Compton read her paper. The train creaked, slowed, and halted infirmly at another station. Blake could see the southbound platform, where a few passengers were waiting to go into the city. There was a workman with a lunch pail, a dressed-up woman, and a woman with a suitcase. They stood apart from one another. Some advertisements were posted on the wall behind them. There was a picture of a couple drinking a toast in wine, a picture of a Cat's Paw rubber heel, and a picture of a Hawaiian dancer. Their cheerful intent seemed to go no farther than the puddles of water on the platform and to expire there. The platform and the people on it looked lonely. The train drew away from the station into the scattered lights of a slum and then into the darkness of the country and the river.

---

[4]See Job 28:12–22 in which Job seeks to understand God's ways, which he cannot find in the natural world.

"I want you to read my letter before we get to Shady Hill," she said. "It's on the seat. Pick it up. I would have mailed it to you, but I've been too sick to go out. I haven't gone out for two weeks. I haven't had any work for three months. I haven't spoken to anybody but the landlady. Please read my letter."

He picked up the letter from the seat where she had put it. The cheap paper felt abhorrent and filthy to his fingers. It was folded and refolded. "Dear Husband," she had written, in that crazy, wandering hand, "they say that human love leads us to divine love, but is this true? I dream about you every night. I have such terrible desires. I have always had a gift for dreams. I dreamed on Tuesday of a volcano erupting with blood. When I was in the hospital they said they wanted to cure me but they only wanted to take away my self-respect. They only wanted me to dream about sewing and basketwork but I protected my gift for dreams. I'm clairvoyant. I can tell when the telephone is going to ring. I've never had a true friend in my whole life. . . ."

The train stopped again. There was another platform, another picture of the couple drinking a toast, the rubber heel, and the Hawaiian dancer. Suddenly she pressed her face close to Blake's again and whispered in his ear. "I know what you're thinking. I can see it in your face. You're thinking you can get away from me in Shady Hill, aren't you? Oh, I've been planning this for weeks. It's all I've had to think about. I won't harm you if you'll let me talk. I've been thinking about devils. I mean, if there are devils in the world, if there are people in the world who represent evil, is it our duty to exterminate them? I know that you always prey on weak people. I can tell. Oh, sometimes I think I ought to kill you. Sometimes I think you're the only obstacle between me and my happiness. Sometimes . . ."

She touched Blake with the pistol. He felt the muzzle against his belly. The bullet, at that distance, would make a small hole where it entered, but it would rip out of his back a place as big as a soccer ball. He remembered the unburied dead he had seen in the war. The memory came in a rush; entrails, eyes, shattered bone, ordure, and other filth.

"All I've ever wanted in life is a little love," she said. She lightened the pressure of the gun. Mr. Watkins still slept. Mrs. Compton was sitting calmly with her hands folded in her lap. The coach rocked gently, and the coats and mushroom-colored raincoats that hung between the windows swayed a little as the car moved. Blake's elbow was on the window sill and his left shoe was on the guard above the steampipe. The car smelled like some dismal classroom. The passengers seemed asleep and apart, and Blake felt that he might never escape the smell of heat and wet clothing and the dimness of the light. He tried to summon the calculated self-deceptions with which he sometimes cheered himself, but he was left without any energy for hope of self-deception.

The conductor put his head in the door and said, "Shady Hill, next, Shady Hill."

"Now," she said. "Now you get out ahead of me."

Mr. Watkins waked suddenly, put on his coat and hat, and smiled at Mrs. Compton, who was gathering her parcels to her in a series of maternal gestures. They went to the door. Blake joined them, but neither of them spoke to him or seemed to notice the woman at his back. The conductor threw open the door, and Blake saw on the platform of the next car a few other neighbors who had missed the express, waiting patiently and tiredly in the wan light for their trip to end. He raised his head to see through the open door the abandoned mansion out of town, a NO TRESPASSING sign nailed to a tree, and then the oil tanks. The concrete abutments of the bridge passed, so close to the open door that he could have touched them. Then he saw the first of the lampposts on the northbound platform, the sign SHADY HILL in black and gold, and the little lawn and flower bed kept up by the Improvement Association, and then the cab stand and a corner of the old-fashioned depot. It was raining again; it was pouring. He could hear the splash of water and see the lights reflected in puddles and in the shining pavement, and the idle sound of splashing and dripping formed in his mind a conception of shelter, so light and strange that it seemed to belong to a time of his life that he could not remember.

He went down the steps with her at his back. A dozen or so cars were waiting by the station with their motors running. A few people got off from each of the other coaches; he recognized most of them, but none of them offered to give him a ride. They walked separately or in pairs—purposefully out of the rain to the shelter of the platform, where the car horns called to them. It was time to go home, time for a drink, time for love, time for supper, and he could see the lights on the hill—lights by which children were being bathed, meat cooked, dishes washed—shining in the rain. One by one, the cars picked up the heads of families, until there were only four left. Two of the stranded passengers drove off in the only taxi the village had. "I'm sorry, darling," a woman said tenderly to her husband when she drove up a few minutes later. "All our clocks are slow." The last man looked at his watch, looked at the rain, and then walked off into it, and Blake saw him go as if they had some reason to say goodbye—not as we say goodbye to friends after a party but as we say goodbye when we are faced with an inexorable and unwanted parting of the spirit and the heart. The man's footsteps sounded as he crossed the parking lot to the sidewalk, and then they were lost. In the station, a telephone began to ring. The ringing was loud, evenly spaced, and unanswered. Someone wanted to know about the next train to Albany, but Mr. Flanagan, the stationmaster, had gone home an hour ago. He had turned on all his lights before he went away. They burned in the empty waiting room. They burned, tin-shaded, at intervals up and down the platform and with the peculiar sadness of dim and purposeless lights. They lighted the Hawaiian dancer, the couple drinking a toast, the rubber heel.

"I've never been here before," she said. "I thought it would look different. I didn't think it would look so shabby. Let's get out of the light. Go over there."

His legs felt sore. All his strength was gone. "Go on," she said.

North of the station there were a freight house and a coalyard and an inlet where the butcher and the baker and the man who ran the service station moored the dinghies, from which they fished on Sundays, sunk now to the gunwales with the rain. As he walked toward the freight house, he saw a movement on the ground and heard a scraping sound, and then he saw a rat take its head out of a paper bag and regard him. The rat seized the bag in its teeth and dragged it into a culvert.

"Stop," she said. "Turn around. Oh, I ought to feel sorry for you. Look at your poor face. But you don't know what I've been through. I'm afraid to go out in the daylight. I'm afraid the blue sky will fall down on me. I'm like poor Chicken-Licken. I only feel like myself when it begins to get dark. But still and all I'm better than you. I still have good dreams sometimes. I dream about picnics and heaven and the brotherhood of man, and about castles in the moonlight and a river with willow trees all along the edge of it and foreign cities, and after all I know more about love than you."

He heard from off the dark river the drone of an outboard motor, a sound that drew slowly behind it across the dark water such a burden of clear, sweet memories of gone summers and gone pleasures that it made his flesh crawl, and he thought of dark in the mountains and the children singing. "They never wanted to cure me," she said. "They . . ." The noise of a train coming down from the north drowned out her voice, but she went on talking. The noise filled his ears, and the windows where people ate, drank, slept, and read flew past. When the train had passed beyond the bridge, the noise grew distant, and he heard her screaming at him, "*Kneel down!* Kneel down! Do what I say. *Kneel down!*"

He got to his knees. He bent his head. "There," she said. "You see, if you do what I say, I won't harm you, because I really don't want to harm you, I want to help you, but when I see your face it sometimes seems to me that I can't help you. Sometimes it seems to me that if I were good and loving and sane—oh, much better than I am—sometimes it seems to me that if I were all these things and young and beautiful, too, and if I called to show you the right way, you wouldn't heed me. Oh, I'm better than you, I'm better than you, and I shouldn't waste my time or spoil my life like this. Put your face in the dirt. *Put your face in the dirt!* Do what I say. Put your face in the dirt."

He fell forward in the filth. The coal skinned his face. He stretched out on the ground, weeping. "Now I feel better," she said. "Now I can wash my hands of you, I can wash my hands of all this, because you see there is some kindness, some saneness in me that I can find and use. I can wash my hands." Then he heard her footsteps go away from him, over the rubble. He heard the clearer and more distant sound they made on the hard surface of the platform. He heard them diminish. He raised his head. He saw her climb the stairs of the wooden footbridge and cross it and go down to the other platform, where her figure in the dim light looked small, common, and harmless. He raised himself out of the dust—warily at first, until he saw by her attitude, her looks, that she had forgotten him; that she had completed what she had wanted to do, and that he was safe. He got to his feet and picked up his hat from the ground where it had fallen and walked home.

1958

Questions

1. Which details suggest that Blake feels not just fear but guilt, too, as he walks from his office to the train?
2. Describe Blake's character. What do you think he is like as a boss? A husband? A father?
3. Describe Miss Dent. Why do you think that she was hospitalized for such an extended period? From what we can tell, was Miss Dent a good worker?
4. Was Blake correct in firing Miss Dent? Why or why not?
5. Miss Dent says that she is "better than" Blake. Is she right? Explain your answer.
6. Explain the ending of the story. Why did Miss Dent follow Blake and make him place his face in the dirt? Why does she not kill Blake?
7. Do you think that Blake will change as a result of his encounter with Miss Dent? Support your answer with references to the details at the end of the story.
8. Is Blake guilty of sexual harassment in his behavior toward Miss Dent? Why or why not?
9. How can this story be interpreted as a satire on the white-collar business world and suburban culture?
10. Do the author's sympathies lie with Blake or Miss Dent? How can you tell? Where do your sympathies lie? Why?

Linda Pastan
(b. 1932)

B orn in the Bronx, one of the five boroughs of New York City, Linda Pastan earned an undergraduate degree from Radcliffe College and graduate degrees from Simmons College and Brandeis University. Married with three children, Pastan writes frequently about domestic life, aging, and mortality. "But I think I've always been interested in the dangers that are under the surface, but seems [sic] like simple, ordinary domestic life," she said. "It may seem like smooth surfaces, but there are tensions and dangers right underneath, and those are what I'm trying to get at."

Her poetry has won many awards, including a Pushcart Prize; the Dylan Thomas Award; the Alice Fay Di Castagnola Award; and the Ruth Lilly Poetry Prize, awarded by *Poetry* magazine along with $100,000. Her poems achieve their clarity and compactness, or what she calls, their "condensed energy," after multiple revisions. "Each poem of mine goes through something like 100 revisions. . . . easily." Her poems have been collected in *PM/AM: New and Selected Poems* (1982) and *Carnival Evening: New and Selected Poems 1968–1998.*

MARKS

My husband gives me an A
for last night's supper,
an incomplete for my ironing,
a B plus in bed.
My son says I am average,
an average mother, but if
I put my mind to it
I could improve.
My daughter believes
in Pass/Fail and tells me
I pass. Wait 'til they learn
I'm dropping out.

1978

Questions

1. What is the controlling metaphor of the poem? Does it seem appropriate to you? Why or why not?
2. What is the tone of the poem? How does the tone affect your interpretation of the last line?
3. What does the poem imply, if anything, about housework?

Chitra Banerjee Divakaruni (b. 1957)

Born in Kolkata (Calcutta), India, Chitra Banerjee Divakaruni graduated from the University of Calcutta before traveling to America to earn a master's degree from Wright State University and a PhD from the University of California, Berkeley, in 1985. She has written in many genres, fiction and nonfiction, and for both children and adults. Her books have been translated into twenty languages. Divakaruni focuses on the plight of women, the South Asian experience, and myth and magic, while celebrating diversity. Two of her novels, *The Mistress of Spices* (1977) and *Sister of My Heart* (1999), have been made into films, and her short story collection, *Arranged Marriage* (1995), won an American Book Award. Her latest novel, *Shadowland* (2009), completes a trilogy in her juvenile fantasy series, which is set in India. "Song of the Fisher Wife" is from her second volume of poetry, *Black Candle* (1991). She currently teaches in the University of Houston's Creative Writing Program.

SONG OF THE FISHER WIFE

He pushes out the boat, black skeleton
against the paie east. His veins
are blue cords. Sun scours the ocean
with its red nails. I hand him
curds and rice wrapped in leaves. Sand
wells over my feet, rotting smell
of seaweed. I sing with the wives.

O husbands, muzzle the great wave,
leap the dark. Bring back boats
filled with fish like silver smiles,
silver bracelets for our arms.

All day I dry the fish, the upturned eyes,
the dead, grinning jaws. How stiff
flesh feels, the flaking layers
under my hand. Salt has cracked
my palms open. The odor crusts me.

My eyes are flecked with sand
and waiting. How well I learn
by the dryness in my mouth
to tell the coming storm.

> *O husbands, no fear*
> *though the sky's breath is black.*
> *We line the calling shore, faithful.*
> *Lip and eye and loin, we keep you*
> *from the jagged wind.*

They say all heard the crack and yell,
the boat exploding into splintered air.
Searched for hours. They strip
my widowed arms, shave off my hair.
Thrust me beyond the village walls.
Nights of no-moon they will come to me,
grunting, heaving, grinding
the damp sand into my naked back,
men with cloths over their faces.

> *O husband, sent by my evil luck*
> *into the great wave's jaw,*
> *do you ride the ocean's boiling back,*
> *eyes phosphorus, sea-lichen hair, gleam*
> *of shell-studded skin, to see*
> *my forehead branded whore?*

1991

NOTE: In many fishing villages in India, residents believe that the wife's fidelity and virtue protect her husband at sea. If a man dies at sea, his widow often becomes an outcast and must turn to prostitution in order to survive.

Questions

1. Define the roles of the husband and the wife in the poem.
2. What is the significance of the women's song?
3. What is the speaker's tone? What does her tone convey about her situation?
4. Do you think that the speaker feels responsible for her husband's death? Why or why not?
5. In an odd way, how do the fishermen yield a mystical and terrifying power to woman?
6. The poem is set in a fishing village. Based on this poem, how completely does the work of fishing dominate the village's culture? Consider fishing in the context of marriage, religion and faith, song, justice, and more.

PART VII

WORK AND ETHICS

Introduction

This section calls upon you to consider the ethical dimensions of work. Of course, many of the readings in the other sections could just as well have been placed here. "A & P," "Waiting Table," "Marks," and "Working in a Public Elementary School" are just a few that come to mind. But as you read these stories and poems, pay special attention to the ethical and moral decisions of the characters and perhaps the moral judgments of the authors.

With "The Prodigal Son," for instance, focus on the ethical considerations that go into the decisions of the father, the prodigal son, and the older brother, who is being asked to accept his brother's return with love and forgiveness rather than pragmatism. Implicitly, the parable calls upon us to think about our decisions from the highest possible perspective. In this way, the parable is not so different from Thoreau's "Life without Principle," but very different from the kind of thinking that drives the city in Wordsworth's "Written in London, September 1802."

In "Bartleby, the Scrivener," the narrator, it seems, is faced with a decision that, for most of us, would require no ethical or moral consideration. Bartleby begins working for the narrator and, within a week, will neither work nor leave the office. The narrator, Bartleby's employer, generously offers him severance pay, but Bartleby refuses to leave. Yet the narrator will not have him forcibly removed. Why not? Consider the narrator's sympathy and moral underpinnings that bring so much discomfort and unrest into his life since Bartleby's arrival. Note that, in many of the readings in this section, the pragmatic and the ethical are in severe conflict.

In Bruce Springsteen's "Highway Patrolman," the singer violates his oath of office, which is something that troubles him. Consider how he struggles to justify his actions or inactions. As you read or listen to the song, ask yourself whether or not, if under similar circumstances, you would act as he does. To you, not to the law, is his violation understandable and acceptable? While the patrolman struggles with himself, Editor Whedon from Masters's *Spoon River Anthology* seems to have little self-conflict during his life. Only in death does he seem more self-reflective and ethically concerned.

In "The Use of Force," the doctor shares his innermost thoughts with the reader regarding his patient and her family. We might, in fact, be surprised by the nature of what he reveals. Do these thoughts alone make him unethical and immoral? Certainly, Lonnie in T. C. Boyle's "The Lie" exhibits very questionable behavior. But would you define him as unethical or immoral? Did he simply speak too spontaneously? Did he trap himself with his first lies? Lonnie's experience dramatizes the consequences of unethical behavior once it is exposed.

What all of the works in this section emphasize is that a moral and ethical dimension is inherent in all work—even in those jobs that seem to require little thought and decision making.

Luke [first century]

L ittle is known about Luke the Evangelist, the author of the third gospel of the New Testament. Luke is thought to have been born in Antioch, to have been a physician, to have traveled widely with the apostle Paul, and to have written the Acts of the Apostles. In Luke 15:11–32, Christ tells the parable of the "The Prodigal Son."

THE PRODIGAL SON

A certain man had two sons: and the younger of them said to his father, "Father, give me the portion of goods that falleth to me." And he divided unto them his living. And not many days after, the younger son gathered all together, and took his journey into a far country, and there wasted his substance with riotous living. And when he had spent all, there arose a mighty famine in that land, and he began to be in want. And he went and joined himself to a citizen of that country, and he sent him into his fields to feed swine. And he would fain have filled his belly with the husks that the swine did eat: and no man gave unto him. And when he came to himself, he said, "How many hired servants of my father's have bread enough and to spare, and I perish with hunger? I will arise and go to my father, and will say unto him, 'Father, I have sinned against heaven, and before thee. And am no more worthy to be called thy son: make me as one of thy hired servants.'" And he arose, and came to his father. But when he was yet a great way off, his father saw him, and had compassion, and ran, and fell on his neck, and kissed him. And the son said unto him, "Father, I have sinned against heaven, and in thy sight, and am no more worthy to be called thy son." But the father said to his servants, Bring forth the best robe, and put it on him, and put a ring on his hand, and shoes on his feet. And bring hither the fatted calf, and kill it, and let us eat, and be merry. "For this my son was dead, and is alive again; he was lost, and is found." And they began to be merry. Now his elder son was in the field, and as he came and drew nigh to the house, he heard music and dancing. And he called one of the servants, and asked what these things meant. And he said unto him. "Thy brother is come, and thy father hath killed the fatted calf, because he hath received him safe and sound." And he was angry, and would not go in: therefore came his father out, and entreated him. And he answering said to his father, "Lo, these many years do I serve thee, neither transgressed I at any time thy commandment, and yet thou never gavest me a kid, that I might make merry with my friends: But as soon as this thy son was come, which hath devoured thy living with harlots, thou hast killed for him the fatted calf." And he said unto him, "Son, thou art ever with me, and all that I have is thine. It was meet that we should make merry, and be glad: for this thy brother was dead, and is alive again: and was lost, and is found."

Questions

1. Summarize the story of the "The Prodigal Son." What is the intended spiritual lesson of the parable?
2. Explain the ethical or moral decisions that the father and his two sons make or need to make in the parable.
3. Compare and contrast the two brothers.
4. What is the older brother's reaction to his father's decision?
5. What might the parable suggest about work and the relationship between a boss and a worker? Is the father in the parable accountable to anyone for his decision?
6. Do you think that the father's decision is fair? Do you think that a similar situation would present most employers and fathers with an ethical and moral dilemma? Why or why not?
7. What practical lesson might a manual laborer take from the parable? What do you think the reaction might be from the workers in O'Neill's *The Hairy Ape*, the illegal immigrants in Guthrie's "Deportees," or the wait staff in Ehrenreich's *Nickel and Dimed?*

William Wordsworth (1770–1850)

William Wordsworth is one of English literature's most important poets. He was born in England's Lake District, where he would live most of his life and whose people and landscape would inspire much of his poetry. As a young man, Wordsworth traveled to France where he met Annette Vallon, with whom he would have a child, but because of political circumstances, which included a war, would never marry. The French Revolution and the rise of the common man fueled Wordsworth's democratic impulses and had a sharp effect on his poetics. In his poetry, Wordsworth celebrates common people often performing ordinary tasks in, what he calls, verse with "the real language of men." In 1798, he and Samuel Taylor Coleridge published the *Lyrical Ballads*, the book often credited with launching the Romantic Age of English literature.

Inspired by nature, Wordsworth loved to walk in the wilderness, and took frequent and long walking tours of the English and European countryside. He was often accompanied by his sister Dorothy, his lifelong intellectual companion. In 1802, Wordsworth married Mary Hutchinson, whom he had known since childhood and with whom he had five children. As Wordsworth aged, his politics became more conservative and, by the time he was forty, his poetic powers had waned. In 1843, however, he was appointed Poet Laureate of England, a post he held until his death.

WRITTEN IN LONDON, SEPTEMBER 1802

O friend! I know not which way I must look
For comfort, being, as I am, oppressed,
To think that now our life is only dressed
For show; mean handiwork of craftsman, cook,
Or groom! We must run glittering like a brook
In the open sunshine, or we are unblessed;
The wealthiest man among us is the best;
No grandeur now in Nature or in book
Delights us. Rapine, avarice, expense,
10   This is idolatry, and these we adore;

Plain living and high thinking are no more;
The homely beauty of the good old cause
Is gone; our peace, our fearful innocence,
And pure religion breathing household laws.

1802

Questions

1. What is the speaker's complaint in this poem?
2. According to the poem's implication, what must we do to correct the situation?
3. What does the poem imply about work?
4. How is the speaker consistent with Thoreau's attitude toward work in "Life without Principle" and the speaker's attitude in Frost's "The Tuft of Flowers"?
5. How is the cultural atmosphere of the London in the poem similar to the atmosphere of Wall Street in Herman Melville's "Bartleby, the Scrivener" and Dublin in Joyce's "Counterparts"?
6. How does the speaker in "Editor Whedon" illustrate the speaker's complaint?

Herman Melville
(1819–1891)

Herman Melville was born into two prominent New York families, but his life took a sharp turn when, at twelve years of age, his father died shortly after declaring bankruptcy. His mother was forced to rely on relatives for support. At nineteen years of age, Melville went to sea, where he had experiences and found material for inclusion in his fiction and poetry. As Ishmael, the narrator of *Moby-Dick*, says, "A whale ship was my Yale College and my Harvard." Melville's first novel, *Typee* (1846), told about life among cannibals and became a best seller. Over the next eleven years, he published ten major volumes to various critical and commercial successes. *Moby-Dick*, his masterpiece and a world classic, was published in 1851. Exhausted by his output and frustrated by his inconsistent success, Melville stopped writing fiction for more than thirty years after he published *The Confidence-Man* in 1857. He continued writing poetry, and although largely underappreciated at publication, his Civil War poetry ranks next to Walt Whitman's war poems for sensitivity, authority, and revelation. Melville returned to fiction near the end of his life and produced another classic, the posthumously published *Billy Budd, Sailor.* Today, Melville is regarded as one of the world's great writers.

"Bartleby, the Scrivener," which was first published in *Putnam's Monthly Magazine* in November and December 1853, stands among Melville's finest works. The story evokes the familiar Melville themes of authority and submission, work and identity, the dehumanization of capitalism, the dangers of isolation, and the omnipresence of ambiguities.

BARTLEBY, THE SCRIVENER

A Story of Wall Street

I am a rather elderly man. The nature of my avocations, for the last thirty years, has brought me into more than ordinary contact with what would seem an interesting and somewhat singular set of men, of whom, as yet, nothing, that I know of, has ever been written—I mean,

the law-copyists, or scriveners. I have known very many of them, profession-
ally and privately, and, if I pleased, could relate divers histories, at which
good-natured gentlemen might smile, and sentimental souls might weep. But I
waive the biographies of all other scriveners, for a few passages in the life of
Bartleby, who was a scrivener, the strangest I ever saw, or heard of. While, of
other law-copyists, I might write the complete life, of Bartleby nothing of that
sort can be done. I believe that no materials exist, for a full and satisfactory biography of this man. It is an irreparable loss to literature. Bartleby was one of
those beings of whom nothing is ascertainable, except from the original
sources, and, in his case, those are very small. What my own astonished eyes
saw of Bartleby, *that* is all I know of him, except, indeed, one vague report,
which will appear in the sequel.

Ere introducing the scrivener, as he first appeared to me, it is fit I make
some mention of myself, my *employés,* my business, my chambers, and general
surroundings, because some such description is indispensable to an adequate
understanding of the chief character about to be presented. Imprimis:[1] I am a
man who, from his youth upwards, has been filled with a profound conviction
that the easiest way of life is the best. Hence, though I belong to a profession
proverbially energetic and nervous, even to turbulence, at times, yet nothing of
that sort have I ever suffered to invade my peace. I am one of those unambi-
tious lawyers who never address a jury, or in any way draw down public applause; but, in the cool tranquillity of a snug retreat, do a snug business among
rich men's bonds, and mortgages, and title-deeds. All who know me, consider
me an eminently *safe* man. The late John Jacob Astor,[2] a personage little given
to poetic enthusiasm, had no hesitation in pronouncing my first grand point to
be prudence; my next, method. I do not speak it in vanity, but simply record
the fact, that I was not unemployed in my profession by the late John Jacob
Astor; a name which, I admit, I love to repeat; for it hath a rounded and orbic-
ular sound to it, and rings like unto bullion. I will freely add, that I was not in-
sensible to the late John Jacob Astor's good opinion.

Some time prior to the period at which this little history begins, my avocations had been largely increased. The good old office, now extinct in the State of
New York, of a Master in Chancery, had been conferred upon me. It was not a
very arduous office, but very pleasantly remunerative. I seldom lose my temper;
much more seldom indulge in dangerous indignation at wrongs and outrages; but
I must be permitted to be rash here and declare, that I consider the sudden and violent abrogation of the office of Master in Chancery, by the new Constitution, as
a—premature act; inasmuch as I had counted upon a life-lease of the profits,
whereas I only received those of a few short years. But this is by the way.

My chambers were up stairs, at No.—Wall Street. At one end, they looked
upon the white wall of the interior of a spacious skylight shaft, penetrating the
building from top to bottom.

---

[1] *Imprimis:* in the first place (Latin)
[2] *John Jacob Astor* (1763–1848) was an extremely wealthy American capitalist.

This view might have been considered rather tame than otherwise, deficient in what landscape painters call "life." But, if so, the view from the other end of my chambers offered, at least, a contrast, if nothing more. In that direction, my windows commanded an unobstructed view of a lofty brick wall, black by age and everlasting shade; which wall required no spyglass to bring out its lurking beauties, but, for the benefit of all near-sighted spectators, was pushed up to within ten feet of my window-panes. Owing to the great height of the surrounding buildings, and my chambers being on the second floor, the interval between this wall and mine not a little resembled a huge square cistern.

At the period just preceding the advent of Bartleby, I had two persons as copyists in my employment, and a promising lad as an office-boy. First, Turkey; second, Nippers; third, Ginger Nut. These may seem names, the like of which are not usually found in the Directory. In truth, they were nicknames, mutually conferred upon each other by my three clerks, and were deemed expressive of their respective persons or characters. Turkey was a short, pursy Englishman, of about my own age—that is, somewhere not far from sixty. In the morning, one might say, his face was of a Fine florid hue, but after twelve o'clock, meridian—his dinner hour—it blazed like a grate full of Christmas coals; and continued blazing—but, as it were, with a gradual wane—till six o'clock, P.M., or thereabouts; after which, I saw no more of the proprietor of the face, which, gaining its meridian with the sun, seemed to set with it, to rise, culminate, and decline the following day, with the like regularity and undiminished glory. There are many singular coincidences I have known in the course of my life, not the least among which was the fact, that, exactly when Turkey displayed his fullest beams from his red and radiant countenance, just then, too, at that critical moment, began the daily period when I considered his business capacities as seriously disturbed for the remainder of the twenty-four hours. Not that he was absolutely idle, or adverse to business then; far from it. The difficulty was, he was apt to be altogether too energetic. There was a strange, inflamed, flurried, flighty recklessness of activity about him. He would be incautious in dipping his pen into his inkstand. All his blots upon my documents were dropped there after twelve o'clock, meridian. Indeed, not only would he be reckless, and sadly given to making blots in the afternoon, but, some days, he went further, and was rather noisy. At such times, too, his face flamed with augmented blazonry, as if cannel coal had been heaped on anthracite. He made an unpleasant racket with his chair; spilled his sand-box; in mending his pens, impatiently split them all to pieces, and threw them on the floor in a sudden passion; stood up, and leaned over his table, boxing his papers about in a most indecorous manner, very sad to behold in an elderly man like him. Nevertheless, as he was in many ways a most valuable person to me, and all the time before twelve o'clock, meridian, was the quickest, steadiest creature, too, accomplishing a great deal of work in a style not easily to be matched—for these reasons, I was willing to overlook his eccentricities, though, indeed, occasionally, I remonstrated with him. I did this very gently, however, because, though the civilest, nay, the blandest and most reverential of men in the morning, yet, in the afternoon, he was disposed, upon provocation, to be slightly rash with his tongue—in fact, insolent. Now, valuing his morning services as I did, and resolved not to lose them—yet, at the same time, made uncomfortable by his inflamed ways after twelve o'clock—and being a man of peace, unwilling by my admonitions to call forth unseemly retorts from him, I took upon me, one Saturday noon (he was always worse on Saturdays) to hint to him, very kindly, that, perhaps, now that he was growing old, it might be well to abridge his labours; in short, he need not come to my chambers after twelve o'clock, but, dinner over, had best go home to his lodgings, and rest himself till tea-time. But no; he insisted upon his afternoon devotions. His countenance became intolerably fervid, as he oratorically assured me—gesticulating with a long ruler at the other end of the room—that if his services in the morning were useful, how indispensable, then, in the afternoon?

5   "With submission, sir," said Turkey, on this occasion, "I consider myself your right-hand man. In the morning I but marshal and deploy my columns; but in the afternoon I put myself at their head, and gallantly charge the foe, thus"— and he made a violent thrust with the ruler.

"But the blots, Turkey," intimated I.

"True; but, with submission, sir, behold these hairs! I am getting old. Surely, sir, a blot or two of a warm afternoon is not to be severely urged against gray hairs. Old age—even if it blot the page—is honorable. With submission, sir, we *both* are getting old."

10   This appeal to my fellow-feeling was hardly to be resisted. At all events, I saw that go he would not. So, I made up my mind to let him stay, resolving, nevertheless, to see to it that, during the afternoon, he had to do with my less important papers.

Nippers, the second on my list, was a whiskered, sallow, and, upon the whole, rather piratical-looking young man, of about five-and-twenty. I always deemed him the victim of two evil powers—ambition and indigestion. The ambition was evinced by a certain impatience of the duties of a mere copyist, an unwarrantable usurpation of strictly professional affairs such as the original drawing up of legal documents. The indigestion seemed betokened in an occasional nervous testiness and grinning irritability, causing the teeth to audibly grind together over mistakes committed in copying; unnecessary maledictions, hissed, rather than spoken, in the heat of business; and especially by a continual discontent with the height of the table where he worked. Though of a very ingenious mechanical turn, Nippers could never get this table to suit him. He put chips under it, blocks of various sorts, bits of pasteboard, and at last went so far as to attempt an exquisite adjustment, by final pieces of folded blotting-paper. But no invention would answer. If, for the sake of easing his back, he brought the table-lid at a sharp angle well up toward his chin, and wrote there like a man using the steep roof of a Dutch house for his desk, then he declared that it stopped the circulation in his arms. If now he lowered the table to his waistbands, and stooped over it in writing, then there was a sore aching in his back. In short, the truth of the matter was, Nippers knew not what he wanted. Or, if he wanted anything, it was to be rid of a scrivener's table altogether. Among the manifestations of his diseased ambition was a fondness he had for receiving visits from certain ambiguous-looking fellows in seedy coats, whom he called his clients. Indeed, I was aware that not only was he, at times, considerable of a ward-politician, but he occasionally did a little business at the Justices' courts, and was not unknown on the steps of the Tombs.[3] I have good reason to believe, however, that one individual who called upon him at my chambers, and who, with a grand air, he insisted was his client, was no other than a dun, and the alleged title-deed, a bill. But, with all his failings, and the annoyances he caused me, Nippers, like his compatriot Turkey, was a very useful man to me; wrote a neat, swift hand; and, when he chose, was not deficient in a gentlemanly sort of deportment. Added to this, he always dressed in a gentlemanly sort of way; and so, incidentally, reflected credit upon my chambers. Whereas, with respect to Turkey, I had much ado to keep him from being a reproach to me. His clothes were apt to look oily, a smell of eating-houses. He wore his pantaloons very loose and baggy in summer. His coats were execrable; his hat not to be handled. But while the hat was a thing of indifference to me, inasmuch as his natural civility and deference, as a dependent Englishman, always led him to doff it the moment he entered the room, yet his coat was another matter. Concerning his coats, I reasoned with him; but with no effect. The truth was, I suppose, that a man with so small an income could not afford to sport such a lustrous face and a lustrous coat at one and the same time. As Nippers once observed, Turkey's money went chiefly for red ink. One winter day, I presented Turkey with a highly respectable-looking coat of my own—a padded gray coat, of a most comfortable warmth, and which buttoned straight up from the knee to the neck. I thought Turkey would appreciate the favor, and abate his rashness and obstreperousness of afternoons. But no; I verily believe that buttoning himself up in so downy and blanket-like a coat had a pernicious effect upon him—upon the same principle that too much oats are bad for horses. In fact, precisely as a rash, restive horse is said to feel his oats, so Turkey felt his coat. It made him insolent. He was a man whom prosperity harmed.

Though, concerning the self-indulgent habits of Turkey, I had my own private surmises, yet, touching Nippers, I was well persuaded that, whatever might be his faults in other respects, he was, at least, a temperate young man. But indeed, nature herself seemed to have been his vintner, and, at his birth, charged him so thoroughly with an irritable, brandy-like disposition, that all subsequent potations were needless. When I consider how, amid the stillness of my chambers, Nippers would sometimes impatiently rise from his seat, and stooping over his table, spread his arms wide apart, seize the whole desk, and move it, and jerk it, with a grim, grinding motion on the floor, as if the table were a perverse voluntary agent, intent on thwarting and vexing him, I plainly perceive that, for Nippers, brandy-and-water were altogether superfluous.

It was fortunate for me that, owing to its peculiar cause—indigestion—the irritability and consequent nervousness of Nippers were mainly observable in the morning, while in the afternoon he was comparatively mild. So that,

---

[3]a jail in New York City

Turkey's paroxysms only coming on about twelve o'clock, I never had to do with their eccentricities at one time. Their fits relieved each other, like guards. When Nippers' was on, Turkey's was off; and *vice versa*. This was a good natural arrangement, under the circumstances.

Ginger Nut, the third on my list, was a lad, some twelve years old. His father was a carman, ambitious of seeing his son on the bench instead of a cart, before he died. So he sent him to my office, as student at law, errand-boy, cleaner, and sweeper, at the rate of one dollar a week. He had a little desk to himself, but he did not use it much. Upon inspection, the drawer exhibited a great array of the shells of various sorts of nuts. Indeed, to this quickwitted youth, the whole noble science of the law was contained in a nut-shell. Not the least among the employments of Ginger Nut, as well as one which he discharged with the most alacrity, was his duty as cake and apple purveyor for Turkey and Nippers. Copying lawpapers being proverbially a dry, husky sort of business, my two scriveners were fain to moisten their mouths very often with Spitzenbergs, to be had at the numerous stalls nigh the Custom House and Post Office. Also, they sent Ginger Nut very frequently for that peculiar cake—small, flat, round, and very spicy—after which he had been named by them. Of a cold morning, when business was but dull, Turkey would gobble up scores of these cakes, as if they were mere wafers—indeed, they sell them at the rate of six or eight for a penny—the scrape of his pen blending with the crunching of the crisp particles in his mouth. Of all the fiery afternoon blunders and flurried rashnesses of Turkey, was his once moistening a ginger-cake between his lips, and clapping it on to a mortgage, for a seal. I came within an ace of dismissing him then. But he mollified me by making an oriental bow, and saying—   15

"With submission, sir, it was generous of me to find you in stationery on my own account."

Now my original business—that of a conveyancer and title hunter, and drawer-up of recondite documents of all sorts—was considerably increased by receiving the Master's office. There was now great work for scriveners. Not only must I push the clerks already with me, but I must have additional help.

In answer to my advertisement, a motionless young man one morning stood upon my office threshold, the door being open, for it was summer. I can see that figure now—pallidly neat, pitiably respectable, incurably forlorn! It was Bartleby.

After a few words touching his qualifications, I engaged him, glad to have among my corps of copyists a man of so singularly sedate an aspect, which I thought might operate beneficially upon the flighty temper of Turkey, and the fiery one of Nippers.

I should have stated before that ground-glass folding-doors divided my premises into two parts, one of which was occupied by my scriveners, the other by myself. According to my humor, I threw open these doors, or closed them. I resolved to assign Bartleby a corner by the folding-doors, but on my side of them, so as to have this quiet man within easy call, in case any trifling thing was to be done. I placed his desk close up to a small side-window in that part of the room, a window which originally had afforded a lateral view of certain grimy brickyards and bricks, but which, owing to subsequent erections, commanded at present no view at all, though it gave some light. Within three feet of the panes was a wall, and the light came down from far above, between two lofty buildings, as from a very small opening in a dome. Still further to a satisfactory arrangement, I procured a high green folding-screen, which might entirely isolate Bartleby from my sight, though not remove him from my voice. And thus, in a manner, privacy and society were conjoined.

At first, Bartleby did an extraordinary quantity of writing. As if long fam-   20
ishing for something to copy, he seemed to gorge himself on my documents. There was no pause for digestion. He ran a day and night line, copying by sunlight and by candle-light. I should have been quite delighted with his application, had he been cheerfully industrious. But he wrote on silently, palely, mechanically.

It is, of course, an indispensable part of a scrivener's business to verify the accuracy of his copy, word by word. Where there are two or more scriveners in an office, they assist each other in this examination, one reading from the copy, the other holding the original. It is a very dull, wearisome, and lethargic affair. I can readily imagine that, to some sanguine temperaments, it would be altogether intolerable. For example, I cannot credit that the mettlesome poet, Byron, would have contentedly sat down with Bartleby to examine a law document of, say five hundred pages, closely written in a crimpy hand.

Now and then, in the haste of business, it had been my habit to assist in comparing some brief document myself, calling Turkey or Nippers for this purpose. One object I had, in placing Bartleby so handy to me behind the screen, was, to avail myself of his services on such trivial occasions. It was on the third day, I think, of his being with me, and before any necessity had arisen for having his own writing examined, that, being much hurried to complete a small affair I had in hand, I abruptly called to Bartleby. In my haste and natural expectancy of instant compliance, I sat with my head bent over the original on my desk, and my right hand sideways, and somewhat nervously extended with the copy, so that, immediately upon emerging from his retreat, Bartleby might snatch it and proceed to business without the least delay.

In this very attitude did I sit when I called to him, rapidly stating what it was I wanted him to do—namely, to examine a small paper with me. Imagine my surprise, nay, my consternation, when, without moving from his privacy, Bartleby, in a singularly mild, firm voice, replied, "I would prefer not to."

I sat awhile in perfect silence, rallying my stunned faculties. Immediately it occurred to me that my ears had deceived me, or Bartleby had entirely misunderstood my meaning. I repeated my request in the clearest tone I could assume; but in quite as clear a one came the previous reply, "I would prefer not to."

"Prefer not to," echoed I, rising in high excitement, and crossing the room   25
with a stride. "What do you mean? Are you moonstruck? I want you to help me compare this sheet here—take it," and I thrust it towards him.

"I would prefer not to," said he.

I looked at him steadfastly. His face was leanly composed; his gray eye dimly calm. Not a wrinkle of agitation rippled him. Had there been the least uneasiness, anger, impatience, or impertinence in his manner; in other words, had there been anything ordinarily human about him, doubtless I should have violently dismissed him from the premises. But as it was, I should have as soon thought of turning my pale plaster-of-paris bust of Cicero out of doors. I stood gazing at him awhile, as he went on with his own writing, and then reseated myself at my desk. This is very strange, thought I. What had one best do? But my business hurried me. I concluded to forget the matter for the present, reserving it for my future leisure. So, calling Nippers from the other room, the paper was speedily examined.

A few days after this, Bartleby concluded four lengthy documents, being quadruplicates of a week's testimony taken before me in my High Court of Chancery. It became necessary to examine them. It was an important suit, and great accuracy was imperative. Having all things arranged, I called Turkey, Nippers, and Ginger Nut, from the next room, meaning to place the four copies in the hands of my four clerks, while I should read from the original. Accordingly, Turkey, Nippers, and Ginger Nut had taken their seats in a row, each with his document in his hand, when I called to Bartleby to join this interesting group.

"Bartleby! quick, I am waiting."

30   I heard a slow scrape of his chair legs on the uncarpeted floor, and soon he appeared standing at the entrance of his hermitage.

"What is wanted?" said he, mildly.

"The copies, the copies," said I, hurriedly. "We are going to examine them. There"—and I held towards him the fourth quadruplicate.

"I would prefer not to," he said, and gently disappeared behind the screen.

For a few moments I was turned into a pillar of salt, standing at the head of my seated column of clerks. Recovering myself, I advanced towards the screen, and demanded the reason for such extraordinary conduct.

35   "*Why* do you refuse?"

"I would prefer not to."

With any other man I should have flown outright into a dreadful passion, scorned all further words, and thrust him ignominiously from my presence. But there was something about Bartleby that not only strangely disarmed me, but, in a wonderful manner, touched and disconcerted me. I began to reason with him.

"These are your own copies we are about to examine. It is labour saving to you, because one examination will answer for your four papers. It is common usage. Every copyist is bound to help examine his copy. Is it not so? Will you not speak? Answer!"

"I prefer not to," he replied in a flute-like tone. It seemed to me that, while I had been addressing him, he carefully revolved every statement that I made; fully comprehended the meaning; could not gainsay the irresistible conclusion; but, at the same time, some paramount consideration prevailed with him to reply as he did.

"You are decided, then, not to comply with my request—a request made 40
according to common usage and common sense?"

He briefly gave me to understand, that on that point my judgment was
sound. Yes: his decision was irreversible.

It is not seldom the case that, when a man is browbeaten in some unprece-
dented and violently unreasonable way, he begins to stagger in his own plainest
faith. He begins, as it were, vaguely to surmise that, wonderful as it may be, all
the justice and all the reason is on the other side. Accordingly, if any disinterested
persons are present, he turns to them for some reinforcement for his own falter-
ing mind.

"Turkey," said I, "what do you think of this? Am I not right?"

"With submission, sir," said Turkey, in his blandest tone, "I think that you are."

"Nippers," said I, "what do *you* think of it?"   45

"I think I should kick him out of the office."

(The reader, of nice perceptions, will have perceived that, it being morning, Turkey's answer is couched in polite and tranquil terms, but Nippers
replies in ill-tempered ones. Or, to repeat a previous sentence, Nippers's ugly
mood was on duty, and Turkey's off.)

"Ginger Nut," said I, willing to enlist the smallest suffrage in my behalf,
"what do *you* think of it?"

"I think, sir, he's a little *luny*," replied Ginger Nut, with a grin.

"You hear what they say," said I, turning towards the screen, "come forth 50
and do your duty."

But he vouchsafed no reply. I pondered a moment in sore perplexity. But
once more business hurried me. I determined again to postpone the consideration of this dilemma to my future leisure. With a little trouble we made out to
examine the papers without Bartleby, though at every page or two Turkey deferentially dropped his opinion, that this proceeding was quite out of the common; while Nippers, twitching in his chair with a dyspeptic nervousness,
ground out, between his set teeth, occasional hissing maledictions against the
stubborn oaf behind the screen. And for his (Nippers's) part, this was the first
and the last time he would do another man's business without pay.

Meanwhile Bartleby sat in his hermitage, oblivious to everything but his
own peculiar business there.

Some days passed, the scrivener being employed upon another lengthy
work. His late remarkable conduct led me to regard his ways narrowly. I observed that he never went to dinner; indeed, that he never went anywhere. As
yet I had never, of my personal knowledge, known him to be outside of my office. He was a perpetual sentry in the corner. At about eleven o'clock though,
in the morning, I noticed that Ginger Nut would advance toward the opening in
Bartleby's screen, as if silently beckoned thither by a gesture invisible to me
where I sat. The boy would then leave the office, jingling a few pence, and
reappear with a handful of ginger-nuts, which he delivered in the hermitage, receiving two of the cakes for his trouble.

He lives, then, on ginger-nuts, thought I; never eats a dinner, properly
speaking; he must be a vegetarian, then; but no; he never eats even vegetables,

he eats nothing but ginger-nuts. My mind then ran on in reveries concerning the probable effects upon the human constitution of living entirely on ginger-nuts. Ginger-nuts are so called, because they contain ginger as one of their peculiar constituents, and the final flavoring one. Now, what was ginger? A hot, spicy thing. Was Bartleby hot and spicy? Not at all. Ginger, then, had no effect upon Bartleby. Probably he preferred it should have none.

55   Nothing so aggravates an earnest person as a passive resistance. If the individual so resisted be of a not inhumane temper, and the resisting one perfectly harmless in his passivity, then, in the better moods of the former, he will endeavor charitably to construe to his imagination what proves impossible to be solved by his judgment. Even so, for the most part, I regarded Bartleby and his ways. Poor fellow! thought I, he means no mischief; it is plain he intends no insolence; his aspect sufficiently evinces that his eccentricities are involuntary. He is useful to me. I can get along with him. If I turn him away, the chances are he will fall in with some less indulgent employer, and then he will be rudely treated, and perhaps driven forth miserably to starve. Yes. Here I can cheaply purchase a delicious self-approval. To befriend Bartleby; to humour him in his strange wilfulness, will cost me little or nothing, while I lay up in my soul what will eventually prove a sweet morsel for my conscience. But this mood was not invariable with me. The passiveness of Bartleby sometimes irritated me. I felt strangely goaded on to encounter him in new opposition—to elicit some angry spark from him answerable to my own. But, indeed, I might as well have essayed to strike fire with my knuckles against a bit of Windsor soap. But one afternoon the evil impulse in me mastered me, and the following little scene ensued:

"Bartleby," said I, "when those papers are all copied, I will compare them with you."

"I would prefer not to."

"How? Surely you do not mean to persist in that mulish vagary?"

No answer.

60   I threw open the folding-doors nearby, and turning upon Turkey and Nippers, exclaimed:

"Bartleby a second time says, he won't examine his papers. What do you think of it, Turkey?"

It was afternoon, be it remembered. Turkey sat glowing like a brass boiler; his bald head steaming; his hands reeling among his blotted papers.

"Think of it?" roared Turkey; "I think I'll just step behind his screen, and black his eyes for him!"

So saying, Turkey rose to his feet and threw his arms into a pugilistic position. He was hurrying away to make good his promise, when I detained him, alarmed at the effect of incautiously rousing Turkey's combativeness after dinner.

65   "Sit down, Turkey," said I, "and hear what Nippers has to say. What do you think of it, Nippers? Would I not be justified in immediately dismissing Bartleby?"

"Excuse me, that is for you to decide, sir. I think his conduct quite unusual, and, indeed, unjust, as regards Turkey and myself. But it may only be a passing whim."

"Ah," exclaimed I, "you have strangely changed your mind, then—you speak very gently of him now."

"All beer," cried Turkey; "gentleness is effects of beer—Nippers and I dined together to-day. You see how gentle *I* am, sir. Shall I go and black his eyes?"

"You refer to Bartleby, I suppose. No, not to-day, Turkey," I replied; "pray, put up your fists."

I closed the doors, and again advanced towards Bartleby. I felt additional 70 incentives tempting me to my fate. I burned to be rebelled against again. I remembered that Bartleby never left the office.

"Bartleby," said I, "Ginger Nut is away; just step around to the Post Office, won't you?" (it was but a three minutes' walk) "and see if there is anything for me."

"I would prefer not to."

"You *will* not?"

"I *prefer* not."

I staggered to my desk, and sat there in a deep study. My blind inveteracy 75 returned. Was there any other thing in which I could procure myself to be ignominiously repulsed by this lean, penniless wight?—my hired clerk? What added thing is there, perfectly reasonable, that he will be sure to refuse to do?

"Bartleby!"

No answer.

"Bartleby," in a louder tone.

No answer.

"Bartleby," I roared. 80

Like a very ghost, agreeably to the laws of magical invocation, at the third summons, he appeared at the entrance of his hermitage.

"Go to the next room, and tell Nippers to come to me."

"I prefer not to," he respectfully and slowly said, and mildly disappeared.

"Very good, Bartleby," said I, in a quiet sort of serenely-severe self-possessed tone, intimating the unalterable purpose of some terrible retribution very close at hand. At the moment I half intended something of the kind. But upon the whole, as it was drawing towards my dinner-hour, I thought it best to put on my hat and walk home for the day, suffering much from perplexity and distress of mind.

Shall I acknowledge it? The conclusion of this whole business was, that it 85 soon became a fixed fact of my chambers, that a pale young scrivener, by the name of Bartleby, had a desk there; that he copied for me at the usual rate of four cents a folio (one hundred words); but he was permanently exempt from examining the work done by him, that duty being transferred to Turkey and Nippers, out of compliment, doubtless, to their superior acuteness; moreover, said Bartleby was never, on any account, to be dispatched on the most trivial errand of any sort; and that even if entreated to take upon him such a matter, it was generally understood that he would "prefer not to"—in other words, that he would refuse point-blank.

As days passed on, I became considerably reconciled to Bartleby. His steadiness, his freedom from all dissipation, his incessant industry (except when he chose to throw himself into a standing revery behind his screen), his great stillness, his unalterableness of demeanor under all circumstances, made him a valuable acquisition. One prime thing was this—*he was always there*—first in the morning, continually through the day, and the last at night. I had a singular confidence in his honesty. I felt my most precious papers perfectly safe in his hands. Sometimes, to be sure, I could not, for the very soul of me, avoid falling into sudden spasmodic passions with him. For it was exceeding difficult to bear in mind all the time those strange peculiarities, privileges, and unheard-of exemptions, forming the tacit stipulations on Bartleby's part under which he remained in my office. Now and then, in the eagerness of dispatching pressing business, I would inadvertently summon Bartleby, in a short, rapid tone, to put his finger, say, on the incipient tie of a bit of red tape with which I was about compressing some papers. Of course, from behind the screen the usual answer, "I prefer not to," was sure to come; and then, how could a human creature, with the common infirmities of our nature, refrain from bitterly exclaiming upon such perverseness—such unreasonableness? However, every added repulse of this sort which I received only tended to lessen the probability of my repeating the inadvertence.

Here it must be said, that, according to the custom of most legal gentlemen occupying chambers in densely populated law-buildings, there were several keys to my door. One was kept by a woman residing in the attic, which person weekly scrubbed and daily swept and dusted my apartments. Another was kept by Turkey for convenience sake. The third I sometimes carried in my own pocket. The fourth I knew not who had.

Now, one Sunday morning I happened to go to Trinity Church, to hear a celebrated preacher, and finding myself rather early on the ground I thought I would walk round to my chambers for a while. Luckily I had my key with me; but upon applying it to the lock, I found it resisted by something inserted from the inside. Quite surprised, I called out; when to my consternation a key was turned from within; and thrusting his lean visage at me, and holding the door ajar, the apparition of Bartleby appeared, in his shirt-sleeves, and otherwise in a strangely tattered *deshabille*, saying quietly that he was sorry, but he was deeply engaged just then, and—preferred not admitting me at present. In a brief word or two, he moreover added, that perhaps I had better walk round the block two or three times, and by that time he would probably have concluded his affairs.

Now, the utterly unsurmised appearance of Bartleby, tenanting my law-chambers of a Sunday morning, with his cadaverously gentlemanly *nonchalance*, yet withal firm and self-possessed, had such a strange effect upon me, that incontinently I slunk away from my own door, and did as desired. But not without sundry twinges of impotent rebellion against the mild effrontery of this unaccountable scrivener. Indeed, it was his wonderful mildness chiefly, which not only disarmed me, but unmanned me, as it were. For I consider that one, for the time, is a sort of unmanned when he tranquilly permits his hired clerk to dictate to him, and order him away from his own premises. Furthermore, I was full of uneasiness as to what Bartleby could possibly be doing in my office in his shirt-sleeves, and in an otherwise dismantled condition of a Sunday morning. Was anything amiss going on? Nay, that was out of the question. It was not to be thought of for a moment that Bartleby was an immoral person. But what could he be doing there?—copying? Nay again, whatever might be his eccentricities, Bartleby was an eminently decorous person. He would be the last man to sit down to his desk in any state approaching to nudity. Besides, it was Sunday; and there was something about Bartleby that forbade the supposition that he would by any secular occupation violate the proprieties of the day.

Nevertheless, my mind was not pacified; and full of a restless curiosity, at last I returned to the door. Without hindrance I inserted my key, opened it, and entered. Bartleby was not to be seen. I looked round anxiously, peeped behind his screen; but it was very plain that he was gone. Upon more closely examining the place, I surmised that for an indefinite period Bartleby must have ate, dressed, and slept in my office, and that too without plate, mirror, or bed. The cushioned seat of a rickety old sofa in one corner bore the faint impress of a lean, reclining form. Rolled away under his desk, I found a blanket; under the empty grate a blacking box and brush; on a chair, a tin basin, with soap and a ragged towel; in a newspaper a few crumbs of ginger-nuts and a morsel of cheese. Yes, thought I, it is evident enough that Bartleby has been making his home here, keeping bachelor's hall all by himself. Immediately then the thought came sweeping across me, what miserable friendlessness and loneliness are here revealed! His poverty is great; but his solitude, how horrible! Think of it: Of a Sunday, Wall Street is deserted as Petra;[4] and every night of every day it is an emptiness. This building, too, which of week-days hums with industry and life, at nightfall echoes with sheer vacancy, and all through Sunday is forlorn. And here Bartleby makes his home; sole spectator of a solitude which he has seen all populous—a sort of innocent and transformed Marius brooding among the ruins of Carthage?[5]

For the first time in my life a feeling of overpowering stinging melancholy seized me. Before, I had never experienced aught but a not unpleasing sadness. The bond of a common humanity now drew me irresistibly to gloom. A fraternal melancholy! For both I and Bartleby were sons of Adam. I remembered the bright silks and sparkling faces I had seen that day, in gala trim, swan-like sailing down the Mississippi of Broadway; and I contrasted them with the pallid copyist, and thought to myself, Ah, happiness courts the light, so we deem the world is gay; but misery hides aloof, so we deem that misery there is none. These sad fancyings—chimeras, doubtless, of a sick and silly brain—led on to other and more special thoughts, concerning the eccentricities of Bartleby. Presentiments of strange discoveries hovered round me. The scrivener's pale form appeared to me laid out, among uncaring strangers, in its shivering winding-sheet.

Suddenly I was attracted by Bartleby's closed desk, the key in open sight left in the lock.

---

[4]Petra is an ancient Arabian city.
[5]Gaius Marius was an exiled Roman general who found refuge in Carthage, a city destroyed by the Romans. Melville may be referencing the famous painting, *Marius amid the Ruins* (1807), by John Vanderlyn.

I mean no mischief, seek the gratification of no heartless curiosity, thought I; besides, the desk is mine, and its contents, too, so I will make bold to look within. Everything was methodically arranged, the papers smoothly placed. The pigeon-holes were deep, and removing the files of documents, I groped into their recesses. Presently I felt something there, and dragged it out. It was an old bandanna handkerchief, heavy and knotted. I opened it, and saw it was a saving's bank.

I now recalled all the quiet mysteries which I had noted in the man. I remembered that he never spoke but to answer; that, though at intervals he had considerable time to himself, yet I had never seen him reading—no, not even a newspaper; that for long periods he would stand looking out, at his pale window behind the screen, upon the dead brick wall; I was quite sure he never visited any refectory or eating-house; while his pale face clearly indicated that he never drank beer like Turkey; or tea and coffee even, like other men; that he never went anywhere in particular that I could learn; never went out for a walk; unless, indeed, that was the case at present; that he had declined telling who he was, or whence he came, or whether he had any relatives in the world; that though so thin and pale, he never complained of ill-health. And more than all, I remembered a certain unconscious air of pallid—how shall I call it?—of pallid haughtiness, say, or rather an austere reserve about him, which had positively awed me into my tame compliance with his eccentricities, when I had feared to ask him to do the slightest incidental thing for me, even though I might know, from his long-continued motionlessness, that behind his screen he must be standing in one of those dead-wall reveries of his.

95   Revolving all these things, and coupling them with the recently discovered fact, that he made my office his constant abiding place and home, and not forgetful of his morbid moodiness; revolving all these things, a prudential feeling began to steal over me. My first emotions had been those of pure melancholy and sincerest pity; but just in proportion as the forlornness of Bartleby grew and grew to my imagination, did that same melancholy merge into fear, that pity into repulsion. So true it is, and so terrible, too, that up to a certain point the thought or sight of misery enlists our best affections; but, in certain special cases, beyond that point it does not. They err who would assert that invariably this is owing to the inherent selfishness of the human heart. It rather proceeds from a certain hopelessness of remedying excessive and organic ill. To a sensitive being, pity is not seldom pain. And when at last it is perceived that such pity cannot lead to effectual succor, common sense bids the soul be rid of it. What I saw that morning persuaded me that the scrivener was the victim of innate and incurable disorder. I might give alms to his body; but his body did not pain him; it was his soul that suffered, and his soul I could not reach.

I did not accomplish the purpose of going to Trinity Church that morning. Somehow, the things I had seen disqualified me for the time from churchgoing. I walked homeward, thinking what I would do with Bartleby. Finally, I resolved upon this—I would put certain calm questions to him the next morning, touching his history, etc. and if he declined to answer them openly and unreservedly (and I suppose he would prefer not), then to give him a twenty dollar bill over and above whatever I might owe him, and tell him his services were no longer required; but that if in any other way I could assist him, I would be happy to do so, especially if he desired to return to his native place, wherever that might be, I would willingly help to defray the expenses. Moreover, if, after reaching home, he found himself at any time in want of aid, a letter from him would be sure of a reply.

The next morning came.

"Bartleby," said I, gently calling to him behind his screen.

No reply.

"Bartleby," said I, in a still gentler tone, "come here; I am not going to ask 100 you to do anything you would prefer not to do—I simply wish to speak to you."

Upon this he noiselessly slid into view.

"Will you tell me, Bartleby, where you were born?"

"I would prefer not to."

"Will you tell me *anything* about yourself?"

"I would prefer not to." 105

"But what reasonable objection can you have to speak to me? I feel friendly towards you."

He did not look at me while I spoke, but kept his glance fixed upon my bust of Cicero, which, as I then sat, was directly behind me, some six inches above my head.

"What is your answer, Bartleby?" said I, after waiting a considerable time for a reply, during which his countenance remained immovable, only there was the faintest conceivable tremor of the white attenuated mouth.

"At present I prefer to give no answer," he said, and retired into his hermitage.

It was rather weak in me I confess, but his manner, on this occasion, nettled me. Not only did there seem to lurk in it a certain calm disdain, but his perverseness seemed ungrateful, considering the undeniable good usage and indulgence he had received from me.

Again I sat ruminating what I should do. Mortified as I was at his behavior, and resolved as I had been to dismiss him when I entered my office, nevertheless I strangely felt something superstitious knocking at my heart, and forbidding me to carry out my purpose, and denouncing me for a villain if I dared to breathe one bitter word against this forlornest of mankind. At last, familiarly drawing my chair behind his screen, I sat down and said: "Bartleby, never mind, then, about revealing your history; but let me entreat you, as a friend, to comply as far as may be with the usages of this office. Say now, you will help to examine papers tomorrow or next day: in short, say now, that in a day or two you will begin to be a little reasonable:—say so, Bartleby."

"At present I would prefer not to be a little reasonable," was his mildly cadaverous reply.

Just then the folding-doors opened, and Nippers approached. He seemed suffering from an unusually bad night's rest, induced by severer indigestion than common. He overheard those final words of Bartleby.

"*Prefer not*, eh?" gritted Nippers—"I'd *prefer* him, if I were you, sir," addressing me—"I'd *prefer* him; I'd give him preferences, the stubborn mule! What is it, sir, pray, that he *prefers* not to do now?"

115 Bartleby moved not a limb.

"Mr. Nippers," said I, "I'd prefer that you would withdraw for the present."

Somehow, of late, I had got into the way of involuntarily using this word "prefer" upon all sorts of not exactly suitable occasions. And I trembled to think that my contact with the scrivener had already and seriously affected me in a mental way. And what further and deeper aberration might it not yet produce? This apprehension had not been without efficacy in determining me to summary measures.

As Nippers, looking very sour and sulky, was departing, Turkey blandly and deferentially approached.

"With submission, sir," said he, "yesterday I was thinking about Bartleby here, and I think that if he would but prefer to take a quart of good ale every day, it would do much towards mending him, and enabling him to assist in examining his papers."

120 "So you have got the word, too," said I, slightly excited.

"With submission, what word, sir?" asked Turkey, respectfully crowding himself into the contracted space behind the screen, and by so doing, making me jostle the scrivener. "What word, sir?"

"I would prefer to be left alone here," said Bartleby, as if offended at being mobbed in his privacy.

"*That's* the word, Turkey," said I—"*that's* it."

"Oh, *prefer?* oh yes—queer word. I never use it myself. But, sir, as I was saying, if he would but prefer—"

125 "Turkey," interrupted I, "you will please withdraw."

"Oh certainly, sir, if you prefer that I should."

As he opened the folding-door to retire, Nippers at his desk caught a glimpse of me, and asked whether I would prefer to have a certain paper copied on blue paper or white. He did not in the least roguishly accent the word "prefer." It was plain that it involuntarily rolled from his tongue. I thought to myself, surely I must get rid of a demented man, who already has in some degree turned the tongues, if not the heads of myself and clerks. But I thought it prudent not to break the dismission at once.

The next day I noticed that Bartleby did nothing but stand at his window in his dead-wall revery. Upon asking him why he did not write, he said that he had decided upon doing no more writing.

"Why, how now? what next?" exclaimed I, "do no more writing?"

130 "No more."

"And what is the reason?"

"Do you not see the reason for yourself?" he indifferently replied.

I looked steadfastly at him, and perceived that his eyes looked dull and glazed. Instantly it occurred to me, that this unexampled diligence in copying by his dim window for the first few weeks of his stay with me might have temporarily impaired his vision.

I was touched. I said something in condolence with him. I hinted that of course he did wisely in abstaining from writing for a while; and urged him to embrace that opportunity of taking wholesome exercise in the open air. This, however, he did not do. A few days after this, my other clerks being absent, and being in a great hurry to dispatch certain letters by the mail, I thought that, having nothing else earthly to do, Bartleby would surely be less inflexible than usual, and carry these letters to the Post Office. But he blankly declined. So, much to my inconvenience, I went myself.

Still added days went by. Whether Bartleby's eyes improved or not, I 135 could not say. To all appearance, I thought they did. But when I asked him if they did, he vouchsafed no answer. At all events, he would do no copying. At last, in replying to my urgings, he informed me that he had permanently given up copying.

"What!" exclaimed I; "suppose your eyes should get entirely well—better than ever before—would you not copy then?"

"I have given up copying," he answered, and slid aside.

He remained as ever, a fixture in my chamber. Nay—if that were possible— he became still more of a fixture than before. What was to be done? He would do nothing in the office; why should he stay there? In plain fact, he had now become a millstone to me, not only useless as a necklace, but afflictive to bear. Yet I was sorry for him. I speak less than truth when I say that, on his own account, he occasioned me uneasiness. If he would but have named a single relative or friend, I would instantly have written, and urged their taking the poor fellow away to some convenient retreat. But he seemed alone, absolutely alone in the universe. A bit of wreck in the mid-Atlantic. At length, necessities connected with my business tyrannized over all other considerations. Decently as I could, I told Bartleby that in six days' time he must unconditionally leave the office. I warned him to take measures, in the interval, for procuring some other abode. I offered to assist him in this endeavor, if he himself would but take the first step towards a removal. "And when you finally quit me, Bartleby," added I, "I shall see that you go not away entirely unprovided. Six days from this hour, remember."

At the expiration of that period, I peeped behind the screen, and lo! Bartleby was there.

I buttoned up my coat, balanced myself; advanced slowly towards him, 140 touched his shoulder, and said, "The time has come; you must quit this place; I am sorry for you; here is money; but you must go."

"I would prefer not," he replied, with his back still towards me.

"You *must.*"

He remained silent.

Now I had an unbounded confidence in this man's common honesty. He had frequently restored to me sixpences and shillings carelessly dropped upon the floor, for I am apt to be very reckless in such shirt-button affairs. The proceeding, then, which followed will not be deemed extraordinary.

"Bartleby," said I, "I owe you twelve dollars on account; here are thirty- 145 two, the odd twenty are yours—will you take it?" and I handed the bills towards him.

But he made no motion.

"I will leave them here, then," putting them under a weight on the table. Then taking my hat and cane and going to the door, I tranquilly turned and added—"After you have removed your things from these offices, Bartleby, you will of course lock the door—since every one is now gone for the day but you—and if you please, slip your key underneath the mat, so that I may have it in the morning. I shall not see you again; so good-bye to you. If, hereafter, in your new place of abode, I can be of any service to you, do not fail to advise me by letter. Good-bye, Bartleby, and fare you well."

But he answered not a word; like the last column of some ruined temple, he remained standing mute and solitary in the middle of the otherwise deserted room.

As I walked home in a pensive mood, my vanity got the better of my pity. I could not but highly plume myself on my masterly management in getting rid of Bartleby. Masterly I call it, and such it must appear to any dispassionate thinker. The beauty of my procedure seemed to consist in its perfect quietness. There was no vulgar bullying, no bravado of any sort, no choleric hectoring, and striding to and fro across the apartment, jerking out vehement commands for Bartleby to bundle himself off with his beggarly traps. Nothing of the kind. Without loudly bidding Bartleby depart—as an inferior genius might have done—I *assumed* the ground that depart he must; and upon that assumption built all I had to say. The more I thought over my procedure, the more I was charmed with it. Nevertheless, next morning, upon awakening, I had my doubts—I had somehow slept off the fumes of vanity. One of the coolest and wisest hours a man has, is just after he awakes in the morning. My procedure seemed as sagacious as ever—but only in theory. How it would prove in practice—there was the rub. It was truly a beautiful thought to have assumed Bartleby's departure; but, after all, that assumption was simply my own, and none of Bartleby's. The great point was, not whether I had assumed that he would quit me, but whether he would prefer so to do. He was more a man of preferences than assumptions.

150   After breakfast, I walked down town, arguing the probabilities *pro* and *con*. One moment I thought it would prove a miserable failure, and Bartleby would be found all alive at my office as usual; the next moment it seemed certain that I should find his chair empty. And so I kept veering about. At the corner of Broadway and Canal Street, I saw quite an excited group of people standing in earnest conversation.

"I'll take odds he doesn't," said a voice as I passed.

"Doesn't go?—done!" said I; "Put up your money."

I was instinctively putting my hand in my pocket to produce my own, when I remembered that this was an election day. The words I had overheard bore no reference to Bartleby, but to the success or non-success of some candidate for the mayoralty. In my intent frame of mind, I had, as it were, imagined that all Broadway shared in my excitement, and were debating the same question with me. I passed on, very thankful that the uproar of the street screened my momentary absent-mindedness.

As I had intended, I was earlier than usual at my office door. I stood listening for a moment. All was still. He must be gone. I tried the knob. The door was locked. Yes, my procedure had worked to a charm; he indeed must be vanished. Yet a certain melancholy mixed with this: I was almost sorry for my brilliant success. I was fumbling under the door mat for the key, which Bartleby was to have left there for me, when accidentally my knee knocked against a panel, producing a summoning sound, and in response a voice came to me from within—"Not yet; I am occupied."

It was Bartleby.

155

I was thunderstruck. For an instant I stood like the man who, pipe in mouth, was killed one cloudless afternoon long ago in Virginia, by summer lightning; at his own warm open window he was killed, and remained leaning out there upon the dreamy afternoon, till some one touched him, when he fell.

"Not gone!" I murmured at last. But again obeying that wondrous ascendancy which the inscrutable scrivener had over me, and from which ascendancy, for all my chafing, I could not completely escape, I slowly went downstairs and out into the street, and while walking round the block, considered what I should next do in this unheard-of perplexity. Turn the man out by an actual thrusting I could not; to drive him away by calling him hard names would not do; calling in the police was an unpleasant idea; and yet, permit him to enjoy his cadaverous triumph over me—this, too, I could not think of. What was to be done? or, if nothing could be done, was there anything further that I could *assume* in the matter? Yes, as before I had prospectively assumed that Bartleby would depart, so now I might retrospectively assume that departed he was. In the legitimate carrying out of this assumption, I might enter my office in a great hurry, and pretending not to see Bartleby at all, walk straight against him as if he were air. Such a proceeding would in a singular degree have the appearance of a home-thrust. It was hardly possible that Bartleby could withstand such an application of the doctrine of assumption. But upon second thoughts the success of the plan seemed rather dubious. I resolved to argue the matter over with him again.

"Bartleby," said I, entering the office, with a quietly severe expression, "I am seriously displeased. I am pained, Bartleby. I had thought better of you. I had imagined you of such a gentlemanly organization, that in any delicate dilemma a slight hint would suffice—in short, an assumption. But it appears I am deceived. Why," I added, unaffectedly starting, "you have not even touched that money yet," pointing to it, just where I had left it the evening previous.

He answered nothing.

"Will you, or will you not, quit me?" I now demanded in a sudden passion, advancing close to him.

160

"I would prefer *not* to quit you," he replied, gently emphasizing the *not*.

"What earthly right have you to stay here? Do you pay any rent? Do you pay my taxes? Or is this property yours?"

He answered nothing.

"Are you ready to go on and write now? Are your eyes recovered? Could you copy a small paper for me this morning? or help examine a few lines? or step round to the Post Office? In a word, will you do anything at all, to give a coloring to your refusal to depart the premises?"

165   He silently retired into his hermitage.

I was now in such a state of nervous resentment that I thought it but prudent to check myself at present from further demonstrations. Bartleby and I were alone. I remembered the tragedy of the unfortunate Adams and the still more unfortunate Colt[6] in the solitary office of the latter; and how poor Colt, being dreadfully incensed by Adams, and imprudently permitting himself to get wildly excited, was at unawares hurried into his fatal act—an act which certainly no man could possibly deplore more than the actor himself. Often it had occurred to me in my ponderings upon the subject that had that altercation taken place in the public street, or at a private residence, it would not have terminated as it did. It was the circumstance of being alone in a solitary office, up stairs, or a building entirely unhallowed by humanizing domestic associations—an uncarpeted office, doubtless, of a dusty, haggard sort of appearance—this it must have been, which greatly helped to enhance the irritable desperation of the hapless Colt.

But when this old Adam of resentment rose in me and tempted me concerning Bartleby, I grappled him and threw him. How? Why, simply by recalling the divine injunction: "A new commandment give I unto you, that ye love one another." Yes, this it was that saved me. Aside from higher considerations, charity often operates as a vastly wise and prudent principle—a great safeguard to its possessor. Men have committed murder for jealousy's sake, and anger's sake, and hatred's sake, and selfishness' sake, and spiritual pride's sake; but no man, that ever I heard of, ever committed a diabolical murder for sweet charity's sake. Mere self-interest, then, if no better motive can be enlisted, should, especially with high-tempered men, prompt all beings to charity and philanthropy. At any rate, upon the occasion in question, I strove to drown my exasperated feelings towards the scrivener by benevolently construing his conduct. Poor fellow, poor fellow! thought I, he don't mean anything; and besides, he has seen hard times, and ought to be indulged.

I endeavored, also, immediately to occupy myself, and at the same time to comfort my despondency. I tried to fancy, that in the course of the morning, at such time as might prove agreeable to him, Bartleby, of his own free accord, would emerge from his hermitage and take up some decided line of march in the direction of the door. But no. Half-past twelve o'clock came; Turkey began to glow in the face, overturn his inkstand, and become generally obstreperous; Nippers abated down into quietude and courtesy; Ginger Nut munched his noon apple; and Bartleby remained standing at his window in one of his profoundest dead-wall reveries. Will it be credited? Ought I to acknowledge it? That afternoon I left the office without saying one further word to him.

Some days now passed, during which, at leisure intervals I looked a little into "Edwards on the Will," and "Priestley on Necessity."[7] Under the circum-

---

[6]During a quarrel in 1842, Samuel Adams was killed by John C. Colt, a brother of the gunmaker. Colt committed suicide rather than face hanging.
[7]Jonathan Edwards, in *Freedom of the Will* (1754), and Joseph Priestley, in *Doctrine of Philosophical Necessity* (1777), argued that human beings do not have free will.

stances, those books induced a salutary feeling. Gradually I slid into the persuasion that these troubles of mine, touching the scrivener, had been all predestined from eternity, and Bartleby was billeted upon me for some mysterious purpose of an all-wise Providence, which it was not for a mere mortal like me to fathom. Yes, Bartleby, stay there behind your screen, thought I; I shall persecute you no more; you are harmless and noiseless as any of these old chairs; in short, I never feel so private as when I know you are here. At last I see it, I feel it; I penetrate to the predestinated purpose of my life. I am content. Others may have loftier parts to enact; but my mission in this world, Bartleby, is to furnish you with office-room for such period as you may see fit to remain.

I believe that this wise and blessed frame of mind would have continued 170 with me, had it not been for the unsolicited and uncharitable remarks obtruded upon me by my professional friends who visited the rooms. But thus it often is, that the constant friction of illiberal minds wears out at last the best resolves of the more generous. Though to be sure, when I reflected upon it, it was not strange that people entering my office should be struck by the peculiar aspect of the unaccountable Bartleby, and so be tempted to throw out some sinister observations concerning him. Sometimes an attorney, having business with me, and calling at my office, and finding no one but the scrivener there, would undertake to obtain some sort of precise information from him touching my whereabouts; but without heeding his idle talk, Bartleby would remain standing immovable in the middle of the room. So after contemplating him in that position for a time, the attorney would depart, no wiser than he came.

Also, when a reference was going on, and the room full of lawyers and witnesses, and business driving fast, some deeply-occupied legal gentleman present, seeing Bartleby wholly unemployed, would request him to run round to his (the legal gentleman's) office and fetch some papers for him. Thereupon, Bartleby would tranquilly decline, and yet remain idle as before. Then the lawyer would give a great stare, and turn to me. And what could I say? At last I was made aware that all through the circle of my professional acquaintance, a whisper of wonder was running round, having reference to the strange creature I kept at my office. This worried me very much. And as the idea came upon me of his possibly turning out a long-lived man, and keeping occupying my chambers, and denying my authority; and perplexing my visitors; and scandalizing my professional reputation; and casting a general gloom over the premises; keeping soul and body together to the last upon his savings (for doubtless he spent but half a dime a day), and in the end perhaps outlive me, and claim possession of my office by right of his perpetual occupancy: as all these dark anticipations crowded upon me more and more, and my friends continually intruded their relentless remarks upon the apparition in my room; a great change was wrought in me. I resolved to gather all my faculties together, and forever rid me of this intolerable incubus.

Ere revolving any complicated project, however, adapted to this end, I first simply suggested to Bartleby the propriety of his permanent departure. In a calm and serious tone, I commended the idea to his careful and mature consideration. But, having taken three days to meditate upon it, he apprised me, that his original determination remained the same; in short, that he still preferred to abide with me.

What shall I do? I now said to myself, buttoning up my coat to the last button. What shall I do? what ought I to do? what does conscience say I *should* do with this man, or, rather, ghost. Rid myself of him, I must; go, he shall. But how? You will not thrust him, the poor, pale, passive mortal—you will not thrust such a helpless creature out of your door? you will not dishonour yourself by such cruelty? No, I will not, I cannot do that. Rather would I let him live and die here, and then mason up his remains in the wall. What, then, will you do? For all your coaxing, he will not budge. Bribes he leaves under your own paperweight on your table; in short, it is quite plain that he prefers to cling to you.

Then something severe, something unusual must be done. What! surely you will not have him collared by a constable, and commit his innocent pallor to the common jail? And upon what ground could you procure such a thing to be done?—a vagrant, is he? What! he a vagrant, a wanderer, who refuses to budge? It is because he will *not* be a vagrant, then, that you seek to count him *as* a vagrant. That is too absurd. No visible means of support; there I have him. Wrong again: for indubitably he *does* support himself, and that is the only unanswerable proof that any man can show of his possessing the means so to do. No more, then. Since he will not quit me, I must quit him. I will change my offices; I will move elsewhere, and give him fair notice, that if I find him on my new premises I will then proceed against him as a common trespasser.

175　　Acting accordingly, next day I thus addressed him: "I find these chambers too far from the City Hall; the air is unwholesome. In a word, I propose to remove my offices next week, and shall no longer require your services. I tell you this now, in order that you may seek another place."

He made no reply, and nothing more was said.

On the appointed day I engaged carts and men, proceeded to my chambers, and having but little furniture, everything was removed in a few hours. Throughout, the scrivener remained standing behind the screen, which I directed to be removed the last thing. It was withdrawn; and, being folded up like a huge folio, left him the motionless occupant of a naked room. I stood in the entry watching him a moment, while something from within me upbraided me.

I re-entered, with my hand in my pocket—and—and my heart in my mouth.

"Good-bye, Bartleby; I am going—good-bye, and God some way bless you; and take that," slipping something in his hand. But it dropped upon the floor, and then—strange to say—I tore myself from him whom I had so longed to be rid of.

180　　Established in my new quarters, for a day or two I kept the door locked, and started at every footfall in the passages. When I returned to my rooms, after any little absence, I would pause at the threshold for an instant, and attentively listen ere applying my key. But these fears were needless. Bartleby never came nigh me.

I thought all was going well, when a perturbed-looking stranger visited me, inquiring whether I was the person who had recently occupied rooms at No.—Wall Street.

Full of forebodings, I replied that I was.

"Then, sir," said the stranger, who proved a lawyer, "you are responsible for the man you left there. He refuses to do any copying; he refuses to do anything; he says he prefers not to; and he refuses to quit the premises."

"I am very sorry, sir," said I, with assumed tranquillity, but an inward tremor, "but, really, the man you allude to is nothing to me—he is no relation or apprentice of mine, that you should hold me responsible for him."

"In mercy's name, who is he?"   185

"I certainly cannot inform you. I know nothing about him. Formerly I employed him as a copyist; but he has done nothing for me now for some time past."

"I shall settle him, then—good morning, sir."

Several days passed, and I heard nothing more; and, though I often felt a charitable prompting to call at the place and see poor Bartleby, yet a certain squeamishness, of I know not what, withheld me.

All is over with him, by this time, thought I, at last, when, through another week, no further intelligence reached me. But, coming to my room the day after, I found several persons waiting at my door in a high state of nervous excitement.

"That's the man—here he comes," cried the foremost one, whom I recog-   190
nized as the lawyer who had previously called upon me alone.

"You must take him away, sir, at once," cried a portly person among them, advancing upon me, and whom I knew to be the landlord of No.—Wall Street. "These gentlemen, my tenants, cannot stand it any longer; Mr. B—," pointing to the lawyer, "has turned him out of his room, and he now persists in haunting the building generally, sitting upon the banisters of the stairs by day, and sleeping in the entry by night. Everybody is concerned; clients are leaving the offices; some fears are entertained of a mob; something you must do, and that without delay."

Aghast at this torrent, I fell back before it, and would fain have locked myself in my new quarters. In vain I persisted that Bartleby was nothing to me—no more than to any one else. In vain—I was the last person known to have anything to do with him, and they held me to the terrible account. Fearful, then, of being exposed in the papers (as one person present obscurely threatened), I considered the matter, and, at length, said, that if the lawyer would give me a confidential interview with the scrivener, in his (the lawyer's) own room, I would, that afternoon, strive my best to rid them of the nuisance they complained of.

Going up stairs to my old haunt, there was Bartleby silently sitting upon the banister at the landing.

"What are you doing here, Bartleby?" said I.

"Sitting upon the banister," he mildly replied.   195

I motioned him into the lawyer's room, who then left us.

"Bartleby," said I, "are you aware that you are the cause of great tribulation to me, by persisting in occupying the entry after being dismissed from the office?"

No answer.

"Now one of two things must take place. Either you must do something, or something must be done to you. Now what sort of business would you like to engage in? Would you like to re-engage in copying for some one?"

200   "No; I would prefer not to make any change."

"Would you like a clerkship in a dry-goods store?"

"There is too much confinement about that. No, I would not like a clerkship; but I am not particular."

"Too much confinement," I cried, "why, you keep yourself confined all the time!"

"I would prefer not to take a clerkship," he rejoined, as if to settle that little item at once.

205   "How would a bar-tender's business suit you? There is no trying of the eye sight in that."

"I would not like it at all; though, as I said before, I am not particular."

His unwonted wordiness inspirited me. I returned to the charge.

"Well, then, would you like to travel through the country collecting bills for the merchants? That would improve your health."

"No, I would prefer to be doing something else."

210   "How, then, would going as a companion to Europe, to entertain some young gentleman with your conversation—how would that suit you?"

"Not at all. It does not strike me that there is anything definite about that. I like to be stationary. But I am not particular."

"Stationary you shall be, then," I cried, now losing all patience, and, for the first time in all my exasperating connection with him, fairly flying into a passion. "If you do not go away from these premises before night, I shall feel bound—indeed, I *am* bound—to—to quit the premises myself!" I rather absurdly concluded, knowing not with what possible threat to try to frighten his immobility into compliance. Despairing of all further efforts, I was precipitately leaving him, when a final thought occurred to me—one which had not been wholly unindulged before.

"Bartleby," said I, in the kindest tone I could assume under such exciting circumstances, "will you go home with me now—not to my office, but my dwelling—and remain there till we can conclude upon some convenient arrangement for you at our leisure? Come, let us start now, right away."

"No; at present I would prefer not to make any change at all."

215   I answered nothing; but, effectually dodging every one by the suddenness and rapidity of my flight, rushed from the building, ran up Wall Street towards Broadway, and, jumping into the first omnibus, was soon removed from pursuit. As soon as tranquillity returned, I distinctly perceived that I had now done all that I possibly could, both in respect to the demands of the landlord and his tenants, and with regard to my own desire and sense of duty, to benefit Bartleby, and shield him from rude persecution. I now strove to be entirely care free and quiescent; and my conscience justified me in the attempt; though, indeed, it was not so successful as I could have wished. So fearful was I of being again hunted out by the incensed landlord and his exasperated tenants, that,

surrendering my business to Nippers, for a few days, I drove about the upper part of the town and through the suburbs, in my rockaway; crossed over to Jersey City and Hoboken, and paid fugitive visits to Manhattanville and Astoria. In fact, I almost lived in my rockaway for the time.

When again I entered my office, lo, a note from the landlord lay upon the desk. I opened it with trembling hands. It informed me that the writer had sent to the police, and had Bartleby removed to the Tombs as a vagrant. Moreover, since I knew more about him than any one else, he wished me to appear at that place, and make a suitable statement of the facts. These tidings had a conflicting effect upon me. At first I was indignant; but, at last, almost approved. The landlord's energetic, summary disposition had led him to adopt a procedure which I do not think I would have decided upon myself; and yet, as a last resort, under such peculiar circumstances, it seemed the only plan.

As I afterward learned, the poor scrivener, when told that he must be conducted to the Tombs, offered not the slightest obstacle, but, in his pale, unmoving way, silently acquiesced.

Some of the compassionate and curious by-standers joined the party; and headed by one of the constables arm-in-arm with Bartleby, the silent procession filed its way through all the noise, and heat, and joy of the roaring thoroughfares at noon.

The same day I received the note, I went to the Tombs, or, to speak more properly, the Halls of Justice. Seeking the right officer, I stated the purpose of my call, and was informed that the individual I described was, indeed, within. I then assured the functionary that Bartleby was a perfectly honest man, and greatly to be compassionated, however unaccountably eccentric. I narrated all I knew, and closed by suggesting the idea of letting him remain in as indulgent confinement as possible, till something less harsh might be done—though, indeed, I hardly knew what. At all events, if nothing else could be decided upon, the almshouse must receive him. I then begged to have an interview.

Being under no disgraceful charge, and quite serene and harmless in all 220 his ways, they had permitted him freely to wander about the prison, and, especially, in the enclosed grass-platted yards thereof. And so I found him there, standing all alone in the quietest of the yards, his face towards a high wall, while all around, from the narrow slits of the jail windows, I thought I saw peering out upon him the eyes of murderers and thieves.

"Bartleby!"

"I know you," he said, without looking round—"and I want nothing to say to you."

"It was not I that brought you here, Bartleby," said I, keenly pained at his implied suspicion. "And to you, this should not be so vile a place. Nothing reproachful attaches to you by being here. And see, it is not so sad a place as one might think. Look, there is the sky, and here is the grass."

"I know where I am," he replied, but would say nothing more, and so I left him.

As I entered the corridor again, a broad meat-like man, in an apron, ac- 225 costed me, and, jerking his thumb over his shoulder, said, "Is that your friend?"

"Yes."

"Does he want to starve? If he does, let him live on the prison fare, that's all."

"Who are you?" asked I, not knowing what to make of such an unofficially speaking person in such a place.

"I am the grub-man. Such gentlemen as have friends here, hire me to provide them with something good to eat."

230   "Is this so?" said I, turning to the turnkey.

He said it was.

"Well, then," said I, slipping some silver into the grub-man's hands (for so they called him), "I want you to give particular attention to my friend there; let him have the best dinner you can get. And you must be as polite to him as possible."

"Introduce me, will you?" said the grub-man, looking at me with an expression which seemed to say he was all impatience for an opportunity to give a specimen of his breeding.

Thinking it would prove of benefit to the scrivener, I acquiesced; and, asking the grub-man his name, went up with him to Bartleby.

235   "Bartleby, this is a friend; you will find him very useful to you."

"Your sarvant, sir, your sarvant," said the grub-man making a low salutation behind his apron. "Hope you find it pleasant here, sir; nice grounds—cool apartments—hope you'll stay with us some time—try to make it agreeable. What will you have for dinner to-day?"

"I prefer not to dine to-day," said Bartleby, turning away. "It would disagree with me; I am unused to dinners." So saying, he slowly moved to the other side of the inclosure, and took up a position fronting the dead wall.

"How's this?" said the grub-man, addressing me with a stare of astonishment. "He's odd, ain't he?"

"I think he is a little deranged," said I sadly.

240   "Deranged? deranged is it? Well, now, upon my word, I thought that friend of yourn was a gentleman forger; they are always pale and genteel-like, them forgers. I can't help pity 'em—can't help it, sir. Did you know Monroe Edwards?" he added touchingly, and paused. Then, laying his hand piteously on my shoulder, sighed, "he died of consumption at Sing-Sing. So you weren't acquainted with Monroe?"

"No, I was never socially acquainted with any forgers. But I cannot stop longer. Look to my friend yonder. You will not lose by it. I will see you again."

Some few days after this, I again obtained admission to the Tombs, and went through the corridors in quest of Bartleby; but without finding him.

"I saw him coming from his cell not long ago," said a turnkey, "may be he's gone to loiter in the yards."

So I went in that direction.

245   "Are you looking for the silent man?" said another turnkey, passing me. "Yonder he lies—sleeping in the yard there. 'Tis not twenty minutes since I saw him lie down."

The yard was entirely quiet. It was not accessible to the common prisoners. The surrounding walls, of amazing thickness, kept off all sounds behind them. The Egyptian character of the masonry weighed upon me with its gloom. But a soft imprisoned turf grew under foot. The heart of the eternal pyramids, it seemed, wherein, by some strange magic, through the clefts, grass-seed, dropped by birds, had sprung.

Strangely huddled at the base of the wall, his knees drawn up, and lying on his side, his head touching the cold stones, I saw the wasted Bartleby. But nothing stirred. I paused; then went close up to him; stooped over, and saw that his dim eyes were open; otherwise he seemed profoundly sleeping. Something prompted me to touch him. I felt his hand, when a tingling shiver ran up my arm and down my spine to my feet.

The round face of the grub-man peered upon me now. "His dinner is ready. Won't he dine to-day, either? Or does he live without dining?"

"Lives without dining," said I, and closed the eyes.

"Eh!—He's asleep, ain't he?"   250

"With kings and counselors," °murmured I.

There would seem little need for proceeding further in this history. Imagination will readily supply the meagre recital of poor Bartleby's interment. But, ere parting with the reader, let me say, that if this little narrative has sufficiently interested him, to awaken curiosity as to who Bartleby was, and what manner of life he led prior to the present narrator's making his acquaintance, I can only reply, that in such curiosity I fully share, but am wholly unable to gratify it. Yet here I hardly know whether I should divulge one little item of rumor, which came to my ear a few months after the scrivener's decease. Upon what basis it rested I could never ascertain; and hence, how true it is I cannot now tell. But, inasmuch as this vague report has not been without a certain suggestive interest to me, however sad, it may prove the same with some others; and so I will briefly mention it. The report was this: that Bartleby had been a subordinate clerk in the Dead Letter Office at Washington, from which he had been suddenly removed by a change in the administration. When I think over this rumor, hardly can I express the emotions which seize me. Dead letters! does it not sound like dead men? Conceive a man by nature and misfortune prone to a pallid hopelessness, can any business seem more fitted to heighten it than that of continually handling these dead letters, and assorting them for the flames? For by the cart-load they are annually burned. Sometimes from out the folded paper the pale clerk takes a ring—the finger it was meant for, perhaps, moulders in the grave; a bank-note sent in swiftest charity—he whom it would relieve, nor eats nor hungers any more; pardon for those who died despairing; hope for those who died unhoping; good tidings for those who died stifled by unrelieved calamities. On errands of life, these letters speed to death.

Ah, Bartleby! Ah, humanity!

1853

°From Job 3:13–14, "then had I been at rest,/with kings and counselors of the earth, which built desolate places for themselves."

Questions

1. "Bartleby, the Scrivener" is subtitled "A Story of Wall Street." What does the story suggest about Wall Street as a business culture? As part of your answer, describe the working conditions of the narrator and his staff.

2. What is the significance of the names of the secondary characters in the story: Turkey, Nippers, Ginger Nut, and Mr. Cutlets?

3. Describe Bartleby's physical appearance. How does it foreshadow his future withdrawal?

4. What kind of worker is Bartleby during his first few days at work? How does he change?

5. What is Bartleby's motivation for his behavior? Is he lodging a social protest? Has he come to a philosophical realization about life and humanity? Is he simply insane? Refer to the text in your answer.

6. How do you think that Bartleby may have been influenced by his work at the Dead Letter Office before coming to New York?

7. How would you describe the narrator as a worker?

8. Describe the narrator's relationships and activities outside of work. Would you say that the narrator has a healthy balance of work, personal relationships, leisure activities, and self-development? Why or why not?

9. Compare and contrast the narrator and Bartleby. Does the narrator experience an ethical or moral dilemma over Bartleby? Why is he so sympathetic toward Bartleby?

10. Does the narrator change as a result of his experience with Bartleby?

11. "Bartleby, the Scrivener" is often humorous. Which scenes are among the most humorous? How does the humor affect the story's meaning?

12. Does Melville sympathize with his characters?

13. Do any of the characters have your sympathy? Why or why not?

14. Compare and contrast the workers in the narrator's office with the speaker in Wayman's "Factory Time," the waiter in Rompf's "Waiting Table," and Mike LeFevre in Terkel's "Who Built the Pyramids?"

15. Imagine that you are the office manager in the narrator's office and that you have to provide orientation to a new employee while Bartleby is still in residence, but not working. Write as if you are delivering the orientation through the voice and character of Orozco's speaker in "Orientation."

Edgar Lee Masters
(1868-1950)

For biographical information, see page 172.

EDITOR WHEDON

To be able to see every side of every question;
To be on every side, to be everything, to be nothing long.
To pervert truth, to ride it for a purpose.
To use great feelings and passions of the human family
For base designs, for cunning ends.
To wear a mask like the Greek actors
Your eight-page paper—behind which you huddle.
Brawling through the megaphone of big type:
"This is I, the grant."
I hereby also living the life of a sneak-thret.
Poisoned with the anonymous words
Of your clandestine soul.
To scratch dirt over scandal for money.
And exhume it to the winds for revenge.
Or to sell papers.
Crushing reputations, or bodies, if need be.
To win at any cost, save your own life.
To glory in demoniac power, ditching civilization.
As a paranoiac boy puts a log on the track
And derails the express train.
To be an editor, as I was.
Then to lie hate close by the river over the place[9]
Where the sewage flows from the village.
And the empty and garbage are dumped.
And abortions are hidden.

1915

---
[9]The speaker is referring to the Spoon River Cemetery, where he is buried.

Questions

1. Explain the speaker's quick downward moral shift from line 1 to line 3. Does such a moral descent continue in the poem? Refer to specific images and lines in your answer.
2. Describe the speaker as an editor and a citizen.
3. Explain the simile in lines 19 and 20 in which the speaker compares himself to "a paranoiac boy" derailing a train. What does this comparison suggest about the unethical life?
4. How does the speaker feel about himself and his work as he reflects on his life?
5. What is the significance of the images in the final three lines?
6. Do you think that Masters sympathizes with Editor Whedon? Do you sympathize with the editor? Why or why not?
7. Compare the ethics of Editor Whedon with that of other characters mentioned in this text, such as Blake in Cheever's "The Five-Forty-Eight" and the patrolman in Springsteen's "Highway Patrolman." Is one character more or less ethical than another? Explain your answer.
8. How does the speaker illustrate Wordsworth's complaint in "Written in London, September 1802"?
9. Do you think that once someone at work is dishonest or unethical—in any way—that it becomes easier and even commonplace for that individual to continue the unethical behavior? Refer to your own experiences, observations, and discussions with others in your answer.

William Carlos Williams (1883-1963)

William Carlos Williams was born in Rutherford, New Jersey, where he practiced pediatrics from 1910 until his retirement in 1951 during which time he published twenty-five volumes of fiction, poetry, and essays, as well as an autobiography. In 1906, he received his MD from the University of Pennsylvania; after which he interned in New York City and then traveled to Germany to practice. He first befriended poet Ezra Pound while both were studying at the University of Pennsylvania, and he renewed the friendship while in Europe. Williams is best known for his highly influential poetry, which championed the rhythms of American speech and drew on the lives of his poor and middle-class patients.

Williams's poetic output culminated in the long poem *Paterson*, published in five books from 1946 to 1958. *Paterson* weaves together local history, newspaper excerpts, letters, interviews, and other documents with lyrical and descriptive passages that mark the town's development into an industrialized city. Like all of Williams's work, *Paterson* resonates with the broad themes of the American experience. Williams's poetry won many awards, including the National Book Award for *Paterson: Book III and Selected Poems* and the Pulitzer Prize for his posthumous collection, *Pictures from Breughel*. "The Use of Force" is from *The Farmers' Daughters: The Collected Stories* (1961).

THE USE OF FORCE

They were new patients to me; all I had was the name, Olson. Please come down as soon as you can, my daughter is very sick.

When I arrived I was met by the mother, a big startled looking woman, very clean and apologetic who merely said, Is this the doctor? and let me in. In the back, she added. You must excuse us, doctor, we have her in the kitchen where it is warm. It is very damp here sometimes.

The child was fully dressed and sitting on her father's lap near the kitchen table. He tried to get up, but I motioned for him not to bother, took off my overcoat and started to look things over. I could see that they were all very nervous, eyeing me up and down distrustfully. As often, in such cases, they weren't telling me more than they had to, it was up to me to tell them; that's why they were spending three dollars on me.

The child was fairly eating me up with her cold, steady eyes, and no expression to her face whatever. She did not move and seemed, inwardly, quiet; an unusually attractive little thing, and as strong as a heifer in appearance. But her face was flushed, she was breathing rapidly, and I realized that she had a high fever. She had magnificent blonde hair, in profusion. One of those picture children often reproduced in advertising leaflets and the photogravure sections of the Sunday papers.

She's had a fever for three days, began the father, and we don't know what it comes from. My wife has given her things, you know, like people do, but it don't do no good. And there's been a lot of sickness around. So we tho't you'd better look her over and tell us what is the matter.

As doctors often do I took a trial shot at it as a point of departure. Has she had a sore throat?

Both parents answered me together, No . . . No, she says her throat don't hurt her.

Does your throat hurt you? added the mother to the child. But the little girl's expression didn't change, nor did she move her eyes from my face.

Have you looked?

I tried to, said the mother, but I couldn't see.

As it happens, we had been having a number of cases of diphtheria in the school to which this child went during that month and we were all, quite apparently, thinking of that, though no one had as yet spoken of the thing.

Well, I said, suppose we take a look at the throat first. I smiled in my best professional manner and asking for the child's first name I said, come on, Mathilda, open your, mouth and let's take a look at your throat.

Nothing doing.

Aw, come on, I coaxed, just open your mouth wide and let me take a look. Look, I said opening both hands wide. I haven't anything in my hands. Just open up and let me see.

Such a nice man, put in the mother. Look how kind he is to you. Come on, do what he tells you to. He won't hurt you.

At that I ground my teeth in disgust. If only they wouldn't use the word "hurt" I might be able to get somewhere. But I did not allow myself to be hurried or disturbed but speaking quietly and slowly I approached the child again.

As I moved my chair a little nearer suddenly with one catlike movement both her hands clawed instinctively for my eyes and she almost reached them too. In fact she knocked my glasses flying and they fell, though unbroken, several feet away from me on the kitchen floor.

Both the mother and father almost turned themselves inside out in embarrassment and apology. You bad girl, said the mother, taking her and shaking her by one arm. Look what you've done. The nice man. . .

For heaven's sake, I broke in. Don't call me a nice man to her. I'm here to look at her throat on the chance that she might have diphtheria and possibly die of it. But that's nothing to her. Look here, I said to the child, we're going to look at your throat. You're old enough to understand what I'm saying. Will you open it now by yourself or shall we have to open it for you?

Not a move. Even her expression hadn't changed. Her breaths however were coming faster and faster. Then the battle began. I had to do it. I had to have a throat culture for her own protection. But first I told the parents that it was entirely up to them. I explained the danger but said that I would not insist on a throat examination so long as they would take the responsibility.

If you don't do what the doctor says you'll have to go to the hospital, the mother admonished her severely.

Oh yeah? I had to smile to myself. After all, I had already fallen in love with the savage brat, the parents were contemptible to me. In the ensuing struggle they grew more and more abject, crushed, exhausted while she surely rose to magnificent heights of insane fury of effort bred of her terror of me.

The father tried his best, and he was a big man but the fact that she was his daughter, his shame at her behavior and his dread of hurting her made him release her just at the critical Moment Several times when I had almost achieved success, till I wanted to kill him. But his dread also that she might have diphtheria made him tell me to go on, go on though he himself was almost fainting, while the mother moved back and forth behind us raising and lowering her hands in an agony of apprehension.

Put her in front of you on your lap, I ordered, and hold both her wrists.

But as soon as he did the child let out a scream. Don't, you're hurting me. Let go of my hands. Let them go I tell you. Then she shrieked terrifyingly, hysterically. Stop it! Stop it! You're killing me!

Do you think she can stand it, doctor! said the mother.

You get out, said the husband to his wife. Do you want her to die of diphtheria?

Come on now, hold her, I said.

Then I grasped the child's head with my left hand and tried to get the wooden tongue depressor between her teeth. She fought, with clenched teeth, desperately! But now I also had grown furious—at a child. I tried to hold myself down but I couldn't. I know how to expose a throat for inspection. And I did my best. When finally I got the wooden spatula behind the last teeth and just the point of it into the mouth cavity, she opened up for an instant but before I could see anything she came down again and gripping the wooden blade between her molars she reduced it to splinters before I could get it out again.

Aren't you ashamed, the mother yelled at her. Aren't you ashamed to act like that in front of the doctor?

Get me a smooth-handled spoon of some sort, I told the mother. We're going through with this. The child's mouth was already bleeding. Her tongue was cut and she was screaming in wild hysterical shrieks. Perhaps I should have desisted and come back in an hour or more. No doubt it would have been better. But I have seen at least two children lying dead in bed of neglect in such cases, and feeling that I must get a diagnosis now or never I went at it again. But the worst of it was that I too had got beyond reason. I could have torn the child apart in my own fury and enjoyed it. It was a pleasure to attack her. My face was burning with it.

The damned little brat must be protected against her own idiocy, one says to one's self at such times. Others must be protected against her. It is social necessity. And all these things are true. But a blind fury, a feeling of adult shame, bred of a longing for muscular release are the operatives. One goes to the end.

In a final unreasoning assault I overpowered the child's neck and jaws. I forced the heavy silver spoon back of her teeth and down her throat till she gagged. And there it was—both tonsils covered with membrane. She had fought valiantly to keep me from knowing her secret. She had been hiding that sore throat for three days at least and lying to her parents in order to escape just such an outcome as this.

Now truly she was furious. She had been on the defensive before but now she attacked. Tried to get off her father's lap and fly at me while tears of defeat blinded her eyes.

1938

Questions

1. Describe the relationship between the physician and Mathilda's family. Does the relationship change as the story develops? Is it a relationship of mutual respect?
2. How would you describe the doctor's feelings toward Mathilda?
3. What do you think is the doctor's attitude toward his work?
4. Do you have any concerns about the doctor's ethics or morality? Why or why not? Do his thoughts trouble you?
5. Why do you think that the narrator is offended by the mother's use of the word "hurt"?
6. Do you think that the doctor approached the situation in the best possible way? What might you have advised?
7. Based on this story, would you recommend this physician to someone in need? Why or why not?
8. Write a paper based on your visit to a physician. Compare your experience with that presented in "The Use of Force."
9. Research diphtheria. What is the nature of the disease? How severe was the threat of death from diphtheria in the first half of the twentieth century?

Bruce Springsteen (b. 1949)

Bruce Springsteen is an American rock music icon. Springsteen's first two albums, *Greetings from Asbury Park* (1973) and *The Wild, the Innocent, and the E Street Shuffle* (1973) met with critical acclaim but sluggish sales. It would be the third album, *Born to Run* (1975), which made Springsteen a major voice on the rock scene.

Born in Long Branch, New Jersey, Springsteen was inspired to play the guitar when, at seven years of age, he saw Elvis Presley perform on *The Ed Sullivan Show*. As a young musician, he played in numerous bands and gained the nickname "The Boss," which he dislikes, when one of his early bands elected him to collect and distribute the band's pay. Springsteen's music ranges from arena rock anthems, like "Thunder Road," to contemplative folk songs like "Highway Patrolman," with much in between. He primarily writes about working-class characters, images, and themes. He has earned numerous honors and awards, including nineteen Grammy Awards, two Golden Globes, and an Academy Award. He has sold more than 125 million albums worldwide. Among his best works are *Darkness on the Edge of Town* (1978), *The River* (1980), *Nebraska* (1982), *Born in the U.S.A.* (1984), *The Ghost of Tom Joad* (1995), *The Rising* (2002), and, most recently, *Working on a Dream* (2009). "Highway Patrolman" is from *Nebraska*.

HIGHWAY PATROLMAN

My name is Joe Roberts I work for the state
I'm a sergeant out of Perrineville barracks number 8
I always done an honest job as honest as I could
I got a brother named Franky and Franky ain't no good

Now ever since we was young kids it's been the same come
down

I get a call over the radio Franky's in trouble downtown
Well if it was any other man, I'd put him straight away
But when it's your brother sometimes you look the other way

Me and Franky laughin' and drinkin' nothin' feels better than
   blood on blood
Takin' turns dancin' with Maria as the band played "Night of the
   Johnstown Flood"

I catch him when he's strayin' like any brother would
Man turns his back on his family well he just ain't no good

Well Franky went in the army back in 1965 I got a farm deferment,
   settled down, took Maria for my wife
But them wheat prices kept on droppin' till it was like we were gettin'
   robbed
Franky came home in 68, and me, I took this job

Yea we're laughin' and drinkin' nothin' feels better than blood on blood
Takin' turns dancin' with Maria as the band played "Night of the
   Johnstown Flood"
I catch him when he's strayin', teach him how to walk that line
Man turns his back on his family he ain't no friend of mine

Well the night was like any other, I got a call 'bout quarter to nine
There was trouble in a roadhouse out on the Michigan line
There was a kid lyin' on the floor lookin' bad bleedin' hard from his
   head there was a girl cryin' at a table and it was Frank, they said
Well I went out and I jumped in my car and I hit the lights
Well I must of done one hundred and ten through Michigan county
   that night

It was out at the crossroads, down round Willow bank
Seen a Buick with Ohio plates behind the wheel was Frank
Well I chased him through them county roads till a sign said Canadian
   border five miles from here
I pulled over the side of the highway and watched his taillights disappear

Me and Franky laughin' and drinkin'
Nothin' feels better than blood on blood
Takin' turns dancin' with Maria as the band played "Night of the
   Johnstown Flood"
I catch him when he's strayin' like any brother would
Man turns his back on his family well he just ain't no good

1982

Questions

1. Summarize the situation in the poem. Who is the singer? What did Franky do?
2. What is the ethical dilemma for the patrolman? What does he decide? How does he justify his decision?

3. Should the singer or the police department be held partially responsible for Franky's acts of violence? Why or why not?

4. Do you sympathize with either Franky or the singer? Explain your answer.

5. How are the highway patrolman and Edgar Lee Masters's Editor Whedon guilty of violating the public trust?

6. Both the highway patrolman and Blake in Cheever's "The Five-Forty-Eight" are guilty of ethical violations. Whose violation do you think is worse? Explain your answer.

7. Write an essay explaining an ethical decision that you may have faced either at work or in school. Explain the dilemma, your struggle, your decision-making process, your decision, and the result.

T. C. Boyle
(b. 1948)

Born in Peekskill, New York, Thomas John Boyle, who, at seventeen years of age, changed his middle name to Coraghessan, graduated from the State University of New York, Potsdam after which he began teaching at the high school where his mother worked as a secretary and his father as a janitor. He left to study at the University of Iowa Writers' Workshop, from which he earned an MFA, before earning his PhD in nineteenth-century British literature, also from the University of Iowa. Through the mid 1990s, Boyle published under T. Coraghessan Boyle, which he still uses occasionally. The author of some twenty books of fiction, he has been honored with many awards. His novels include *World's End* (1987), *The Road to Wellville* (1993), *The Tortilla Curtain* (1995), and *The Women* (2009), and his short story collections include *Greasy Lake and Other Stories* (1985), *After the Plague* (2001), *Tooth and Claw* (2005), and *Wild Child and Other Stories* (2010). He has taught at the University of Southern California since 1978. His fiction, a mixture of humor and social satire, frequently explores the struggle of a directionless individual in a confusing and sometimes brutal world. "The Lie" was first published in *The New Yorker* in 2008 and is included in *Wild Child and Other Stories.*

The New Yorker Fiction

I'd used up all my sick days and the two personal days they allowed us, but when the alarm went off and the baby started squalling and my wife threw back the covers to totter off to the bathroom in a hobbled two-legged trot, I knew I wasn't going in to work. It was as if a black shroud had been pulled over my face: my eyes were open but I couldn't see. Or no, I could see—the pulsing L.E.D. display on the clock radio, the mounds of laundry and discarded clothes humped round the room like the tumuli of the dead, a hard-driving rain drooling down the dark vacancy of the window—but everything seemed to have a film over it, a world coated in Vaseline. The baby let out a series of scaled-back cries. The toilet flushed. The overhead light flicked on.

Clover was back in the room, the baby flung over one shoulder. She was wearing an old Cramps T-shirt she liked to sleep in and nothing else. I might have found this sexy to one degree or another but for the fact that I wasn't at my best in the morning and I'd seen her naked save for one rock-and-roll memento T-shirt for something like a thousand consecutive mornings now. "It's six-fifteen," she said. I said nothing. My eyes eased shut. I heard her at the closet, and in the dream that crashed down on me in that instant she metamorphosed from a rippling human female with a baby slung over her shoulder to a great shining bird springing from the brink of a precipice and sailing on great shining wings into the void. I woke to the baby. On the bed. Beside me. "You change her," my wife said. "You feed her. I'm late as it is."

We'd had some people over the night before, friends from the pre-baby days, and we'd made margaritas in the blender, watched a movie and stayed up late talking about nothing and everything. Clover had shown off the baby, Xana—we'd named her Xana after a character in one of the movies I'd edited, or, actually, logged—and I'd felt a rush of pride. Here was this baby, perfect in every way, beautiful because her parents were beautiful, and that was all right. Tank—he'd been in my band, co-leader, co-founder, and we'd written songs together till that went sour—had said she was fat enough to eat and I'd said, "Yeah, just let me fire up the barbie," and Clover had given me her little drawn-down pout of disgust because I was being juvenile. We stayed up till the rain started. I poured one more round of margaritas, and then Tank's girlfriend opened her maw in a yawn that could have sucked in the whole condo and the street out front, too, and the party broke up. Now I was in bed, and the baby was crawling up my right leg, giving off a powerful reek of shit.

The clock inched forward. Clover got dressed, put on her makeup, and took her coffee mug out to the car and was gone. There was nothing heroic in what I did next, dealing with the baby and my own car and the stalled nose to tail traffic that made the three miles to the babysitter's seem like a trek across the wastelands of the earth—it was just life, that was all. But as soon as I'd handed Xana over to Violeta at the door of her apartment, which threw up a miasma of cooking smells, tearful Telemundo dialogue, and the diachronic yapping of her four chihuahuas, I slammed myself into the car and called in sick. Or no: not sick. My sick days were gone, I reminded myself. And my personal days, too. My boss picked up the phone. "Iron House Productions," he said, his voice digging out from under the "r"s. He had trouble with "r"s. He had trouble with English, for that matter.

"Hello, Radko?"

"Yes, it is he—who is it now?"

"It's me, Lonnie."

"Let me guess—you are sick."

Radko was one of that select group of hard chargers in the production business who kept morning hours, and that was good for me because with Clover working days and going to law school at night—and the baby, the baby, of course—my own availability was restricted to the daylight hours when Violeta's own children were at school and her husband at work operating one of the cranes that lifted the beams to build the city out till there was nothing green left for fifty miles around. Radko had promised me career advancement, moving up from logging footage to actual editing, but that hadn't happened yet. And on this particular morning, as on too many mornings in the past, I felt I just couldn't face the editing bay, the computer screen, the eternal idiocy of the dialogue repeated over and over through take after take, frame after frame, "No, Jim, stop / No—Jim, stop! / No! Jim, Jim: *stop!!"* I used to be in a band. I had a college degree. I was no drudge. Before I could think, it was out: "It's the baby," I said.

There was a silence I might have read too much into. Then Radko, dicing the interrogative, said, "What baby?"

"Mine. My baby. Remember the pictures Clover e-mailed everybody?" My brain was doing cartwheels. "Nine months ago? When she was born?"

Another long pause. Finally, he said, "Yes?"

"She's sick. Very sick. With a fever and all that. We don't know what's wrong with her." The wheel of internal calculus spun one more time and I made another leap, the one that would prove to be fatal: "I'm at the hospital now."

As soon as I hung up, I felt as if I'd been pumped full of helium, giddy with it, rising right out of my seat, but then the slow seepage of guilt, dread, and fear started in, drip by drip, like bile leaking out of a liver gone bad. A delivery truck pulled up next to me. Rain beat at the windshield. Two cholos rolled out of the apartment next to Violeta's, the green block tattoos they wore like collars glistening in the light trapped beneath the clouds. I had the whole day in front of me. I could do anything. Go anywhere. An hour ago it was sleep I wanted. Now it was something else. A pulse of excitement, the promise of illicit thrills, started up in my stomach.

I drove down Ventura Boulevard in the opposite direction from the bulk of the commuters. They were stalled at the lights, a single driver in every car, the cars themselves like steel shells they'd extruded to contain their resentments. They were going to work. I wasn't. After a mile or so, I came to a diner where I sometimes took Clover for breakfast on Sundays, especially if we'd been out the night before, and I pulled into the lot. I bought a newspaper from the machine out front and then I took a copy of the free paper, too, and went on in and settled into a seat by the window. The smell of fresh coffee and home fries made me realize how hungry I was, and I ordered the kind of breakfast I used to have in college after a night of excess—salt, sugar, and grease, in quantity—just to open my pores. While I ate, I made my way through both newspapers, item by item, because this was luxurious, kingly, the tables clean, the place brightly lit and warm to the point of steaming with the bustle of the waitresses and the rain at the windows like a plague. Nobody said a word to me. Nobody even looked at me, except for my waitress. She was middle-aged, wedded to her uniform, her hair dyed shoe-polish black. "More coffee?" she asked for the third or fourth time, no hurry, no rush, just an invitation. I glanced at my watch and couldn't believe it was only nine-thirty.

That was the thing about taking a day off, the way the time reconfigured itself and how you couldn't help comparing any given moment with what you'd be doing at work. At work, I wouldn't have eaten yet, wouldn't even have reached the coffee break—*Jim, stop! No, no!*—and my eyelids would have weighed a hundred tons each. I thought about driving down to the ocean to see what the surf looked like under the pressure of the storm. Not that I was thinking about surfing; I hadn't been surfing more than a handful of times since the baby was born. It was just that the day was mine and I wanted to fill it. I wound my way down through Topanga Canyon, the commuter traffic dissipated by now, and I saw how the creek was tearing at the banks and there were two or three places where there was water on the road and the soft red dough of the mud was like something that had come out of a mold. There was nobody on the beach but me. I walked along the shore till the brim of my baseball cap was sodden and the legs of my jeans as heavy as if they'd just come out of the washing machine.

I drove back up the canyon, the rain a little worse, the flooding more obvious and intense, but it wasn't anything, really, not like when the road washes out and you could be driving one minute and the next flailing for your life in a chute full of piss-yellow water. There was a movie at two I was interested in, but since it was only just past twelve and I couldn't even think about lunch after the Lumberjack's Special I'd had for breakfast, I went back to the condo, parked the car, and walked down the street, getting wetter and wetter and enjoying every minute of it, to a bar I knew. The door swung in on a denseness of purpose, eight or nine losers lined up on their barstools, the smell of cut lime and the sunshine of rum, a straight shot of Lysol from the toilet in back. It was warm. Dark. A college basketball game hovered on the screen over the cash register. "A beer," I said, and then clarified by specifying the brand.

I didn't get drunk. That would have been usual, and I didn't want to be usual. But I did have three beers before I went to the movie and after the movie I felt a vacancy in my lower reaches where lunch should have been and so I stopped at a fast-food place on my way to pick up the baby. They got my order wrong. The employees were glassy-eyed. The manager was nowhere to be seen. And I was thirty-five minutes late for the baby. Still, I'd had my day, and when I got home I fed her her Cream of Wheat, opened a beer, put on some music, and began chopping garlic and dicing onions with the notion of concocting a marinara sauce for my wife when she got home. Thoughts of the following morning, of Radko and what he might think or expect, never entered my mind. Not yet.

All was well, the baby in her crib batting at the little figurines in the mobile over her head (the figurines personally welded to the wires by Clover's hippie mother so that there wasn't the faintest possibility the baby could get them lodged in her throat), the sauce bubbling on the stove, the rain tapping at the windows. I heard Clover's key in the door. And then she was there with her hair kinked from the rain and smelling like everything I'd ever wanted and she was asking me how my day had gone and I said, "Fine, just fine."

Then it was morning again and the same scene played itself out—Clover stutter-stepping to the bathroom, the baby mewling, rain whispering under the soundtrack—and I began to calculate all over again. It was Thursday. Two more days to the weekend. If I could make it to the weekend, I was sure that by Monday, Monday at the latest, whatever was wrong with me, this feeling of anger, hopelessness, turmoil, whatever it was, would be gone. Just a break. I just needed a break, that was all. And Radko. The thought of facing him, of the way he would mold the drooping doglike folds of his Slavic flesh around the suspicion in his eyes while he told me he was docking me a day's pay and expected me to work overtime to make up for yesterday, was too much to hold on to. Not in bed. Not now. But then the toilet flushed, the baby squalled and the overhead light went on. "It's six-fifteen," my wife informed me.

The evening before, after we'd dined on my marinara sauce with porcini mushrooms and Italian-style turkey sausage over penne pasta, in the interval before she put the baby down for the night, while the dishwasher murmured from the kitchen and we lingered over a second glass of Chianti, she'd told me she was thinking of changing her name. "What do you mean?" I was more surprised than angry, but I felt the anger come up in me all the same. "My name's not good enough for you? Like it was my idea to get married in the first place?"

She had the baby in her lap. The baby was in high spirits, grinning her toothless baby grin and snatching for the wineglass my wife held just out of reach. "You don't have to get nasty about it. It's not your name that's the problem—it's mine. My first name."

"What's wrong with Clover?" I said and even as I said it I knew how stupid I sounded. She was Clover. I could close my eyes and she was Clover, go to Africa and bury myself in mud and she'd still be Clover. Fine. But the name was a hippie affectation of her hippie parents—they were glassblowers, with their own gallery—and it was insipid, I knew that, down deep. They might as well have named her Dandelion or Fescue.

"I was thinking of changing it to Cloris." She was watching me, her eyes defiant and insecure at the same time. "Legally."

I saw her point—she was a legal secretary, studying to be a lawyer, and Clover just wouldn't fly on a masthead—but I hated the name, hated the idea. "Sounds like something you clean the toilet with," I said.

She shot me a look of hate.

"With bleach in it," I said. "With real scrubbing power."

But now, though I felt as if I'd been crucified and wanted only to sleep for a week, till Monday, just till Monday, I sat up before she could lift the baby from the crib and drop her on the bed, and in the next moment I was in the bathroom myself, staring into the mirror. As soon as she left I was going to call Radko. I would tell him the baby was worse, that we'd been in the hospital all night. And if he asked what was wrong with her I wasn't going to equivocate because equivocation—any kind of uncertainty, a tremor in the voice, a tonal shift, playacting—is the surest lie detector. Leukemia, that was what I was going to tell him. "The baby has leukemia."

This time, I waited till I was settled into the booth at the diner and the waitress with the shoe-polish hair had got done fussing over me, the light of recognition in her eyes and a maternal smile creasing her lips—I was a regular, two days in a row—before I called in. And when Radko answered, the deepest consonant-battering pall of suspicion lodged somewhere between his glottis and adenoids, I couldn't help myself. "The baby," I said, holding it a beat, "the baby

. . . passed." Another beat. The waitress poured. Radko breathed fumes through the receiver. "Last night. At—at 4 A.M. There was nothing they could do."

"Past?" his voice came back at me. "What is this *past?*"

"The baby's dead," I said. "She died." And then, in my grief, I broke the connection.

I spent the entire day at the movies. The first show was at eleven, and I killed time pacing round the parking lot at the mall till they opened the doors, and then I was inside, in the anonymous dark. Images flashed by on the screen. The sound was amplified to a killing roar. The smell of melted butter hung over everything. When the lights came up, I ducked into the men's room and then slipped into the next theatre and the next one after that. I emerged at quarter of four, feeling shaky.

I told myself I was hungry, that was all, but when I wandered into the food court and saw what they had arrayed there, from chapatis to corn dogs to twice-cooked machaca, pretzels and Szechuan eggplant in a sauce of liquid fire, I pushed through the door of a bar instead. It was one of those oversanitized, too bright, echoing spaces the mall designers, in their wisdom, stuck in the back of their plastic restaurants so that the average moron, accompanying his wife on a shopping expedition, wouldn't have to kill himself. There was a basketball game on the three TVs encircling the bar. The waitresses were teenagers, the bartender had acne. I was the only customer and I knew I had to pick up the baby, that was a given, that was a fact of life, but I ordered a Captain-and-Coke, just for the smell of it.

I was on my second, or maybe my third, when the place began to fill up and I realized, with a stab of happiness, that this must be an after-work hangout, with a prescribed happy hour and some sort of comestibles served up gratis on a heated tray. I'd been wrapped up in my grief, a grief that was all for myself, for the fact that I was twenty-six years old and going nowhere, with a baby to take care of and a wife in the process of flogging a law degree and changing her name because she wasn't who she used to be, and now suddenly I'd come awake. There were women everywhere, women my age and older, leaning into the bar with their earrings swaying, lined up at the door, sitting at tables, legs crossed, feet tapping rhythmically to the canned music. Me? I had to pick up the baby. I checked my watch and saw that I was already late, late for the second day running, but I was hungry all of a sudden and I thought I'd just maybe have a couple of the taquitos everybody else was shoving into their mouths while I finished my drink, and then I'd get in the car, take the back streets to Violeta's and be home just before my wife and see if we could get another meal out of the marinara sauce. With porcini mushrooms. And turkey sausage.

That was when I felt a pressure on my arm, my left arm, and I lifted my chin to glance over my shoulder into the face of Joel Chinowski, who occupied the bay next to mine at Iron House Productions. At first, I didn't recognize him—one of those tricks of the mind, the inebriated mind, especially, in which you can't place people out of context, though you know them absolutely. "Joel," I said.

He was shaking his head, very slowly, as if he were tolling a bell, as if his eyes were the clappers and his skull the ringing shell of it. He had a big head, huge—he was big all around, one of those people who aren't obese, or not exactly, but just overgrown to the extent that his clothes seemed inflated, his pants, his jacket, even his socks. He was wearing a tie—the only one of the seventy-six employees at Iron House to dress in shirt and tie—and it looked like a toy trailing away from his supersized collar. "Shit, man," he said, squeezing tighter. "Shit."

"Yeah," I said, and my head was tolling, too. I felt caught out. Felt like the very essence he was naming—like shit, that is.

"We all heard," he said. He removed his hand from my arm, and peered into his palm as if trying to divine what to say next. "It sucks," he said. "It really sucks."

"Yeah," I said.

And then, though his expression never changed, he seemed to brighten around the eyes for just an instant. "Hey," he said, "can I buy you a drink? I mean, to drown the sorrow—I mean, that's what you're doing, right? And I don't blame you. Not at all. If it was me . . ." He let the thought trail off. There was a girl two stools down from me, her hair pulled up in a long trailing ponytail, and she was wearing a jumper over a little black skirt and red leggings. She glanced up at me, two green swimming eyes above a pair of lips pursed at the straw of her drink. "Or maybe," Joel said, "you'd rather be alone?"

I dragged my eyes away from the girl. "The truth is," I said, "I mean, I really appreciate it, but like, I'm meeting Clover at the—well, the funeral parlor. You know, to make the arrangements? And it's—I just stopped in for a drink, that's all."

"Oh, man"—Joel was practically erupting from his shoes, his face drawn down like a curtain and every blood vessel in his eyes gone to waste—"I understand. I understand completely."

On the way out the door, I flipped open my cell and dialled Violeta to tell her my wife would be picking up the baby tonight because I was working late, and then I left a message to the same effect at my wife's law office. Then I went looking for a bar where I could find something to eat and maybe one last drink before I went home to lie some more.

The next day—Friday—I didn't even bother to call in, but I was feeling marginally better. I had a mild hangover, my head still clanging dully and my stomach shrivelled up around a little nugget of nothing, so that after I dropped the baby off I wasn't able to take anything more than dry toast and black coffee at the diner that was fast becoming my second home, and yet the force of the lie, the enormity of it, was behind me, and here, outside the windows, the sun was shining for the first time in days. I'd been listening to the surf report in the car on the way over—we were getting six-foot swells as a result of the storm— and after breakfast I dug out my wetsuit and my board and let the Pacific roll on under me until I forgot everything in the world but the taste of salt and the smell of the breeze and the weird, strangled cries of the gulls. I was home by three and I vacuumed, washed the dishes, scrubbed the counters. I was twenty minutes early to pick up Xana and while dinner was cooking—meat loaf with baked potatoes and asparagus vinaigrette—I took her to the park and listened to her screech with baby joy as I held her in my lap and rocked higher and higher on the swings.

When Clover came home she was too tired to fight and she accepted the meat loaf and the wine I'd picked out as the peace offerings they were and after the baby was asleep we listened to music, smoked a joint, and made love in a slow deep plunge that was like paddling out on a wave of flesh for what seemed like hours. We took a drive up the coast on Saturday, and on Sunday afternoon we went over to Tank's for lunch and saw how sad his apartment was with its brick-and-board bookcases, the faded band posters curling away from the walls, and the deep-pile rug that was once off-white and was now just plain dirty. In the car on the way home, Clover said she never could understand people who treated their dogs as if they'd given birth to them, and I shook my head—tolling it, but easily now, thankfully—and said I couldn't agree more.

I woke on Monday before the alarm went off and I was showered and shaved and in the car before my wife left for work, and when I pulled up in front of the long windowless gray stucco edifice that was home to Iron House Productions I was so early that Radko himself hadn't shown up yet. I took off my watch and stuffed it deep in my pocket, letting the monotony of work drag me down till I was conscious of nothing, not my fingers at the keyboard or the image on the screen or the dialogue I was capturing frame by frozen frame. Log and capture, that was what I was doing, hour, minute, second, frame, transcribing everything that had been shot so the film's editor could locate what he wanted without going through the soul-crushing drudgery of transcribing it himself.

At some point—it might have been an hour in, two hours, I don't know—I became aware of the intense gland clenching aroma of vanilla chai, hot, spiced, blended, the very thing I wanted, caffeine to drive a stake into the boredom. Vanilla chai, available at the coffeehouse down the street, but a real indulgence because of the cost—usually I made do with the acidic black coffee and artificial creamer Radko provided on a stained cart set up against the back wall. I lifted my head to search out the aroma and there was Jeannie, the secretary from the front office, holding a paperboard Venti in one hand and a platter of what turned out to be homemade cannoli in the other. "What?" I said, thinking Radko had sent her to tell me he wanted to see me in his office. But she didn't say anything for a long excruciating moment, her eyes full, her face white as a mask, and then she shoved the chai into my hand and set the tray down on the desk beside me. "I'm so sorry for your loss," she said, and then I felt her hand on my shoulder and she was dipping forward in a typhoon of perfume to plant a kind of sobbing kiss just beneath my left ear.

What can I say? I felt bad about the whole business, felt low and despicable, but I cracked the plastic lid and sipped the chai, and, as if I weren't even conscious of what my fingers were doing, I started in on the cannoli, one by one, till the platter was bare. I was just sucking the last of the sugar from my fingertips when Steve Bartholomew, a guy of thirty or so who worked in special effects, a guy I barely knew, came up to me and without a word pressed a tin of butter cookies into my hand. "Hey," I said, addressing his retreating shoulders, "thanks, man, thanks. It means a lot." By noon, my desk was piled high with foodstuffs—sandwiches, sweets, a dry salami as long as my forearm—and at least a dozen gray-jacketed sympathy cards inscribed by one co-worker or another.

Just before quitting time, Radko appeared, his face like an old paper bag left out in the rain. Joel Chinowski stood beside him. I glanced up at them out of wary eyes and in a flash of intuition I realized how much I hated them both, how much I wanted to jump to my feet like a cornered animal and punch them out, both of them. Radko said nothing. He just stood there gazing down at me and then, after a moment, he pressed one hand to my shoulder in Slavic commiseration, turned and walked away. "Listen, man," Joel said, shifting his eyes away from mine, "we all wanted to . . . Well, we got together, me and some of the others, and I know it isn't much, but—"

I saw now that he was holding a plastic grocery sack in one hand. I knew what was in the sack. I tried to wave it away, but he thrust it at me and I had no choice but to take it. Later, when I got home and the baby was in her high chair smearing her face with Cream of Wheat and I'd slipped the microwave pizza out of its box, I sat down and emptied the contents of the bag on the kitchen table. It was mainly cash, but there were maybe half a dozen checks, too. I saw one for twenty-five dollars, another for fifty. The baby made one of those expressions of baby joy, sharp and sudden, as if the impulse had seized her before she could process it. It was five-thirty and the sinking sun was pasted over the windows. I sifted the bills through my hands, tens and twenties, fives—a lot of fives—and surprisingly few singles, thinking how generous my co-workers were, how good and real and giving, but I was grieving all the same, grieving beyond any measure I could ever have imagined or contained. I was in the process of counting the money, thinking I'd give it back—or donate it to some charity—when I heard Clover's key in the lock and I swept it all into the bag and tucked that bag in the deep recess under the sink where the water persistently dripped from the crusted-over pipe and an old sponge smelled of mold.

The minute my wife left the next morning, I called Radko and told him I wasn't coming in. He didn't ask for an excuse, but I gave him one anyway. "The funeral," I said. "It's at 11 A.M., just family, very private. My wife's taking it hard." He made some sort of noise on the other end of the line—a sigh, a belch, the faintest cracking of his knuckles. "Tomorrow," I said. "I'll be in tomorrow without fail."

And then the day began, but it wasn't like that first day, not at all. I didn't feel giddy, didn't feel liberated or even relieved—all I felt was regret and the cold drop of doom. I deposited the baby at Violeta's and went straight home to bed, wanting only to clear some space for myself and think things out. There was no way I could return the money—I wasn't that good an actor—and I couldn't spend it either, even to make up for the loss of pay. That would have been low, lower than anything I'd ever done in my life. I thought of Clover then, how furious she'd be when she found out my pay had been docked. If it had been docked. There was still a chance Radko would let it slide, given the magnitude of my tragedy, a chance that he was human after all. A good chance.

No, the only thing to do was bury the money someplace. I'd burn the checks first—I couldn't run the risk of anybody uncovering them; that would really be a disaster, magnitude 10. Nobody could explain that, though various scenarios were already suggesting themselves: a thief had stolen the bag from the glove box of my car; it had blown out the window on the freeway while I was on my way to the mortuary, the neighbor's pet macaque had come in through the open bathroom window and made off with it, wadding the checks and chewing up the money till it was just monkey feces now. *Monkey feces.* I found myself repeating the phrase over and over, as if it were a prayer. It was a little past nine when I had my first beer. And for the rest of the day, till I had to pick up the baby, I never moved from the couch.

I tried to gauge Clover's mood when she came in the door, dressed like a lawyer in her gray herringbone jacket and matching skirt, her hair pinned up and her eyes in traffic mode. The place was a mess. I hadn't picked up. Hadn't put on anything for dinner. The baby, asleep in her molded-plastic carrier, gave off a stink you could smell all the way across the room. I looked up from my beer. "I thought we'd go out tonight," I told her. "My treat." And then, because I couldn't help myself, I added, "I'm just trashed from work."

She wasn't happy about it, I could see that, lawyerly calculations transfiguring her face as she weighed the hassle of running up the boulevard with her husband and baby in tow before leaving for her eight-o'clock class. I watched her reach back to remove the clip from her hair and shake it loose. "I guess," she said. "But no Italian." She'd set down her briefcase in the entry hall, where the phone was, and she put a thumb in her mouth a moment—a habit of hers; she was a fingernail chewer—before she said, "What about Chinese?" She shrugged before I could. "As long as it's quick, I don't really care."

I was about to agree with her, about to rise up out of the grip of the couch and do my best to minister to the baby and get us out the door, en famille, when the phone rang. Clover answered. "Hello? Uh-huh, this is she."

My right knee cracked as I stood, a reminder of the torn A.C.L. I'd suffered in high school when I'd made the slightest miscalculation regarding the drop off the back side of a boulder while snowboarding at Mammoth.

"Jeannie?" my wife said, her eyebrows lifting in two perfect arches. "Yes," she said. "Yes, *Jeannie*—how are you?"

There was a long pause as Jeannie said what she was going to say and then my wife said, "Oh, no, there must be some mistake. The baby's fine. She's right here in her carrier, fast asleep." And her voice grew heartier, surprise and confusion riding the cusp of the joke: "She could use a fresh diaper judging from the smell of her, but that's her daddy's job, or it's going to be if we ever expect to—"

And then there was another pause, longer this time, and I watched my wife's gaze shift from the form of the sleeping baby in her terry-cloth jumpsuit to where I was standing, beside the couch. Her eyes, in soft focus for the baby, hardened as they climbed from my shoetops to my face, where they rested like two balls of granite.

Anybody would have melted under that kind of scrutiny. My wife, the lawyer. It would be a long night, I could see that. There would be no Chinese, no food of any kind. I found myself denying everything, telling her how scattered Jeannie was and how she must have mixed us up with the Lovetts—she remembered Tony Lovett, worked in SFX? Yeah, they'd just lost their baby, a little girl, yeah. No, it was awful. I told her we'd all chipped in—"Me, too, I put in a fifty, and that was excessive, I know it, but I felt I had to, you know? Because of the baby. Because what if it happened to us?" I went on in that vein till I ran out of breath, and when I tried to be nonchalant about it and go to the refrigerator for another beer she blocked my way. "Where's the money?" she said.

We were two feet apart. I didn't like the look she was giving me because it spared nothing. I could have kept it up, could have said, "What money?," injecting all the trampled innocence I could summon into my voice, but I didn't. I merely bent to the cabinet under the sink, extracted the white plastic bag and handed it to her. She took it as if it were the bleeding corpse of our daughter—or no, of our relationship that went back three years, to the time when I was up onstage, gilded in light, my message elided under the hammer of the guitar and the thump of the bass. She didn't look inside. She just held my eyes. "You know this is fraud, don't you?" she said. "A felony offense. They can lock you up for this. You know that."

She wasn't asking a question, she was making a demand. And I wasn't about to answer her because the baby *was* dead and she was dead, too. Radko was dead, Jeannie the secretary whose last name I didn't even know, and Joel Chinowski, and all the rest of them. Very slowly, button by button, I did up my shirt. Then I set my empty beer bottle down on the counter as carefully as if it were full to the lip and went on out the door and into the night, looking for somebody I could tell all about it.[10]

2008

Questions

1. Describe Lonnie, the narrator. Why do you think that he tells such a huge lie to his employer? Does he consider the ethical or moral dimensions of his lie? Would you define Lonnie as unethical and immoral? Why or why not?

2. How is "The Lie" a story of lost dreams? What was Lonnie's dream career? How does his lost dream affect his behavior and attitude?

3. What is the significance of Lonnie's detailed descriptions? What do the descriptions reveal about him and about the culture in which he lives?

4. What is the significance of Lonnie's statement as he enters the bar and notices "a denseness of purpose"?

---

[10]The Cramps were an American punk band formed in the late 1970s.

5. Interpret the final paragraph of the story. What do you think is going through Lonnie's mind? Why does he say that the "the baby *was* dead and she was dead, too."

6. As the story ends, what would you advise Lonnie to do?

7. At work or at school, have you ever experienced what Lonnie refers to as "the monotony of work drag[ging] me down till I was conscious of nothing" and work's "soul-crushing drudgery"? How did you get through it?

8. Does Lonnie see himself becoming like one of the workers in Shu Ting's "Assembly Line"?

9. Does Lonnie have your sympathy? Why or why not?

10. Have you or someone you have known ever escaped work or school through a lie and then been caught? Explain the situation.

11. Compare and contrast Lonnie with Daniels's Digger, the speaker in Wayman's "Factory Time," and Terkel's Mike LeFevre.

12. Compare and contrast Lonnie's attitude toward work with the singer's in Cam'ron's "I Hate My Job."

PART VIII

WORK: FULFILLMENT AND DISILLUSIONMENT

Introduction

We spend much of our lives at work. In fact, during an average week, most of us will spend more time at work than with our families. If we have a job that we find uninteresting or one that we dislike, our lives tend to be much less satisfying and fulfilling. Many of the readings in this section peer into the lives of individuals and study them at work and on their way to and from work, as well as look at the impact of work on the other parts of their lives.

In the opening selection, William Wordsworth's "The Solitary Reaper," the speaker comes across a woman cutting and binding grain. She sings a beautiful but sad song, the words of which the speaker cannot understand. Can she be happy at work if she is singing a sad song? Spellbound by the beauty of the song, the speaker does not raise the question. However, if we consider the solitary reaper alongside the industrial workers depicted in this text, we realize that her work provides her with an opportunity for self-expression, which assembly line workers in Shu Ting's poem, for instance, lack.

Walt Whitman draws on the image of song for "I Hear America Singing," a poem, which catalogues various American laborers joyously at work. Whitman's workers find self-expression and solidarity, as the central metaphor suggests, as they move America forward with boundless energy—an energy that the speaker strives to capture in the one very long sentence that forms the poem.

However, many individuals have little opportunity for self-expression at work. "Assembly Line" depicts not the drudgery of work (as Wayman's "Factory Time" does), but the effects that such drudgery can have on individual lives. Transformed by the monotony of routine, the exhausted workers become dehumanized, robotic, and insensitive to the surrounding natural beauty. The poem depicts a terrifying reality and possibility. Although the setting may be different in Adriane Giebel's "Working in a Public Elementary School," consider the situation of the narrator, who finds little opportunity and no encouragement to develop methods to benefit her students—students trapped, it seems, in an inferior education system and doomed to a life of limited possibilities.

Similarly, a profound sullenness engulfs James Wright's "Autumn Begins in Martins Ferry, Ohio," in which the speaker sits in a football stadium and contemplates his working-class community with its shattered dreams and unhappy marriages. The unfulfilled parents can only hope that football will provide their sons with the opportunities that they never had. However, athletic heroism, excessively celebrated in high school, can lead to false expectations and disillusioned lives. In Updike's "Ex-Basketball Player," the former high school star now pumps gas and tries to relive his past glory at the pinball machine.

Other images of work are more ambiguous. Ezra Pound's "In a Station of the Metro" depicts commuters with an image that is essentially indefinite. In Gary Snyder's "Hay for the Horses," a worker on the job for fifty-one years recalls his very first day. "I sure would hate to do this all my life," he thought at the time. "And dammit, that's just what / I've gone and done." But is he disappointed with his career and life? He never says directly, but the reader may find the answer in the details that the author provides. Certainly, there is no ambiguity in the speaker of Heaney's "Digging," who through labor comes to a deeper understanding, appreciation, and acceptance of his father and himself. However, the son in Stephen Paul Miller's "Dr. Shy," while he greatly admires his father's dedication to his career and profession, recalls youthful feelings of neglect and disconnection from his father.

Collectively, the works in this section remind us of the importance of Thoreau's statement in "Life without Principle": "If the laborer gets no more than the wages which his employer pays him, he is cheated, he cheats himself." Of course, the full challenge of Thoreau's imperative does not emerge until we find ourselves reliant on the pay, benefits, and security of a particular job.

William Wordsworth
(1770–1850)

For biographical information, see page 253.

THE SOLITARY REAPER

Behold her, single in the field,
Yon solitary Highland Lass!
Reaping and singing by herself;
Stop here, or gently pass!

Alone she cuts and binds the grain,
And sings a melancholy strain;
O listen! for the Vale profound
Is overflowing with the sound.

No Nightingale did ever chaunt
More welcome notes to weary bands
Of travelers in some shady haunt,
Among Arabian sands;
A voice so thrilling ne'er was heard
In springtime from the Cuckoo bird,
Breaking the silence of the seas
Among the farthest Hebrides.[1]

Will no one tell me what she sings?[2]
Perhaps the plaintive numbers flow
For old, unhappy, far-off things,
And battles long ago;
Or is it some more humble lay,
Familiar matter of today?
Some natural sorrow, loss, or pain,
That has been, and may be again?

---

[1] The Hebrides are a group of islands off the west coast of Scotland.
[2] The speaker does not understand Scots Gaelic, the woman's language.

Whate'er the theme, the Maiden sang
As if her song could have no ending;
I saw her singing at her work,
And o'er the sickle bending—

I listened, motionless and still;
And, as I mounted up the hill,
The music in my heart I bore,
Long after it was heard no more.

1807

Questions

1. How would you identify the speaker? What catches his attention?
2. Summarize the speaker's description of the work and the song of the woman. Do you think that she likes her work? Why or why not?
3. Generally, work songs have a strong and steady rhythm to accompany repetitious work. Would you say that she is singing a work song? Why or why not?
4. What impresses the speaker about the song?
5. Explain the speaker's command in line 4.
6. Compare and contrast the solitary reaper with the speaker in Wayman's "Factory Time" and the protagonists in Sandburg's "Washerwoman" and McKay's "Harlem Dancer."
7. Compare and contrast "The Solitary Reaper" with the cumulative image of Whitman's "I Hear America Singing."
8. Most scholars believe that Wordsworth was inspired to write "The Solitary Reaper" after reading the passage below from Thomas Wilkinson's *Tour in Scotland*:

> Passed a female who was reaping alone: she sung in Erse [Gaelic], as she bended over her sickle; the sweetest voice I ever heard: her strains were tenderly melancholy, and felt delicious long after they were heard no more.

Compare and contrast the poem and Wilkinson's passage. Is Wordsworth guilty of plagiarism?

Walt Whitman (1819–1892)

Walt Whitman was the first great poet to emerge in America. He was born in Huntington in Long Island, New York, but when he was four years old, his father moved the family to Brooklyn, where Whitman attended the local public schools. From 1836 to 1841, Whitman taught school in Long Island. He then moved to Manhattan to work as a printer and to write for various newspapers. In 1842, he became the editor of the *Brooklyn Daily Eagle*, from which he was fired for his liberal politics. Afterwards, he traveled to New Orleans where he worked on the *Crescent* for several months before returning to Brooklyn via a circuitous and adventurous route.

In 1855, Whitman issued his poems in the first of nine editions of *Leaves of Grass*. This first edition met with a disappointing reception, although Whitman did find a champion in Ralph Waldo Emerson, America's foremost man of letters. During the Civil War, Whitman worked as a nurse for the North and wrote America's greatest Civil War poetry. He then worked briefly for the U.S. Bureau of Indian Affairs. In 1873, he suffered a stroke from which he would never fully recover. He moved to Camden, New Jersey, where he would spend the rest of his life.

Whitman is noted for his grand, democratic vision of America, his bold celebration of himself, his compassion, his rough and frank language, and his experiments with rhythm and sound. Whitman's poetry sounded fresh and dynamic next to the popular genteel poets of his day. As he writes in "Song of Myself": "I sound my barbaric yawp over the roofs of the world."

I HEAR AMERICA SINGING

I hear America singing, the varied carols I hear:
Those of mechanics—each one singing his, as it should be,
   blithe and strong;
The carpenter singing his, as he measures his plank or beam,
The mason singing his, as he makes ready for work, or leaves
   off work;
The boatman singing what belongs to him in his boat—the
deckhand
   singing on the steamboat deck;

The shoemaker singing as he sits on his bench—the hatter singing as he
   stands;
The wood cutter's song—the ploughboy's on his way in the morning, or
   at noon intermissions, or at sundown;
The delicious singing of the mother—or of the young wife at work—or
   of the girl sewing or washing—
Each singing what belongs to him or her and to none else;
The day what belongs to the day—at night, the part of young fellows,
   robust, friendly,
Singing, with open mouths, their strong melodious songs.

1867

Questions

1. How does "America singing" and "song" serve as a metaphor for Whitman?
2. How does Whitman idealize work in this poem?
3. What does the poem imply about America?
4. Why is it significant that the poem is one sentence?
5. Compare and contrast "I Hear America Singing" with Cam'ron's "I Hate My Job" and Daniels's "Digger Laid Off."
6. Compare and contrast the cumulative image of "I Hear America Singing" with that of "The Solitary Reaper."
7. How does Whitman combine the idealism of Thoreau and the pragmatism of Franklin?

Ezra Pound
(1885-1972)

B orn in Idaho, Ezra Pound earned a bachelor's degree in philosophy from Hamilton College, New York, and a master's in romance languages from the University of Pennsylvania. He spent most of his life, however, in Europe, living in London, Paris, and Italy. He was an influential modernist and the prime figure in the poetic movement of Imagism, which stressed clarity, precision, and the image. During World War II, he broadcast pro-Italian fascist propaganda and anti-American messages from Rome. He was arrested, imprisoned, and prosecuted for treason after the war. He was exonerated on the grounds of insanity. His major work was *The Cantos*, a complex set of poems, which he began as early as 1915 and worked on for the remainder of his life.

IN A STATION OF THE METRO

The apparition of these faces in the crowd;
Petals on a wet, black bough.

1916

Questions

1. What is suggested by the use of "apparition"? Remember that the poem is set in the Paris subway.
2. Is the image of the "wet, black bough" positive or negative? Why? What do you think happened to the petals?
3. The poem is in the tradition of Japanese haiku, which usually contains seventeen syllables in three lines of five, seven, and five syllables each. A haiku will juxtapose two images to create a distinct picture that could arouse an emotion, offer a spiritual insight, or suggest something about life. Write a haiku to describe the commuters who you see around you.

Seamus Heaney
(b. 1939)

Born just northwest of Belfast, Ireland, Seamus Heaney was educated at Queen's College and St. Joseph's College, both in the city. He published his first collection, *Eleven Poems*, in 1965, followed by *Death of a Naturalist* in 1966, which won several awards. By his third volume, *Door in the Dark* (1969), he was recognized as a significant contemporary poet. Among his later volumes are *North* (1975), *Station Island* (1984), *The Spirit Level* (1996), and *District and Circle* (2006). Heaney has held various teaching positions—among others, at St. Joseph's College; Carysfort College (Dublin); the University of California, Berkeley; Harvard University; and Oxford University. In addition to poetry, he has published collections of essays and translations, including his celebrated translation of *Beowulf* (2000). He writes frequently about his Northern Irish roots, including his family and the culture and its history. His poetry tends to explore the large in the small, or the profound in the mundane. In 1995, he became the first Irish poet since William Butler Yeats to win the Nobel Prize for Literature. The citation praised him "for work of lyrical beauty and ethical depth, which exalt everyday miracles and the living past."

DIGGING

Between my finger and my thumb
The squat pen rests; snug as a gun.

Under my window, a clean rasping sound
When the spade sinks into gravelly ground:
My father, digging. I look down

Till his straining rump among the flowerbeds
Bends low, comes up twenty years away
Stooping in rhythm through potato drills
Where he was digging.

The coarse boot nestled on the lug, the shaft
Against the inside knee was levered firmly.
He rooted out tall tops, buried the bright edge deep

To scatter new potatoes that we picked
Loving their cool hardness in our hands.

By God, the old man could handle a spade,
Just like his old man.

My grandfather could cut more turf in a day
Than any other man on Toner's bog.
Once I carried him milk in a bottle
Corked sloppily with paper. He straightened up
To drink it, then fell to right away
Nicking and slicing neatly, heaving sods
Over his shoulder, digging down and down
For the good turf. Digging.

The cold smell of potato mold, the squelch and slap
Of soggy peat, the curt cuts of an edge
Through living roots awaken in my head.
But I've no spade to follow men like them.

Between my finger and my thumb
The squat pen rests.
I'll dig with it.

1966

Questions

1. What prompted the speaker to write this poem? Where is he when he writes the poem? What does he see?
2. How does the speaker reveal his pride in his father?
3. Explain the last three lines of the poem.
4. What is the tone of the poem? What is the speaker's attitude toward his and his father's work?
5. Explain the title of the poem. Who is digging? How does digging unite three generations of the speaker's family?
6. How can work or the work ethic unite more than one generation of a family? Draw on your own observations and refer to specific families.

James Wright (1927–1980)

James Wright was born and raised in Martins Ferry, Ohio, a steel-producing town not far from the West Virginia and Pennsylvania borders. His father worked in a glass factory for fifty years and his mother in a laundry. Wright served in the military and then studied at Kenyon College, the University of Vienna, and the University of Washington, where he earned a PhD. He taught at several colleges, but settled at Hunter College in New York City, where he taught from 1966 until his death. In 1972, he received the Pulitzer Prize in Poetry for his *Collected Poems*.

AUTUMN BEGINS IN MARTINS FERRY, OHIO

In the Shreve High football stadium,
I think of Polacks nursing long beers in Tiltonsville,
And gray faces of Negroes in the blast furnace at Benwood,
And the ruptured night watchman of Wheeling Steel,
Dreaming of heroes.

All the proud fathers are ashamed to go home.
Their women cluck like starved pullets,
Dying for love.

Therefore,
Their sons grow suicidally beautiful
At the beginning of October,
And gallop terribly against each other's bodies.

1963

Questions

1. Describe the speaker of the poem. What tone does he assume?
2. How would you define the communities considered in the poem?
3. Why are the fathers "ashamed" to go home?

4. How do you interpret the description of the women in lines 6–8?

5. Explain the closing stanza with its image of suicide and clashing bodies.

6. What do you think that the speaker would predict for the futures of the football players?

7. How decidedly American is this poem? Would it be different if it were set in another country?

8. Do you think that most of the other spectators in the stadium are having the same thoughts as the speaker? Why or why not?

9. How can this poem be interpreted to be about other individuals in the text, fictional or nonfictional? Consider, for instance, the narrator in "I Stand Here Ironing," Digger in Daniels's "Digger Laid Off," the speaker in Wayman's "Factory Time," Jim LeFevre in Terkel's *Working*, the workers in Shu Ting's "Assembly Line," and others.

10. "Autumn Begins in Martins Ferry, Ohio" and Boyle's "The Lie" are about lost dreams. What dreams were lost? How do the speaker in the poem and the narrator in the story respond to the realization that their dreams have been lost?

John Updike
(1932–2009)

For biographical information, see page 35.

EX-BASKETBALL PLAYER

Pearl Avenue runs past the high-school lot,
Bends with the trolley tracks, and stops, cut off
Before it has a chance to go two blocks,
At Colonel McComsky Plaza. Berth's Garage
Is on the corner facing west, and there,
Most days, you'll find Flick Webb, who helps Berth out.

Flick stands tall among the idiot pumps—
Five on a side, the old bubble-head style,
Their rubber elbows hanging loose and low.
One's nostrils are two S's, and his eyes
An E and O.[4] And one is squat, without
A head at all—more of a football type.

Once Flick played for the high-school team, the Wizards.
He was good: in fact, the best. In '46
He bucketed three hundred ninety points,
A county record still. The ball loved Flick.
I saw him rack up thirty-eight or forty
In one home game. His hands were like wild birds.

He never learned a trade, he just sells gas,
Checks oil, and changes flats. Once in a while,
As a gag, he dribbles an inner tube,
But most of us remember anyway.
His hands are fine and nervous on the lug wrench.

---

[4]This is a reference to old-style gas pumps marked with the company name *ESSO,* now Exxon.

It makes no difference to the lug wrench, though.
Off work, he hangs around Mae's luncheonette.
Grease-gray and kind of coiled, he plays pinball,
Smokes those thin cigars, nurses lemon phosphates.
Flick seldom says a word to Mae, just nods
Beyond her face toward bright applauding tiers
Of Necco Wafers, Nibs, and Juju Beads.[5]

1958

Questions

1. In the first stanza, why is it significant that Pearl Avenue is cut off after only two blocks?
2. What is the speaker's attitude toward Flick Webb?
3. Explain the contrast between Webb's present and past.
4. What is the significance of Webb's playing pinball? What does he gain from pinball?
5. Do you sympathize with Webb? Do you know anyone who has had a similar fate?
6. Create a biography for Flick Webb that is consistent with the poem.
7. What do "Ex-Basketball Player" and "Autumn Begins in Martins Ferry, Ohio" imply about sports in American culture?

---

[5]candies and sweets

Gary Snyder
(b. 1930)

Born in San Francisco, Gary Snyder said that he was "raised on a feeble sort of farm just north of Seattle." He did his undergraduate work at Reed College before studying at the University of California, Berkeley, where he studied Japanese and Chinese cultures. He lived in Japan from the mid 1950s until the 1970s. A translator, essayist, and author of sixteen volumes of poetry, Snyder won the American Book Award for *Axe Handles* (1983), the Pulitzer Prize for Poetry for *Turtle Island* (1974), and numerous other awards and honors, including the Bollingen Prize, a Guggenheim Foundation fellowship, and the Robert Kirsch Lifetime Achievement Award from *The Los Angeles Times*. His poems, influenced by non-Western poetic traditions, often draw on his experiences working on a farm, in the forest as a logger and ranger, at sea as a crewman, and as a student of Zen. He has taught at Berkeley; the Naropa Institute of Colorado; and the University of California, Davis.

HAY FOR THE HORSES

He had driven half the night
From far down San Joaquin
Through Mariposa, up the
Dangerous mountain roads,
And pulled in at eight a.m.
With his big truckload of hay
      behind the barn.
With winch and ropes and hooks
We stacked the bales up clean
To splintery redwood rafters
High in the dark, flecks of alfalfa
Whirling through shingle-cracks of light,
Itch of haydust in the
      sweaty shirt and shoes.
At lunchtime under Black oak
Out in the hot corral,
—The old mare nosing lunchpails,

Grasshoppers crackling in the weeds—
"I'm sixty-eight" he said,
"I first bucked hay when I was seventeen.
I thought, that day I started,
I sure would hate to do this all my life.
And dammit, that's just what
I've gone and done."

1958

Questions

1. Describe, in your own words, the work portrayed in this poem.
2. What is the speaker's attitude toward the work and the sixty-eight-year-old man? Which details in the poem communicate his attitude?
3. What is the older worker's attitude toward his work? How can you tell?
4. What might you find satisfying in this kind of work?
5. Compare and contrast the camaraderie of the laborers and the setting in "Hay for the Horses" with what the other workers mentioned in this text experience as they work, for instance, in the engine room in O'Neill's *The Hairy Ape*; in the offices of Melville's "Bartleby, the Scrivener," Cheever's "The Five-Forty-Eight," or Orozco's "Orientation"; in the cafés and restaurants in Rompf's "Waiting Table," Terkel's "Dolores Dante, Waitress," Rodas's "El Olor de Cansansto (The Smell of Fatigue)," and Nelson's "Goodfellows"; or in the factories of Wayman's "Factory Time," Terkel's "Who Built the Pyramids?," and Shu Ting's "Assembly Line."

Shu Ting
(b. 1952)

Shu Ting, the pen name of Gong Peiyu, is a Chinese poet born in Jinjiang, Fujian Province. During the Cultural Revolution in China (1966–1976, a time of economic stress and governmental oppression of individual freedoms), she was forced to work in the countryside for three years before being assigned to construction sites, a textile mill, and a lightbulb factory. In 1979, she published her first poem and, in 1983, became a professional writer and later deputy chairperson of the Writers' Association, Fujian Branch. Her collections include *Brigantines* (1982) and *Selected Lyrics of Shu Ting and Gu Cheng* (1985). She is considered one of China's Misty Poets—poets who reject formulaic language and structures and whose work has been declared "misty" and "obscure." Her work, like that of many of the Misty Poets, was attacked during China's Anti-Spiritual Pollution Campaign of the early 1980s. As a result, she stopped writing poetry for a few years. She is especially popular in China for her tender poems of romance—romance was repressed in the arts for many years in China. Her *Selected Poems* was published in 1994.

ASSEMBLY LINE
Translated by Carolyn Kizer

In time's assembly line
Night presses against night.
We come off the factory night-shift
In line as we march towards home.
Over our heads in a row
The assembly line of stars
Stretches across the sky.
Beside us, little trees
Stand numb in assembly lines.

The stars must be exhausted
After thousands of years
Of journeys which never change.

The little trees are all sick,
Choked on smog and monotony,
Stripped of their color and shape.
It's not hard to feel for them;
We share the same tempo and rhythm.

Yes, I'm numb to my own existence
As if, like the trees and stars
—perhaps just out of habit
—perhaps just out of sorrow,
I'm unable to show concern
For my own manufactured fate.

1991

Questions

1. How does the speaker feel about himself or herself? How has the job shaped these feelings?
2. Why does the speaker say "we" instead of "I"? Who does "we" represent?
3. How does the speaker's work influence his/her interpretation of nature?
4. Why does the speaker say of the trees that "it's not hard to feel for them"?
5. Explain the speaker's feeling of numbness. How did it result? How does the rhythm of the poem reflect this numbness?
6. Compare and contrast the speaker in this poem with other factory workers: the speaker in Wayman's "Factory Time," the workers in Wright's "Autumn Begins in Martins Ferry, Ohio," and Terkel's Mike LeFevre.
7. Compare and contrast the speaker with Jorge in Martin Espada's "Jorge the Church Janitor Finally Quits."

Stephen Paul Miller
(b. 1951)

S tephen Paul Miller is the author of *The Seventies Now: Culture as Surveillance* (1999), an examination of American culture in the 1970s, and several volumes of poetry: *The Bee Flies in May* (2002), *Skinny Eighth Avenue* (2005), *Being with a Bullet* (2007), *Art Is Boring for the Same Reason We Stayed in Vietnam* (1992), and, most recently, *Fort Dad* (2009). He co-edited, with Terence Diggory, *The Scene of My Selves: New Work on New York School Poets*, and, with Daniel Morris, *Radical Poetics and Secular Jewish Culture*. He is a professor of English at St. John's University, and he was a Senior Fulbright Scholar at Jagiellonian University in Krakow, Poland.

Dr. SHY

I want to thank the Staten
Island Pharmaceutical Society
on behalf of my mother, sister,
and brothers for the great
honor you bestow upon my
father. Although he is not here
in body we are sure he is
in spirit. We remember how
happy he was when he learned that
he was receiving this award—
he had an immense love
and respect for the pharmaceutical
profession and its variously
related functions and thought
of you, his peers, as family.

As you well know my father
was a humble man who
honestly valued being of
service over making a profit.
In 1957, he turned an
abandoned donut shop
into a Staten Island landmark.

Unlike an international hero,
who is known for one act
or function, my father's
brand of heroism was
constant. Because he was
so kind and considerate and
trusting to everyone, in such
an unassuming and direct way,
his lifetime achievement is a
fond and guiding remembrance
to us all and his loss is
felt by so many.

"I argued with my father
about Vietnam but the man
helped build America after all."

The night before my father
had his colostomy I was
reading a detailed account
of the battle for Okinawa to him for
hours beside his hospital
bed. The marines of
World War II were one of
the few subjects that
immediately pushed my
father's interest
button—that and things like
being on the look out for a new
drug which
he could order months
before he received a
prescription for it—
or for that matter months before
any other Staten Island
druggist, or even the
Staten Island Hospital's
pharmacy, received a
prescription for it

Because none of them
would ever order a
drug until someone
wanted it and even then
the hospital would call my
father for that drug

until enough other doctors
prescribed it.
Once I was watching
a Yankee game while
my father was sitting in his easy chair
doing paperwork
on a folding dinner stand.
When the trainer came
out to home plate my
father looked up.
I never saw
anyone concentrating
more intently than my
father seeing what the
trainer was putting on Graig Nettles.
A medic during the war,
my father recalled
it vividly. He
anticipated each development
and depiction in the
history I read to him.
At first he refused all sedatives
and painkillers, I
think because he was a
pharmacist he simply didn't see
any medical purpose in them.
His thinking remained
clear and lucid as his
body was shutting down
and it became hard for him to speak.
I didn't know how amazingly
bloody and gory Okinawa
was. All his life, my father
was an amazingly untalkative
     man and
he didn't think of his past—
growing up on Staten Island,
the war, owning a drug store,
being married, having a family,
and everything else—
as anything to be talked about.
He never wanted to talk about dying,
not even with my mother.
Any mention of it would
upset him and make him turn away
or hiccup—a big symptom of colon cancer.

His only orientation was towards survival.
After his colostomy he came out of the
anesthesia tor the operation quickly
and asked it he'd be able to
swim with his colostomy bag.
We all supposed he would.
My father couldn't see the point
or potential point in dying.
He never seemed to think about
that kind of stuff.
Talking about it wouldn't
change a thing and
he made the idea that
it would seem like some sort
of silly faddish notion.
It was as if he was in the
dead center of sanity and
the moderns and ancients
were playing with mirrors.
Of course he would have
hated this kind of family album
poem more than the least
sentimental member of you,
my audience. But still,
I feel as if I owe it to myself
to owe it to my father.
I mean God knows I have,
without exaggeration, over a hundred
other books or texts for books
in my file cabinet
typeset and everything, supposedly
for a poetry art book
with my illustrations and calligraphy
but I chose this for Lucio Pozzi's series
not because most of you don't have
wonderful fathers who care or cared
about you. Actually mine cared
about me only to the extent
that he knew me and knowing
me didn't mean descending
into unspeakable bullshit.
He didn't even know how to
give me the benefit of the doubt,
and he didn't have to, because
he didn't have to try to be nice,
he was the personification of niceness,

and he never got in my way within
his epistemological limits.
He was hard to be a kid under
because he didn't realize I
needed any more attention
than an occasional movie
after a pre-McDonald's hamburger
with all the trimmings.
He was more a soft skin than a father.
He was a sensitivity within limits which were
defined by what he loved most—
running a drug store all day
the way he wanted to run one.
He was fairly fixed in his ways
and couldn't stand anything exotic.
He was the only person I know who
didn't like the Marx Brothers.
My father wasn't like anyone else on Staten Island.
I'm not saying that because he was my father.
I never met anyone who reminded me of him and
I'm reasonably objective and always
noticing the features of other people in the
people I'm with, but
his face, features, and voice were so soft
they were hard to distinguish.
I still don't have a clear picture of him in my mind.
It's almost as if he were from another planet or
the Eastern hemisphere. Once while sitting on
the radiator beside his hospital bed
I said, "You know, I believe that
we only use our bodies." "Huh?" he said.
"You know, I believe in reincarnation."
"Makes sense," he said. I don't know how
it made sense but it didn't seem to be a
comforting idea or anything. It wasn't
worth thinking about; it just made sense.
That about half of the marines my father
landed in Okinawa with died, as
well as both the American and Japanese
commanders in chief, is only indicative
of how freakish all the hand-to-hand
deaths in the monsoon mud were. "I
had to sleep under water with my nose
sticking out," my father said. At
one point the narrator noted the officers'
great displeasure with the enlisted men

for their lack of discipline and decorum.
I asked my father if that was true.
"Everyone did their best," he said. It
bothers me that this is more about my
father than to him. But the very
impulse to make a book look like
a sixties record album sounds—with illustrations
    and meticulous lettering
(even if you cannot see them in this form)—
is as much my father's as mine. I'm personally
and idiosyncratically producing the
written word the way my father did a
drug store. In 1975, when I was
living in Little River, South Carolina,
a friend of mine, Jim Fresino, and
I were interested in a horse running
in the Triple Crown because his name
was Avatar. (We felt as if Meher Baba
might be the avatar.) Diablo tripped up Avatar
in the Kentucky Derby so that

Foolish Pleasure won,
I remember there was a horse
    named Bombay Duck
who was hit in the head with a beer
can and couldn't finish.
I don't know for sure who won the Preakness
but I think it was Master Derby. But
not only did
Avatar win the Belmont
but that was the only race that Jim
and I bet on him,
through an acquaintance
who was going to India through New York.
We had told him to give away any
winnings to the Avatar
Meher Baba Trust. (My father had
sent a huge cardboard box,
the size of a trunk,
full of spare drugs and medicines
and vitamin
samples to the Meher Free
Dispensary in Ahmednagar.
Before leaving his
house for the last time
my father noticed some old clothes

that had to be thrown out.
"Does Meher Baba need any clothes?" he asked
    and then left.)
Since Avatar was a fourteen to one shot,
about a hundred dollars and a few weeks later
I received a pink sheet of paper in the mail from
Meher Baba's sister Mani. Above
her drawing of a little man she wrote,
"Dear Steve, Thank you for
your love donation straight from the horse's mouth.
Regards from everyone in Babatown, Mani."
I don't think Mani was thinking of me as a poet
when she wrote "straight
from the horse's mouth"
but the next time I visited India
she greeted me as "Poet" more often than "Steve."
Mani's letter was dated June 12, 1975,
the same day on which my father's
picture appeared in the *Staten Island*
Advance feeding a horse
from the other side of a corral.
The caption read: "Alfred Miller,
President of the Staten Island Lions' Club
with horse "Poet"
at Annual Lions'
Club Horse Show." No big
coincidence, but, you know.

I want to thank
the Staten Island Lions'
Club on behalf of my mother, sister, and brothers
for the great honor you bestow
upon my father. Although
he is not here in body we are sure he is in spirit.
He had an immense love and respect for
    the Lions' Club,
in its functions and what it stands
for and thought of you, his peers, as family.
That the Wednesday lunches
were perhaps the only
occasions he regularly fit into his
pharmacy schedule speaks for itself.

2002

Questions

1. Who is the speaker of the poem? Does he reveal as much about himself as he does about his subject?
2. What portrait of the speaker's father (Alfred Miller) emerges from the poem? What kind of pharmacist and person was he? What kind of father? What is the significance of the title?
3. How did the father's dedication to his work affect his parenting and his relationship with the speaker? How did the father's work as a pharmacist influence his son's work as a poet?
4. Characterize the tone of the poem. Where does the tone shift? What do the tonal shifts reveal?
5. Consider the setting and the occasion of the poem, which indeed was read as part of a tribute to Alfred Miller at a luncheon. Do the setting and the occasion affect your evaluation of either the subject or the speaker?
6. Compare and contrast the pharmacist's commitment to his work with that of other individuals, fictional and nonfictional, mentioned in this text. Compare Alfred Miller with, for example, the old waiter in Hemingway's "A Clean Well-Lighted Place," Dolores Dante from Terkel's "Waitress," the farmers in "Under the Lion's Paw," and the narrator in Williams's "The Use of Force."

Adriane Giebel
(b. 1977)

R aised in Rochester, New York, Adriane Giebel studied art and film at Harvard and New York universities. A filmmaker and writer, she has worked on independent documentaries, including *Theater of War* (2008), *Some Assembly Required* (2004), and *Capitalism: A Love Story* (2009). She lives in New York City's East Village.

WORKING IN A PUBLIC ELEMENTARY SCHOOL

"This is only temporary," I told myself as I entered the decaying brick elementary school near a large public housing complex in the Bronx. "The projects." Temporary for me, maybe. A temporary job. But the school didn't feel temporary at all. The echoing hallways smelled of vomit, a stench that proved to be perpetual and pervasive, dank residue of decades of grime and cleaning products. The school was old enough to have wooden moldings and wainscoting on its walls, their surfaces smoothed by generations of little fingers. I climbed four floors to my classroom.

I was twenty-three and a graduate student at New York University, getting a Masters in Cinema Studies. I had no intention of becoming a teacher. I didn't even particularly like children. But I'd been lured there by the pay. I was poor. I'd always been poor. I'd qualified for reduced price lunches at my public high school, and I'd felt out of place amongst the Dalton- and Exeter-educated scions of old families at Harvard, where I'd earned my BA. Now I was living in a shared apartment in deep Brooklyn, commuting 90 minutes each way to grad school, and subsisting on oatmeal and the occasional twenty-cent banana. So when I was offered $12 an hour for a part-time job, I accepted. I was to be a kind of teaching assistant through Bill Clinton's America Reads literacy program, a scheme to match university students with underprivileged schools. Because I was willing to go to an outer borough, taking three hours' worth of subways each day, I received an extra $2 an hour for my work, a grand total of $14 an hour, more than any other work-study jobs on offer. But I was taken aback by what I found. The school's neighborhood made my Midwood block look posh by comparison. And I soon realized that my $14 was probably twice what my class' parents were making. Of those parents who had jobs. I guessed that the employed parents were in the minority.

My class was thirty fourth-graders. Twenty-three were African American, six were Latino, and one was a recent immigrant from Oman. Their teacher was a sixtyish Jamaican woman, heavy with dignity. Always dressed impeccably in suits and bright dresses, Mrs. Jackson carried herself haughtily erect, as though personally affronted by all she encountered. These students, these shabby classrooms, all were an insult to her pride. She was not used to working in such conditions, despite twenty years of hard service teaching in the Bronx. Mrs. Jackson was on the verge of retirement; this was her last year, a fact she mentioned at least daily.

Although it was 2001, hardly the dawn of the computer age, Mrs. Jackson's classroom had only two computers, placed at the back of the room. These were antiquated Macs that were not connected to the Internet, and which Mrs. Jackson never allowed the children to use. Every morning, while the children were taking off their coats, Mrs. Jackson would turn on the computers. And at the end of each day, Mrs. Jackson would turn off the computers, like extinguishing the lights in the room. This inexplicable daily ritual never varied: those computers were always on during class time, ready for use. Yet Mrs. Jackson never once incorporated the computers into a lesson, or allowed students to experiment with them during a study period. The kids were very interested in these forbidden treasures; they were constantly being reprimanded for stroking a keyboard or a mouse on their way to the cloakroom.

Mrs. Jackson had an old-fashioned sense of how children ought to behave. Propriety and fine manners were priorities for her, and she was continually disappointed by her class. "Children, you are dirty! You are filthy! You have dirty habits!" she'd declaim in her booming voice, glaring at the children. She'd halt the history lesson in mid-sentence for a twenty minute lecture on manners. The class deflated visibly under her censure, slumping deeper into their broken metal chairs, still young enough to crave the approval of authority figures.

The children were, it is true, constantly sucking their pencils and chewing their cuticles, licking their braids if hair length permitted, worrying buttons and zippers, and scratching themselves as though a plague of bedbugs had overtaken the projects they all lived in. Surveying the squirming roomful, I'd often wonder what Freud would have made of these kids. A class full of neurotic symptoms. But Mrs. Jackson saw only poorly disciplined little savages who needed correction, and probably a good spanking, too. "Your parents don't spank you enough, children," she sermonized. "If you were my children, I would give you a good spanking. That would straighten you out all right!" But detention was the only option open to her. And that was singularly ineffective. Every time a child was sentenced to spend his lunch hour at his desk, with me standing prison guard, four or five other voices would chime out, "Can I have detention, too?" Spending time alone with an adult, even a stern one determined to lecture through the period, was an enticement, not a deterrent.

Likewise, during small group reading time, when I'd take ten kids to the back of the classroom to take turns reading aloud, there would be huge squabbles over who got to sit next to me in the circle. The kids would climb over each other to hold my hands, to rest their hands on my arms and thighs. It was unprofessional—and maybe illegal?—to cuddle the children, I told myself, and I'd try to swat their little hands away, asking them to please sit in their own chairs. I felt a sick mixture of revulsion and pity. The kids' noses were constantly running, and their skin was flecked with scabs and sores, and sometimes visible dirt. A lifelong hypochondriac and germophobe, I'd imagine bacteria swarming over their hands, flu viruses spiking the kisses they surreptitiously planted on my neck and cheeks. Yet they seemed so eager, so neglected. I couldn't understand why they were so hungry for adult attention. How could they be so flirtatious and affectionate with a total stranger? Clues slipped out here and there. When Mrs. Jackson asked why kids hadn't asked their parents for help with a challenging homework assignment, they would usually reply that their parents hadn't been home last night. Or that their books were at Grandma's, but they had spent the night at Dad's new girlfriend's. The glimpses I received were of lives of instability and chaos. Mrs. Jackson's reply: "Children, I am so tired of your excuses!"

On parent-teacher nights, the only parents who ever showed up were four or five Latina mothers, recent immigrants who spoke no English whatsoever, but who smiled and nodded as we displayed their kids' drawings and papers. As a child of what the *New York Times* terms "helicopter parents," it was hard for me to imagine how this could be. How could the other twenty-five kids' parents simply trust the city schools to care for their sons and daughters? Didn't they want to inspect the adults who spent every day with their children? How difficult their lives must be, that talking to their kids' teachers was such a low priority. I imagined horrifying scenarios: prison, addiction, depression, unemployment, mental illness, domestic abuse. Or perhaps they simply had jobs where they had no control over their schedules: shift work or multiple jobs.

The school's beleaguered administration was unable to fill the gaping holes in these children's lives. The school didn't provide any type of counseling and guidance to help stanch the wounds of absent parents and neglect. Thanks to budget cuts, even the school nurse was part-time, so a sick child could get help only if he planned his illness to fall on certain days of the week. The children who spoke English as a second language received help for a few hours each week, but these ESOL classes began several months into the school year, which meant that Abdul, our little Omani immigrant, was forced to sit in class for weeks, although he spoke not a word of English. And during prep periods, when Mrs. Jackson left the classroom to work on lesson plans, the kids were handed into the care of stand-ins, whose teaching credentials were very dubious. One such sub was a female security guard with the demeanor of a wronged cop, who clearly viewed the children as future murderers and car thieves. She spent periods screaming at the children for imagined infractions, and writing on the chalkboard with such poor spelling and grammar that the fourth-graders would pipe up to correct her. I was incredulous that the school would place the children in the hands of someone so ill-equipped to teach them. Mrs. Jackson urged me to come to the teachers' lounge with her to relax during these prep periods, but I was afraid to leave the class alone with the security guard. Though what could I do? How could any teacher shield these children from their difficult family lives, their neighborhood, and the inadequacy of the schools themselves?

Even in the brief months that I knew these children, I witnessed changes that I feared would send these young lives off in terrible directions. Halfway through the school year, the smartest, most advanced child in the class—the only one who could read at a fourth grade level—disappeared. Mrs. Jackson informed me that his mother had him switched into special education. "Michael isn't special needs!" I exclaimed, horrified. Mrs. Jackson rolled her eyes and explained that Michael's mother had decided that he would get more attention in the smaller class size of the special ed track. Another of the brightest kids, an adorable cornrowed Trini named Thomas, had behavioral problems that were worsening. Mrs. Jackson told me he was living with relatives, and that both his parents had returned to Trinidad. He'd gaze at me with lovestruck, long-lashed eyes and do precisely what I'd forbidden so that I'd be forced to stop class and speak to him. His need for attention was so great that he was acting out, just so he could be corrected. I wanted to pay for him to go into therapy, wanted to find him a proper home with loving parents who provided the adult interaction and affection he obviously craved.

I often wondered what my role truly was at this school. Was I backup enforcement, another adult in the room to command the children's attention, silencing whispers while Mrs. Jackson hectored them about chewing on their pencils or their poor penmanship? That hardly seemed worthwhile. I didn't want to be a cop, and I didn't feel that Mrs. Jackson's lectures were really addressing the issue at hand. Even if the kids listened, would Mrs Jackson's advice do them any good? All the adults in the school seemed to be neglecting the catastrophic problems in these children's lives—namely, the lack of concerned, loving parents with time and resources to care for them—in favor of haranguing them over minutia. I wasn't surprised that they weren't learning their lessons, when their most basic needs were so clearly unmet.

Was I teaching them literacy? Very little of my time was actually spent reading with the children. I spent most of the day standing at the sidelines, watching Mrs. Jackson hold court. And the children's reading level was so low that the books the school provided were hopelessly ambitious, making progress nearly impossible even when we did sit in small groups. We would only make it through a couple of sentences in a half-hour's work, because the students' reading skills were still at the sounding out and guessing stage.

Or was I there as the butt of a sick joke? Had some frustrated bureaucrat dreamed up the program as a means to lure outsiders in to bear witness to this Kafkaesque mess, a mess hidden away in the slums, the peripheries? Someone who had despaired of fixing the educational system's problems, and wanted only to mutely point at them? I felt like the computers that idled in the back of the classroom, an untapped resource, present but never utilized. I wished I could spend time one-on-one with the children, asking them about their home lives and showing them that I cared about their well-being. But nearly every minute of the school day was filled with structured activities, and how could I justify giving extra attention to just one student, pulling him out of class to chit chat?

I felt sick leaving the school each day. I'd watch the kids disperse in small packs, walking home through a neighborhood so troubled that my colleagues were horrified to hear that I walked more than a mile to get to my subway line. "You can't walk around here. Don't you know that? You can't be walking the streets around this place!" Yet five and six year-olds were walking them daily, without any adult supervision. Watching their sweet faces in this inhospitable context, I wondered where my students would be in five or ten years time.

Ultimately, I quit my job at that elementary school before the end of the school year. I had two other part-time jobs, on top of full-time coursework, and I was very busy. But I really left the school because it was too sad and too stressful to be there. It was too painful to witness the results of the profound in-equity in our society. These sweet children were on a dead-end track, inade-quately prepared for an unwelcoming world. Their neighborhood had no good jobs to offer them when they left school, and their educational institutions were certainly not readying them for college careers—which their families would be unable to afford in any case. I didn't want to think about these massive societal problems, which I felt helpless to address. Or rather, I wanted to think about these problems in the tidy abstract, not face them in all their concrete misery. But "my kids"' faces still haunt me.

Today, I live comfortably in Manhattan and work in documentary film. Researching foreign educational systems for a movie recently, I thought again of these kids from the Bronx, comparing their fates to those of poor and immi-grant children in other nations. In Finland, for instance, such a school would re-ceive just as much funding per student as a school in the wealthiest, whitest neighborhoods. The child of recent immigrants in Finland is almost as likely to complete university as the child of native-born parents. And what a difference economic security such as is offered by "social welfare states" could have made for my Bronx children's families!

Sometimes I fantasize about returning to New York's public schools. I read the ads in the subway exhorting young professionals to make a difference, become a teacher, after all, "You always remember your first grade teacher's name." I wonder whether one dedicated teacher really could help children in dire straits clamor out into another world, another social class. I wonder if I abandoned those kids. I think of those children's children, now biding their time in those same classrooms with semi-literate security guards. Most of the time, though, I think that what is really needed is profound changes in our so-cial safety net on a national level. I left the dank halls of that Bronx school be-hind me. But I can't efface the memory of those sticky little hands groping for my own during story time.

2010

Questions

1. What were Giebel's initial impressions of the students and the school? As time passed, did the author's feelings toward the children change?

2. Do you think that Giebel was adequately prepared and trained for her position? What do you think her training program should have included?

3. Giebel writes that she "often wondered what my role truly was at this school." If a job description existed, what do you think it said? Write a job description based on what the author actually did. Do you think that she was being used most effectively?

4. How would you describe the author? Do you think that she changes as a result of her work in the school? Is your opinion of her affected because she left her job before the school year ended?

5. What did the author find most and least satisfying about her job?

6. According to the essay, what are the main problems that the school's students face? Is this school able to solve these problems? Could any school solve them? What solutions would you propose to help these children?

7. What are the political and social implications of the essay?

8. What portrait of Mrs. Jackson emerges from the essay? What are her strengths and weaknesses as a teacher?

9. Does the essay suggest that one teacher in this particular school could have a beneficial and life-changing impact on the lives of these students? Do you think that a teacher could have such an effect on these elementary school students? Why or why not?

10. If you were hiring teachers for his particular school, what qualities would you look for in your candidates?

Credits

Index